PILGRIMAGE OF ANASTASIUS

JEROME GRACIÁN *of the* MOTHER OF GOD

(1545–1614)

PILGRIMAGE OF ANASTASIUS

The Autobiography of the First Provincial of the Discalced Carmelites

TRANSLATED BY STEPHEN WATSON, O.C.D.

ICS Publications
Institute of Carmelite Studies
Washington, D.C.

ICS Publications
2131 Lincoln Road NE
Washington, DC 20002-1199

www.icspublications.org

Cover and text design and pagination by Rose Design
Printed in the United States of America

Cover image (background): Benito Mercadé y Fábregas, *Santa Teresa de Jesús*, 1868, oil on canvas, 300 x 412 cm, Museo Nacional del Prado, Madrid; (portrait): *Fray Jerónimo Gracián*, c. 1594, Monastery of Consuegra.

ISBN: pbk: 978-1-939272-62-1 ebook: 978-1-939272-64-5

Library of Congress Cataloging-in-Publication Data

Names: Gracián, Jerónimo, 1545-1614, author. | Watson, Stephen, Father, O.C.D., translator. | Gracián, Jerome, 1545-1614. Peregrinación de Anastasio.
Title: Pilgrimage of Anastasius : the autobiography of the first Provincial of the Discalced Carmelites / Jerome Gracián of the Mother of God (1545-1614) ; translated by Stephen Watson, O.C.D.
Other titles: Peregrinación de Anastasio. English
Description: Washington, D.C. : ICS Publications, Institute of Carmelite Studies, [2022] | Includes bibliographical references and index. | Summary: "Seventeenth-century autobiography and apologia of the great collaborator and confidant of St. Teresa of Ávila"-- Provided by publisher.
Identifiers: LCCN 2021058497 (print) | LCCN 2021058498 (ebook) | ISBN 9781939272621 (trade paperback) | ISBN 9781939272645 (ebook)
Subjects: LCSH: Gracián, Jerónimo, 1545-1614. | Monks--Spain--Biography. | Monks--Italy--Biography. | Discalced Carmelites.
Classification: LCC BX4705.G617548 A3 2022 (print) | LCC BX4705.G617548 (ebook) | DDC 271/.7302 [B]--dc23/eng/20220107
LC record available at https://lccn.loc.gov/2021058497
LC ebook record available at https://lccn.loc.gov/2021058498

10 9 8 7 6 5 4 3 2

Contents

Acknowledgments vii
Introduction ix
A Note on the Translation xxxv
Abbreviations xxxix
Chronology of the Life of Jerome Gracián xli

DIALOGUES

Preface 3
Prologue 5
First Dialogue: Vocation 9
Second Dialogue: Discalced 21
Third Dialogue: Visitator 36
Fourth Dialogue: Expulsion 55
Fifth Dialogue: Appeal 69
Sixth Dialogue: Captive 77
Seventh Dialogue: Freedom 96
Eighth Dialogue: Afflictions 108
Ninth Dialogue: Calced 123
Tenth Dialogue: Consolations 135
Eleventh Dialogue: Succor 162
Twelfth Dialogue: Writings 185
Thirteenth Dialogue: Foundations 193
Fourteenth Dialogue: Fruits 239
Fifteenth Dialogue: Prayer 259
Sixteenth Dialogue: Revelations 292

Appendixes

Appendix I: Letter to a Friend 319

Appendix II: Letter 185 to Francisca de Las Llagas and María de San José 342

Appendix III: Letter 222 to Alfonso de Narvaez, Captain of the Artillery of Pamplona 346

Appendix IV: Illness and Happy Death of Jerome Gracián 350

Appendix V: Official Declaration of the Rehabilitation of Father Jerome Gracián of the Mother of God, O.C.D. 355

Notes 359

Bibliography 399

Biblical Index 403

Index 407

Acknowledgments

Since the time I first read *Peregrinación de Anastasio* I have had it in mind to translate this autobiographical work of Jerome Gracián. I have to thank the late Father Pascal Perini, O.C.D., of the California-Arizona Province for his constant encouragement and for never letting me renege on this intention.

My study of Father Gracián and his works was undoubtedly made possible by the scholarly work of two outstanding Teresian Carmelites, Father Ildefonso Moriones, O.C.D., and Father Juan Luis Astigarraga, O.C.D. Father Moriones is arguably the most ardent promoter and defender of the person of Jerome Gracián as an authentic and irreplaceable witness of the Teresian charism. Of his many books and articles, two are of particular importance for understanding Gracián: *Ana de Jesús y la Herencia Teresiana* (Rome, 1968) and *El Carisma Teresiano* (Rome: Teresianum, 1972; Eng: *The Teresian Charism*, trans. Christopher O'Mahoney, Rome: Teresianum, 1972). Father Astigarraga has done an inestimable job of promoting the study of Jerome Gracián with his impressive three-volume series called *Monumenta Hieronymi Gracian*. In fact, I must acknowledge my indebtedness to the team of historians and researchers who comprise the *Monumenta Historica Carmeli Teresiani*, which over many years worked to collect and edit, always with abundant and informative notes, the documents pertinent to the early history of the Teresian Carmelites. Their work is a great credit to the Discalced Carmelite Order.

I particularly want to thank Father Antonio Fortes, O.C.D., who was very generous with his time in helping me grasp the sense of some difficult sentences, expressions, and words of the *Peregrinación de Anastasio*. I also thank Father Patrick Sugrue, O.C.D., Father Donald Kinney,

O.C.D., Father James Goeghegan, O.C.D., Deacon David A. Lopez of Sioux City, Brother Luis David Perez, O.C.D., and Sister Mary Elizabeth, O.C.D., of Loretto Carmel, for their editorial advice and skills; and especially Father John McGowan, O.C.D., from whom I have received help and encouragement in this rather long and drawn-out translation project. I must also express my profound gratitude to Sister Marie Therese, O.C.D., of Sioux City Carmel, for managing the manuscript, compiling the chronology, providing the cross-references, and for offering many good suggestions as to readability, all of which I deeply appreciate. Finally, I want to thank our previous superior general, Father Luis Arostégui, O.C.D., who very much wanted me to complete this translation. The fact that I was doing something that the superior general wanted me to do gave me the extra determination I needed to persevere in an undertaking that has been perhaps a little too ambitious for my talent (but not my zeal)!

Introduction

The *Pilgrimage of Anastasius* that you have here in its English translation is an autobiographical writing by Jerome Gracián, first provincial of the Discalced Carmelites.[1] In this work, Gracián tells the story of his life and adventures—his "pilgrimage"—by adopting the voice of St. Anastasius of Persia, a monk who was martyred in Jerusalem in 628,[2] and putting him in dialogue with St. Cyril of Constantinople, who was allegedly a hermit of Mount Carmel in the thirteenth century and general of the order for many years.[3] Gracián's account spans from the time he joined the Discalced Carmelites at Pastrana in 1572 to the time he went to Brussels in 1607, where he would die seven years later.

The *Pilgrimage of Anastasius* consists of sixteen "dialogues." This was a style of writing that was meant to be pedagogical. In the case of the *Pilgrimage*, it was also autobiographical and apologetic. Gracián explains his purpose in writing it: "What I mainly intend is to defend the honor of many holy persons and religious who are suspected of some imperfection by whomever has spoken about my failures, for they have been judged to be accomplices of my weaknesses."[4] Of course there is a lot more to Gracián's story than his supposed "failures" and "weaknesses," as the reader will see. He dedicated this work to four of his siblings—one brother

1. Originally published in Spanish as *Peregrinación de Anastasio,* ed. Juan Luis Astigarraga, MHCT 19; MHG 2 (Rome: Institutum Historicum Teresianum, 2001).

2. St. Anastasius's January 22 feast was observed by the Carmelites, and his relics are venerated in the abbey church of Saints Vincent and Anastasius in Rome. The collect for his Mass says, "God, who called blessed Anastasius from the solitude of Carmel to receive the palm of martyrdom. . . . ."

3. The first college of the Discalced Carmelites took Cyril for its patron in honor of the Separation Brief of 1581 issued on March 6, which is St. Cyril's feast day.

4. See Gracián's Preface (PA Pref.4.).

and three sisters—each of them also Discalced Carmelites, reserving it for circulation among family and friends until after his death.

The *Pilgrimage of Anastasius* will be of interest to the sons and daughters of St. Teresa of Jesus as well as to all who study Carmelite history and spirituality, since Gracián was Teresa's closest collaborator in the work of establishing communities of the Discalced Carmelites the last seven years of her life. St. Teresa tells us of his importance in chapter 23 of the *Book of Her Foundations*, a chapter that can be read as a fitting introduction to this edition. She was convinced that the Blessed Virgin Mary chose this young man, half Teresa's age, of "much learning, intelligence, and modesty along with other great virtues," to help the Order of Carmel (F 23.1). St. Teresa concludes this chapter by saying, "I begged her [the Blessed Virgin Mary] very much to intercede that her Son always favor this Father and give him grace to advance far in His service" (F 23.13).

JEROME GRACIÁN

Jerome Gracián was born on June 6, 1545. He was the third child of Diego Gracián and Juana Dantisco. After Jerome, seventeen more children were born to this good Christian couple.

Diego Gracián (1510–1600) was an important secretary of the king of Spain, Philip II. A humanist who studied under Juan Luis Vives at the famed University of Louvain, Diego was an accomplished classicist who taught his son Greek and Latin from an early age. He was a devout Catholic and a loving husband to Juana, who was many years younger than he.

Juana was the daughter of Jan Dantyszek (1485–1548), the famous Polish-Latin poet often regarded as "the father of Polish diplomacy."[5]

5. Also known as Johannes Danticus or Juan Dantisco, he was at King Sigismund I's side at the Convention of Vienna in 1515 for which he was knighted and ennobled. He never married and was ordained in 1533 after returning to Poland. As bishop, he resisted Reformation encroachment by ousting all such sympathizers from his diocese of Warmia and burning heretical books.

His name was taken from his place of origin, Danzig (Gdańsk) of the Kingdom of Poland, where he was brought up, the son of a brewer. He was appointed the Polish ambassador to Spain, where he met but never married Juana's mother Isabel and left them both when he was called back to Poland for other diplomatic duties; Juana was four years old. Dantisco later became the bishop of Kulm and then Ermland (Warmia), the latter being the same diocese of Nicolaus Copernicus. It is interesting to note that this grandfather of Jerome was attended to medically (for gout in the spring of 1538) by Copernicus, who, besides being an astronomer, was also a canon and skilled physician.

Gracián's family lived close to the royal court, but they did not necessarily benefit from the wealth of the most powerful monarch on earth. However, King Philip did favor his loyal secretary with some help for his sons' tuition. Jerome thus received a first-class education. At the age of fifteen, he began studies at the University of Alcalá de Henares, earning a bachelor of arts degree in 1563 and his master of arts a year later. His father and the king were expecting him to follow a career as a royal secretary, but Jerome wanted to study theology and become a priest. After finishing his studies in the arts, he enrolled in the school of theology and studied under some illustrious Jesuit professors. After receiving his licentiate in theology, he began a four-year course for his doctorate. In 1570, Jerome was ordained a priest.[6] He was completing the last of a series of examinations for the doctorate when he suddenly left Alcalá to join the Discalced Carmelites, much to the consternation of his family. Actually, as he tells us in the first dialogue, he had struggled for a year and a half as to whether he should join the Discalced. He had already been accepted by the Jesuits, but he was captivated by the Blessed Virgin Mary to whom he was so devoted. He became convinced that the Virgin wanted him to join "her order," which the Carmelite Order was

6. Gracián was ordained a priest on March 25, 1570, which was Holy Saturday. He sang his first Mass in Madrid at the Poor Clare monastery of Descalzas Reales ("the Royal Discalceds"), the former palace of King Charles I. See Carlos Ros, *El hombre de Teresa de Jesús: Jerónimo Gracián* (Seville, Spain: Rosalibros, 2006), 101.

commonly considered,[7] causing him to abandon his intention to join the Jesuits.

> But I made up my mind, for I was not able to suffer the impetus of the thoughts that came to me from love of our Lady. I was saying to myself, "If there have been many noble men who, for love of a woman of this world, have become blind, allowing their homes, honor, and lives to be lost, getting knifed, and all the rest, why should I take heed of anything, blinded as I am by the love I have for such a Lady? I would die a happy man if, even after a few months of entering the order, I died because of the austerity of the life! I will gladly give my life to my Lady, the Virgin Mary." (PA 1.5)

From the time Gracián at age 27 entered the novitiate in Pastrana on April 25, 1572, he was marked for singular service to the order.[8] When the novice master had to be removed because of the imprudent penitential practices he was employing with the novices, Jerome, already a priest, was made novice master. And since he was a priest, he preached and gave spiritual direction to the Discalced Carmelite nuns in Pastrana. It was Teresa's intention that the nuns there should obey him as they would herself. This was, as he says, the beginning of his troubles with the brethren. "This confidence that she placed in me alone—on account of which she changed obedience from the bishops to the friars—was a small ember in the hearts of many that smoldered until it started the great fire about which I will later speak" (PA 1.8).

Gracián made his profession on April 25, 1573, and within six months he was delegated by a Dominican named Francisco de Vargas,

7. St. Teresa refers to the Carmelite Order as "her [our Lady's] order" in F 23.13, which I quote further on.

8. The Discalced still belonged to the Carmelite Order at this point and became a separate order on December 20, 1593. I use the term "order" here and throughout my comments in the sense that Jerome Gracián does, as referring to the Discalced Carmelites, whether they held the status of a province (June 22, 1580) or a congregation (July 10, 1587). In the case above, they are not yet a separate province but are on the way to becoming so, particularly through Gracián's efforts.

apostolic visitator of all the religious of Andalusia, to make the visitation of the Carmelites of Andalusia. "Here I am, twenty-eight years old and professed six months, and I am made the superior of all the Calced Carmelites of Andalusia, in opposition to the general and the protector of the whole order of the Calced" (PA 1.20).[9]

It was at this time that Gracián made his first foundation of the Discalced Carmelite friars. This was the monastery of Nuestra Señora de los Remedios (referred to in the order as "Los Remedios") in Seville. The following year, Vargas named Gracián the vicar provincial of all the Calced and Discalced of Andalusia. It was while he was carrying out these duties that Gracián met St. Teresa in Beas where she had gone to make a foundation.[10] It would be hard to overestimate the importance of this meeting for the advancement of Teresa's work. Referring to Gracián, Teresa writes, "Our Lord truly saw the great need there was for a person like this to carry on the work that He had begun" (F 23.3). She elaborates further on:

> Although he was not the one who first began, he came along at the right moment. . . . Those [houses] of the friars were not going badly, but the basis was there for a very quick collapse. Since the Discalced didn't have their own province, they were governed by the Calced. Those who could have governed, such as Fray Antonio de Jesús,[11] the one who began the renewal, were not given the power to do so. Nor did the friars have constitutions given by our most Reverend Father General. In each house they did as they saw fit. . . . Our Lord provided a remedy through the Father Maestro Fray Jerónimo de la Madre de Dios, because they made him apostolic commissary

---

9. It is important to note that the Carmelites of the Ancient Observance (O.Carm.) do not call themselves "Calced Carmelites." It is a term used by Gracián, St. Teresa, and others as a means of distinguishing them from those who joined St. Teresa's renewal. See my translation notes for more details on the usage of "Discalced" and "Calced."

10. Beas de Segura is the town's full name, of Jaén province, not to be confused with Beas of Huelva province which lies 270 miles southwest.

11. *Fray* is the Spanish word for friar, which is used for religious priests and brothers of mendicant orders.

> and gave him authority and rule over the Discalced friars and nuns. He drafted constitutions for the friars . . . through the apostolic power he had and the talents that the Lord has given him as I have mentioned. In his first visitation of the friars, he arranged everything with such moderation and harmony that it indeed seemed he was helped by the Divine Majesty and that our Lady had chosen him to help her order. (F 23.12–13)

Since the town of Beas was in the ecclesiastical jurisdiction of Andalusia, Gracián became Teresa's ecclesiastical superior. Wanting to do something more in the service of the Lord, on Pentecost 1575, Teresa made a special vow to obey Gracián in all things.

Gracián's authority was contested by the Calced of Andalusia, and the general of the Carmelite Order got involved.[12] A general chapter of the order revoked all of Gracián's faculties. Countering this decision, the papal nuncio Nicolò Ormaneto expanded the faculties of Gracián, naming him commissary and reformer of the Andalusian Carmelites and of the Discalced friars and nuns of Castile. The lives of Gracián and Teresa were anything but tranquil. The persecution from the Calced was so bad that it became clear the only solution was to create a separate jurisdiction for the Discalced, that is, a separate province with its own superiors. The creation of a separate province was due in no small part to Gracián's sacrifices and labors. At one point, for more than a year he was deprived of all authority and confined to a monastery to do penance. Of course he was totally backed by Teresa and her consummate skill in dealing with men in authority.

On June 22, 1580, the pope granted a separate province to the Discalced Carmelites. At the first provincial chapter of the Discalced

12. Father General Juan Bautista (John Baptist) Rubeo, as he was called by the Spaniards, was an Italian by the name of Giovanni Battista Rossi (1507–1578). Elected general of the order in 1564, he made an extensive visitation of Spain in 1566–1567, during which he met St. Teresa in Ávila and permitted her to proceed with more Discalced foundations, including two houses of friars. See E. Allison Peers, *Handbook to the Life and Times of St. Teresa and St. John of the Cross* (London: Burns Oates, 1954), 12.

Carmelites in March 1581, Gracián was elected provincial. During his four-year term, there was significant growth within the order. In addition to the half dozen foundations he made as apostolic visitator before his election, he made a half dozen more in Spain as provincial. He also had an important foundation made in Genoa, Italy, and he sent missionaries to Africa and Mexico. At the end of his term, he presented to the provincial chapter held in Lisbon a defense of his leadership that had been criticized by some rather influential friars. Accusing Gracián of being too lenient regarding abuses and too easy with dispensations, his critics implied that he was excessively oriented to the apostolic life and not concerned enough with the ascetical-contemplative life.

In 1586, Gracián published a work on the missions, leading to contention with the new provincial, Nicolás Doria.[13] This was, in fact, the beginning of Gracián's slide into disfavor with Doria that ultimately led to his expulsion from the order in 1592. What really doomed Gracián was his opposition to Doria's newly instituted and highly centralized form of government called the *consulta,* as well as his support of some of the nuns in their efforts to preserve St. Teresa's constitutions from changes that Doria wanted to make. Doria intended to send him to Mexico but had to yield to the wishes of the king and Cardinal Archduke Albert who wanted Gracián back in Portugal where he had been assigned at the end of his term as provincial. During this time, Sir Francis Drake, leading the English Armada, tried to invade Portugal. Gracián showed himself a fearless spiritual leader during the assault on Lisbon.

When Gracián finished his assignment in Portugal as visitator of the Calced Carmelites, Doria called him to Madrid. He was imprisoned in the Discalced Carmelite monastery of San Hermenegildo and subjected to six months of investigations and interrogations. On February 17, 1592, the sentence was pronounced against Gracián, expelling him from the Discalced Carmelite Congregation of the Carmelite Order that owed him so much.

---

13. Nicolás Doria (Nicolao de Oria) de Jesús María (1539–1594) was born in Genoa, Italy, moved to Spain in 1570, and joined the Discalced Carmelites seven years later.

JEROME AND TERESA

Gracián was disgracefully expelled from the very order of which he was the first provincial. The *Pilgrimage* is an apologia of his life written to justify his actions based on his understanding of St. Teresa's work and his collaboration with her. At the same time, he wants to clear of any blame those who have been defamed on account of association with him. He even seems to want to exonerate those who expelled him from the order. There are those who will say the work is too much about self-justification. Each person who reads this work is free to think what he or she wishes. But it is good to keep in mind what this man meant to St. Teresa and what she meant to him, as he writes in dialogue 16.30: "In order for you to understand this properly, you need to know that she loved me most tenderly and I loved her more than any other creature on earth. . . ." Teresa's vow of obedience to Gracián, which she made very soon after meeting him for the first time, was quite extraordinary, especially when one remembers that she had already attained the highest degree of union with God, called spiritual marriage. Teresa says she had seen the Lord in a vision: "The Lord took [Gracián's] right hand and mine and joined them, and He told me that He wanted me to take him in His place for the rest of my life and that there should be conformity between us in everything because this was fitting" (PA 16.7). Their collaboration was such that Gracián can say that "in whatever business she or I had to undertake, whether of the order or other particular things, we were always in agreement" (PA 16.14).

Teresa wrote to Mother Isabel de Santo Domingo,[14] prioress at Segovia, telling her that she found Gracián "perfect" and asking that the sisters pray he be appointed the superior of the nuns and so relieve her of the burden "of the government of these houses, for I have never seen perfection combined with so much gentleness" (LE 1.81.2). When you read the letters of St. Teresa to Gracián, you can understand why he so

14. Mother Isabel (1537–1614) knew Gracián when her community was located at Pastrana and he was studying at the University of Alcalá de Henares.

confidently assures us that Teresa "loved me most tenderly." It should be pointed out that Teresa's letters to him are the largest part of the collection of over 450 of her extant letters. One reason for this is that he valued her letters and kept them safe, binding them together like a book. The content of Teresa's letters to Gracián could be the subject of a book on love and friendship. One example will suffice to give an idea of what her love was like: "I was wondering which of the two loves Your Paternity more: Doña Juana[15] who I see has a husband and her other children to love, or poor Lorenza who has no one else in the world but this father. May it please God to preserve him to her, amen, for I need this consolation" (LE 1.124.7; (PA 16.29). Doña Juana was Gracián's mother and Lorenza was a code name that Teresa gave herself.[16]

Likewise, Gracián says that his greatest consolation was the friendship and love of Teresa. Just as she supported him when she was alive on earth, so he experienced her loving presence after she died. He says that the memory of all he experienced with her puts other joys and honors in the shade, as the sun by its brightness does to the stars (see PA 10.36).

The relationship of St. Teresa and Gracián ranks as one of the most extraordinary friendships of holy men and women. I have in mind such friendships as Blessed Jordan of Saxony and Blessed Diana degli Andaló, St. Francis and St. Clare, St. Catherine of Siena and Blessed Raymond of Capua, and St. Francis de Sales and St. Jane Frances de Chantal. Francis de Sales and Gracián were much alike in many respects, especially in their gentle direction of women, their apostolic zeal, and their devotion to and theological study of St. Joseph. They might very well have met in Rome in the fall of 1599, where Gracián lived at the time and Francis spent three months obtaining various petitions. It is interesting to note

---

15. *Doña* (dō-nyä) is a Spanish title of respect for a lady or married woman.

16. St. Teresa used code names for herself and several others in her correspondence in case her letters fell into the hands of the Calced or others who wanted to undo the efforts of the Discalced. Such precaution is the reason we have no surviving letters of Teresa to John of the Cross. He burned them all to protect her and the Discalced movement.

that St. Francis de Sales found Teresa's vow of obedience to Gracián very helpful in his spiritual guidance of Madame Chantal.[17]

Gracián was unfailingly loyal to the memory of St. Teresa. It is amazing how much of her writing he seems to have memorized. It can even be said that he is the first great student of the teaching of St. Teresa as put forth in her writings. Indeed, he was the one responsible for her writing *The Interior Castle,* her masterpiece. Not only that, he enthusiastically promoted her writings and always believed in her great sanctity. He deserves no small amount of credit for her beatification and canonization. As he lay dying, he recited her poetry and invoked her intercession.[18] Gracián helps us understand something very personal and special about St. Teresa, but most particularly her unique spiritual charism. He always maintained that she was the foundress of the Discalced friars and nuns. For these reasons, Gracián is worthy of our attention and respect.

Can Gracián stand on his own merits apart from St. Teresa? St. Teresa certainly thought he could. She wrote in his defense that he possessed surpassing honesty and purity of conscience and was one of the greatest servants of God with whom she dealt.[19] Considering the fact that St. Teresa dealt with some of the most learned, holy, and renowned men of her time, it is no small tribute that she praises Gracián as one of the greatest. Even though Gracián is of interest to us apart from Teresa, it has to be admitted that his relationship to Teresa is what sets him apart from the other great servants of God and learned men of his time. She defended him when she was alive and he continued to invoke her in his defense after she died. He understood that his reputation was safeguarded by his relationship to her and the confidence she had always had in him and that she expressed in her letters and manifested in the

17. See Maurice Henry-Coüannier, *St. Francis de Sales and His Friends,* trans. Veronica Morrow (New York: St. Paul Publications, 1964), 180.

18. See Appendix IV, "Illness and Happy Death of Jerome Gracián."

19. See letter 269 to Padre Pablo Hernández (dated October 4, 1578), in *The Collected Letters of St. Teresa of Avila,* trans. Kieran Kavanaugh, vol. 2 (Washington, D.C.: ICS Publications, 2007), no. 4.

vow of obedience she made to him. She wrote an account about her vow, like a document, and asked that it be given to Gracián after she died. He carried this document with him until the end of his life.

The only thing I have ever come across that could undermine Teresa's avowed defense and support of one she liked to think of as her son is something written by Blessed Ana de San Bartolomé (García, 1549–1626), who was Teresa's nurse and secretary and in whose arms she died. Blessed Ana claims that after the foundation of Soria in 1581 (on which Teresa was escorted by Nicolás Doria), Teresa's love of Doria grew while her love for Gracián diminished, such that she came to esteem Doria more than Gracián.[20] Although Blessed Ana was a privileged witness to the life and words of St. Teresa, this statement simply does not ring true given the evidence of Teresa's love for Gracián to the very end of her life. It is true that Teresa was much disturbed and hurt when Gracián left her after the foundation in Burgos to go to Seville, and she says as much in her last letter to him a little more than a month before she died (see LE 2.465.2). In that same letter, however, she also says that knowing he is well is a great comfort to her. How much she wanted to have him near her.

JEROME AND HIS BROTHERS

Gracián understood Teresa's originality and believed he was being faithful to her spirit in promoting missionary activity as part of the friars' vocation. In dialogue 3.22 he writes,

> There are those who think that the sum total of Carmelite perfection consists in not leaving one's cell or missing a moment of choir, even if the entire world were ablaze, and that the welfare of the order lies

---

20. Ana de San Bartolomé, *Ana de San Bartolomé obras completas,* ed. Julián Urkiza (Burgos, Spain: Editorial Monte Carmelo, 1999), 444–45. And yet, Blessed Ana had written of Gracián (in this same work), "Because of the great purity of soul that God has granted him, I believe he is one of the most outstanding persons of our times" (116).

> in multiplying the number of monasteries in tiny Spanish villages and neglecting everything else. They call any other spirit restless and lax. God has not led me by that road but by the road of saving souls. The friars whom they want to use for foundations in small places I would use to found monasteries in the most important cities of diverse kingdoms for the true expansion and good of the order. And since I communicated for a long time and with such familiarity with Mother Teresa, whose spirit was zealous for the conversion of the whole world, I was even more convinced of this way.

Unfortunately for Gracián there were others in the order who vehemently disagreed with his interpretation of the Discalced Carmelites. One of these persons was the man who was to succeed him as provincial, Nicolás Doria. At the first interim chapter of the newly erected province, Doria accused Gracián of having "destroyed the order by his easy ways and lack of rectitude in government."[21] Doria was to become Gracián's main antagonist. These two Discalced Carmelites of the first generation understood the Discalced Carmelite movement in fundamentally different ways. According to Doria, St. Teresa's purpose was to reform the ancient prophetic Order of Carmel founded on Mount Carmel. Simply put, he thought that the Discalced Carmelites were the true reform of the Carmelite Order and there was nothing more to it. This understanding of Discalced Carmelites as returning to the rigors of the primitive Rule in a strictly contemplative life with a strong emphasis on regular observance would prevail under Doria.

St. Teresa was not recognized as founder or leader by the friars except Gracián and his sympathizers, one of whom was St. John of the Cross. According to Doria's way of understanding, Teresa was chiefly the teacher of the nuns, who shared in the perfection of the friars as far as their supposed "womanly frailty" allowed them to. The friars,

21. Joachim Smet, *The Mirror of Carmel: A Brief History of the Carmelite Order* (Darien, Ill.: Carmelite Media, 2011), 113. See also *Gracián's* Apología *y avisos acerca del gobierno* (Rome: Institutum Historicum Teresianum, 1977), 61–62.

according to this view, had their own teacher in John of the Cross. After Gracián was expelled from the order, he was effectively left out of the Discalced Carmelite Order's official history. His understanding of the work and charism of St. Teresa was forgotten.

JEROME AND THE TERESIAN CHARISM

Gracián wrote a history of the foundations of the friars in which he complements and continues Teresa's *Book of Foundations,* which describes the establishment of the nuns' monasteries.[22] From Gracián's work we get a very different idea of the life and purpose of the Discalced Carmelite friars: they are apostolic contemplatives. Gracián was considered a danger because he advocated an apostolic contemplative life that was also ready to engage in the work of the missions. Although the main cause of Gracián's expulsion was his objection to Doria's *consulta,* another reason he had to be expelled (in the view of his superiors) was to prevent others from being "contaminated" with his apostolic and missionary ideas. For Gracián, the reforming activity of St. Teresa was only a secondary aspect of her work. He looked on her work not as a simple reform—the elimination of abuses and the restoration of regular observance—but as something far more significant because it responded to the needs of the times. Gracián was the first to really grasp what we now call the "Teresian charism." He saw her work as a new form of Carmelite life that draws its inspiration from both the contemplative ideal and the deep evangelical spirit of Carmel, and so deserves to be called a founding and creative work rather than a reform.

It is important to appreciate Gracián's understanding of Teresa's charism. Because he knew her intimately, he grasped what she was trying to do and his life became one of fidelity to her ideals. This is the principal defense, as it were, that he gives in the *Pilgrimage of Anastasius* regarding his style of leadership and his commitment to the missions. At the provincial chapter held in Lisbon in May 1585, he delivered a defense

22. Jerome Gracián, *Historia de las fundaciones,* MHCT, Fontes selecti 1; MHCT 3, doc. 423, (Rome: Institutum Historicum Teresianum, 1977), 533–694.

of his four years as the first provincial of the Discalced Carmelites since calumnies about him had already been circulating. One of the accusations against him was that he was not rigorous enough in punishing faults. He says it is true that he is inclined more to gentleness than to rigor and to peace rather than to punishment. Another calumny was that he spent too much time preaching, to the neglect of his duties as provincial. He denies that he was remiss in his duties. On the contrary, he says it is his nature to always be occupied. But the calumny that most perturbed him was the accusation that he spent too much time with the nuns: "Nuns, nuns, much dealing and much friendship with nuns."[23] He says that God is so desirous of the holiness of his spouses that it is never a waste of time to help them, especially considering that the nuns were the first Discalced Carmelites. He concludes his defense at the chapter by giving some advice to those who are superiors in the order. He says that the most important thing a superior has to do is attend to the good and well-being of those under his care. Furthermore, a superior's principal duty is to lead by giving a good example. He should foster virtue, console the downhearted, instill fervor, and defend the vulnerable and persecuted. A superior must be like a judge, a doctor, and a father. The three principal virtues of a superior are charity, patience, and humility.[24] As he will say in the *Pilgrimage,* he was confirmed in this manner of governing by St. Teresa.[25]

JEROME'S PILGRIMAGE

As you will read in his autobiography, after Gracián was expelled in February of 1592 from the very order he helped establish under St. Teresa of Jesus, he becomes like a pilgrim,[26] going, albeit of necessity, from place

23. Gracián, *Apologia y avisos,* 70.

24. Gracián, *Apologia y avisos,* 89.

25. See PA 1.8. St. Teresa even gives Gracián charge over her nuns in Pastrana.

26. A pilgrim, strictly speaking, is a person who journeys to a sacred place for religious reasons. While Gracián uses the term broadly, referring to much of his life as a "pilgrimage," he, like the 19th century holy Russian of *Way of a Pilgrim,* was a mendicant pilgrim, a traveler on a journey of faith, when he left Spain after his expulsion from the order.

to place. In 1593, Pope Clement VIII ratified the sentence of the Discalced superiors. Gracián was forbidden to enter any Carmelite house. After searching unsuccessfully for an order that would accept him, he was told to join the Discalced Augustinians. On his way to Rome from Naples to receive the Discalced Augustinian habit, his ship was captured by Barbary pirates on October 11, 1593. He was taken to Tunis, where he experienced firsthand the hardship of the Christian captives in North Africa. He tells us that the worst prison in Spain would have been better than life in the *baño*, as the dungeon-like pit holding the captives was called. He carried out his priestly ministry to the Christian prisoners even at the risk of being burned alive. Through the resourcefulness of a Jewish merchant indebted to Gracián's family, he was finally ransomed and released in April 1595. When he arrived in Rome, Pope Clement VIII—the same pope who had upheld his expulsion from the order—exclaimed after meeting with him, "This man is a saint."[27] On March 5, 1596, the pope issued a brief revoking the sentence of expulsion and restoring Gracián to the Discalced Carmelites with full rights and privileges. But the papal brief caused such an uproar among the Discalced Carmelites that the superior general, Elías de San Martín (Hériz, d. 1614), who was an old companion and friend, was obliged to write to Gracián, asking him to accept being separated for the peace of the order. "I needed to find out," he wrote, "if receiving Your Reverence back would keep the peace among the friars. And there are clear indications that doing this would create many problems and divisions, which I, as the head, albeit unworthy, am obliged to avoid insofar as I can." [28] He quotes St. Paul's letter to the Romans (9:3, NAB): "Indeed, I could even wish to be separated from Christ for the sake of my brothers." They were so fearful of being forced to take him back that they themselves

27. This story appears in several places. For instance, a Calced Carmelite repeats it in a funeral address he delivers in the city of Madrid after news of Jerome's death arrives there. See Ros, *El hombre de Teresa de Jesús*, 511.

28. Ildefonso Moriones, *The Papal Rehabilitation of Father Jerome Gracián in 1595*, trans. John McGowan (Rome: Postulazione Generale O.C.D., 2006), 52.

wanted the Discalced Carmelite friars in Italy—where Gracián resided at the time—to be made into a separate congregation. This did happen in 1600. Although there were other issues as well that led to the division of the new Order of Discalced Carmelites into the two congregations of Spain and Italy, each having its own superior general, the problem about Gracián was certainly one of them.

Gracián remained in Rome from 1595 to 1600. As the pope directed, he lived with the Calced, who treated him with great reverence and respect, and spent most of that time in service to Cardinal Pedro Deza of the Holy Office (precursor of the Congregation for the Doctrine of the Faith) as a theologian. Even though the pope had allowed him to wear the Discalced habit and follow their constitutions, he wore the Calced habit. It was providential that he was in Rome during those years because he was able to do much to promote St. Teresa's beatification. The pope also gave him permission to raise funds to pay the debt from his ransom and to help other Christian captives in North Africa. Gracián was a zealous promoter of missionary activity and was behind the idea of starting a Vatican congregation to oversee the church's missions. In 1600 he was commissioned to preach in Morocco during the holy year for the benefit of the captives there. Since he needed to obtain safe conduct from the Spanish authorities, he had the opportunity to return to Spain and be at the deathbed of his mother, Doña Juana. After fulfilling his commission, he spent the next seven years in Spain engaged in ministry, especially helping various religious orders on behalf of reforming bishops, one of whom was St. Juan de Ribera, archbishop of Valencia. The Discalced objected so strongly to his presence that it was not possible for him to wear the Discalced Carmelite habit. During his time in Spain, he was under the provincial superior of the Calced of the province of Aragon.

In May 1607, by order of the papal nuncio and the express wish of the king of Spain, Philip III, he accompanied the newly appointed Spanish ambassador to the Spanish Netherlands. Arriving in Brussels in July 1607, he met Ana de San Bartolomé and Ana de Jesús (Lobera,

1545–1621). For Gracián it was like old times. He kept very busy preaching, publishing, and promoting the works of St. Teresa. He lived in a hermitage in the garden of the monastery of the Calced in Brussels, once again wearing the habit of a Discalced Carmelite. Gracián was nominated bishop of the Armenians and was to join the Discalced Carmelites of the Italian congregation. This congregation had sent friars to Persia in 1607, where there was a large Christian Armenian population, but for some reason Gracián's appointment never materialized. Three years later, in 1610, the Discalced Carmelite friars of the Italian congregation went to Brussels and Gracián was again invited to join them. But after serious consideration, he decided not to do so; he believed that the existence of two congregations was against the mind of Teresa. Nevertheless, Gracián helped the Italian congregation and was a great supporter of their missionary activity. Still in Brussels, Gracián had the joy of knowing of Teresa's beatification on April 24, 1614. Less than five months later, zealous to the end, he was returning from ministering to souls beyond the city walls when he fell ill on the evening of September 20. The next morning, he was taken to the monastery of the Calced where he died that day. He was sixty-nine.

JEROME'S ZEAL FOR SOULS AND HIS WRITINGS

Whenever I read the *Pilgrimage of Anastasius,* I cannot help but be struck by the extent of Gracián's involvement in the world of his day. That his father and brothers were royal secretaries certainly gave him knowledge of and access to many important people. But what is praiseworthy is that a man who was so well positioned for a high career in the king's service was intent on serving Jesus Christ alone. His devotion to Christ and His Mother is sincere and profound. It is his devotion to Christ, and surely the influence of his Jesuit formation as a young man, that made him an ardent apostle desirous of saving souls. It is the same devotion that makes him want to plunge into the interior life of the spirit with such serious commitment.

He was a man of prayer and ever dedicated to the interior life of souls, beginning with his own. What impresses me about Gracián is how attentive he was to the spiritual needs of his time and his desire to play an active part in bringing light, healing, and sound doctrine into the lives of all he could reach with his apostolic activity.

Gracián was an exemplary writer. Father Joseph Chorpenning writes of Gracián, "His refined elegant humanistic prose is comparable to the best-known writers of the Spanish Golden Age."[29] Commenting on *Pilgrimage* in particular, Father Silverio de Santa Teresa (Gómez) says: "Like all of the works of this genius, it is a true model of the exactness, naturalness, and purity of the language and of the narrative style."[30]

Gracián was not only an excellent writer but also a prolific one. He was a veritable apostle with a pen. In dialogue 12, he enumerates sixty titles of works he wrote. Father Silverio claims that if the memorials are included,[31] Gracián could have written over five hundred works, not including his letters. It is only natural that from the immense amount of writing Gracián did, we can discern his vast knowledge. All the books and authors he refers to are enough to make a sizable bibliography. He said he devoted time every day to reading and study, which is remarkable considering how busy he was. When did he find time to write? He tells us that he needed only a few hours of sleep. He was certainly one of the most learned and well informed of the Discalced Carmelites of his generation.

Gracián was very attentive to the publication of his works because he considered it part of his ministry for the good of souls. One of the reasons he was persuaded to go to the Spanish Netherlands was the

---

29. Jerome Gracián, *Just Man, Husband of Mary, Guardian of Christ: An Anthology of Readings from Jerónimo Gracián's Summary of the Excellencies of St. Joseph (1597)*, ed. and trans. Joseph Chorpenning, 2nd ed. (Philadelphia: St. Joseph's University Press, 1993), 17. Father Chorpenning provides a fine short biography of Gracián.

30. See Gracián, *Peregrinación de Anastasio*, xix.

31. A memorial in this context is a written statement of facts accompanying a petition presented to an authority such as the bishop or the pope.

high-quality printing that was done there. He personally oversaw the printing of his books in Spain, Portugal, Italy, and the Spanish Netherlands. He was such a good writer that he had no trouble finding benefactors to help with printing costs. Some of his works were so popular that they were reprinted numerous times during his lifetime. His most successful work, with twenty-eight editions to date, was a book on St. Joseph to which he gave the title *Josefina*.[32] Gracián must be counted with St. Teresa as one of the great promoters of devotion to St. Joseph.

The most voluminous and widely read were his devotional works, particularly *Lámpara encendida* (*The Burning Lamp*).[33] Gracián, who had the good fortune to intimately know the soul of St. Teresa, indisputably one of the greatest mystics in the history of Christianity, also wrote many books on the theme of the spiritual life. Perhaps the most significant of these was *Dilucidario del verdadero espíritu* (Elucidation of the true spirit), written in Rome in 1599 and printed in Madrid and later in Brussels. It is an explanation and defense of the doctrine of Mother Teresa of Jesus.[34] Furthermore, Gracián was the first Discalced Carmelite to publish books on the theme of mission, imbued as he was with St. Teresa's missionary spirit. In fact, after his work as collaborator with St. Teresa, his greatest glory is perhaps his zeal for the missions. His *Estímulo de la propagación de la fe* (Stimulus for the propagation of the faith), first published in Seville and later in Naples and Brussels, led to the establishment of the Congregation for the Propagation of the Faith in Rome. Finally, there are his works about the Carmelite Order, its rule, history, and saints. Unfortunately, few of Gracián's works have been translated into English. Perhaps this present translation of his autobiography will encourage an interest in his writings.

---

32. See Gracián, *Just Man.*

33. The English edition is Father José L. Morales, ed., *The Burning Lamp, or A Short Summary of Christian Perfection,* trans. Mary Regina Larkin (Brooklyn Carmel of New York, 1971).

34. Teresa was not yet canonized a saint and was known by everyone as Madre Teresa, much like Mother Teresa of Kolkota in the late twentieth century.

JEROME'S ACQUAINTANCES AND GOOD WORKS

The life, work, and writings of Gracián will be of interest to students of sixteenth- and early seventeenth-century Spanish history, an epoch called the Golden Age because of the flourishing of literature, art, and exploration. Gracián is a window into this period through the wide circle of people of all classes with whom he dealt and the amount of detailed information he provides about the current events of his time. Referring to *Pilgrimage*, Father Silverio—the great twentieth-century historian of the order—says, "I know of no other work of his where his pen has deposited so many biographical sketches, or so much reliable and interesting information about the beginning times of the Discalced. This is its principal merit."[35]

If we were to make a list of all the people with whom Gracián had dealings—in his religious community life, personal meetings, spiritual direction, and correspondence—it would be a "Who's Who" of the sixteenth century. We have a collection of 231 letters of his, the earliest one written in 1571 and the last written less than a week before he died. One of his correspondents was Cardinal Federico Borromeo, the cousin of St. Charles Borromeo. The saintly Federico was the model for one of the main characters in the most famous and widely read novel of the Italian language, *I Promessi Sposi* (published in English as *The Betrothed*), by Alessandro Manzoni. The cardinal expressed great friendship for Gracián and wanted him to come to Milan to help with the reform of religious orders there. Another saint whom Gracián met in Rome soon after his expulsion from the Discalced Carmelites was Philip Neri, who gave Gracián one of the greatest consolations he ever felt: "This saint, seeing me thus, placed his hand on my face, saying, 'Brother, do not doubt,' as if he understood the desolation I then felt. From that touch of affection and the words he spoke, I felt such great consolation and peace descend into my heart, greater than any I have ever had in my life" (PA 13.103).

It would be too long to detail in this introduction all of Gracián's various relationships and acquaintances. Suffice it to say, Gracián was no retiring hermit. And yet, he was in no way a busybody, interfering in other

35. See the introduction to Gracián, *Peregrinación de Anastasio*, xix.

people's affairs. He had quite enough of his own work to do and to be concerned with. He was forever occupied in doing good. In the spirit of the Council of Trent that called for the renewal of the priesthood and religious life, he worked hard in the renewal of religious orders, and he was instrumental in the foundation of new ones such as the Discalced Mercedarians and the Discalced Trinitarians. Gracián also helped establish houses for repentant prostitutes in the cities of Seville, Lisbon, and Naples. He worked to improve hospital care in Lisbon and Madrid. He served as chaplain to Spanish soldiers in the Spanish Netherlands. And he made a "Bond of Brotherhood" between the Discalced Carmelites and the Franciscans of St. Peter of Alcántara to give reciprocal help in their missionary endeavors.

As I have said earlier, Gracián had a tremendous awareness of what was going on in the church and the world of his times. In an inventory of his books were found letters from Japan, a grammar of the Mexican language Nauatl, and a book about Africa. He knew about events on all the continents: Africa, where he sent the first Discalced Carmelite missionaries; North America, where he sent the first Discalced to Mexico; the Philippines, China, and Japan, where the Franciscan missionaries with whom he had made a pact were martyred; the Holy Land, where he hoped to regain Mount Carmel for the Carmelites; Persia, where he was almost sent to be a bishop; India, where his nephew was a Jesuit missionary and where Gracián himself nearly went; and of course Europe, where he advocated for the expansion of the Discalced Carmelite Order to Germany and Poland, where the nuns and friars went with his encouragement. At the end of his life, he became concerned about the Catholics in England. He corresponded with Luisa Carvajal, a Spanish noblewoman living in London who ministered to the persecuted Catholics. She asked Gracián for copies of his devotional works and those of Teresa to support the faith of the English Catholics.

Gracián, an indefatigable apostle of Jesus Christ, was out preaching and ministering right up to the end of his life. He was forever a devoted son of the Blessed Virgin Mary and Teresa of Jesus. He always wore around his neck images of both women, his beloved spiritual mothers. He wanted to see these images one last time before he died, but being too weak to pull them out from under his tunic, he asked for help to retrieve them.

JEROME'S REHABILITATION

Reading the *Pilgrimage of Anastasius,* one might be tempted to think that Gracián is some sort of spiritual Don Quixote. In fact, there is something quixotic about him, in the sense that he was trusting and chivalrous. One of the things Teresa loved most in Gracián was his *llaneza,* that is, his sincere, simple, and trusting nature. But unlike Don Quixote, Gracián's adventures were real and he truly touched the lives of many people who were the better for it. Even though he was treated unjustly by his own religious brothers, he was much loved by all who really knew him. Teresa found him irresistible. Reading his letters and writings and the *Pilgrimage of Anastasius,* you realize what a greathearted person he was.

Jerome's brother Thomas wrote touching lines about his long-suffering saintly brother to accompany a small portrait of him that is now in the possession of the Carmelite nuns of Seville:

Here is seen portrayed
Goodness persecuted,
Patience tested,
Perfection that forgives with meekness.
Lies, envy, and ambition
By divine permission
Attempting to overthrow him
Strengthened the innocent
In grace and holiness.[36]

Fortunately, in God's providence, time and grace often have a way of making things right. Gracián, first provincial of the Discalced Carmelites and collaborator of our Holy Mother St. Teresa, was expelled from the order on February 17, 1592. Four centuries later, on December 15, 1999, that sentence was revoked by a formal declaration promulgated by

36. This poem also appears on the reverse side of the first page of the Toledo manuscript of the *Peregrinación de Anastasio.*

the general definitory of the Discalced Carmelite Order.[37] This declaration was made in the spirit of the then forthcoming Great Jubilee of 2000, following the example of Pope John Paul II who made and encouraged gestures of reparation and repentance for past injustices committed in the name of the church. The pope desired to bring about a healing of the wounds caused by unjust and even morally wrong actions suffered by so many in the name of the church. It is likewise hoped that the declaration of the general definitory of the Discalced Carmelite Order will lead to a healing of its historical memory, especially regarding the rightful place of Jerome Gracián in the history and life of the Discalced Carmelites.

A year or so after this Declaration was made, I was at supper with perhaps the most distinguished historian of the Order of Carmel of the Ancient Observance. I felt very privileged to be in his company. Somehow our conversation got around to Jerónimo Gracián. I admit I was leading him on since Gracián is of such great interest to me, and I expected that this scholar would be interested in him as well. After all, when Gracián was expelled from the Discalced, he found welcome and acceptance among the Calced. So, when this historian wondered out loud what in the world the Discalced were thinking by rehabilitating Jerónimo Gracián, I was taken aback. Of course, I defended my man with the strongest argument I knew, namely, that Gracián was the favored son of our Holy Mother, Teresa of Jesus, who, after all, is a saint. He countered that even saints have their weaknesses. He went on to describe my hero as a bragging buffoon and a whiner who deserved to be cast out from the Discalced. Then he added an argument from authority, saying that this judgment of his was the same as that of Fr. Louis Bouyer. For heaven's sake, what does Fr. Bouyer, one of the great scholars of the Church to be sure, know about Jerónimo Gracián? So my confrere took me up to the library to see a book by the prodigious scholar: ". . . Gracián, obviously, was so

37. See Appendix V, "Official Declaration of the Rehabilitation of Father Jerome Gracián of the Mother of God, O.C.D." (1999). See also Moriones, *Papal Rehabilitation.* Original text: Burgos, Spain: Monte Carmelo, Num. 103 (1995). A section of this study is titled "The Problem of Our Historical Memory."

amusing—what John must not have been, so subtle, so refined!—and the Madre, with all her cares, had great need of a clown in order not to explode. It is merely a shame that she made a clown her director . . ."[38]

Though Fr. Bouyer wrote these words thirty years ago, long before Gracián was rehabilitated, their prejudicial effects remain to this day. Gracián is still maligned and misunderstood. However, with the passage of time, Gracián is gaining a wider acceptance. On the fourth centenary of his death (September 21, 2014), the two superiors general of the respective orders of Carmel, the Discalced (Saverio Cannistrà) and the Ancient Observance (Fernando Millán Romeral), wrote a joint circular letter about him. They conclude (#26): "Dear brothers and sisters, charity triumphs, abounds, and loves all . . . Gracián invites us to be artisans of peace and reconciliation, so that seeing our good works, our heavenly Father will be glorified (see Mt 5:16). The *Pilgrimage* of Jerónimo Gracián is an expression of his profound spiritual way, which is his response to the love of God put into his heart through Our Lady in his desire to embrace the Rule of Carmel according to the teachings of Teresa of Jesus and the passion to give himself to others for their salvation." Such is an apt and succinct description of *Pilgrimage*. May we follow the example of such a pilgrim as Jerome Gracián in our own response to God's love for us.

READING THE *PILGRIMAGE OF ANASTASIUS*

The *Pilgrimage of Anastasius* is a complex work, similar to the Bible in that it consists of a variety of "books" containing interesting and even amazing anecdotes and details. Gracián organizes this varied material by linking each subject to a particular element—or "hieroglyph" as he calls it—in his shield or spiritual coat of arms (see PA Pref.5). His shield is like a treasure map, leading readers to find countless gems that shed light on the person of Jerome Gracián, his great virtue and love of Carmel, St. Teresa and her charism, and the early history of the Discalced Carmelites.

38. Louis Bouyer, *Women Mystics*, trans. Ann E. Nash (San Francisco: Ignatius Press, 1993), 107.

THE DIALOGUES AND THEIR CORRESPONDING ELEMENTS IN GRACIÁN'S SHIELD

Dialogue 1: Novitiate, profession, and visitation	*Unshod feet*
Dialogue 2: Hardships and persecutions from the Discalced	*Unshod feet*
Dialogue 3: Hardships as apostolic visitator and provincial	*Unshod feet*
Dialogue 4: Expulsion from the congregation of the Discalced	*Unshod feet*
Dialogue 5: Appeal of the sentence in Rome and capture by Turks	*Unshod feet*
Dialogue 6: Life in a Tunisian dungeon	*Chains*
Dialogue 7: Freedom and acceptance by the Calced	*Chains*
Dialogue 8: Interior tribulations	*Cross in heart*
Dialogue 9: Desires to return to the Discalced	*Shield and stars*
Dialogue 10: Consolations mixed with labors and tribulations	*Thorns and jewels*
Dialogue 11: Twelve interior comforts	ACFRIC
Dialogue 12: Studies and writings	*Twelve stars*
Dialogue 13: Foundations of Discalced friars and nuns	*Jewels in crown*
Dialogue 14: Reformations of orders and conversions	*Jewels in crown*

Dialogue 15:
Spirit and manner of prayer *Name of Jesus*
Dialogue 16:
Revelations of St. Teresa and other nuns *Name of Mary*

CONCLUSION

I first read *Peregrinación de Anastasio* when I was a newly professed student friar, in order to fulfill a summer study assignment. I felt that I had found someone who could give me a deeper understanding of my vocation. St. John of the Cross had brought me into the Discalced Carmelite Order, and I will always owe my first allegiance to him; St. Teresa of Jesus has been my "Holy Mother" since I was a novice; and St. Thérèse of the Child Jesus is a constant source of encouragement in my attempt to fulfill the Discalced Carmelite vocation. But it is Jerome Gracián who has given me the widest and deepest vision of this same vocation, a vision that is exhilarating and breathtaking. Since that summer nearly forty years ago, I have wanted to translate Gracián's *Peregrinación* in order to share this vision with other English speakers, especially our Carmelite family. It is my hope that this translation will awaken interest in this friend and confidant of St. Teresa who has so much to share with us today. I also believe Jerome Gracián of the Mother of God is a saint in his own right.

At the end of this translation, you will find Gracián's "Letter to a Friend," which is a very short version of what he has written in *Pilgrimage* and includes other interesting details of his life. There are also two letters of his wherein he writes of his circumstances in the Spanish Netherlands. I wish I had more time to translate his many collected letters for they give further insight into the zeal of this holy man.

FATHER STEPHEN WATSON, O.C.D.
OCTOBER 15, 2022

Note on the Translation

As far as I know, the book you have in your hands is the only translation in any language of the *Peregrinación de Anastasio*.[1] This is a translation of the *Peregrinación* edited and prepared by Father Juan Luis Astigarraga. His edition was published as volume 19 of Monumenta Historica Carmeli Teresiani (MHCT) in 2001.

Four manuscripts were used for the edition prepared by Father Astigarraga. Variations between the manuscripts are numerous but not particularly significant with regard to the narration. In any case, Father Astigarraga has done a masterful job of collating the manuscripts in order to provide us with the best Spanish edition of the *Peregrinación de Anastasio* in print. In his Spanish edition, he has placed the variant reading at the bottom of the page with a letter that corresponds to one of the four manuscripts, A, B, C, and D. These variant readings are minor, often consisting of a difference in spelling or verb tense or some additional phrase.

Father Astigarraga was the one to discover the existence of a manuscript ("A") of the *Peregrinación* in the National Historical Archives (AHN) in Madrid, written in Gracián's own hand. It was complete up to and including the seventh dialogue. At the end of dialogue 7, Gracián writes, "I was sent to Pamplona to preach during Lent; from there I came to Flanders."[2] We know from Gracián's letters that he left Pamplona for the Spanish Netherlands at the end of May 1607, so we can

1. There was a French translation of selected passages printed in the *Annales du Carmel* in 1880–1884.

2. I.e., the Spanish Netherlands. I chose to retain Gracian's use of "Flanders" wherever he mentions it in the dialogues since that is how he and his contemporaries referred to the Dutch-speaking region that comprised present-day northern Belgium and neighboring parts of France and the Netherlands.

conclude that at least the first half (dialogues 1–7) of the *Peregrinación* was written by this time. Father Jerome Gracián finally finished his autobiographical work when he was in the Spanish Netherlands. Based on his letters to his sisters, who were Discalced Carmelite nuns in Spain, we can be certain that he finished his great work by 1612. However, we do not know when he began writing it.

In the archives of the Discalced Carmelite nuns of Brussels is found a complete manuscript ("B") of the *Peregrinación*. In fact, this was the only manuscript known to Father Silverio and two other editors of the work. Thus all three previous editions of *Peregrinación de Anastasio* were based exclusively on the Brussels manuscript.[3] The first two editions were made from the transcribed and modernized copy made by Father Gregory of St. Joseph. It was Father Gregory who first discovered the existence of the Brussels manuscript, leading to his monumental study of the expulsion of Gracián that appeared in French in 1904 (Rome: Postulazione Generale O.C.D.) with the title "Le P. Jerome Gratien de la Mere de Dieu et Ses Juges" (Father Jerome Gracián of the Mother of God and his judges). Father John McGowan, O.C.D., recently translated this work.[4]

Those three editors thought that the Brussels manuscript was written in the hand of Gracián. Father Astigarraga, however, is convinced that it was not written by Gracián. His judgment is based on the fact that there are many misspelled words, and worse still, incorrect Latin, mistakes that Gracián would have never made. Astigarraga has studied many manuscripts in Gracián's own hand and can be considered the foremost expert in Gracián's writings. The primary merit of the Brussels manuscript is that it is the only complete text of the *Peregrinación*. It is therefore the basic text used by Astigarraga for dialogues 8–16.

---

3. Angel María de Santa Teresa (Burgos, Spain: El Monte Carmelo, 1905); Silverio de Santa Teresa, Biblioteca Mística Carmelitana 17 (Burgos, Spain: El Monte Carmelo, 1932–1933); Giovanni Maria Bertini (Barcelona: Juan Flors, 1966).

4. Gregory of St. Joseph, *Father Jerome Gratian O.C.D. and Those Who Judged Him*, trans. John McGowan (Oxford, UK: Joshua Horgan Print and Design, 2014).

In the Historical Archives of the civil province of Toledo, there is a manuscript ("C") of the *Peregrinación* that had been in the possession of Father Lorenzo Gracián, the younger brother of Jerome who entered the Discalced Carmelites.[5] Although it is very old and valuable, Father Astigarraga is of the opinion that it is not an autograph copy.

Finally, in the Silveriano Archives of Burgos (O.C.D. province) is found the shortest and briefest of the manuscripts ("D"). The copyist was the official historian of the order, Father Jerónimo de San José (Ezquerra), who probably made the copy around 1630 when he was gathering material for his history. In fact, it contains only parts of dialogues 9, 10, and 13, omitting entire paragraphs that were of no interest to him for his history. Astigarraga asks the question: What is the source of this copy made by Ezquerra? Although there are variations from the Toledo manuscript, the curious fact is that both of these manuscripts end abruptly at the same place in dialogue 13. Could the copyist have carried off the remainder of the Toledo manuscript to finish copying it and never returned it, and what's more, never even finished copying it?

At the beginning of each dialogue is a description of its contents. These descriptions were written by Gracián, but in them I substituted "Gracián" for "Anastasius" to make clear that these are Gracián's real-life experiences. The dialogues themselves, however, remain as Gracián intended, which is to use the voices of "Anastasius" and "Cyril" to express his thoughts and feelings. The superscriptions within the dialogues were originally written in the margins by Gracián, and Father Astigarraga in his Spanish edition placed them at the beginning of each section in which they occur. I have done likewise and have also numbered each paragraph to make it easier to study and refer to various passages of Gracián's autobiographical work.

I freely translated most of Gracián's Scripture quotations (from the Latin Vulgate) or else used the New American Bible which I had with me in Rome at the time. Quotes from the New American Bible are indicated in the citation.

---

5. See Enrique Llamas Martínez, "La 'Peregrinación de Anastasio' del Padre Jerónimo Gracián de la Madre de Dios: Nuevo manuscrito," *EphCarm* 28, no. 2 (1977): 278–310.

Regarding usage, the only thing I need mention is that Gracián uses the terms *Calced* and *Discalced* very frequently throughout the *Peregrinación*. They are always capitalized regardless of their historical context. For the sake of simplicity, ease of reading, and especially for the practical purpose of distinguishing one group from the other, I've done the same. It should be noted that present-day Carmelites of the Ancient Observance are referred to not as Calced, but as "O.Carms."

Gracián died September 21, 1614. He did not want anyone but members of his family to read his *Peregrinación* until after his death. A dear friend of the family, Andrés del Mármol, published a book titled *Excellencias, vida y trabajos del padre fray Gerónimo Gracián de la Madre de Dios, carmelita* (The excellences, life and work of Father Jerome Gracián of the Mother of God, Carmelite [Valladolid, Spain, 1619]).[6] In this biography are extensive quotations from the *Peregrinación*. Gracián also wrote an account of his captivity in the form of a dialogue, called *Dialogos de Eliseo* (Dialogues of Elisha), recounting in much more detail what he experienced and endured during that time. Finally, there is the *Carta a un amigo* (Letter to a friend) that Gracián wrote sometime in the middle of 1612. It is not a letter to anyone in particular but rather a lovely little work written in the form of a letter. It is a résumé of the *Peregrinación de Anastasio*. Astigarraga includes it in his edition of the *Peregrinación de Anastasio*, and my translation of it appears at the end of this work as well.

6. The author of this book is Father Cristóbal Márquez, O.Carm.

Abbreviations

Works by Jerome Gracián

Cartas	*Cartas* (Letters)
Escolias	*Escolias*
Peregrinación	*Peregrinación de Anastasio* (Spanish edition)
PA	*Pilgrimage of Anastasius* (This edition)

Works by St. Teresa of Jesus

ST	*Spiritual Testimonies*
F	*The Book of Her Foundations*
LE	*The Collected Letters of St. Teresa of Avila*

Works by St. John of the Cross

A	*Ascent of Mount Carmel*

Others

EphCarm	*Ephemerides Carmeliticae*
MHCT	Monumenta Historica Carmeli Teresiani
MHG	Monumenta Hieronymi Gracian

Chronology of the Life of Father Jerome Gracián[1]

1545	June 6	Jerome Gracián is born in Valladolid
1559		Moves with his family to Toledo where he begins his study of philosophy
1560		Studies at the University of Alcalá de Henares; receives master of arts
1566		Receives minor orders
1569	September 25	Is ordained a subdeacon
	December 17	Is ordained a deacon
1570	January 1	Preaches his first sermon in Canillejas (Madrid)
	March 25	Is ordained a priest
1571	October 4	Preaches about St. Francis to the Discalced Carmelite nuns of Alcalá de Henares, thinking they were Poor Clares, and reads their constitutions
1572	April 25	Enters the novitiate of the Discalced Carmelite friars at Pastrana
1573	April 25	Makes his profession
	August 4	Is named subdelegate apostolic visitator of the Discalced of Andalusia by Baltasar Nieto, who was given authority (in April) by Francisco de Vargas, O.P.

1. The primary sources for this material are Peers's *Handbook to the Life*, Rohrbach's *Journey to Carith*, and Smet's *Mirror of Carmel*, not to mention Gracián's own *Pilgrimage of Anastasius*.

	September	Travels to Seville with Father Ambrosio Mariano de San Benito (Azaro) and meets Vargas, who makes him apostolic visitator of the Calced of Andalusia
	October 18	Returns San Juan del Puerto monastery to the Calced
1574	January 5	Founds the Discalced monastery of Nuestra Señora de Los Remedios in Seville
	June 13	Is named vicar provincial of all the Calced and Discalced Carmelites of Andalusia by Vargas
	August 13	A papal brief obtained by General Juan Bautista Rubeo (Rossi) revokes the powers of the apostolic visitators in Spain
	September 22	The nuncio Nicolò Ormaneto makes Vargas and Gracián joint reformers of Andalusia (confirmed December 27 by Gregory XIII)
1575	April	Gracián meets Teresa of Jesus in Beas de Segura for the first time
	May 22	The general chapter of the Carmelite Order convenes at Piacenza (Italy) and decides to close the Discalced houses of Andalusia
	May 24	Mother Teresa makes a special vow of obedience to Gracián
	August 3	Gracián is named apostolic visitator of the Calced of Andalusia and commissary of the Discalced by the nuncio Ormaneto
	November 21	Attempts to make a visitation of the Calced at Seville
	December 10	General Rubeo appoints Portuguese Carmelite Jerome Tostado visitator, reformer, and commissary general of the Spanish provinces
1576	February 21–April 1	Gracián makes a visitation of the Calced at Seville

	May 12	A Calced provincial chapter at Moraleja (Castile) confirms the Piacenza resolutions
		The king annuls the Moraleja decisions shortly afterward
	August 3	Gracián writes patent letters in which he declares his intention to create a separate province of the Discalced, confirms the three Discalced houses in Andalusia, and plans a chapter (to be held August 26) for the election of a provincial and definitors
	August 5	Tostado arrives in Madrid; Ormaneto advises him to start his visitation with Portugal
	September 1	Gracián issues decree reasserting intention to establish a Discalced province and deferring election of a provincial while he is still apostolic commissary and visitator
	September 9	Discalced chapter at Almodóvar del Campo presided over by Gracián adopts constitutions, rejects Moraleja chapter decisions, and decides to send deputies to Rome to work for the creation of a separate province (their departure is delayed two years)
		Antonio de Jesús (Heredia) is made Gracián's deputy and first definitor
		Teresa of Jesus, the nuncio, and the king are pleased with the chapter acts
	October	Gracián resumes his visitation of Andalusia
1577	June 18	Continues with the visitation of the Discalced in Castile following the death of Ormaneto
	August 29	Offers to resign his commission to papal nuncio Filippo Sega, but Sega tells him to

		continue his visitations provided that he report to him
		Consults the archbishop of Toledo and the king, whereupon the king intervenes with the pope, who declares that the nuncio is not to interfere with religious orders unless requested by the king
		Fearing Sega's wrath, discontinues his visitations for nearly a year
		Tostado decrees that no new Discalced foundations are to be made, all Discalced houses are to have Calced superiors, and Discalced superiors (friars) are to report to him
		Calced friars of Andalusia accuse Gracián of gross misbehavior during his visitations
	September	Discalced friars Baltasar and Miguel de la Columna accuse Gracián of grave misdeeds but soon retract their accusations
	November 5	The royal council forbids Tostado to conduct visitations in Andalusia and Castile
	December 3	John of the Cross is imprisoned at the Calced monastery in Toledo upon Tostado's orders
1578	May	The king orders Gracián to resume his visitations
	July 23	Sega annuls all patents and faculties given by Ormaneto to Gracián, forbids the Discalced to obey him, and assumes governance of the Discalced (via the Calced)
	August 9	The royal council forbids the Discalced to obey Sega and confirms Gracián as visitator

August 17–18	John of the Cross escapes from the Toledo Carmelite prison
September 4	Carmelite General Rubeo dies; succeeded by Giovanni Battista Caffardo
September	Gracián submits to Sega's "counterbrief" of July 23 by handing over Ormaneto's patents, effectively resigning his office as visitator, which annoys the king
	Sega excommunicates and imprisons Gracián, Antonio, and Mariano in separate monasteries for many weeks; Gracián is sent to the Calced at Madrid.
October 9	Antonio as first definitor convenes a chapter at Almodóvar del Campo and is elected "provincial"
	Pedro de Los Ángeles is chosen to go to Rome to seek independence for the Discalced (Pedro gets sidetracked in Naples and joins the Calced).
October 16	Sega excommunicates the chapter's participants, annuls their decisions, places the Discalced friars and nuns under the Calced provincials, and forbids the Discalced to receive more novices
October–November	Sega banishes or imprisons the Discalced leaders.
	Gracián is confined again at the Calced monastery in Madrid
	The king intervenes; Sega promises to help establish a separate province for the Discalced if Gracián is first sentenced (on charges from the Calced of Andalusia)

	December	Gracián is tried by three judges appointed by Sega
	December 20	Is sentenced by Sega and deprived of the office of visitator, confined to the monastery at Alcalá de Henares where he is to do penance, and forbidden to write or receive letters
1579		A committee appointed by the king examines the whole matter and concludes that the Discalced ought to have their own province and superior
	April 1	Sega revokes all previous briefs and removes the Discalced from under Calced government, naming Angel de Salazar, Calced prior of Valladolid, their vicar general until a separate province can be made for them
	Mid-May	Juan de Jesús (Roca) and Diego de la Trinidad are sent to Rome to work toward obtaining the brief for a separate province
	July 15	Sega and the royal committee petition King Philip II to ask the pope to create a separate Discalced province
	November 11	Sega forwards the king's request for a separate province to the pope, accompanied by his own recommendation
1580	February	Gracián is freed from imprisonment through the intervention of the king and Salazar
	February 19	Is reelected, unanimously, prior of Los Remedios in Seville (takes office in October)
	April 10	Salazar makes Gracián a delegate visitator of the Discalced in Andalusia
	June 22	The Brief of Separation *Pia consideratione* is issued by Gregory XIII, establishing the

		Discalced as a separate province within the order
	August 30	The brief *Nuper iustis* names Pedro Fernández, O.P., to execute the Brief of Separation
	October 26	The king sends for a new brief naming Juan de las Cuevas, O.P., to execute the Brief of Separation due to Fernández's illness and impending death (dies November 22)
	November 20	Gregory XIII issues the new brief
1581	March 3	The "Chapter of the Separation" opens in Alcalá, and the Discalced province is erected; Gracián is elected provincial (receives eleven of twenty votes; Antonio receives seven); four definitors are elected (Doria, Antonio, John of the Cross, and Gabriel de la Asunción); and laws and constitutions for both friars and nuns of the new province are promulgated
	May 4	The new province of the Discalced Carmelites makes its first foundation of friars in Valladolid
	June 1	A college of the friars is founded in Salamanca
	October 14	The foundation of the friars in Lisbon is made
1582	April 5	Gracián sends the first Discalced Carmelite missionaries to the Congo; they drown at sea
	October 4	Teresa of Jesus dies
1583	May 1	The Discalced province holds its second chapter in Almodóvar and elects as definitors Juan de Jesús Roca, Mariano, Agustín de los Reyes (Carrasco y Góngora), and Ambrosio de San Pedro; sends a second missionary expedition to the Congo (they are captured by English pirates, are dumped on an

		island off Africa, and eventually return to Spain); and sends Nicolás Doria to found a house in Genoa
		At the last session, Doria criticizes Gracián for preaching too much outside community life
	May	The foundation of the friars in La Fuensanta is made
	July 25	The foundation of the friars in Daimiel is made
1584	April 10	A third missionary group is sent to the Congo; they arrive successfully
	June 27	A foundation of the friars is made in Málaga by Gabriel de la Peñuela
	December 10	A foundation is made in Genoa by Doria
1585	March 24	The foundation of the friars in Guadalcázar is made
	April 9	Gracián, on behalf of the Discalced Carmelites, signs the Concord of Missionary Brotherhood with the Franciscans
	May 10–17	At chapter in Lisbon, Gracián defends his past term as provincial and proposes Doria, in Genoa at the time, as his successor (receives twenty-six of twenty-eight votes); new definitors are Gracián, John of the Cross, Juan Bautista el Rondeño (after Antonio declines to accept), and Gregorio Nacianceno (Martínez)
	May 17	The definitors decide to send twelve friars to the Indies (Mexico) and three friars to the Congo
	July 11	The missionaries leave for Mexico
	Summer	Gracián writes *Estímulo de la propagación de la fe* (Stimulus for the propagation of the faith)

	October 17	At reconvened chapter in Pastrana, Doria increases the vicariates to four, placing Old Castile and Navarre under Gregorio, New Castile under Juan Bautista, Andalusia under John of the Cross, and Portugal under Gracián; Genoa, Africa, and Mexico remain under the provincial
	October 26	Gracián is made prior of the monastery in Lisbon
1586	January 19	A foundation is made in Mexico City
		Estímulo de la propagación de la fe is published in Lisbon
		Gracián writes and circulates the tract "Apology in Defense of Charity against Some Who, under the Pretext of Observance of Rules, Weaken and Disturb It in Religious Orders"
	August 13–September 4	A definitory meeting is held in Madrid, approving the publication of Teresa's writings, total separation of the Discalced from the Calced, a permanent procurator in Rome, and use of the Roman liturgy in place of the Carmelite liturgy of the Holy Sepulcher; Gracián is not in attendance
	September 20	Sixtus V confirms the definitory's resolutions
1587	April 18–25	The provincial chapter is held in Valladolid; Elías de San Martín (New Castile), Antonio de Jesús (Portugal), Agustín de los Reyes (Andalusia), and Juan Bautista el Remendado (Old Castile) are elected definitors; Doria proposes that the definitors not merely be consultants but also have deciding votes in

	meetings with the provincial; following Gracián's lead, the chapter rejects the *consulta* (Doria later obtains the king's support and uses his connections in Rome to petition the Holy See directly for approval of the *consulta*)
April 23	Doria appoints Gracián vicar provincial of Mexico (Gracián waits for a ship at Seville until September, but no ships are sailing that year due to piracy and King Philip's armada preparations)
July 10	Sixtus V in his brief *Cum de statu* approves of the Discalced Carmelite province being formed into a congregation of five provinces within the Carmelite Order, of its being governed by a vicar general (six-year term), and of Doria's *consulta* (the six councillors would be over the vicars provincial)
July 27	The pope issues a bull (petitioned by Doria) granting the congregation power to expel contumacious friars
September	Gracián goes to work in the diocese of Jaén
September 14	A foundation of the friars is made in Úbeda by Gracián
October 18	Gracián is examined by Elías de San Martín in Úbeda on ten charges having to do with frequent visits with the nuns, eating meat, wearing linen, using sheets, and sleeping on a mattress; Gracián responds to these allegations in a twenty-four page statement
November 25	Doria meets with the definitors in Madrid, obtains sufficient support for the *consulta*, and

		makes a case against Gracián based on the recent charges and a book that Gracián wrote against his superiors
	November 28	The *consulta* sends Gracián a formal admonition to amend his behavior
1588	February	Gracián returns to Portugal
	May 2	Writes the *consulta* that he is willing to resign as vicar of Mexico, renounce active and passive voice, and devote himself to prayer and study at any monastery
	May 12	The *consulta* orders Gracián to Seville (to leave for Mexico)
	June 17	The *consulta* orders that the contents of Gracián's letter of submission be adopted: he is deprived of his vote and his right to hold office in the next two chapters and is to go to Mexico as a simple friar
	June 19	At general chapter of the congregation in Madrid, John of the Cross, Agustín de los Reyes, Antonio de Jesús, and Elías de San Martín are elected definitors; the brief *Cum de statu* is implemented: Doria is elected vicar general and the *consulta* is established; new councillors are John of the Cross, Antonio de Jesús, Mariano, Juan Bautista el Rondeño, Luis de San Jerónimo, and Bartolomé de Jesús
	June 27	Doria sends Gracián to Evora upon pressure from the king and Portuguese prelates, particularly Archbishop Teutonio de Braganza and Cardinal Archduke Albert, who want him

		back in Portugal (rebellion occurs in Portugal as Don Antonio seeks the crown)
	October 13	The nuncio Cesare Speziano confirms and approves the Alcalá constitutions and declares their perpetual stability (the nuns had feared they would be changed or revoked by the *consulta*)
	November 2	Gracián appeals to the king against Doria and asks that the *consulta* and its laws be examined
	November 24	Cardinal Albert makes Gracián visitator and reformer of the Calced in Portugal for fear that the many friars of Lisbon who supported Don Antonio would aid the English
1589	January	Doria writes the king about how good the *consulta* is and how Gracián is disturbing it
	February 20	The royal chaplain notifies Doria of the king's satisfaction with the *consulta*
		Cardinal Albert summons Gracián to Lisbon
	May 30	The English Armada encamps at Alcántara, assails the walls of Lisbon for three days, and then withdraws
1590	June 5	Sixtus V in the brief *Salvatoris* confirms St. Teresa's Alcalá constitutions (which Ana de Jesús had petitioned for in early 1589) and creates for the nuns an office of commissary general, to be subject to the vicar general alone
	June 10	Doria convenes an extraordinary general chapter in Madrid to publish new constitutions that give the councillors a decisive vote and place governance of the nuns under the

		consulta; the chapter also restricts Gracián's correspondence
	June 27	Sixtus V appoints Luis de León and Archbishop Braganza to execute the June 5 brief (Doria refuses to call a chapter for the election of a commissary general)
	July–August	Gracián reviews the laws of the *consulta* and sends a list of its drawbacks to Rome to have them examined
	August 21	Doria writes the nuns that he has to appeal the papal brief or else dissociate from them
	August 27	Sixtus V dies
1591	January 26	Doria declares that Ana de Jesús, María de San José (Salazar), and Gracián are to blame for the papal brief and asks the king to admonish the two nuns to obey their superiors and to urge the pope to declare the Sixtine Brief null and void
	April 25	Gregory XIV issues a brief *Quoniam non ignoramus*, by which the office of commissary is abolished and the communities of nuns are made subject to their own provincials, as opposed to the *consulta*
	May 14	Gracián finishes his visitation of the Calced in Lisbon and around the province
	June 1	At general chapter in Madrid, John of the Cross, who is not reelected to any office due to his increasing opposition to Doria and the *consulta*, speaks out against the excess of laws and the recent treatment of Gracián and the nuns, and volunteers to go to Mexico
	June 3	The *consulta* sends for Gracián

	June 25	A patent is drawn up authorizing John of the Cross to go to Mexico (it is dropped when the definitory learns of Gregory XIV's brief; John of the Cross goes to La Peñuela in late July)
	June–July	Gracián arrives in Madrid (June 28)
		After the *consulta* offers him a patent as vicar general of the Indies, which he refuses, he is arrested, charged, and imprisoned
		After days of solitary confinement as well as coercive threats and false promises from Diego Evangelista, Gracián makes a confession and is brought to trial; he retracts his confession and is sentenced to various restrictions and harsh penances
	November	New charges are read to Gracián and a new tribunal sentences him
	December 14	John of the Cross dies in Úbeda
1592	February 17	Gracián receives the sentence of expulsion from the order for being incorrigible and is stripped of his habit
	February 19	Clement VIII issues a brief approving Doria's new constitutions for the friars and for the nuns; the nuns' constitutions were taken from Gregory's brief
	February 27	Gracián goes to Rome to appeal the sentence (for which the nuncio absolves the censures in the sentence for six months)
	August	Petitions Clement VIII for two judges to examine his case
		Is told to join another order, but no order accepts him

		Father José Acosta tells him to write to the pope and wait elsewhere for a reply
1593	February	Gracián goes to Palermo and stays there writing books
	June	A delegation of Discalced friars attend the general chapter of the Carmelite Order at Cremona and petition to be given their own general; the chapter agrees
	June 22	A brief is issued stating that Gracián is to enter the Augustinian order
	August	Gracián goes to Naples, visits his relatives in Gaeta, and boards a frigate for Rome
	October 11	The frigate is captured by the Turks; Gracián is taken to Bizerte and then to Tunis
	Mid-November	Gracián is put in chains and placed in the dungeon
	December 20	Clement VIII issues the bull *Pastoralis officii*, establishing the Discalced as a separate order and appointing Doria as interim superior general
	Christmas	Gracián is spared being burned alive on suspicion of being an inquisitor
1594	April 1	Gracián is spared being burned alive for converting a renegade
	May 9	Doria dies en route to the general chapter at which he is expected to be elected superior general of the new order
	May 23	The general chapter at Madrid elects Elías de San Martín superior general

	Early June	Diego Evangelista dies en route to take up his duties as provincial of Upper Andalusia (Granada)
1595	April 11	Ransom for Gracián is arranged by a Jewish merchant indebted to his family
		Gracián stays with the French consul for one month
	August 18	Gracián arrives in Genoa and goes to Rome; he is refused admittance by the Augustinians due to his debt for the ransom
	October 25	Writes the Discalced, asking for readmittance
1596	January 9	Receives a papal brief allowing him to beg in order to pay his debt
	March 6	Receives a papal brief readmitting him to the Discalced Order
	March 21	Receives a reply from Father Elías de San Martín saying he will not be readmitted to the Discalced Order due to the objections of some of the friars and his desire to keep peace
	April 6	Receives a patent (issued by papal order) from the vicar general of the Calced allowing him to live with them as a Discalced; serves Cardinal Pedro Deza (protector of Spain) in Rome for the next five years
1597		*Josefina* (Joseph) and *Tratado de la redención de cautivos* (Treatise concerning the redemption of captives) are published in Rome
1600		*El devoto peregrino* (The devout pilgrim) is published in Rome

	June 10	Gracián is commissioned to preach the holy year jubilee in Africa and help the Christian captives there
1601		*Mística teología* (Mystical theology) is published in Madrid
	October 1	Gracián's mother, Juana Dantisco, dies in Madrid; Gracián is there obtaining letters of safe conduct in Africa from King Philip II
1602	May 15	Gracián goes to the monastery of the Calced in Madrid
1604		*Dilucidario del verdadero espíritu* (Elucidation of the true spirit) is published in Madrid
	November 19	Gracián goes to Valencia
1607	Lent	Goes to preach in Pamplona
	May	The first half of *Peregrinación de Anastasio* (*Pilgrimage of Anastasius*) is written by this time
	Summer	Goes to the Spanish Netherlands
1609		*Lámpara encendida* (*The Burning Lamp*) and *Vida del alma y verdadera imitación de Cristo* (Life of the soul and true imitation of Christ) are published in Brussels
1611		*Declamación en que se trata de la perfecta vida y virtudes de la B. M. Teresa de Jesús, y de las fundaciones de sus monasterios* (Declamation about the perfect life and virtues of blessed Mother Teresa of Jesus and the foundation of her monasteries) and *Diez lamentaciones del miserable estado de los ateístas de nuestro tiempo* (Ten lamentations concerning the miserable

		state of the atheists of our time) are published in Brussels
1612		The remainder of *Peregrinación de Anastasio* is written or compiled by this time
1614	April 24	Teresa of Jesus is beatified by Paul V
	September 21	Jerome Gracián dies at the Calced monastery in Brussels
1792		The French Revolution spreads violently to Belgium, destroying the Carmelite priory in Brussels; Gracián's resting place to this day has never been found
1999	December 15	At their 47th session, the general definitory officially revokes the sentence of expulsion from the order issued against Gracián, with an apology for the way he had been treated at the time and indeed since

Dialogues

These dialogues describe the labors, tribulations, persecutions, and crosses that Father Jerome Gracián of the Mother of God [Jerónimo de la Madre de Dios] has suffered ever since he received the Discalced Carmelite habit and the many consolations and mercies he has received from our Lord. They include his manner of proceeding in the spirit and some revelations of Mother Teresa of Jesus and other servants of God foretelling some things that have happened to him.

Addressed to his brother and sisters, Fray Lorenzo de la Madre de Dios and Mothers María de San José, Juliana de la Madre de Dios, and Isabel de Jesús, of the Order of Our Lady of Carmel of the Discalced.

Interlocutors

Anastasius who responds and **Cyril** who questions

Composed by the same Father Fray Jerome Gracián
of the Mother of God

Preface

This section provides the reason this book is written and explains its style and manner of proceeding.

"We glory in our tribulations," says the apostle [Rom 5:3]. Just as the soldier, according to St. Macarius, likes to recount his battles and show his wounds; and one who sails the seas, says Chrysostom, recalls the storms and tempests he has gone through; and the farmer tells of the cold winter he has endured in order to plant, so it is not burdensome for me to recount my tribulations, afflictions, labors, affronts, dangers, and pilgrimages by sea and by land, especially if this is some consolation, exhortation, and help for whoever might read it, because this is why God brings us by way of the cross.

2. I do not think that recounting the affronts I have suffered will detract from what I owe in recognizing my miseries, sins, and faults, since—as St. Augustine says—just as the same fire that refines and makes resplendent the gold first darkens it with smoke, so too the fire of tribulation, which in others produces the gold of virtue, perfection, and an exemplary life, has produced in me—because I am more vile than straw and dung—impatience, sins, and bad example.

3. The truth is—as St. Gregory of Nyssa says—to reveal one's wounds gives glory to God and sings of His everlasting mercy. Just as a barren field that yields a treasure is good, and putting grapes and olives in the press to make wine and oil is good, as is scraping a civet cat so that it gives musk, likewise it is good that God permits tribulations and labors in this life for the great good brought forth by the one who

recounts them and sings His mercies. Being the fruit of the cross of Christ, such tribulations and labors should be esteemed more than honors, riches, rest, and all temporal goods and spiritual delights that can come to a man.

4. I am writing this discourse as a dialogue since it is a more pleasant style and manifests with greater clarity all that has happened to me, without mentioning my name. What I mainly intend is to defend the honor of many holy persons and religious who are suspected of some imperfection by whomever has spoken about my failures, for they have been judged to be accomplices of my weaknesses.

5. To proceed with greater order, I will follow the parts of a badge and emblem that seemed fitting for me to take as a coat of arms: the shield of the Order of Carmel. Through the unshod feet accompanying it,[1] I tell what happened to me from the time I was clothed in the Discalced habit (I do not deal with events of my childhood or when I was a layperson) and the labors, affronts, and contradictions I received in this habit. The chains serve to remind me of what I suffered as a slave and captive of the Turks and all the time I went about as a pilgrim and exile. The cross in the middle of the shield reminds me of the interior afflictions I experienced. As for the other parts of the shield, which I do not want to take time to mention here, I refer you to the table of contents of the dialogues of this book.[2] I beg whoever reads this book to give the glory to God and hold me as the vilest person in the world, and procure the improvement of his spirit.

Prologue

THIS PROLOGUE SHOWS IT IS WORTHWHILE FOR A SOUL TO MANIFEST THE TRIALS SHE HAS SUFFERED AND THE MERCIES SHE HAS RECEIVED FROM GOD, ALTHOUGH IT IS NOT GOOD TO REVEAL ONE'S VIRTUES OR SINS.

1. **Cyril:** *Tell me, Anastasius, about this shield you have drawn and the significance of the unshod feet in prison chains, the heart with a cross in the center, the three stars in the cross, and the other twelve stars above a crown woven from thorns and precious stones with six letters: A.C.F.R.I.C., and in the middle, the names of Jesus and Mary.*[1]

2. **Anastasius:** If this hieroglyph pertains to secret things that have happened to me, and I drew it in order to remember them, why do you want me to tell you about it? Don't you know that St. Bernard says, "My secret for myself,"[2] and that it is tasteless and ignorant to reveal one's business? If they are good and virtuous things, revealing them would leave one open to the imputation of arrogance, and he who has nothing good to say of himself would be lying and sinning in speaking of

his virtue. If they are bad things like my sins (which I would gladly tell you about), it is better to keep quiet because I would never come to an end in telling you about them and it doesn't help anyone to discover the faults of a public man, unless perhaps in order to manifest the mercy of God by the amendment he has made of his faults. This is not found in me. As a *beata* [holy woman] in Elche once said to me, "It is a great harm for people to know the sins of confessors and preachers because they look at them as mirrors for their good, and obscuring them with stains diminishes the fruit of their ministry."

3. **Cyril:** *There are four things a soul can speak about: virtues practiced, sins committed, trials suffered, and mercies received from God. I am not asking you to tell me about your virtues or your sins, for I agree with what you said. Tell me about the trials you have suffered and the mercies you have received from God, because in this way you will be put to shame: the world will know how little you have benefited from these two great gifts and the Lord will be glorified when we sing His mercies. St. Paul is holier and more discreet than you, and in his Second Letter to the Corinthians, chapter 1* [*vv.* 3–6], *he says, "Blessed be the God and Father of our Lord Jesus Christ, Father of mercies and the God of all consolations, who consoles us in all our trials that we may console others when they experience trials; so that if we are afflicted it is for your consolation and salvation; if we are encouraged it is for your encouragement, and our consolations are for your good." Thus, in chapter 11 he recounts his afflictions and dangers at sea and on land, beatings, persecutions of false brothers, and the rest, and in chapter 12 he says it is not tasteless or ignorant if he glories in having suffered trials and having received mercies: "Even if I were to boast it would not be folly in me"* [*2 Cor 12:6, NAB*]. *If St. Paul recounts so frankly and sincerely the persecutions he suffered and the mercies and revelations he received, what scruple could you possibly have? On the contrary, be aware of the opposite, like one who is happy with the good things of his neighbor, for—as we were saying in reference to the apostle—God did not give these things to you except for my benefit. Surely St. Jerome is not in error, or St. Bridget and the other saints who tell of their revelations, or Mother Teresa of Jesus who wrote a book about her revelations and her life.*

4. **Anastasius:** You have convinced me with this reason. Therefore, briefly will I tell you of my trials and the mercies I have received on condition that you take me for the worst person in the world, because if the least thing God has granted me were received by a Turk of Barbary, it would be enough to make him a great saint whereas I have destroyed the household of the Lord. But for the sake of greater clarity, I shall proceed according to the order of the six parts that you have noted in the shield.

First Dialogue: Vocation

Gracián recounts what he suffered when he entered the Discalced Carmelites at San Pedro of Pastrana, how his vocation was put to the test in the year of his novitiate when he bore the burden of governing while being a novice of that monastery, along with the discomfort of hunger, cold, rumors, calumnies, and the envy of some others because Mother Teresa had entrusted him with the government of the nuns. He also recounts what he suffered at the beginning of his profession in the visitation of the Calced Carmelite fathers of Andalusia that he made by commission of Pope Pius V as a substitute for Fray Francisco de Vargas and also by commission of the nuncio [Nicolò] Ormaneto. Last, Gracián describes the life-threatening dangers he experienced and further slanders and false testimonies that were raised against him.

VOCATION TO THE ORDER AND DIFFICULTIES THAT WERE SURMOUNTED

1. **Anastasius:** The unshod feet bring to mind all that I suffered as a Discalced Carmelite. I received the habit in Pastrana in the year 1572,[1] having struggled for over a year and a half with my vocation, which is no small torment. All my natural reasons were contrary to this religious state: lack of health, natural weakness, fatigue from

studies, and obligations to my parents and siblings. Those who serve at the royal court, especially my parents,[2] have no other property or rentals for their patrimony other than the favors the king makes to their children in payment of their services, unless they are unworthy of it. I have twelve siblings. One of them held the office of secretary of the king and would have been able to help me obtain an ecclesiastical benefice,[3] for the king was already mindful of me and asking when I would receive the doctorate, perhaps in order to employ me. With such an appointment, I could have helped my family. Another reason I struggled with my vocation was that I had studied and experienced some of the difficulties that exist in religious orders, and I was quite put off desiring to enter any of them. All this was fighting, on the one hand, against a burning desire I had to serve our Lady. On the other hand, as the reformation of her order was just beginning,[4] it seemed that my Lady was calling me for it. This thought was so forceful that for many months I had to cover a beautiful statue of the Virgin I had with a veil, because it seemed to say to me visibly that I was to serve her in this new ministry.

THE PRAYER OF MOTHER TERESA THAT GRACIÁN MIGHT BECOME A FRIAR

2. My confessors, especially one to whom I gave great credit and obedience, were no help at all, telling me that this was clearly a temptation. However, I later heard from the mouth of Mother Teresa herself that it cost her a year of prayers to bring me into the order, convinced as she was that my entering would help it.

3. **Cyril:** *A great battle often occurs in coming to the right vocation! But tell me, how and why did you make up your mind to be a Discalced Carmelite?*

4. **Anastasius:** If you only knew! These skirmishes put me in such a state of unhappiness as to lose both health and life, even though I had a sweet and easy life at that time since I was in the company of Don Andrés de Bobadilla. He later became the archbishop of Zaragoza and had persevered in his studies on my account, for he had wanted to join

a religious order at once. Changing his mind, he finished his college studies, and his parents, the count and countess of Chinchón, were so grateful that they generously regaled me. In spite of this, every good mouthful of food seemed like arsenic and every honor received, which were not few at the University of Alcalá, seemed like an abomination.

HIS DETERMINATION TO SERVE THE VIRGIN

5. But I made up my mind, for I was not able to suffer the impetus of the thoughts that came to me from love of our Lady. I was saying to myself, "If there have been many noble men who, for love of a woman of this world, have become blind, allowing their homes, honor, and lives to be lost, getting knifed, and all the rest, why should I take heed of anything, blinded as I am by the love I have for such a Lady? I would die a happy man if, even after a few months of entering the order, I died because of the austerity of the life! I will gladly give my life to my Lady, the Virgin Mary."[5] This determination was so strong that if I had to enter by sword fighting—I was going to Pastrana to the Discalced Carmelite monastery of San Pedro that had just begun[6]—I would have had the same determination.

COARSE BUT EFFICACIOUS WORDS OF THE OLD LADY OF SAN BÁBILAS

6. A little while before this, I encountered a very rustic old woman in a village and reproached her for doing too much penance when she had a fever.[7] She replied to me, "Oh! That is one of the devil's cleverest tricks in this life! How this cursed body will have to suffer—with worms crawling in through the eyes and mouth—after it is no longer useful, and it cannot suffer a little now when it does so much good to suffer? Pray to God that our sweet Jesus hide us in the holy wound of His side so that we will not be put with the goats on His left on the Day of Judgment." These words, which I have never forgotten, and the perfection of life and spirit I saw in that good old woman, and the way she looked at me with sunken eyes from an emaciated body of seventy years with such effect, moved me to make up my mind without further consideration.

DUTIES DURING THE YEAR OF NOVITIATE

7. I received the habit and then began my duties and the most arduous labors of preaching and hearing confessions in the monastery, the town of Pastrana, and all the nearby towns where we were given alms.[8] There was no one else to do this work since the prior, Fray Baltasar Nieto,[9] had gone to Madrid to help the Calced with their foundation. I was left to instruct thirty novices, who later became the flower of the whole order, and we were so left to ourselves that I had to shield them from the indiscretions of some of the professed who were governing them. I expended no little effort to keep them from leaving.

THE GOVERNMENT OF THE NUNS AND THE CONFIDENCE OF MOTHER TERESA

8. But what pressured me most during the year of my novitiate—and that was the beginning of many of my troubles—was that Mother Teresa of Jesus, seeing me in her order, sent a command to the Discalced Carmelite nuns of Pastrana that they were to obey me as her very person.[10] Until then she had not consented that any friar, Calced or Discalced, should have any authority over the nuns. As she later told me with tears, she feared the oppression with which the friars used to treat the nuns in the name of obedience, taking from them the holy liberty of spirit that the Council of Trent gave them, which she greatly esteemed and others despised.[11] This confidence that she placed in me alone—on account of which she changed obedience from the bishops to the friars—was a small ember in the hearts of many that smoldered until it started the great fire about which I will later speak. At that time, it caused such a conflagration in the souls of the senior professed, not only in the monastery of Pastrana but in other monasteries as well, that they began to murmur and persecute me because I, being only a novice, exercised offices of a professed religious and even of a superior (though they knew full well that at that time there was no one else to exercise these offices).

THE HARM CAUSED BY IGNORANT HOLY PEOPLE

9. Father Mariano [Ambrosio Mariano de San Benito (Azaro)] was the oldest, but he was not ordained nor did he want to be anything but a lay friar. After many years, however, at my insistence and in obedience to the superior general, he was ordained [in September 1573]. Other recently professed friars, although ordained, lacked proper education, and still others lacked experience and prudence. Prudence was lacking to such an extent that someone once took a novice and was flogging his bare shoulders until a wet log should burst into flames by prayer alone—without setting a fire—as it did for our Father Elijah [see 1 Kings 18:30–38], saying that perfection is known in this way. It is by things like this that holy rusticity is wont to destroy the spirit and credit of religion, as St. Jerome says.[12]

10. Finally, this storm had become so terrible that I was on the verge of leaving the novitiate and not making my profession. Also, it seemed to me that a time would come when I would see myself in the habit of the Calced. These two things brought me such disquiet—the likes of which I have never since experienced—that if it were not for Mother Isabel de Santo Domingo, who was then the prioress of the monastery of nuns in Pastrana and later the foundress of Zaragoza, I would not have been consoled.

THE COLD AND HUNGER HE SUFFERED

11. At that time it was very cold, and I went about in the snow without shoes. I used to go preaching in the town and surrounding villages with my feet swollen like eggplants, so much so that the civic officials asked my religious superiors to make me wear shoes. But this was not possible because the Discalced were in their first fervor, and socks and sandals were not introduced until sometime later. Since there were so many of us, we lacked food to such a degree that we went months, especially one Lent, without anything to eat but soup and turnips. When we received a little rotten codfish at Easter, it seemed like food for kings.

MURMURS AND OPINIONS

12. I suffered no less during this year from the murmurs of relatives and secular friends about my entering the order. Few of them, if any, thought well of it. This was because they did not know my primary motive, and all natural reasons were contrary to my decision.

WORDS OF HIS MOTHER JUANA DANTISCO

13. My mother, who was pregnant at the time, felt my departure so much that she was on the verge of dying. At this time, however, God willed that I secretly find out about something that necessitated my going to Madrid, although I was still a novice. If I had not gone, Prince Ruy Gómez [de Silva] would have died. But my trip saved his life, and during this trip, I was able to see my mother who was near death.[13] Seeing me so content and receiving my assurance that I did not enter the order because of some unhappiness but only in order to serve our Lady, she turned to an image of her. In the presence of Fray Baltasar Nieto—my prior who had accompanied me to Madrid (this occurred before he went to the foundation of the Calced)—she said these words: "My Lady, I have been foolish for feeling that you had taken my son for your service. Now I give him to you with all my heart—my son and myself and all my children and my husband." Turning to the prior, she said, "Father Prior, do not lighten or lessen for him any work in the order." She spoke to our Lady as she did because that is how she responded to the women who would say to her, "Be consoled, Señora Doña Juana, for you have given a son to our Lady." They were trying to console her for my joining the order. My mother's reply to them was that our Lady had taken her son: "I did not give him to her; she just took him." But this is enough about the labors of my novitiate.

14. **Cyril:** *Tell me about the trials you went through after your profession.*

15. **Anastasius:** There is no reason to spend time in stories and details. I only want to tell you two things from all the time I was a Discalced friar: first, what I suffered with the Calced until the Discalced Order

was established and foundations and a province were made; second, what I suffered with the Discalced.

THE REASON FOR GOING TO MADRID AS A NOVICE

16. After I made my profession [April 25, 1573], Ruy Gómez died [July 29], although not from the sickness that caused me to go to Madrid as a novice.

17. **Cyril:** *Will you not tell me what the sickness was that necessitated your going to Madrid as a novice to save his life?*

18. **Anastasius:** It is not necessary for you to know everything. It could be that he was given some poison to eat and that this was revealed to me in the secrecy of the confessional; that not knowing he was sick from poison, the wrong remedy was used; and that when the doctors found out what it was, they changed the treatment and he was cured.

THE OCCASION FOR GOING TO SEVILLE

19. As I was saying, the princess of Éboli,[14] being now a widow, came to Pastrana on account of her great grief and joined the monastery of the Discalced Carmelite nuns. Hence Father Mariano (who had been present at the death of the prince when the princess made him remove his habit so that she could put it on herself) and I gathered that it was necessary, in order to avoid inconveniences, to absent ourselves and go to Seville to close a monastery of Discalced Carmelite friars. It had been poorly founded by some Calced who, in emulation of others, became Discalced and took for themselves a monastery at San Juan del Puerto.[15]

COMMISSION OF APOSTOLIC VISITATOR

20. Well, we arrived and asked Fray Francisco de Vargas, provincial of the Dominicans, for permission and assistance to close the monastery. At that time, he was apostolic visitator of the Calced Carmelites of Andalusia by a brief of Pope Pius V. Not only did he give us permission, but he also substituted me in his place as apostolic visitator, giving me the original brief, the very one. Here I am, twenty-eight years old

and professed six months, and I am made the superior of all the Calced Carmelites of Andalusia, in opposition to the general and the protector of the whole order of the Calced. And Andalusia was the unruliest province we had. This alone is enough for you to gather what I would go through with this new and very heavy responsibility, with so many and such rivals and so little strength on my part.

DISSOLVING THE MONASTERY OF SAN JUAN DEL PUERTO AND COMING TO SEVILLE

21. The monastery of San Juan del Puerto was closed. I put shoes back on those who were Calced and brought the Discalced novices with me to Seville. Not having any other monastery to stay in, we came to the Carmen of the Calced,[16] where something terrible occurred.

A DANGEROUS CASE; THE BEDS OF THE DISCALCED

22. I recall that we all arose for Matins. We Discalced left the choir first and then, after us, the Calced novices. One night, I stayed in bed sick (at that time, we had no beds other than some straw mattresses on the ground, with permission to use our capes for pillows and our habits for covers if we wished, or vice versa). The place I usually had coming from the choir was taken by a Calced novice who looked a lot like me in body size and bearing. It so happened that in a dark corridor near the choir, somebody stabbed him in the thigh—not realizing who it was—and might have even killed him except that God held back the hand of whoever did it. There was no lack of "contemplatives" who said the knifing was intended for me, because the novice was good, peaceable, and well liked by everyone, and his father was a great benefactor of the monastery.

THE FAVOR OF THE ARCHBISHOP OF SEVILLE, DON CRISTÓBAL DE ROJAS; THE FOUNDATION OF LOS REMEDIOS OF SEVILLE AND THE POVERTY AND CONTRADICTION WITH WHICH IT WAS FOUNDED

23. With this stabbing and other insolent treatment they gave us, Don Cristóbal de Rojas, uncle of the duke of Lerma and archbishop of Seville,

who favored us, was moved to give us a hermitage called Nuestra Señora de los Remedios. There we founded the first monastery of the Discalced in Andalusia with so much poverty that we ate nothing but sardines, which were then very cheap.[17] Slices of bread served as our plates since we had no other dishware. We entered the monastery with no more than eighteen *reales*, which was all that was left from two doubloons.[18] I had given one of the doubloons to a poor passenger I knew who was going to the Indies, saying to myself that one doubloon was as good as two in order to found a monastery.

24. The Calced did not stop challenging this foundation, alleging that the brief I had was to reform them and not to found new monasteries of the Discalced. I based myself on the fact that there was no better way of reformation than to found new monasteries where the religious would live according to the observance of the ancient founders of the order. Their opposition did not have much force because they feared the archbishop who, because of some serious cases in which they had been involved in Seville, had arranged with the king to obtain the brief from Pius V for their reform.

CESSATION OF THE COMMISSION OF PIUS V

25. But it so happened that at this time the Lord took Pius V,[19] leaving me without support. Thus I had to get away and seek help in sustaining the new plants of the Discalced, which the Calced wanted to destroy. Although, on the one hand, I was free of the duty of visitator of the Calced, on the other hand, I desired the preservation of the Discalced. Well, it so happened that upon my arrival in Madrid, King Don Philip II, seeing that it was necessary to continue the visitations of the Calced Carmelites, Trinitarians, Mercedarians, Minims, and Calced Franciscans of Andalusia that had begun with the brief of Pius V, sent Father Olea of the Company of Jesus to find out for himself how necessary this continuation of the visitations was, and he told him that he wanted the fathers of the Company to carry them out. Not wanting to get involved in this conflict with friars, however, the

Jesuits insisted that it was better if the visitations were done by friars of the same orders.

COMMISSION OF THE NUNCIO ORMANETO

26. And so, with a new commission from the nuncio Ormaneto[20]—who had faculties from Gregory XIII for the visitations—I was sent as apostolic visitator of all the Discalced Carmelites and of the Calced Carmelites of Andalusia.[21] The first part of this commission pleased me because the Discalced, not being subject to the Calced, could not be undone by them, and I was able to make foundations. I founded twenty Discalced monasteries with which the congregation of the Discalced put down roots.[22] However, fearing death, my weakness refused the second part of the commission since infamies and affronts I had already swallowed.

CARDINAL QUIROGA

27. I spoke about this fear to Cardinal [Gaspar de] Quiroga so that he might intercede with the king to relieve me of the responsibility of the visitation of the Calced, and with holy anger he told me, "Let them kill you. Let them kill you! To whom are we to confide this commission if not to a man of noble blood who is known to us as you are? Fear not death." And so, with this resolve to lose my life, and with the brief of the nuncio Ormaneto and letters of the king in hand, I turned around and walked back to Andalusia.

OCCUPATIONS AND FATIGUES

28. Who can tell of the fatigues of the road, the inconveniences of having to carry forward the good example of the Discalced, and the demands of business and study? I remember having carried on for years without sleep in the midst of work, study, prayer, and Mass from twelve at night until twelve at noon without raising my head. On top of all this, when would I finish if I were to tell you of the calumnies, affronts, and false testimonies that have befallen this miserable sinner?

CALUMNIES OF THE CALCED

29. One day we had to walk from Carmona to Córdoba. The Calced prior had along two mules of the monastery with which they were going to haul firewood from a mountain four leagues away. He decided that we and the other Calced who were with us should all go there to eat. They brought a turkey he had raised in the monastery and I don't know how many chickens. They immediately wrote to the king that he should take a look at the visitator he had sent to them who traveled with mules loaded with turkeys and chickens and see whether he was a good Discalced.

30. I carried with me, as I always do, a night scapular that had on it an image of Our Lady of the Conception. They spread it around that I slept with an image of our Lady, using such awful words that, for anyone listening, were a source of the most horrendous and accursed blasphemy imaginable.

31. While I was away on business concerning the visitation, they preached publicly in the pulpit of the monastery of Seville that they had denounced the evil deeds and abominations of "that evil man," that they had me burned at the stake, and that they would provide certification of my ashes.

FEAST OF THE PRESENTATION; WHY THE NUNS CELEBRATE IT

32. When I presented the brief of the visitation to them, they shut the doors of the monastery, not wanting to obey. There was such a scandal and commotion that Mother Teresa ordered all the nuns to celebrate the feast of the Presentation of Our Lady, which occurred the day the brief was presented.[23]

33. Because I tried to get them to hold books and other things of value in common—as the council says[24]—they accused me of pocketing more than three thousand ducats. There is no reason to tire you in telling you of more calumnies. It is enough to say that not a day went by when there were not new affronts to me. By then, I was never without them.

DANGERS OF BEING POISONED

34. I always carried a bezoar stone around my neck because I ate in their monasteries; I could do no less.[25] But I was careful to eat only eggs that were baked or cooked in their shells (food tastes very bad when it is flavored with the sauce of fear of what is eaten). One day, a companion found a salamander in a water jar we had for drinking. It did not seem possible for it to have gotten in by itself.

35. In order to defend some Calced nuns from slander, I sent three Discalced nuns to their monastery to reform them. The same Calced nuns whom I defended raised such false testimony against me themselves that it is a horror to speak of it.[26] But let this be enough now of this material.

Second Dialogue: Discalced

Gracián, continuing the explanation of the unshod feet found in the hieroglyph, begins to describe the hardships and persecutions that came to him from the Discalced Carmelites. Excusing himself at the outset for dealing with this matter but convinced he is obligated to speak the truth, he tells of some visions of ghosts or demons that announced these persecutions and the threat Lucifer made to him, a threat he realizes caused all these upheavals. He mentions in particular some false charges made against him by some of the Discalced and the even greater tribulation he had when he was sentenced by the nuncio Filippo Sega, for the congregation of the Discalced was at the point of disappearing if he did not let himself be sentenced and accept the sentence given.

1. **Cyril:** *As for what you suffered with and from the same Discalced Carmelites in order to establish their province, you can do nothing less than recount it. When Caesar was stabbed in the Senate by many men, he only complained of Brutus who was like his son.*[1] *And Christ said in the person of David, "If an enemy had reviled me, I could have borne it" [Ps 55:13, NAB].*[2] *If one is persecuted by his enemies, it is not a great trial. But when one's own beloved sons are the cause of such grief, it must be intolerable. Therefore, I would like you to tell me slowly what you have suffered with them and from them.*

THE REASON PERSECUTION FROM ONE'S BROTHERS HURTS SO MUCH, ESPECIALLY IF THEY ARE SERVANTS OF GOD

2. **Anastasius:** When you fight with sons and brothers whom you love as life itself, it is a most difficult battle because they strike sharp blows in order to wound and you cannot hit them back except lightly in order to defend yourself. Any wound of those you dearly love hurts you more than your own. Besides, it is not licit to hurt the honor and holiness of such servants of God whose discredit would harm the good things they do or can do for the church. That is why, in all this time, I have not opened my mouth to speak of this matter, nor do I want to talk about it now, so do not ask me anything.

THAT IT IS AN OBLIGATION FOR ONE WHO HOLDS A PUBLIC OFFICE, ESPECIALLY IN THE CARE OF SOULS, TO DEFEND HIS HONOR

3. **Cyril:** *You have no reason to keep quiet like that since you are obliged under pain of sin to remove the scandal caused to those who hold you in disrepute on account of your silence. You are obliged to speak the truth because, being a public person, the honor is not yours but that of the church so that it can bear fruit. The Holy Spirit says, "Take care of your good name" [Sir 41:12], which is more valuable than all the world's riches. Christ said plainly, "I have not a demon" [Jn 8:49]. And the saints defend themselves. Do you wish to make yourself humbler than they? How much the rumors born of these sentences and expulsion of yours redound to the dishonor of such great servants of God as the Discalced Carmelite nuns, whose honor you have the obligation to restore and which your silence has taken from them.*

4. **Anastasius:** Ever since these disturbances with them began, I have firmly resolved to leave this whole matter to the tribunal of God and place it before Him, who is judge; He is also a witness who knows what is public and what is secret. Thus, do not importune me anymore for I am resolved in what I have always said, which are three propositions: First, they are true servants of God and acted properly in what they did.

Second, the Discalced nuns are great servants of God, and neither with me nor anyone else have they failed in their vocation, and what some have murmured and judged about them is false. Third, although I am the worst person in the world, I am not guilty of what has been imputed to me and for which I was sentenced. I mean the things imputed to me that are important and weighty, for there is no one so holy of whom it cannot be said, "The just man falls seven times daily" [see Prov 24:16]. These three things I will swear on a consecrated altar.

5. **Cyril:** *How is it possible that you were expelled from such a holy order as an incorrigible—a sentence that is given only for the gravest offenses—and that they are saints and you are without fault? If they have raised false charges, they are most guilty. If not, you have been most evil.*

MANY TIMES MISTAKES ARE MADE WITHOUT FAULT OF ANY PARTY

6. **Anastasius:** Do you not know that the Child Jesus was lost without any fault of Mary or Joseph? That is because she, so perfectly obedient, kept the precepts of the priests who mandated that children, when they reach the age of twelve, should go with their fathers. Joseph, as a most devout father, went ahead to buy provisions, and he did not want to bring the Child so as not to tire him. Although he too kept the precepts of the priests, he considered that since the Child had no earthly father, he was not obligated by that precept to take the Child along.

THE WORDS OF NICHOLAS OF ANTIOCH THAT WERE SAID WITHOUT ANY FAULT ON HIS PART, YET WERE THE CAUSE OF GREAT HARM AND SCANDAL

7. Many times God permits events—or the devil plots them—from which arise great harm without the fault of any party. Remember what happened to Nicholas of Antioch when St. Peter and the other apostles reprimanded him for treating his wife, who was very beautiful, with too much severity. He said, "I do not do it on account of jealous love, but only for her good. As for jealousy, let whoever desires her take her."[3] St. Peter did not sin in reprimanding him and charging him to be kind. And,

according to St. Ignatius, Tertullian, and other holy men, Nicholas did not sin in the words he spoke because he said them with good purpose and he was holy. Thus, many authors defend him, even though from his words came the heresy of the Nicolaitans and the Gnostics, who gave a bad meaning to them, saying that in the church of the apostles, it had been decided that married women should be held in common.

8. Once there were two blacksmiths who were hammering the same iron bar to work it well, and someone closed the window on them. Being without light, instead of striking the iron, they struck each other's skull. They are not at fault for their injuries to one another. Rather, he who closed the window with the bad intention that they hurt each other is to blame.

THE SOURCE OF THE UPHEAVAL AND PERSECUTIONS OF THE DISCALCED; THE CONSULTA AND ITS HARMS

9. I desired the perfection of the order, that it continue as it had been from the beginning, and that the laws so wisely ordained for the nuns by Mother Teresa of Jesus be kept, as well as those ordained for the friars by the Alcalá Chapter and Fray Juan de las Cuevas with the bull of Gregory XIII. And it seemed to me—as if I could see it with my very eyes—that from the new government they wanted to introduce, called the *consulta*, great harm to the friars would follow. The sincerity of their spirit would be lost and many would leave the order, to its discredit and ruin. I saw that it [the *consulta*] would oppress the nuns too much by taking away the holy liberty that Mother Teresa left them—and about which she spoke to me in tears—and that harm would come if the laws their mother left them were changed. Seeing myself with an apostolic commission from Cardinal Albert,[4] I sent a friar to the pope and to the protector of the order that they might examine this new mode of governing of the *consulta*.[5] I also wrote to many persons, explaining to them the great inconveniences and harm that would come from it. And since, until then, I had governed the order[6] and had experience and had read much about religious orders—while those who wanted to introduce

the *consulta* were new and inexperienced—it seemed to me that I was obligated to do what I did. I am not sorry nor will I repent of having written to some of the prioresses, telling them to do all in their power to have Pope Sixtus V confirm the constitutions of Mother Teresa and order that they be left unchanged. They did so, and although Sixtus V gave this brief, it was not accepted.[7] So, you see, I am without fault for what I did regarding this matter.

10. They thought that all the good of the order consisted in introducing this new government of the *consulta* and that if I stayed in the order, they would not be able to conserve it. Therefore, the good of the order depended on getting rid of me, which could not be done without passing a sentence. Carried away by this zeal and taking advantage of the words and calumnies of the Calced and other persons and concluding that it is expedient that one man die [see Jn 11:50], they gave that sentence that has so much resounded.[8] It imputed to me great disobedience and rebellion against the superiors—which is the greatest offense one can commit in a religious order—for having sent a letter of complaint to the pope. Since they were superiors and had gained the favor of the king for other reasons [i.e., services],[9] they used this favor against me and, because they had the upper hand, succeeded with their intentions. I believe no hatred or rancor moved them but only zeal for the order. Thus, only the devil has the guilt in this case, for he closed the window and blocked the light.

A STRANGE CASE AND THREAT OF LUCIFER

11. As an example of what I mean, I want to tell you about a strange case that has given me great consolation in my trials and tribulations. I once dealt with the soul of a person who was compelled every day by Lucifer to call him "omnipotent" ninety times while kneeling. I said to tell Lucifer for me that if he held himself omnipotent, he was to come to my cell at midnight, and I, with a stick in hand, would give him a great many strikes that would make him understand if he were omnipotent or not. It seems this person told him this. He told me that Lucifer responded, "You tell him that I said he is taking on Lucifer and that within eight

days he will experience who Lucifer is." Within five days my troubles began, troubles that have continued for twenty-five years and that I believe will last until the end of my life. There have been so many entanglements, upheavals, and intrigues that even I—who have passed and am passing through them—do not understand them nor would I know what else to say other than they have been the intrigues of Lucifer.

MANY TIMES GOD PERMITS PERSECUTIONS FOR A GREATER GOOD; DIVERSE VOCATIONS

12. **Cyril:** *How do you know it hasn't been the plan of God to keep your talents from being submerged in retirement, which is how some of the Discalced conduct themselves in the name of recollection and perfection? God does not give talents in vain, for them to be enclosed in a cell or desert. Although that life is good for some, God wishes to lead others by another way, and vocations are diverse. St. John the Baptist was holy in his hermitage, and he lost his head in coming to court [see Mt 14:1–12]. Jesus Christ was no less holy, though He ate with Zacchaeus and let His feet be washed, kissed, and dried with the tears, mouth, and hair of a sinner [see Lk 19:1–10 and Lk 7:37–38 respectively]. St. John in his hermitage was esteemed and had a good reputation, while Christ was murmured against, persecuted, and placed on a cross. According to what I know about the many varied services you rendered after you put on shoes—which you were not able to wear as a Discalced—I cannot get these words out of my mind: "How beautiful are your feet in sandals" [Song 7:2, NAB]. But I will admit that they are without fault, those who hammered your head in order to hammer the iron of the order. What I am asking you—and you must not refuse me for any reason—is that you show me your head injuries and tell me about the trials that have come to you from the Discalced and for the Discalced.*

WORKS OF THE DEVIL, USING THE DISCALCED FRIARS AS AN INSTRUMENT

13. **Anastasius:** You sure are persistent. So that you will be quiet and leave me alone, I will recount some of them. That you will understand that these things come from the devil and not from men, the first one

I will tell you about is the time I was in Seville at the beginning of the monastery there.[10] The devil gave a novice such a great temptation to kill me that, day and night, he was unable to get rid of the thought. While I was sleeping, he took a knife, and it seemed that, although he did not want to, those thoughts were leading him to kill me. But God willed that he speak with me about it, dissolving in tears. I consoled him, and I went about without fear and without caution because I knew that the devil could do no more than what God allowed, and he is such a coward that he flees from anyone who stands up to him.

14. **Cyril:** *Having raised this point, don't refuse to answer me: have you encountered him in visible form?*

15. **Anastasius:** Don't drag me into this conversation. Don't you know what an enemy I am of revelations and apparitions? Instead, I believe that most of them are phantoms and imaginings produced by fear and that there is no reason to pay attention to them.

VISION IN ASTORGA

16. Such a thing happened to me in Astorga when I was eleven years old, coming down a deserted side street around midnight. Some distance before coming to a crossroad, I became very afraid. My hair stood up so much that it raised a velvet cap I had on, and I did not know what this fear meant. When I came to the end of the street and entered the crossroad, I saw—about four steps from me—a bulky object the size of a donkey and the shape of a billy goat. It was the color of black pitch speckled with spots of fire, and its eyes, which were like two big red-hot coals, were staring at me. I did not turn my head away. Instead, I walked backward, keeping my eyes fixed on his. I entered a house that was being built, and there I blessed myself and recited the Creed. Feeling in the dark with my feet, I found two rocks to my liking. I threw my cape over my left arm, and with one rock in my left hand and the other in my right, I came out with such spirit and desire to charge that phantom and give him a whack between the eyes with the rocks. It seemed that never in my life had I so great a desire to do anything as I had then. But when I

came out, I did not see it, and I ran to my house with my rocks without fearing anything, surprised how I could be so brave at that age.

THE VOICES OF MONDÉJAR

17. Another time, when the troubles with the nuncio Sega began—of which I will speak later[11]—Father Mariano and I were in Mondéjar [Guadalajara] in the home of a secular brother, the father of one of our friars, who gave us lodging. At midnight, we heard many shouts of different voices complaining, "Ay! Ay!" and so forth. It sounded as though they were coming from above our heads, no matter what part of the house we were in. These voices awakened us; everyone in the house was awakened and came to us disturbed, not knowing what it was. It could be that the devils were complaining, because following that commotion—as I will later tell[12]—was the establishment of the Discalced province and the strengthening of the order, which was at the point of being undone.

VISION IN TOLEDO; VISION OF BROTHER ALBERTO IN THE HOSPITAL

18. Another time, Father Fray Antonio de Jesús and I were in Toledo spending the night at the Hospital de Tavera. While reciting Compline in the basement below the infirmary, we saw a very large figure with many tails—like an octopus—standing by the garden fence. It frightened us so much that we fled immediately. We ran so fast that Brother Alberto—a lay brother we had brought with us—was surprised at our speed. It seemed to him that we had made a bet on who could run the fastest.

19. On another occasion, I came to stay in the same hospital with this friar, Brother Alberto, since we did not have a monastery in Toledo yet. I slept in a room at the end of the basement, and he had a room next to mine. One morning when I asked him why he looked so pale, he asked me what happened to me. I said that nothing happened to me and why did he ask. He responded that he had heard a muted sound like

"hu, hu," at the door of his room and had seen two large cats, one black and the other reddish-brown, with heads as big as those of men. They removed his covers and held him down so that he could not budge until he said, "Jesus of Nazareth." Then he heard me making loud groans, but he didn't have the courage to look in on me. This must have been a nightmare—as it is called—but it is nevertheless true that on those two occasions two great trials happened to us from which came two great benefits for the Discalced.

VISION OF A DISCALCED NUN

20. **Cyril:** *I was told by a nun—not the least holy of the Discalced*[13]*—that she had seen a serpent with seven heads come up behind you, remove your habit, and carry you away naked. She did not know where you were taken.*

21. **Anastasius:** Come on, all these things must be imaginings. I have heard so many such things that we would never finish if I recounted them all. Let's move on to my head wounds.

PERSECUTION FROM A FALSE REPORT

22. A Discalced Carmelite lay brother [Fray Miguel de la Columna] who had accompanied me for a long time was persuaded by some of the Calced to sign an affidavit against me regarding abominable things that he had seen in me. Since he was a Discalced and my own companion, he was considered a credible witness. Later, however, having confessed his weakness, he asked pardon and recanted in writing, sending various copies written in his own hand to all those who had received his first affidavit. This was no small head wound.

ANOTHER HEAD WOUND FROM A CRAZY FRIAR WHO WAS THOUGHT TO BE HOLY AND SANE

23. But an even worse defamation came from another Discalced friar [Pedro de San Angel (de Balboa)] who, although crazy, appeared to be quite sane. His madness was that his depraved imagination would distort whatever he heard about the Discalced, and he would prepare

memorials of what he fancied to be cases of heresy and take them to the Holy Office [of the Spanish Inquisition]. One time, when Father Mariano was the prior of the monastery in Lisbon, the porter—who was this lay brother—came to his room when he was in bed and said there were some women who wanted to go to confession. Father Mariano responded, "Tell them their confessions will be heard." He distorted these words to mean that the Discalced friars, without even being priests, heard confessions and that Father Mariano had sent a lay brother to hear them. He wrote down his accusation and sent it to the inquisitors. One of them, a friend of Father Mariano's, seeing that it was not true, sent for Father Mariano and told him about the case. Realizing what was behind it, Father Mariano had the friar who had made the accusation stripped of his habit and dismissed from the order. As the superior at that time, I gave the habit back to him, treated him well, and calmed him down. In payment of this kindness, he wrote memorials against me of the most abominable and horrendous things imaginable. These were placed in the hands of the king, who in turn gave them to his secretary, [Gabriel de] Zayas, who was very disturbed to read these things since he knew me. Zayas shared them with Fray Juan de las Cuevas,[14] who later became the bishop of Segovia. By order of the king, I was sent for; I was in Andalusia at the time. God willed that Fray Juan de las Cuevas ask Father Gregorio Nacianceno [Martínez][15] who this friar was, and not remembering his name, he took out the documents to read the signature. Father Gregorio recognized the handwriting and explained to Fray Juan de las Cuevas that this friar was crazy; nevertheless, when it comes to defamation of character, the first information always makes an impact. This friar was not at fault since he was without judgment. The devil took advantage of his insanity and melancholy as an instrument to hurl these defamations. Later, Father Nicolás de Jesús María [Doria], when he was provincial, sentenced him as crazy because he did not cease to write to the Inquisition against the Discalced Carmelites. In the end, he died a recluse in his cell with the same fixation as always.

THE NUNCIO'S JURISDICTION IMPEDED; CAUSE OF HIS INDIGNATION

24. I do not want to discuss any other particular trifles in order that I might come to the principal tribulations I have suffered for the sake of the Discalced, one of which has to do with the nuncio Sega. The nuncio Ormaneto, who gave me his commission to govern the Discalced and the Calced of Andalusia as apostolic visitator, died.[16] The nuncio Sega came to court and claimed to have the same jurisdiction over religious orders as he had over the secular clergy.[17] He sent for me and with much indulgence told me that I should continue with my visitation and that I was to inform him of what I was doing. I went to the king, who had given me the brief of Ormaneto and letters for the visitation, and reported to him what the nuncio Sega told me and asked him what I should do. He responded that I should not do anything until he wrote to the pope about whether it was necessary for the nuncio to have a special commission from the pope as Ormaneto had. Here I was caught between the king and the nuncio over this difficult business of jurisdiction: the king said I was not to go to the nuncio until a reply came from Rome, while the nuncio bellowed because I did not come to him, charging me with obstructing his apostolic jurisdiction. Then word came from the pope that the nuncio should not intervene in matters concerning the friars except for those cases requested by the king. The nuncio was so stung by this that he said if I were not turned over to be burned for impeding his jurisdiction he would return to Rome.

WHAT REALLY INCREASED HIS ANGER

25. The nuncio's indignation was further increased by the calumnies and charges that the Calced were bringing against me, now that I was finished with the visitation and no longer had authority over them.[18] His indignation was no less on account of some memorials I had given to the king, specifying the great inconveniences that would come upon the religious orders of Spain if the nuncios were giving briefs contrary

to the ordinances of the superiors. The king had sent these reports to several important people in Spain who in turn had shown them to the nuncio. These two things infuriated him so much that I greatly feared being burned at the stake and considered any other form of death preferable to that.

THE ARREST OF THREE FATHERS AND THEIR EXCOMMUNICATION

26. He excommunicated me and Father Fray Antonio de Jesús and Father Mariano until we presented ourselves to him. We had nowhere to hide, nor was there anyone to whom we could make an appeal. We came into his presence. Father Mariano was sent to [the monastery of] Our Lady of Atocha and imprisoned there. Father Antonio was imprisoned at St. Bernard's of the Discalced Franciscans. And I (for being the worst offender) was sent to the Calced Carmelites, who, still aggrieved about my visitation, treated me even worse in their prison.[19] So there we were, excommunicated and unable to hear or say Mass, which is no small penalty, awaiting the terrible punishment that was to come. I recalled how St. Paul once said, "That I might be accursed and cut off from Christ if this could benefit my brothers" [Rom 9:3].

FEAR OF THE INQUISITION; FEAR THEY WOULD DISSOLVE THE CONGREGATION OF THE DISCALCED

27. In addition to this grief, there were many other things happening, such as the arrival of an inquisitor from Seville who sent for my mother to come to his house. She was alarmed to think there was some reason for my rivals to make charges against me about my faith. My pain was also increased at seeing that the general, the protector of the order, and many cardinals were writing to the nuncio that the Discalced should be dissolved and placed under the Calced, as was done.[20] To have the whole congregation of the Discalced dissolved at once was the greatest of my sufferings.

28. Things being in this state of affairs, God willed that the king gather opinions to be given to the pope as to whether it was better to dissolve

the Discalced or to separate them from the Calced and make a separate province for them, and that the nuncio Sega should come to think that the Discalced should not be dissolved, saying they were good and that it was because of me that they were in turmoil and ruin.[21] Coming right to the point with the king, he said he was upset not that the pope had taken the ordinary jurisdiction of the religious orders away from him but rather because of the great harm that he had been informed I had done. He told him that before anything else was done, I should first be sentenced. And then, after my case was over, he would attend to the cause of the Discalced and ask the pope that the province be established.

PERPLEXITY OF CONSCIENCE IS A GREAT CROSS

29. This was the greatest conflict I have ever had or will have in my life. If I let myself be sentenced solely for the charges that the Calced from Andalusia had been sending against me, without a reexamination of the truth of the matter, I feared two things: one, the harsh sentence of the nuncio; two—and this I feared much more—to let myself be condemned without fault and remain defamed the rest of my life, thus losing the fruit I could bear in the service of the church with my talents. I also knew from theology that it is a mortal sin to let oneself be defamed if one is a public man and obliged to defend one's honor.

30. On the other hand, in order that I might be vindicated, the nuncio said that I should ask for a commission to go to Andalusia on my behalf in order to review the charges that had been sent from there and to see to my defense. But there were three very great disadvantages to my doing this. First, I did not have the money nor could I expect to get it from the friars, nor did it make sense to ask my relatives to pay someone sent by the nuncio to get this new information. Second, I feared that once the commission arrived, those who had sent these calumnies in the first place would convince them to take their side and my innocence would not be made clear. The third and greatest of these disadvantages—the others are nothing in comparison—was that during the

delay, the Calced would destroy the Discalced who would be subject to them in the meantime. With the passage of time, the king and the nuncio would forget about their previous intention to make a separate province for the Discalced, and it would not be made. The Discalced were not strongly rooted enough in the Discalced reform, and many of them were still weak. With the passage of time in the company of their Calced superiors and novice masters, the rigor of the Discalced would be lost.

31. Finding myself in this perplexity of conscience, I commended myself much to God and discussed the matter with theologians. Although there were different opinions, some assured my conscience that at least I would not be committing a mortal sin if I let myself be condemned without defending my innocence. Moved by my zeal for the good of the Discalced and as a result of prayer and these opinions, I was determined to suffer whatever sentence I was given, even if it were death, if in exchange the Discalced province would be made. I chose before anything else to lose my life and my honor for my province rather than have the Discalced be harmed. Although the Discalced might not thank me for my determination and the fruits that followed, I hope in God and the Virgin Mary—whose order it is—that they save my reward for me in the place of heavenly crowns because in this world there is nothing to hope for except crosses and more crosses.

THE SENTENCE OF THE NUNCIO

32. The nuncio sentenced me, depriving me of voice and office and confining me to the college of the Discalced Carmelites of Alcalá with I don't know what fasts, disciplines, and prayers.[22] He was careful that the sentence was not for having impeded his jurisdiction—which was what upset him—since it was the king who petitioned the pope, who then limited his authority. Rather, he based it on the charges that the Calced had sent from Andalusia. Although they were of things very abominable, twisted, and ugly, there was no reason for the sentence to be more severe than it was because my defense was not heard.

DISCALCED WHO ACCUSED HIM AS A REBEL TO THE NUNCIO

33. I went to Alcalá, contenting myself to pray to God and say Mass, but even there I did not lack things to suffer. Father Elías [de San Martín (Hériz)], the rector, loved me very much, and, being sick, commanded me to preside at the chapter of the friars. Three of them, without telling me anything, wrote to the nuncio that, in spite of the sentence, I was interfering in the government of the monastery.[23] This made him indignant, and Father Elías and I were no less upset. As it turned out, those three died a disgraceful death that summer.

FRAY ANGEL DE SALAZAR, PROVINCIAL OF THE CALCED, A VERY PIOUS AND PRUDENT MAN

34. Many other things occurred during this persecution by the nuncio that I have not recounted. Following this persecution, after I was sentenced, the nuncio and the king wrote to Pope Gregory XIII their opinion and reasons a province should be established and why the Discalced should not be dissolved. While waiting for the brief, the Calced Father Angel de Salazar, a prudent and worthy man, governed.[24] As he knew it would not be a long wait and that it was the good pleasure of the king and the nuncio that the Discalced continue, he did not want to change anything nor allow any Calced to interfere in their government. But I will tell you later about the tight spot I was in when we gave him our obedience.[25]

Third Dialogue: Visitator

GRACIÁN CONTINUES WITH THE TRIBULATIONS, CONTRADICTIONS, AFFRONTS, FATIGUES, LIFE-THREATENING DANGERS, AND OTHER VERY SERIOUS PERSECUTIONS THAT HE SUFFERED AS A DISCALCED CARMELITE FROM THE TIME HE FINISHED HIS COMMISSION OF APOSTOLIC VISITATOR AND OF BEING PROVINCIAL UNTIL THE LAWS OF THE CONSULTA WERE MADE. HE DESCRIBES HIS EXPERIENCES NOT ONLY OF FORMING THE DISCALCED PROVINCE BUT ALSO IN EXERCISING THE OFFICE OF APOSTOLIC VISITATOR TO THE CALCED CARMELITES OF PORTUGAL WHEN THE ENGLISH BESIEGED LISBON, AND OTHER GRAVE AFFAIRS THAT WERE PRESENTED TO HIM.

1. **Cyril:** *Now I want to know what the sentence was and how long the infamy, annihilation, isolation, and demoralization lasted.*

THE NUNCIO REVOKES THE SENTENCE

2. **Anastasius:** It did not last very long because not many months later the nuncio Sega went to speak with the king, and His Majesty told him that I had been punished enough. So the sentence was revoked, the penance was lifted, and I was restored to the same rank of honor as I had before. I had no rest, though, because the Discalced did not make a move unless I guided them. They turned to me for direction as to how to solicit the Brief of Separation so that our province could be erected.

FRAY JUAN DE JESÚS AND FRAY DIEGO DE LA TRINIDAD TRAVEL TO ROME

3. So, I sent Fray Juan de Jesús Roca and Fray Diego de la Trinidad—who was formerly a Jeronimite friar—to Rome. They were the most zealous and experienced friars we had at that time. It was very necessary that they go to Rome because although the king and the nuncio had written why the Discalced should be juridically separated from the Calced, the general, cardinal protector, and many cardinals in Rome were against it. Therefore, the ambassador to Rome and the cardinals who were favorable to the affairs of the king would not have been able to succeed in the matter unless someone was there to personally inform them and look after it.

FRAY ANGEL MADE GRACIÁN HIS COMPANION AND CONFERRED WITH HIM ABOUT THE AFFAIRS OF THE DISCALCED

4. Also at this time, Fray Angel de Salazar, a Calced (who governed the Discalced as their vicar general with a brief of the nuncio), chose me for his companion.[1] Although he had the title, the responsibility of governing was laid upon my shoulders because he referred everything possible to me; he only signed the patents I presented to him. He also conferred with me about many affairs of the Calced.

GRACIÁN TAKES THE BRIEF OF SEPARATION TO SALAMANCA

5. The Brief of Separation came.[2] Suffering some difficulty on the road because it was the middle of winter, I took the brief by order of the king to Master Fray Pedro Fernández, provincial of the Dominicans, who was charged with carrying it out.[3] All was done secretly so that the Calced would not learn of it and try to interfere. (Although Fray Angel de Salazar knew very well what was going on, he pretended not to know and gave me permission to travel wherever necessary and to do whatever was necessary for the good of our province. We therefore owe much to this holy man.)

6. I arrived in Salamanca with the brief and letters of the king at the very time Fray Pedro Fernández was dying. God took him, and the brief could not be executed.[4] I went with this news to Portugal where the king was just then taking possession of that kingdom. I arrived at Elvas on the same day that God took the queen, Doña Ana,[5] and that same day His Majesty sent a dispatch to the pope, asking for a new commission that would give Fray Juan de las Cuevas authority to execute the brief. They wanted me to attend the queen's funeral, but I excused myself saying that I was on the king's business. I went from there to the monastery of Los Remedios in Seville, which had need of a prior and for which Fray Angel had named me.[6] It cost me a little effort to reform it because in all the commotion it had lost much of its observance.

7. The commission for Fray Juan de las Cuevas arrived from Rome.[7] I took it in very rainy weather to Talavera [de la Reina] where Fray Juan was prior. I informed him of all that had transpired and did so in secret so that no friar, neither Dominican nor that of any other order, would know what it was about. Although they wanted me to stay in their monastery, it seemed more appropriate under the circumstances to stay at an inn. Working there day and night with the secrecy and diligence that was so important, all the notifications and letters were written to every Discalced monastery over which I was superior. There is no little work involved in such grave business.

ERECTION OF THE PROVINCE

8. The [Discalced] fathers met for their chapter in Alcalá [March 1581]. The province was erected [March 3, 1581], laws and constitutions were promulgated [March 13, 1581], and I was elected provincial [March 4, 1581].[8] I governed the province for four years, founding monasteries of friars and nuns in company with Mother Teresa of Jesus, with the usual work and responsibility involved in traveling, business, correspondence, confessions, sermons, studies, and so forth.

9. **Cyril:** *Is it possible that during all this time you don't have some notable tribulations to tell me about?*

TRIBULATIONS HE SUFFERED BEFORE HE WAS MADE PROVINCIAL; THE DUKE OF ALBA, DON FERNANDO DE TOLEDO

10. **Anastasius:** They were never lacking. The duke of Alba, Don Fernando de Toledo, called me from Alcalá to Uceda [Guadalajara], where he was, so that I could hear his confession. There I contracted the tertian fever [malaria]. During my convalescence from this, he wanted to take me with him on the conquest of Portugal,[9] where I would be able to have some honor and rest away from conflicts of the friars. The duke was by this time so holy you would be surprised at certain things I could tell you about him. But I did not go with him. It was enough at that time that I had abandoned my honor and peace—and there is no greater peace than to get away from fraternal persecutions—in order not to fail in the affairs of my Discalced, choosing to die for them rather than be lord of the whole world. And all this was nothing. The tertian fever and the loss of peace are of little account compared to an extraordinary affliction that beset me before the erection of the province.

ANGUISH AT THE PRESENTATION OF THE BRIEF OF THE NUNCIO AND IN GIVING OBEDIENCE TO THE CALCED

11. The nuncio Sega issued a brief to the effect that the Discalced were to be subject to the Calced.[10] It seemed to all the Discalced that they were as good as dissolved because the Calced, having them under their feet, would annihilate them. Therefore, some of them went to the king for help. The king ordered the royal council to issue a proviso [dated August 9, 1578] to counter this brief of the nuncio so that it would not be carried out.

12. Father Mariano brought the proviso to the monastery of Pastrana where the principal leaders of the Discalced were assembled. I was brought there as well. At this point, two fathers, Masters Fray Hernando Xuárez and Fray Coria, arrived at the monastery door with the nuncio's brief to present it to the Discalced and receive their obedience. Father Mariano—with his proviso of the council—and many of the Discalced were ready to take it from them and not give obedience, thinking that

their preservation lay in this way. They called me to determine what was to be done. I told them to leave me be, that I was fed up with suffering at the nuncio's hands and fighting with him, and that they should do as they wished. They insisted that nothing would be done without my order. I found myself greatly constrained and confused about what was to be done. Almost all the Discalced were of the opinion that obedience should not be given to the nuncio's brief. Meanwhile, the Calced were knocking on the doors for us to open up.

FRAY BENITO DE JESÚS Y LA VIRGEN

13. God willed that in the monastery there was a holy lay brother named Fray Benito de Jesús y la Virgen, of whom I could tell you great things.[11] He had come to such simplicity that he even forgot the name of his father and where he was from. He did not know how to do anything other than make acts of love of God and our Lady and be devoted to the Blessed Sacrament and the souls in purgatory. I had confidence that God would give me light in such a serious matter by the tongue of this saint. I closed myself in a cell with him and, as though he were the most grave, wise, and prudent man in the world, told him about all this business, giving him the positions of both sides. He began to hit his head on the floor, saying, "I am a bad thing, a bad thing," excusing himself humbly. I insisted that for God's sake he tell me what he thought.

THE JUDGMENT OF FRAY BENITO IN HIS MANNER OF SPEAKING

14. He responded in these words: "Look, pretty boy,[12] if you now anger the little treasurer, the big treasurer will get angry; and the little black one, neither thing nor thing. One little step and another little step, one little effort and another little effort, you will see thing and thing." I received these words as if from an angel from heaven, and they imprinted themselves in my heart. I understood them to mean in this language of his that if the nuncio gets angry now, then the pope will get angry, and the province will not be made nor will they give a brief for its creation. And the king—whom he called "the little black one" because he was a

secular—although he shows favor now and has given the proviso annulling the nuncio's brief, will afterward leave us, and nothing good will come of it. To give obedience to the Calced now is a step and an effort. Giving obedience and having the laws and customs of the Discalced removed is another step and an effort. Being dissolved is yet another step and an effort. From one momentous step to the next, there is time to negotiate. What is important now is not to disgrace the nuncio by annulling the brief with the royal proviso because he might help us with the pope, and this way our affairs will go well.

GIVING OBEDIENCE TO THE CALCED

15. So I decided to go down immediately and open the door to the two Calced masters, speaking to them with much humility and love. I asked the Discalced to give me the royal proviso. I put it in my breast pocket and called a meeting. The Calced came in, gave notice of the brief, and I obeyed with much submission and humility, and the rest of the Discalced did not dare do less. I brought them into the refectory, gave them lunch, and told them to tell the nuncio that although the king had sent a proviso—which I showed them—the Discalced did not want to do anything else but obey His Lordship and our most dear Calced fathers in every point. They went away very content with this. The nuncio must have lost some of the dislike he had for me, for everything went very well, as this saint prophesied. Many other prophecies of his were likewise later fulfilled.

TURMOIL AT THE TIME OF THE FOUNDATION OF VALLADOLID

16. Other pesky troubles befell me when I was provincial, such as the turmoil surrounding the foundation of Valladolid: the Calced came in the middle of the night to force us out of the monastery, I was excommunicated by the abbot provisor,[13] and we had to go to the chancery for the absolution.[14] Other similar things happened that makes one believe there is much suffering in making foundations of new monasteries and reforming an order. If the apostle says that whoever wants to serve God

must be prepared—"All those who live devotedly in Jesus Christ will be persecuted" [2 Tim 3:12]—then what could be expected for one who has desired that a community serve as a source and spring from which have sprung so many monasteries with so much fruit as you can see this order brings forth in the church? For this reason, you will not be surprised by what I have suffered ever since God and our Lady called me to break the ice. I have been taken by extraordinary roads, not only in the affairs of the order but also in business outside the order.

THE BUSINESS OF THE PRINCESS OF ÉBOLI, WIFE OF RUY GÓMEZ

17. The king gave permission to me alone to speak with the princess of Éboli and deal with her concerns, when he had her imprisoned in Santorcaz. There was plenty of opportunity for gaining merit. Since this servant of God was of a terrible disposition and her adversaries were the most powerful of all, it was necessary to proceed with much prudence, tact, and courage.[15]

A MOST GRAVE SECRET AFFAIR

18. One time I was at the College of Alcalá,[16] when I was provincial, and a very solemn and illustrious person arrived late one night to talk to me. Not wanting any friar to see him or to know anything, he made me climb onto a mule, and we rode all that night in order to undo a very difficult and devilish entanglement. Although the harm could not be entirely prevented, if they had listened to me, the outbreak of fighting and killing that occurred later would not have happened. I cannot say what it was about, but it is enough to tell you that for more than a week I dressed with a belt of gold and precious stones—covered with canvas and worth more than a hundred thousand ducats—girded around my waist. It was given to me for safekeeping. I did what I could and remedied much harm. The man whose life was in danger wanted to thank me with a present worth more than a thousand ducats. I did not want it nor was it prudent to accept it because men who appear to be seeking some gain are not taken into confidence in these kinds of situations.

WHEN HE FINISHED HIS OFFICE OF PROVINCIAL; FRIARS HE SENT TO NEW SPAIN AND GUINEA; FRAY FRANCISCO DE JESÚS EL INDIGNO

19. I finished my term of provincial, having sent Nicolao de Oria [Nicolás Doria] to found the monastery in Genoa, from which came the monasteries of Italy. I held the chapter in Lisbon [May 1–17, 1585], and as the senior definitor, I sent twelve friars to the Indies. They have founded monasteries in New Spain [Mexico]. I sent friars to the Congo for the conversion of the people there, and they had great success.[17] Two of them alone baptized more than a hundred thousand Congolese. One of these friars was Fray Francisco de Jesús, 'el Indigno' [the Unworthy], of whose holiness, spirit, and zeal much could be said. I had sent missionaries to Ethiopia two other times by order of the king of Spain at the request of Don Alvaro, king of the Congo. The first group drowned at sea, and the second group returned stripped and robbed by Lutherans. Finally, the third group, which was Fray Francisco, Fray Diego del Sacramento, and another friar, arrived and bore the fruit I mentioned. At the chapter in Lisbon, they elected a man of much holiness and prudence for provincial, Father Fray Nicolás Doria, who was not present. I desired to rest a little from the burden of governing, but I could not have my wish because very shortly afterward they sent me to Portugal as vicar provincial.[18]

20. **Cyril:** *It was a great work, it seems to me, to expand the order by sending friars to Italy, the Indies, and the Congo of Ethiopia.*

21. **Anastasius:** Well then, that you may know how greatly diverse vocations, opinions, and passions are, it was imputed to me as a very bad work to have sent these friars.

THE SPIRIT OF RETIREMENT AND RECOLLECTION IN SOME MAKES THEM JUDGE THE SPIRIT OF ZEAL FOR SOULS AS SOMETHING BAD

22. There are those who think that the sum total of Carmelite perfection consists in not leaving one's cell or missing a moment of choir, even

if the entire world were ablaze, and that the welfare of the order lies in multiplying the number of monasteries in tiny Spanish villages and neglecting everything else. They call any other spirit restless and lax. God has not led me by that road but by the road of saving souls. The friars whom they want to use for foundations in small places I would use to found monasteries in the most important cities of diverse kingdoms for the true expansion and good of the order. And since I communicated for a long time and with such familiarity with Mother Teresa, whose spirit was zealous for the conversion of the whole world, I was even more convinced of this way.[19]

23. **Cyril:** *Who can doubt that since Christ and His apostles were the holiest of all, the imitation of them is the best spirit, for of them it is said, "Their voice has gone out to the entire world" [Ps 19(18):4(5); Rom 10:18]. When the religious were in uninhabited places, for themselves alone, it was well and good that they did not communicate with people, not even to go out to hear confessions, assist the dying, preach, or anything else. But after the councils made them leave the deserts to help the bishops and priests for the well-being of souls, there is no reason to turn back to ancient modes of solitary existence.*

24. **Anastasius:** Let us set this question aside since the Carthusians are a very good order and do not have the care of souls.

25. **Cyril:** *That was their institution, but not that of the Carmelites. Elijah and Elisha—the very austere founders of the Carmelites—went out to Samaria and other places, and they had their sisters, like the Shulammite of Zarephath.[20] But tell me now, I beg you, when you were vicar provincial in Portugal, did anything happen that can be recounted?*

MINISTRY IN JAÉN WITH THE DELUDED

26. **Anastasius:** The bishop of Jaén, Don Francisco Sarmiento,[21] called me to examine many souls of extraordinary spirits who were in his diocese. It was then that the true spirit of Gaspar Lucas was discovered and a stop was put to a new fabrication of the devil whereby those who were deceived into carnal relations with him [the devil] were thought to be

holy.[22] Many other things of this nature were stopped as well, a work into which I put no little effort, having recourse to the Inquisition in Córdoba.[23] Also, the foundation of the monastery of the Discalced Carmelite friars of Jaén began at this time.

MINISTRY IN EVORA WITH OTHER SOULS WHO WERE DECEIVED

27. The archbishop of Evora, Don Teutonio de Braganza,[24] likewise brought me to his archbishopric in order to bring other extraordinary spirits of revelations and visions under control. God knows what was suffered there because they were disquieting the kingdom with news—given by way of revelations—of the coming of King Don Sebastián.[25]

TROUBLES IN LISBON ON ACCOUNT OF THE NUN WITH THE STIGMATA

28. And all this was nothing compared to what I went through in Lisbon with the unrest caused there by false spirits, and where, among other things, I examined the case of the prioress of the Annunciation convent who had the stigmata.

29. **Cyril:** *I would be so pleased if you would tell me the whole story.*

30. **Anastasius:** It is too long to tell and beyond our purpose.[26]

DANGER OF DEATH FROM THE ANTONISTAS

31. It suffices to say that having informed Cardinal Albert[27] of certain secret things upon which hung the peace of that kingdom [Portugal], and in order to keep the Lutherans, who had heard about the affair of the prioress with the stigmata, from gaining influence,[28] I was forced to leave for Castile. Hurrying to notify the king, I left by night and had to avoid the main roads so that I might not be killed by the Antonistas (which is what those of the party of Don Antonio call themselves;[29] they are against King Philip, whose followers they call Filipistas). At El Escorial, the king asked me through Don Cristóbal de Moura (after my having given much information about the affairs of that kingdom) if I thought it was a good idea for the Inquisition to investigate whether the

wounds of the stigmatic were true or false.[30] I responded that the case did not really concern the faith but was a matter for the bishop, and yet, because it was so serious and rare and there was reason to fear that the Lutherans could invade and cause harm to the faith, it would be good if the Inquisition got involved.

THE DANGEROUS RETURN TO PORTUGAL; THE DANGER WHEN THE WOUNDS OF THE STIGMATIC WERE FOUND TO BE FAKE

32. The king then ordered my superiors to send me back to Lisbon. I returned, and soon after my arrival, the wounds were discovered to be fake when the inquisitors washed them away with soap and hot water.[31] The Portuguese rose up against me, especially those devoted to the prioress and the Antonistas. They said, "A devil of a Carmelite friar brought some kind of powder that King Don Philip gave him, and he used it to remove the wounds our Lord God was pleased to send from heaven to our holy prioress."[32] Once again, a second persecution was directed against me. But since the Inquisition was now involved and Cardinal Albert defended me, I did not have much to fear.

THE COMING OF DON ANTONIO AND DRAKE TO PORTUGAL; THE YEAR 1588; OCCUPATIONS AT THAT TIME

33. Occurring at this time was the rebellion in the kingdom of Portugal and the assault on Lisbon by [Sir Francis] Drake and Don Antonio with their armada.[33] This was the year 1588, foretold to be a year of terrible events. I believe that all the stars and their bad influence were aligned against me, because I suffered in a strange way there, and the sum of my troubles and persecutions was forged at that time.[34] I will leave aside the fatigue I experienced of hearing the confessions of all those imprisoned in castles by Don Antonio, a duty the cardinal would not entrust to the Portuguese or any Castilian but me; of going out and assisting the soldiers condemned to death; of interceding with the marquis of Santa Cruz [Don Alvaro de Bazán] and afterward the count of Fuentes [Don Pedro Enríquiz de Azevedo] for the pardon of other soldiers; of

delivering messages entrusted to me by Father Fray Luis de Granada,[35] who was then very old and sick, in order to tend to many things concerning the souls of Portuguese and Castilians alike; of continuous preaching and hearing confessions; of arranging the foundation and administration of a home for converted prostitutes, which God granted me the favor to establish there in Lisbon whereby many sins have been avoided;[36] of having to deal with many people of this type of life, either already converted or intending to convert; of assisting the Inquisition and the archbishop with special cases, such as healers using incantations and other things of that sort; of tending to secret matters, in which the cardinal got me involved, that had to do with the rebellion; of governing and maintaining my monastery of San Felipe of the Discalced Carmelites and assisting the nuns of San Alberto;[37] and of many other similar occupations.

THE OCCASION OF THE VISITATION OF THE CALCED OF PORTUGAL

34. Let us turn to what is more important. News arrived that the armada was approaching Lisbon.[38] The Calced monastery, which was founded by Count Don Alvarez Pereira who had defeated the Castilians in the famous Battle of Aljubarrota, had a hundred friars.[39] It was feared that they might start a revolution because those who caused the most harm in these situations were friars and clerics. (Of our own, Father Master Calderón had been in prison, another very valiant friar had been the captain of Don Antonio, and some friars in the monastery had "eaten the bread" [taken the side] of those who were most rebellious.) Since the monastery was like a fortress and near the city wall, it was feared they would let the English enter through there. A rumor circulated that six thousand harquebuses were hidden in the Carmen [the monastery of the Calced Carmelites], where the plot of treason was said to originate.[40] This fear reached the point where the artillery of the castle was aimed at the Carmen and each night a company of Castilian soldiers quietly surrounded it. In order to verify this rumor about the harquebuses, restrain the friars and have them subdued when the enemy was

to come, and discover and banish any troublemakers, Cardinal Albert gave me the apostolic commission—with the faculties he had from the pope—to be the visitator and reformer of the Calced Carmelites of Portugal [November 24, 1588].

THE CARRYING OUT OF THE VISITATION

35. Here I was burdened with the office of superior of the Portuguese Calced—having experienced the taste of turpentine from the Andalusians—and, at the same time, I was made a captain of negotiations of war. I entered the Carmen with only my Discalced companion [Fray Bautista de la Trinidad], though not without great opposition from the Castilian seculars. Fearing that I would be killed, they said I should not go there without being accompanied by harquebusiers for surely the friars would kill me. Disregarding the risk involved, I ate, slept, and lived with them for a long time. I discovered that what was rumored about the harquebuses was not true, and I sent some friars away from there with honorable offices, those who would have caused trouble if they stayed in Lisbon.

FEAR OF DEATH WHEN THE ENEMY ARRIVED AT LISBON

36. The enemy arrived and camped in Alcántara, a half league from Lisbon, where they thought the battle was to take place.[41] I went out very early one morning with two *donados*[42] to hear the confessions of the soldiers—as was my custom—since the cardinal would not grant faculties to hear confessions to any Portuguese priest. A strange fear came over me. My nerves contracted and my throat tightened, like someone who sees himself in clear danger of death. I realized that when the battle broke out against us—who were not more than three thousand five hundred at our best—the enemy—who were thirty thousand—would spread out, surround us, and enter the city, trapping us in the middle. The first to die would be those in the rear guard, where I would be while the others were fighting. I had no doubt this would happen. The cardinal and our men, realizing the same danger, returned to the city, closed the gates, and fortified themselves within the walls. And thus, a

lieutenant who came upon me on the road told me that I should return to the city (and my soul returned to my body).

THE DEPARTURE OF THE DISCALCED FRIARS AND NUNS, WHOSE MONASTERIES OF SAN FELIPE AND SAN ALBERTO WERE OUTSIDE THE WALLS, AND HOW THEY ENTERED THE CITY

37. By that time the Discalced Carmelite friars had already gone into the city and were staying at the Carmen of the Calced, and the Discalced nuns of San Alberto had been brought to the castle, which was a sight worthy to see. Following a large crucifix, they went in procession with their crosses in their hands and their veils covering their faces, accompanied by the Discalced and Calced friars and a company of soldiers guarding them. Passing through the squadrons, they gave great courage to the soldiers. It so happened that the nuns were placed in the same part of the castle as the artillery. Every time the cannon was fired, they got down on their knees and prayed the *Veni, Sancte Spiritus* [Come, Holy Spirit] with the intention that the cannonball be guided in defense of Christendom.

OCCUPATIONS DURING THE SIEGE OF LISBON

38. When the enemy saw that they were not going to be engaged in battle in Alcántara, they drew near the walls of Lisbon and stationed themselves in all the outlying districts. The monasteries in those places, such as San Felipe and San Alberto of the Discalced Carmelites and La Esperanza of the saintly Franciscan nuns, and the remaining parishes and churches were used by them as lodgings and dormitories since all the people had fled into the city. Only the Company of Jesus, whose house was outside the walls, gave orders that the Spanish soldiers could use their place to fight from. This was a big help on account of the many English they killed from there.

39. For three days, the enemy assailed the walls of Lisbon. The life I was leading at that time was to go at night to my monastery, the Carmen, which had a hundred friars. They were enclosed in a dormitory on the

top floor because the rest of the house, including the church, cells, and offices, was full of seculars, more than two thousand men and women who had taken shelter there with their households. It was sobering to see what these poor people suffered from hunger and misfortune. Because of their fear, they had forgotten to eat or to bring any food with them, and it was necessary to assist them lest they perish. And during the day, my Discalced friars and I went among the soldiers hearing confessions. Since our soldiers were greatly outnumbered, they had little hope of life.

40. One of those three days, when it already seemed that the enemy had entered and all was lost, my Portuguese Calced friars began to get restless and to leave the dormitory against my orders. When I saw this, I asked for a squadron of up to fifty Portuguese harquebusiers to visit the upper dormitory under the pretext of removing the women—family members of the friars—who had gone up there. I told the soldiers, "Load your guns," commanding them to put balls in the harquebuses, in case they were carrying them unloaded. They were stunned by the words "load your guns" and glared at me for a long time.

DANGER OF DEATH

41. There were tremendous things happening during these days, with few hours to sleep and much danger of death. Without any fear, I threw out the *cabezones* [pigheads],[43] many of whom were Portuguese soldiers who came into the monastery to escape the fighting. God knows what they were up to, but this was our greatest danger: all eight thousand armed Portuguese disappeared, leaving only the Castilians on the battlefield, and we had reason to believe that—as their officers had told us—in seeing the English prevail, they would help them by cutting the throats of us all. Thus we had thirty thousand Portuguese enlisted soldiers, but we were ignorant of the whereabouts of eight thousand armed ones. Well, what would it matter to one of them just to knife me when I was chasing him out of the monastery with force and insults to go and fight? Or when I went out at night on the roof with a torch to

keep watch over my monastery, how difficult would it be for the enemy to fell me with a bullet, as our Castilian soldiers said to me, laughing at my daring? But the truth is, in a situation like this, when a man is determined to face even death, he fears no danger.

42. The enemy entered the outskirts of the city on Thursday morning, the day of Corpus Christi, and were there the whole day. Instead of the Corpus Christi procession that we usually had, there were skirmishes of soldiers who went out through the gate of San Antonio and other skirmishes on the ramparts. It was necessary to hear the confessions of the soldiers who went out because not even half of them returned alive. The attack continued Friday, Saturday, and Sunday until, after midnight, the enemy withdrew to Oeiras, two leagues away.

THE ENGLISH WITHDRAW

43. Drake, who had remained aboard his ship in Cascais, saw that the Portuguese were not fulfilling the promise they had made to the Queen of England, which was that when the English arrived at the walls of Lisbon, the gates would be opened to them, they would be received with peace, and each English soldier would be given eight doubloons. Instead, he saw the Castilians defending the walls, killing many English soldiers, and hanging some of the Portuguese who were trying to carry out the agreement. He concluded that to win Lisbon was of little importance, whereas to lose his armada was to lose everything valued by the queen. He lost many soldiers, some—not very many—at the hands of the Castilians but many more at the hands of God due to a sudden sickness he gave them. The cause of this sickness in most cases was that, as the soldiers came off the ships hungry and unable to taste, they had a great desire for the marmalade of Portugal. Finding shops in the surrounding districts where soap is sold—a watery soap was used there, which looked like marmalade—they filled themselves with it and then drank water. With the fever and dysentery it gave them, they were dead in one day, or at least sick and useless.

DANGER IN GOING OUT TO IDENTIFY THE DEAD

44. Monday morning, the enemy having withdrawn, Cardinal Albert sent me—since I knew all the Castilian soldiers—with a company of harquebusiers to identify the dead in order to bury the Catholics and burn the heretics. Going out from the city, I saw a miserable spectacle of death. There were more than three hundred Castilians, whom we laid face up with their arms crossed to show they were Catholics, and more than eight hundred Lutherans, whom we turned face down—looking at hell where their souls were already burning—in order to burn their bodies.[44]

45. There was no little danger in going out like this because we came across many Lutherans hidden in the houses. Since I went in front of the harquebusiers, it was easy for one of them to fell me with a shot from a window without us knowing where it came from. Many of those Lutherans were killed by the harquebusiers who went out with me. Others I protected, saying they should not be killed but be sent back to the city as prisoners. I hope in God that this outing was a great service to Him because we also encountered many Portuguese, men and women alike, who lived in the outlying districts or who had come there to help and serve the English. One of the soldiers wanted to shoot the first one we found, who was a woman. I shouted to him not to do it, that he could not kill her because she was a Christian. They argued that they were traitors who helped the enemy. We shouted back and forth about this. I threatened and commanded them in the name of God and the cardinal not to kill anyone, adding that since they had been sent under my orders, they were to obey me. Since the Castilian people are punctilious in observing obedience, no one was ever shot again. I believe everyone we met would otherwise have been killed, and there were more than three hundred.[45]

PERILOUS RISKS

46. Some perilous risks were taken at this time, such as going out on behalf of the cardinal to the Bernardine nuns of Odivelas, who are a

league and a half from the city. Their superiors had ordered them to stay in their monastery, and I was to order them to leave. They departed, escorted by a squadron of light cavalry that was sent for them. Some of the nuns, however, of the band of Don Antonio, remained waiting for him with conserves and refreshments as for their king. But the others, who were Filipistas and feared the insolence of the Lutherans, had written to me earlier to negotiate with the cardinal permission for them to leave their monastery and come to the city. When I returned with this license, alone in those fields, the army of the enemy was not more than half a league away. For this reason, many friends reprimanded me, saying I was wrong for going out alone. But I was blinded by zeal that the Lutherans not defile the spouses of Jesus Christ. Another time, I went out alone in the open country as far as the Castle of San Gian with another important message while the Lutherans were in Oeiras, which was a league from there.

THE COMING OF MASTER CARRANZA

47. The war ended and we were at peace, although it did not end for me. Rather, new wars began because Father Master Carranza, a Calced Carmelite, who came by order of the general and the protector, was offended that I was making a visitation of their Portuguese Calced friars. I received him in the monastery with the recognition customary for receiving the general (because he carried a patent of the vicar general of Portugal). He fell ill upon arrival and was at the point of dying. I took care of him and treated him kindly. When he got well, I informed him that I had accepted the visitation only so that the order could be freed of the infamy of treason, and I turned over to him the documents of the case. I told him—as was true—that I had not entered into examining their customs or regular observance because in this there was no province in the order of the Calced that excelled theirs. I said that I wanted to return to my monastery of the Discalced and that he alone, with his companion, Master [Diego] Heredia, should make the ordinary visitation, since I was in charge just during the turmoil of the war. He thanked

me for this good outcome. Having recourse to the cardinal however, he did not give his consent for me to return to my Discalced monastery. He said that since I had begun the visitation, the two of us should finish it together, and he would write to the general about the service I would be rendering the order in accepting. We went around the province. When the visitation was finished [on May 14, 1591], he returned to Aragon, at the same time the rebellion of Antonio Pérez began.[46] I returned to my Discalced with much peace and quiet, although this was like the silence of children who rest so they can cry all the more, as I shall recount later.

Fourth Dialogue: EXPULSION

THIS DIALOGUE CONCERNS THE SENTENCE OF EXPULSION FROM THE ORDER OF CARMEL THAT THE SUPERIORS GAVE TO GRACIÁN: HOW DEEPLY HE FELT SUCH GREAT DISHONOR AT SEEING HIMSELF STRIPPED OF THE HABIT AND EXPELLED FROM THE ORDER HE LOVED SO MUCH AND FOR WHICH HE HAD GREATLY LABORED, BY THE HANDS OF THE SAME FRIARS TO WHOM HE HAD GIVEN THE HABIT AND RECEIVED INTO THE ORDER. HE STATES THE REASON THIS SENTENCE WAS GIVEN, THE CHARGES THAT WERE MADE IN ORDER TO GIVE IT, AND THE AWFUL RUMORS THAT FOLLOWED. WHILE DEFENDING HIS INNOCENCE AND DECLARING THAT HE WAS SEVERELY SENTENCED WITHOUT FAULT, GRACIÁN IS ABLE WHOLEHEARTEDLY TO EXCUSE HIS JUDGES, DECLARING THAT THOSE WHO SENTENCED HIM ARE SERVANTS OF GOD AND HOLY MEN.

LAWS OF THE CONSULTA AND THEIR DISADVANTAGES

1. **Anastasius:** At this time [summer of 1590], the new laws of the *consulta* came into my hands, and I saw clearly the harm that would come to the Discalced from that mode of governing. I wrote down their disadvantages and sent them to Rome with Father Fray Pedro de la Purificación.[1] I had an apostolic license from Cardinal Albert and a license from the protector of the order [Cardinal Domenico Pinelli] that gave me the authority to send Father Pedro to Rome.[2]

TRIP TO MADRID WITH HUMILITY AND OBEDIENCE

2. The Discalced superiors in Madrid sent for me.[3] I was mistrustful about going and could easily have gone to Rome from Lisbon, but I was fooled by my innocence and obedience, and my desire for peace and humility. It seemed to me that if I went to the *consulta* and explained to them my thoughts regarding the disadvantages in that new way of governing, they would believe me. If and when they did not believe me and I saw that they were holding to their opinion, I would tell them that I would submit and speak no more about the subject. Rather, I would serve and obey them in everything (because I had already done what I owed my conscience in writing to the pope, the cardinal protector, and the general, and telling them what I thought). I would peacefully stay in whatever monastery they wanted, serving the order in my office as preacher and confessor and putting my studies to use.

WHAT MOVED THEM TO EXPEL HIM FROM THE ORDER

3. They did not believe me. On the contrary, they were set upon two things: one, all the good of the Discalced consisted in this new mode of governing; two, in no way would they be able to establish it if I remained in the order, for they could already see that the rest of the Discalced were not going along with that novelty.

SENDING HIM TO THE INDIES TO GET HIM OUT OF THE ORDER

4. In order to remove this hindrance [to their plans for the *consulta*], they gave me a patent to be vicar general of the Indies, requesting with much peace and obsequiousness that I go there.[4] But a secular friend of mine, in whom they confided, warned me that it was a ploy to throw me out of Spain to that faraway New World. At the same time they ordered that I not be received there so that, not having supporters, I would not be able to raise my head.

HE WANTED TO GO TO THE EAST INDIES BUT THE KING DID NOT CONSENT

5. This secular, who was on friendly terms with the nuncio, had compassion for me. Without my knowing it, he negotiated with the nuncio to give an order that I not be sent to the Indies. The nuncio gave the order.[5] Would to God that he had not given it and that I had then gone to the West Indies, or that when I was in Lisbon, I had gone to the East Indies with Matías de Albuquerque who was viceroy of India and a great friend of mine who was going there at that time. I had permission from the cardinal to accompany him, but when the king found out about it, he stopped me from going. Or would to God that I had gone to Rome with the licenses I had, without appearing before the *consulta,* so that such a disastrous affair—as I will now recount—would never have occurred. But the king and the nuncio and the deception of my own innocence, and God by means of all these, led me to what I will speak about now.

THE SENTENCE OF EXPULSION FROM THE ORDER OF CARMEL, FROM THE DISCALCED AND THE CALCED ALIKE

6. As they saw that I was not going to the Indies and that they had no remedy other than to expel me from the order to ensure their new laws and government, they began the process against me. They arrested me. I did not pay much attention to the charges they laid on me because even if they were true, they were not of much importance. Thus I was fooled by my innocence, never believing that the case would reach the point that it did, which was a sentence of expulsion from the order [February 17, 1592], written in loaded,[6] grave, and offensive words.

7. **Cyril:** *Many things must have happened before it came to that. I don't want you to hide anything from me.*

8. **Anastasius:** On the contrary, I don't intend to say anything other than summarize all this in three points. First, that those who did this were servants of God—as I have said—and they did not err, nor did

they do anything wrong. Second, that the author of this sentence and everything that followed was God and none other. Third, that—as I have also said—my conscience does not accuse me nor will ever accuse me of a grave fault in those things they imputed to me or in what has been judged about me by people who do not know the facts of the case.

9. **Cyril:** *How is this possible? That God should persecute, and that, in such grave matters so public and scandalous, you are innocent and they have proceeded with justice and rectitude?*

10. **Anastasius:** I would like you to read the book of Job attentively. You will see how the Lord ordained his trials and gave the devil a free hand to persecute him. Job complained to God for treating him as though He were against him and shooting His arrows into his heart like a target. He said that when persecution comes from God, there is no remedy whatsoever.

ZEAL IS THE REASON PERSECUTION OF THE INNOCENT CAN BE JUST, ALTHOUGH IN ERROR AND NOT ACCORDING TO KNOWLEDGE

11. So that you may understand how God can persecute when He wants, He not only allows those who are evil to mistreat those who are not—since it is clear that a leaf on a tree does not move without the will of God—but even aids persecution by means of good people. When a just person is of the opinion that something is for the service of God and the opposite is harmful, the zeal born of that opinion is a zeal that is good, just, and holy. And although the understanding errs and the will is blind (because it is not obligated to follow any course other than the one marked out by the understanding), the will, in desiring to pursue that path, merits and does well. This merit and good intention of the will, as well as zeal, grows stronger in holy persons, with the fruit of Holy Communion, confession, mental prayer, and all the other exercises of virtue. Once it is conceived as something holy and for the good of the order to expel a man who will hinder its increase and perfection, then Holy Communion, mental prayer, spiritual fruits, and all the rest (which usually restrain those who persecute with malice) increase the

zeal and strength of those who, without malice, think they are offering service to God.[7] Therefore, I say that the persecution was unstoppable because it came from God by means of the prayer, spirituality, Communions, and merits of those who persecuted me. They gained glory in this, and I got the grief.

12. As to how they can be saints and gain merit in persecuting me while I am innocent and persecuted without fault and that this is not a contradiction (although I have just finished saying something about this), something remains to be said: the difference lay in the understandings of each, for which there is neither merit nor demerit, and the wills were in accordance with what each understood. Just as is the case with the speculative understanding—that two men who are wise, grave, and holy, holding diverse opinions, can argue and shout, as did St. Augustine and St. Jerome—so it is with the practical understanding that you can have diverse opinions and end up quarreling and going separate ways without there being any fault of the parties. This is seen in the quarrel between St. Paul and St. Barnabas over whether to take St. Mark with them. St. Paul claimed he was useless and would hinder the fruit of their evangelizing, because he judged, from what he had seen, that Mark did not undertake the work with the zeal and rigor that he expected. St. Barnabas saw the fruit Mark was going to have in all Egypt. So they argued and fought obstinately and separated. God permitted that division and quarrel for the greater good of each and of the church because St. Paul was fruitful in Antioch, and St. Barnabas and St. Mark in Egypt. And as I will later relate, incredible fruits have come from my pilgrimage, which would not have happened if I had remained with the Discalced.

13. **Cyril:** *I am still not satisfied because St. Paul did not impute faults to St. Barnabas as the* consulta *imputed faults and failings to you. In fact, they condemned you for them. And St. Barnabas did not make excuses for St. Paul's innocence as you have done for the* consulta. *It is either one or the other: you are evil and guilty, or they are blaming and defaming an innocent person. My understanding does not come to any other logic. Either they are lying or you are.*

14. **Anastasius:** Oh, if you only knew the subtlety of the designs of God and how He is accustomed to persecuting somebody by means of just and holy brothers—which is the greatest of all persecutions—without anyone being at fault! Read the book of Job again, slowly. This book has really sustained me. You will find that his friends are just, holy, and good friends. They come to visit him with the very good intention of consoling him. In almost the whole of that book, there is nothing other than the reasoning of Job's friends who try to persuade him that there is no man so just that he never falls and to recognize this and do penance and let himself be condemned. All the reasons and arguments they give are most holy and true. For his part, Job, in defense of his innocence, replies that he is not aware of any grave sin and that if his faults were weighed in the balance against the pains he suffers, without a doubt the pains weigh more, being as innumerable as the sand of the sea.

HUMAN WORKS ARE LIKE PICTURES

15. You see how both sides speak truthfully, both speak well, and yet they are saying opposite things. To understand this more clearly, consider that human actions are like pictures that, when seen from different angles and with different eyeglasses, present diverse images. If the glasses are crystal and for viewing close up, they enlarge what is little. If they are red, they make what is white look red. If green, the thing looks green. If the glasses reflect, the image looks distorted, and what is really nice-looking will, with those glasses, seem ugly. The picture is always one and the same; the eyes are not at fault but rather the glasses are. The scribes and Pharisees were devout men of the law; nevertheless, they judged Mary Magdalene kissing the feet of Christ [see Lk 7:36–50], Christ making mud on the Sabbath to give sight to a blind man [see Jn 9], and the disciples not washing their hands before eating bread [see Mt 15:1–20] as bad things—even though they were perfection—because they wore glasses that made their neighbor's straw look like a beam of a wine press [see Mt 7:3–5; Lk 6:41–42].

16. **Cyril:** *You have just contradicted yourself. The Pharisees were evil and full of malice, yet you say that your adversaries were just and holy and did not sin in condemning you. The Pharisees certainly sinned in condemning Christ.*

17. **Anastasius:** There are two kinds of reflecting eyeglasses. One kind is made from the glass of malice and hatred; such were the glasses of the Pharisees. The other kind is made from the glass of zeal. This second type usually exaggerates, enlarges, and distorts the images more than the eyeglasses of malice because they are born of virtue and good desires—although with a deceived understanding—which have greater strength than passion and malice.

EXAMPLES OF WORDS AND THINGS WRONGLY UNDERSTOOD BY HOLY PEOPLE WHO HAVE AN OPINION CONTRARY TO THOSE WITH ZEAL FOR SOULS

18. I want to give you some examples:

THE OCCASIONS FROM WHICH THE MAIN CHARGES AROSE

19. One night, having finished supper, we were at recreation. We heard a man stab another man and the wounded man was crying out and asking for confession. I said, "Let's go out and hear his confession." Someone—not the least saintly—responded, "The door cannot be opened because it is against obedience." I said with anger, "That obedience is not obedience! Let's go out before he dies." And we went out to hear his confession. He who had the other opinion accused me of saying that there is no vow of obedience in religious life or some such words that smacked of heresy.

20. On one occasion, when I was provincial, I entered a monastery, and a holy and very simple Discalced Carmelite nun embraced me with I don't know what impetus. She put her mouth on my heart where I wore a crucifix and remained enraptured, aware that Christ was there. This was seen with such eyeglasses and was related with such words as to make one think that something impure—mixed with the heresy of the illuminists [*alumbrados*]—was done.

21. Mother Teresa of Jesus gave me some relics. A prioress, one of the holiest and purest that I have known in the order, placed them in a reliquary made in the form of a heart, which I carried with me. Having given me this heart-shaped reliquary, it was said that the prioress had an improper affection for me.

22. When the monastery of the nuns in Lisbon was being constructed, I used to look after those in charge of the work. During the summer, I liked to take a little siesta in the afternoon when it was hot. The nuns would bring out a mattress for me (obviously the mattress belonged to the nuns, not the carpenters). It was written about me that I used to sleep in the nuns' beds and so on, with words that were very prejudicial.

23. I entered the cloister to anoint and prepare for a good death one of the holiest nuns we have. Having sat up in bed so that she could take a sip of water or something, she fell in a faint. I extended my arms to hold her head. They said that I embraced the nuns when they were in bed.

24. I arrived to hear a nun's confession. It seemed to another nun that my mouth was very close to her face, and since she related her observation in accordance with her rash judgment, it was imputed to me that I used to kiss the Discalced nuns.

25. Sometimes I entered the cloister for necessary things, such as to look at the plans with the builders, and so forth. Being asked whether I entered the cloister on those occasions, I answered yes and told them why. They wrote that I confessed to entering the cloister, and they judged that there was not sufficient reason for my doing so, that it was enough for the builders to enter the cloister. In the end, they charged me with entering the cloister of the nuns without sufficient reason and that I had already confessed to this.

26. In Seville, there were many mosquitoes during the summer. To remedy the situation, the nuns sent me a lightweight toque that, by

propping it up with sticks, made a kind of canopy that covered my face. They charged that I used to sleep with a canopy sent by the nuns.

27. Many other things of this kind were commonly said without being specific except to say "things concerning the nuns," which made a bad impression on the king, the pope, and many people.

28. When I sent a petition to Rome asking that the laws of the *consulta* be examined, I was charged with the fault of *erigentibus se contra superiores* ["rising up against superiors"], as if the pope were not the greater superior. This was one of the greatest faults of which they accused me. To this charge, they added the sentence of the nuncio [Sega] along with other admonitions they had given me. From all this, they concluded I was incorrigible.

29. All these things and others besides are seen with the eyeglasses of erroneous zeal. It might be that you or others do not believe it. That is why I said from the start that I have reserved this cause for the tribunal of God, and I have been just fine remaining quiet and hidden until the time comes when all will be revealed in the next life.

TAKING AWAY THE HABIT

30. Finally, after a long imprisonment,[8] they took the habit from me. It hurt me very much to see myself dressed in a cassock and mantle of fine material, which had belonged to a novice who had just entered. These nice clothes lasted until I got from the monastery to my parents' house [in Madrid]. Then I removed them and had a long cape extending to the feet made for me, with a habit of the coarsest brown fabric that could be found. These gave me the look of a hermit or a pilgrim. Only someone who suffered it could say what it felt like to have entered the order of the Discalced with the calling I had when I entered, to have suffered so much to establish the province, and to have given the habit of the order to the same ones who took it from me.

RUMORS THAT FOLLOWED HIS EXPULSION

31. **Cyril:** *I have heard it said by many—some of them very holy people and very good friends of yours—that you yourself wanted to leave, that they gave you a lighter sentence keeping you in the order, but you did not accept it.*

32. **Anastasius:** Some said that since the sentence was given by such holy men and that two of the judges were from other orders, one Dominican and the other Jeronimite,[9] they must have had good reasons for it. They were astonished that hypocrisy has such power that, being such a person, I was able to deceive Mother Teresa of Jesus and many others up to that time and that these judges have uncovered it. Others attributed passion to the judges. Still others said that even though there might have been some faults, it would have been reasonable to conceal them and keep quiet so as not to defame the order. For it was a great humiliation for such a holy order to have always had for its superior a man who is now discovered to be so evil; it would have been more sensible to pardon me than to defame it. Others were saying it was very foolish to make this public and that it would have been better to keep me in a well of silence without anyone knowing of it. Some asked the friars what my faults were for meriting such a severe punishment that was so public, harsh, and scandalous. Most of the friars responded that they knew nothing other than that the judges who gave the sentence were very holy and so must have looked at the case very well; and they would shrug their shoulders. Other religious, and even the judges, said and would even swear that in all these things there was not a mortal sin; rather, at the beginning stages of religious orders, such punishments were necessary in order to introduce "perfection," which ought not to be hindered (they understood by "perfection" the government of the *consulta*). They concluded that it was impossible for those laws to remain as long as I remained in the order. Others said I was obnoxious and that if I had humbled myself and asked pardon of them, the affair would not have come to the breaking point. Many of them disclosed the sentence and trial proceedings, for which reason the transcript was printed, a thing rarely done. It is filled with words so loaded and grave

that whoever sees it—however great a friend of mine he might be—will shrug his shoulders and be silent. Not realizing there is a kind of zeal different from that of passion and malice and that exaggerates things, many of my closest friends (and even I myself) said to themselves that it would serve God better to believe that a man was really as bad as they said rather than believe the church of God had come to the state where an order so holy and so perfect would be guilty of such perjury. Finally, there were so many different opinions and rumors that it was not possible for me to do anything other than be silent and draw close to God.

THEY WANTED TO TRY TO MAKE HIM A BISHOP

33. What hurt me most at this time was that the very ones who took the habit from me tried to have me made a bishop so that I would remain in the habit of the secular clergy. I do not know their intentions or what their consciences accused them of after they saw so much murmuring.

34. **Cyril:** *And could they have had you made a bishop?*

35. **Anastasius:** Very easily, because at that time Father Fray Nicolás Doria, who was a most holy and prudent man, was rendering a notable service for the king and all Christendom. He was undoing the damage that came to Spain from contracts with the Genoese who, with their exchanges and so forth, ate up all the money.[10] It was by his order that the decree was then made against the Genoese. The king was so grateful that, if Doria had wanted, he would have made him an archbishop and given him whatever he might request. Doria wanted nothing more than royal favor for the good of the order and to go forward with the *consulta* and his government. With his lively ingenuity and vigorous reasons, he convinced the king and his ministers that in this [the *consulta*] consisted all the perfection of the order and that I was disturbing it.[11] Consequently, the king turned against me with regard to my remaining in the order, and all the ministers who knew me abandoned me; yet, had Father Nicolás asked for it, they might have favored me with any other position. My mother, who knew well how things worked at court,[12] also suffered from this while I was in Madrid because

my disgrace was a cause of great humiliation. All my relatives and friends would rather have seen me dead than in this awful situation.

HOW HE LEFT MADRID

36. Thus, without anyone seeing me, I left Madrid and headed for Rome, with much hardship, misery, and discouragement. The sentence carried such threats of excommunication that it was necessary to go to the pope.[13]

37. **Cyril:** *I am still not satisfied, even though you have given good reasons and examples, such as the Child Jesus lost in the temple without fault of His mother or St. Joseph, the dissension between Saints Paul and Barnabas, the vision through different eyeglasses, the diverse view of the same picture, and everything else you have said. How can it be reconciled that you are innocent and without fault and that the judges, your fathers, are saints who did well in giving you such a serious and shameful sentence of expulsion, a sentence that is not given except to religious who are most criminal and incorrigible* ne morbida pecus . . . [*"lest the infected sheep"* (. . . *infect the flock*)].[14] *"Was it his sin or that of his parents that caused him to be born blind?"* [*Jn 9:2, NAB*]. *Since there is no punishment if not for some fault, either you were found guilty and justly sentenced or you were not guilty and they are, for sentencing you with passion contrary to justice.*

38. **Anastasius:** I can respond to you as Christ responded to His disciples when they asked that question: "It was no sin, either of this man or of his parents" [Jn 9:3, NAB]. Neither did I sin so as to merit such a sentence.

TWO KINDS OF FAULTS IMPUTED TO HIM

39. Two kinds of faults were imputed to me. One kind was of things that touched the honor of the Discalced Carmelite nuns and smacked of immorality. As for this, the Lord lives in whose presence I stand, and I swear, with all I can swear by, that I never had a serious fault in all the time I dealt with them. I say serious since the Holy Spirit says, "The just man falls seven times a day" [Prov 24:16]. I would be very foolish and proud if I were to swear that I have been free all my life of slight faults

and venial sins—which can be absolved with holy water—into which the just man falls seven times a day.

A SENTENCE OF EXPULSION IS GIVEN FOR SERIOUS REASONS TO FRIARS WHO ARE CRIMINAL AND INCORRIGIBLE

40. But those sins, what do they have to do with a sentence of expulsion, which is given only for sins that are crimes?

REASONS WITH WHICH GRACIÁN PROVES HIS INNOCENCE

41. You want me to prove clearly that this is true? First, if I were as incorrigible as the sentence says, why didn't they notice my evil life before they decreed the laws of the *consulta*? And why, before then, did they always elect me a superior? Second, even if I were the worst person in the world, the Discalced Carmelite nuns are so holy that they would have never consented to any of the things stated—with words so offensive and full of insinuations—in so severe a sentence. Third, if they regard Mother Teresa of Jesus as holy and most wise, prudent, zealous, and discreet, how could she have let me deal with her nuns and not realize what sort of person I was before her death? And never did she hold them back from me or look down on me. On the contrary, she praised and esteemed me and had such affirming revelations about me, as you know and of which we will later speak [in dialogue 16]. Fourth, the same judges who sentenced me told many important persons (the duke of Infantado among others will tell you[15]) that they never found a mortal sin in me in all these things, affirming this with an oath.

WHEN FATHER TOMÁS DE AQUINO DIED

42. Some of them said publicly, when they were dying,[16] that I was innocent. They did so in order to restore my good name as best they could and be freed of the fear that oppressed them for having defamed and humiliated me. There is no testimony more insistent of your innocence than that of those who were once against you.[17]

THEY WERE SAYING GRACIÁN WAS RISING UP AGAINST THE SUPERIORS, AND THERE ARE GRAVE PUNISHMENTS IN THE ORDER CONCERNING REBELLION AGAINST SUPERIORS.[18]

43. The second kind of fault they imputed to me had to do with my having sent Fray Pedro de la Purificación to Rome with my objections to the laws of the *consulta*. But this—if we have the Catholic faith that the pope and the protector are superior to those fathers who made the laws—was not a fault but a merit because in doubtful things, especially when motivated by good zeal, it is meritorious to go to the superiors. And at that time, when I sent Fray Pedro to Rome, I was the apostolic visitator of Portugal, and my commission was superior to theirs.[19]

44. "Nor his parents" [Jn 9:3, NAB], said Christ, and I say that my fathers did not sin in giving me the sentence because sin is in the will, and their wills were motivated by holy zeal for the perfection of the order and the removal of whatever would hinder this perfection, which they thought was in this new government of the *consulta*. With this zeal—seeing that if I were in the order, the *consulta* would not last—they wanted to expel me. Since they could not expel me without a sentence, and one that merited expulsion, they believed that everything they did against me was holy.

45. **Cyril:** *Even now, much harm has arisen from this sentence because some judge you to be guilty and a bad sheep while others judge them to be impassioned.*

46. **Anastasius:** This is nothing new. From now until the end of the world, the Jews judge and will judge that the death of Christ was for His crimes, and Christians that it was for the glory of God for He was raised up to the Eternal Father by that road and given the name above all names. Likewise, my expulsion was for the glory of God, the good of my soul, and for many good things—as I will afterward recount—that would not have come about if I had persevered as a Discalced, crushed and enclosed in a monastery. Therefore, I conclude that this unfortunate, humiliated, and disgraced blind man, Anastasius, did not sin, nor did his superiors sin. Rather, God ordained it in order to manifest His works in him.

Fifth Dialogue: Appeal

This concerns the great affronts, dangers, fears, peregrinations, and labors that Gracián suffered in going to Rome, Naples, and Sicily so the defense of his innocence would be heard: how they did not want to hear him but instead confirmed the sentence and threatened him with the galley if he did not enter some other order; how no order wanted to accept him since he was an infamous and expelled friar; and how, returning to Rome to join the Discalced Augustinians, he fell into the hands of the Turks who captured him near Gaeta.

1. **Cyril:** *Why didn't you appeal the sentence?*

2. **Anastasius:** It's a long story. I had no one to appeal to except the pope. So, it seemed that the best thing to do was to get free of their grasp any way possible and walk to Rome, turning my back on Spain. They had treated me so badly there, in my own country and in the presence of my relatives, friends, and others I knew. Wearing the clothes of a pilgrim, I arrived in Alicante to board a ship. I saw the sea, I feared its waves, and the two seculars traveling with me left me there alone.[1] It was Lent. I missed being able to preach and hear confessions, but because I wasn't wearing a habit, I could not go up into the pulpit and appear before the people. In the sentence, they had ordered that I was not to preach or hear confessions until I received the habit and professed in

another order, an order other than the Calced Carmelites, because they did not want me to go over to the Calced.

3. **Cyril:** *Well now, can those who expel someone from one order tell him what to do outside of that order, he no longer being their subject?*

4. **Anastasius:** Let us leave that question aside for now. It was enough for me that *excomunicatio, iusta vel iniusta, semper est timenda* ["just or unjust, excommunication is a dreaded thing"] and that for all my affairs it was well to present myself to the pope.

HE IS PAINED AT NOT BEING ABLE TO PREACH OR EXERCISE HIS OFFICE

5. As I was saying, it pained me very much not being able to help souls, thus losing out on all the work I put into my studies. For this reason, I hope in God to see myself counted among those who will ask justice against those who afflict them and deprive them of the fruit of their labors. As the wise man says, "Then shall the just one with great assurance confront his oppressors who set at naught his labors" [Wis 5:1, NAB]. The age I was then, forty-something,[2] was the best age to exercise my learning in the pulpit and the confessional and in writing books. All this was denied me.

6. There were no ships leaving from Alicante; thus it was necessary to go and look for a ship that was docked in Tortosa. I passed through Valencia during Holy Week, and at a talk I gave at the Hospital of St. Lucy, seven women from the public house converted; it was customary to invite them to the hospital during those days.

MASTER MONTESA DIES

7. I left Valencia on Easter Sunday. In route, I encountered the master of Montesa who was lying dead upon a litter that was carrying him to his burial.[3] I envied him because he was not going my way, for I desired to end my life's hardships. After making arrangements with the ship and gathering the supplies I would need for the sea voyage, I received a message to call on a friend from Vinaroz. He was going to carry two million doubloons to Italy in the galleys of Genoa.[4]

EMBARCATION IN THE GALLEYS; FRIENDSHIP WITH THE DISCALCED FATHERS WHO WERE GOING TO ROME TO WORK AGAINST HIS APPEAL

8. I embarked in Vinaroz, and in the same galley were two Discalced fathers who were going to Rome with all the documentation of my trial in order to justify their sentence and testify against me in case I were to make an appeal.[5] We dealt with each other familiarly as if nothing had happened, not saying a word about this business because the others on the galley knew nothing of it. We arrived in Genoa. I went to the Carmen of the Calced, and they were surprised to see how I was dressed. We sailed on to Civitavecchia, walking from there to Rome through the countryside, which was rife with bandits.

THE SHIP HE WAS SUPPOSED TO GO ON FROM TORTOSA SANK

9. I heard that the ship I was supposed to sail on from Tortosa sank soon after leaving port.[6]

THEY DID NOT WANT TO HEAR HIM IN ROME

10. I arrived at Rome. All the money I had carried with me was gone. I saw myself alone, poor, and disgraced, with powerful adversaries who were favored. I asked for judges who would examine my case.[7] They gave me to Father Toledo, who later became a cardinal, and, soon afterward, to Father Alexandre, a Dominican, who was later made a bishop.[8] My opponents made appointments with all the cardinals, showing them the sentence and the memorials they carried for the purpose of proving my guilt. They resolved not to hear me, and instead decided that the sentence of the Discalced should be executed. Father Toledo could not suffer this, asking why they would not listen to a man even if he were the most evil in the world. Although at first Father Alexandre thought the same as Father Toledo, he afterward turned against me. It was he who most insisted that I enter another order and if I did not, I should be thrown into the galley. I could not understand this reserve until the ambassador, who was the duke of Sessa, feeling sorry for me, explained

it by showing me a letter of the king. With words written in his own hand, it said, "If Father Gracián comes calling there, ask the pope not to listen to him or to deal with his case in any way." As I saw such a terrible wind against me, I took in my sails, shrugged my shoulders, shut my mouth, and drew close to God.

AFFRONTS SUFFERED IN ROME

11. Those Discalced fathers spread my offenses and infamies around Rome to such an extent that the ambassador ordered them to leave. My friends in Rome were affronted and embarrassed, and I did not dare raise my head.

12. **Cyril:** *There is one thing I do not understand. Granted that those who sentenced you were moved by zeal, how can you excuse these other Discalced who divulged your infamies in Rome and in other parts of Spain? Even if such faults were true, it is not licit to harm one's neighbor by revealing his faults.*

13. **Anastasius:** Those friars who went to Rome were only doing what they were ordered by their superiors. They showed the offensive sentence and the memorials of infamy that they had been given, and they defended the honor of the order and their superiors by giving the whole world to understand that they were moved not by passion but rather by justice. Many people—not only seculars and those who knew me but also religious of all orders who never even met me—were saying and still say that they were acting from passion. When a man is whipped for stealing, those who publicize his crime are not guilty of sin. Neither are those who believe it, since it is better to believe that someone has robbed than that many judges defamed an innocent man with a false judgment.

HE ASKED TO JOIN OTHER ORDERS BUT THEY DID NOT WANT TO ACCEPT HIM ON ACCOUNT OF HIS INFAMOUS REPUTATION

14. But returning to my disgraces . . . I went to the Capuchins, the Carthusians, the Discalced Franciscans, and all the other religious orders to ask to be received. Not one wanted to accept me, and I saw myself rejected by all the orders as the most disgraced religious in the

world. I asked them, when they rejected me, to give me a signed statement from the superior saying that I had asked to join them but they did not want to receive me, and that it was not my fault I did not stay. I returned with these documents and asked what I should do, thinking that such diligence in seeking to enter an order should be enough to make one free to go where he wished. Nevertheless, Father Alexandre still insisted that I join another order, and if I did not, I would be thrown into the galleys. Those who took the side of the Discalced said that I should not mention having been expelled. Obviously, if I confessed having been expelled from one order for being evil, I was not a good candidate to be received in another order. But lying in so serious a matter is a mortal sin. The first thing you are asked when seeking to enter a religious order is whether you have been expelled from another order. To say no in such a case is a pernicious lie, not to mention that if the truth were discovered, I would be thrown out, which would only add to my disgrace.

HIS OPPONENTS SUCCEEDED IN GETTING A MANDATE FROM THE POPE THAT THE DOMINICANS TAKE HIM

15. Their negotiations were so skillful that they obtained a mandate from the pope requiring the Dominicans to receive me at the monastery of the Minerva.[9] Upon being notified, the vicar general of Spain—who at that time was Master Fray Juan Vicente—threw himself at the feet of the pope. He said that if I had sinned, was an evil man, and deserved to be expelled by the Carmelites from their order, then what sin had the Order of St. Dominic committed that it would be forced to accept someone expelled from the Carmelites? The pope was silent. For the time being, receiving the Dominican habit was thwarted because the Virgin Mary and Holy Mother Teresa must have seen from heaven that to be a religious of another order, as holy as it might be, against my will and joining an order as a result of human negotiations and not through a divine calling was no path to my salvation. At this time, I found myself in the greatest desolation I can remember because I feared the galley

and I surely could have been sent there. They already wrote to Spain that the pope had thrown me in the galley for rebellion against the Apostolic See, and the galleys of the pope were full of difficult friars like me, who for almost no reason at all were sent to row [in the galleys].

THE ADVICE OF FATHER JOSÉ DE ACOSTA

16. God willed at this time to bring Father José de Acosta of the Company of Jesus to Rome.[10] He had been a student with me in Alcalá de Henares. I went to him for confession and asked his advice on whether I could deny being expelled from the Order of Carmel in order to be received into another order and thus avoid the galley with which I was threatened. He responded that I could not. He advised me to draft a memorial in which I petitioned that, considering I was not being accepted into any order, I was ready to obey whatever was demanded of me, and that when His Holiness, in commanding me to join another order, negotiated with another order to accept me, I would very willingly take it. Once I wrote this memorial, I was to leave Rome, letting it be known where they could reach me.

AFFRONTS IN NAPLES

17. With this I went to Naples, suffering inconveniences on the road on account of winter. I expected to find favor with an important person who was there while I waited for the reply from Rome, but he did not want to see me or listen to me, saying that since I was in disgrace with the king, Don Philip, it was not fitting that he favor me.[11] So I turned to seek the good graces of the King of heaven. Just as books of chivalry tell of knights who, despairing of unrequited love, let loose the reins of their horse so that it goes where it wants, in such a way I left Naples.[12]

EMBARCATION TO SICILY

18. Seeing that some ships were sailing to Sicily, I went aboard the first one that accepted me. God willed that a lieutenant, without knowing me, put me in the skiff where women of ill repute are placed.[13] These women had pity on me. The things I said motivated some of them

afterward to marry those with whom they were living as concubines and others to reform themselves. I took from this the beginnings of what was later done, which was to found convents for repentant women in Naples,[14] thus preventing innumerable sins. God knows how to do His works with such weak instruments.

THE COUNTESS OF OLIVARES CONSOLES HIM

19. We arrived in Messina, and from there I embarked for Palermo in a frigate. Because of a storm, I disembarked in Cefalù, and from there I arrived at Palermo by land. I had recourse to the countess of Olivares, who was the viceroy's wife. Her husband did not want to see me for the same reason the viceroy of Naples gave. The countess consoled me and ordered that I be received at the hospital for Spanish soldiers in Palermo. She wrote to Rome that any dispatches for me should be sent to her because she had me in that city serving the soldiers in the hospital. I was secluded there for eight months, writing a book titled "Flores Carmeli" [Flowers of Carmel] and finishing another called *Armonía mística* [Mystical harmony].[15]

THE DISPATCH FROM ROME THAT HE ENTER THE DISCALCED AUGUSTINIANS; TRIP TO GAETA

20. The papal brief and the license of the general of the Augustinians arrived.[16] I was to join the Discalced Augustinians who were then starting up in Italy. With interior contradiction and affliction of spirit, about which I will later speak, I departed with this dispatch to enter that order.[17] I arrived in Naples and met with a Discalced Augustinian who had letters and patents for me,[18] but we parted there, he staying in Naples for various reasons that needn't be mentioned, while I went on to Gaeta to see some relatives I had there.[19]

FALLING INTO THE POWER OF THE TURKS

21. I waited in Gaeta for the galley of the pope going to Rome (although it was going to stop in Civitavecchia). I had just finished saying Mass when, going against the strong inclination caused in me by the Virgin

Mary and Holy Mother Teresa not to leave their order, I resolved to join the Discalced Augustinians. Then, since I wanted to shorten my journey, I boarded a frigate of the Inquisition that was going directly to Rome. The wind had calmed somewhat, so the sailors went a little out to sea to catch it again. I saw a ship in the distance. The sailors saw smoke in its towers—a signal that pirates use—and they began to cry.

22. Because the Discalced feet of my shield come to an end here and the irons and chains begin,[20] so as to avoid making mistakes and to catch my breath a little, let us leave the tale of my captivity for another day.

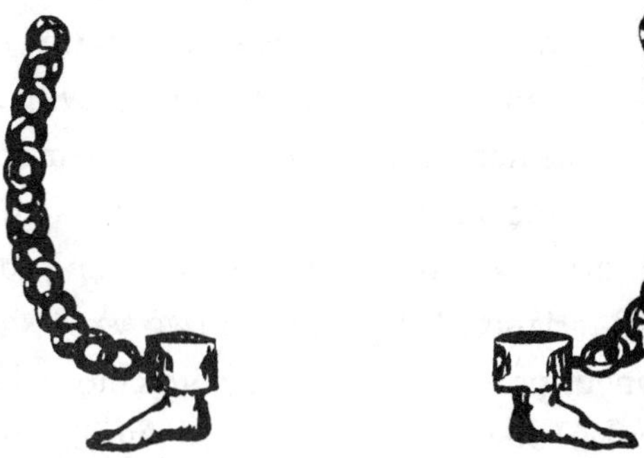

Sixth Dialogue: Captive

Gracián tells of how he was captured by the Turks and taken to Tunis under the mastery of Mami, the pasha of Tunis; the great trials he suffered and what he learned being a captive; how they were going to burn him alive, thinking he was an inquisitor; the times he was in danger of drowning at sea; and some predictions regarding his shipwrecks and dangers.

VISION OF ANTONIA DEL ESPÍRITU SANTO, WHO WAS ONE OF THE FIRST DISCALCED CARMELITE NUNS

1. **Anastasius:** I remember that many years before the troubles in the order began, at its very beginning, one of the holiest nuns we had, while at prayer, saw a turbulent sea and me drowning in the waves.[1] Although at the time I laughed heartily at this nun and teasingly called her "the prophet Perogrullo,"[2] from the things that later happened, I saw that although we should not make too much of these revelations, we should not despise everything.

PREDICTIONS OF A HEALER

2. Once when I was having supper in Malagón with two of the city councillors and four or five of our friars—one of whom was the son of one of the councillors—a man from the Indies came in with a rosary and a large crucifix around his neck. He told us to keep them safe because he wanted to go and heal the sheep (he was a healer).[3] I chuckled at him and invited him to drink. He began to stare at us and said very determinedly to Father Mariano, "It hasn't been two years since you had a fall and were in danger of death." And to a councillor whose name was Alonso Ruiz, he said, "You were a healer like me until your mother took away the grace." And to the others, he revealed other similar secrets. He looked at me intently and asked me to give him my hand. He wanted to see the lines in my palms. I laughed and refused to give it to him. He said very angrily, "Well, be careful of water!" What he said to the others was true—as I found out afterward—but as for me, I forgot about the danger of the water.

WORDS OF ANA RODRÍGUEZ IN EVORA

3. One day when I was in Evora and thinking of going to the East Indies in the company of Matías de Albuquerque,[4] a very holy woman (whom I will say more about later [see PA 14.34]) said to me, "Do not fear that you are going to where you are thinking about but to somewhere else, to a people outside the faith, where you never imagined."

DANGERS OF DROWNING AT SEA EIGHT TIMES[5]

4. From things that have happened I now understand these words, because I have been in real life-threatening situations at sea [at least] five times[6] and can say in all truth, [there are] "dangers at sea" [see 2 Cor 11:26]: (1) When I wanted to embark in Tortosa, for I found out later that the ship had sunk, as I said above.[7] (2) Going to Sicily in a frigate during a storm, when I disembarked at Cefalù. (3) Boarding the galley of Elizarráez on San Pedro [Pietro] Island when I was a captive, for it was a miracle I didn't fall off the ladder into the sea, where I would have

drowned because not for anything do I know how to swim. (4) Going from Bizerte to Tabarka in a *sandal*—which is a long, low boat—that was loaded with hides, for the Moors and Jews on board thought they were as good as dead because of a huge storm; but God willed that we take, with great difficulty, a cove near La Torre de la Pesquería del coral.

THE MERCY GRACIÁN FOUND IN MORATERRÁEZ

5. (5) Going in a small ship from Tabarka to Genoa when we were sighted by Moraterráez,[8] who was in the port of Tabarka with three galleys. A calm came upon us, and the Turks said, "Let us go, Master, and take that boat." Moraterráez responded, "Let them be. What do you think they are carrying besides wheat and barley from people in Tabarka, who are our friends,[9] and the unfortunate Papaz,[10] who was the slave of Mami and is now rescued? Let him go with God to his land."

6. **Cyril:** *Well then, could you have been captured again?*

7. **Anastasius:** Yes, since it is the law of that land that if a slave, in leaving the land of the Moors—after he has left the port—is captured again, the one who captures him gets half the price and the other half goes to the former owner, even though he has already once received all the ransom money. But I found pity with Moraterráez, which I might not have found in others. (6) After this calm, such a severe storm came upon us that it was a great miracle to get into port near Genoa; it was the vigil of Our Lady of August.[11] (7) Going to Spain in a galleon named the *de Salinier* when in view of the two islands[12] a strong wind threatened to sink us, and all the people—there were three hundred of us—were confessing at once without any hope of life; suddenly, the wind shifted and we were out of danger. (8) Going in a boat from Sanlúcar de Barrameda to Puerto de Santa María when such a storm came upon us that the mast broke, the sailors lost courage, and four other boats sailing with us sank, whereas, by some great miracle, ours found a cove; it was the eve of Our Lady of the Purification.[13]

HOW AND BY WHOM AND WHERE GRACIÁN WAS CAPTURED

8. I will leave out other storms and tempests that were not so dangerous. Finally, on the day of St. Dionysius the Areopagite (Monday, October 11, 1593) at ten o'clock in the morning, I was aboard a frigate of Master Antonio de Leiva, ten miles from Gaeta, near Monte Circeo, and saw a *galeota*[14] of Turks in the distance; smoke was coming from its towers. However hard the sailors of the frigate tried to get to land, in the space of a Creed they were upon us, shouting, "Take in the sails, take in the sails," and balls fired from their *escopetas*[15] were whizzing past our ears. In a flash, they robbed the frigate of everything and took the nine sailors, five passengers, my armed servant,[16] and me aboard their *galeota*. When I saw these people dressed in blue and red with white turbans on their heads—well, this did not seem good to me, especially when two or three surrounded me, saying "ásperos, ásperos," which means money, and ordering me to hand over whatever I had. I did not understand anything other than that I was in an unpleasant situation.[17]

9. They stripped me, leaving me nothing but linen underwear. They manacled my hands and put me in the hold.[18] I gave thanks to God and the Virgin who punished me so quickly for deciding four hours earlier, when I said Mass, to relinquish her habit by my own choice. And I was content with the habit Adam gave me, which no one could take from me without skinning me. Then I gulped, thinking that I would die in that life—which more truly is death—because rowing in the Christian galleys (especially those of the pope that I greatly feared when I was in Rome) is life, whereas rowing in the galleys of the Turks is death.

HE FELT GREAT SORROW BECAUSE OF THE DESTRUCTION OF HIS PAPERS

10. I soon saw them cleaning their *escopetas* with the paper on which I had written *Armonía mística*, which had cost me no small labor and was of no little value. I was carrying it with me in order to have it printed in Rome.

11. The meal, which was served from time to time, consisted of a little black *bizcocho,*[19] fetid and full of bugs, and a cupful of water, but the water was so foul-smelling that it was necessary to hold your nose to get it down. We did not go to the deck to relieve nature when our body needed to but only once a day at sundown. The bed I occupied was the *escopetas* of the Turks, and for a pillow a powder keg. When they had occasion to fight against Christians, they asked me to hand them the harquebuses, which I never wanted to do since I was scrupulous not to cooperate in the death or capture of Catholics.

A PITY TO SEE THE NEW CAPTIVES COMING EACH DAY

12. The torment in seeing new Christian captives coming aboard was alleviated by having to immediately hear the confessions of some who were mortally wounded and having to admonish others—although not without fear of the infidels—to keep their faith, which they were ready to deny, and to support them in it. Others were crying and asking me for bread and water—for they were dying of thirst—as if I had a great dispensary and were their father or mother and not a suffering captive like themselves.

THE ISLAND OF VENTOTENE; THEY HAD STOLEN A FLOCK OF SHEEP

13. In those first days, we arrived at the Island of Ventotene, off the coast of Naples, in order to make *arache*—as they call it—which is to auction off the stuff they had robbed, and to take shelter from a contrary wind and get water from some holes they dug in the sand. We Christians went ashore with the Turks. They prepared their *tíngers,* or copper pots, for cooking their rice and the meat they got from a flock of sheep they had stolen on the mainland.

THEY MADE CROSSES ON THE SOLES OF HIS FEET WITH A HOT IRON; A TURKISH CEREMONY

14. As I was sitting on a rock looking up to heaven and considering my misfortune, a Turk came over and asked for my right foot. I gave it to

him. He made a cross in the sole with a hot iron he carried in his hand. A little while later, he came back with the same iron reheated and made another cross in the sole of my left foot. I asked the older Christian slaves what this was all about. One said to me, "Father, it is the practice of the Turks that when there is bad weather and they see themselves in some danger, in opprobrium of the cross of Jesus Christ, they find a priest and brand a cross on the sole of his foot. And if good weather does not come, get ready, for surely they will burn you alive, this being their devotion." I prayed to God to give them good weather because I feared the fire.

THE THREE GALEOTAS AND SIX BRIGANTINES ARRIVED AT GAETA

15. Just then, they discovered two *galeotas* and six brigantines coming toward them. They thought they were Christians and that they would not be able to escape them, so they prepared at once to fight or to flee. But as the *galeotas* and the brigantines got closer, they could see that the two *galeotas* belonged to the pasha of Tunis and that the brigantines were from Bizerte.[20] As they arrived, those of my *galeota* made a great hurrah and cheered, because the newcomers would give them *bizcocho,* for theirs was all gone.

16. The weather improved a little, and all three *galeotas* and the brigantines set out again for Gaeta. They robbed the countryside and, if they had not been spotted, would have plundered the city. How much it grieved me to see the houses I had left only recently, with many gifts of food and linen clothes given to me by my relatives who lived there.

THEY WENT TO NAPLES; 190 CHRISTIANS WERE CAPTURED

17. From Gaeta, they sailed to Naples, and on the way they robbed a church and seized I don't know how many Christians and livestock. They arrived at the Gulf of Naples before sunrise and robbed the boats that were coming with provisions for the city. During those days while I was on the *galeota,* 190 Christians were taken captive, not to mention all the other things.

TWO IMAGES GRACIÁN CARRIED WITH HIM THAT HAD WORKED MIRACLES; THE FOUR GALLEYS OF FLORENCE THAT RESCUED MASTER MARK AND HIS COMPANIONS

18. We went to San Pedro [Pietro] Island where three Christians disembarked. One of them was named Master Mark, a Venetian and the only master builder of *galeotas* in all of Barbary. He bought two copper images for one *escudo* from the Turks, images that I used to carry. One is the face of Christ at the age of twelve, and the other is that of our Lady when she lost him. Accompanied by three renegades for guards, they went quite some distance with axes in their hands in order to cut trees for their shipbuilding. They saw four galleys coming from afar that they recognized as Florentine. Master Mark bid the renegades goodbye, because those galleys meant their freedom, but the renegades insisted that they return with them to the *galeota*. However, these Christian men were courageous and, seeing themselves with steel axes in their hands, replied that they should leave and not force them to bloody their axes with their heads. With that they signaled the galleys, which sent a Florentine brigantine to them. Thus they escaped to freedom. Master Mark had said to his companion, Nicolás, "I hope in God that by means of these two images that had belonged to our father, I will have freedom within eight days." And so it was.[21]

19. Well, when the Turks saw the four Florentine galleys in the distance, they made us board so quickly that I almost fell from the ladder—as I already said—which is a plank of wood thrown from the *galeota* to the land. Without waiting for more than thirty Turks who had gone further inland to hunt, they fled, giving chase to the Florentine galleys.[22] The Turks were so disheartened, for they would have surely been caught if God had not permitted the rigging of the Florentine flagship to break, which allowed the Turks to escape.

THE TURKS ARRIVE IN BIZERTE

20. They arrived in Bizerte, their own land, which seemed like heaven to me as I was so exhausted by the bad treatment of the sea.

CAPTAINS DURALÍ AND ELISBEY; THE BAÑO OF ELISBEY AND THE HUNGER EXPERIENCED THERE

21. In Bizerte, they divided the Christians two by two between the two captains of the *galeota* in which I came. One was named Duralí who was from Algiers, and the other was Elisbey, who got me. Since he was poorer, I hoped to be ransomed sooner. He brought me to his *baño*, which was a broken-down corral made of a few logs.[23] In the middle was a millstone that was turned by a little donkey guided by a blind renegade. That is where Elisbey put his Christians. We were more than thirty. For a long time, we were given nothing to eat or drink. At last, we were brought a great treat of a big bowl of soup from a pot in which half a cow's head was cooking for all thirty of us. I got part of the snout. In truth, those Christians who promised to renounce the faith and those with whom they had begun to practice sodomy were fed separately, and not bad food, but they forgot about us.

THE DEATH OF ANTONIO DE LEIVA ON ACCOUNT OF THE MELANCHOLY OF SUCH A LIFE

22. This sort of life gave Antonio de Leiva, the captain of the frigate that took me aboard, such melancholy that he died of pure sadness. I was consoled at seeing a young lame boy, the son of my patron Elisbey, come around, and I began to show him respect, thinking that I would have to serve him as his slave for the rest of my life.

FALSE TESTIMONY OF HONOR THAT THE TURKS SPREAD ABOUT GRACIÁN

23. But blessed be God who restores honor! Whereas in the land of Christians, they affronted me and knocked me down to the point where I was not even worthy to be a cook in any religious order in the world, here in the land of the Moors they took me for a great archbishop going to Rome to be made a cardinal, and then, within a few days, I would become the great *papaz*, which is what they called the pope. Here I am an archbishop, a cardinal, and a pope in the making. They called me "*papazquivir*," as if to say "great prelate."

THE PASHA SENT AN AMBASSADOR OF THE GRAND TURK FOR HIM

24. This rumor reached the ears of the pasha in Tunis, which is ten or twelve leagues from Bizerte. He sent Zambalí, the head man or *chauz*—which means the ambassador of the Grand Turk in the kingdom of Tunis—accompanied by lancers and harquebusiers, to get me.[24] There is a law that when a great personage is taken captive, the pasha can take him from whichever Turk has him, regardless of who the Turk is, in order to send him to the Grand Turk.

HE LOSES HOPE OF RESCUE

25. My new title of archbishop only served to take away every hope I had of being rescued from the power of Elizarráez [Elisbey] because the Christians told me that principal captives were taken to Constantinople, to the towers overlooking the Black Sea, and held there as great prizes until the end of their lives. Just as other kings exhibit grandeur by having cages of lions and exquisite birds, the Grand Turk has a wooden cage—surrounded by a strong wall—of great persons. In the end, I lost my hope of rescue and gave myself up to the thought of being like a bird in that cage. The Christians said it is so cold there that they cut off frozen feet, where the flesh is dead already, so that they don't die all at once.

WORDS EXCHANGED BETWEEN DURALÍ AND ZAMBALÍ ABOUT NOT WANTING TO HAND OVER GRACIÁN

26. Well, Zambalí arrived with this message from the pasha, and my patron Elisbey sent me to the *baño* of Duralí, his partner, since he was from Algiers and therefore not a subject of the pasha of Tunis. In this way, he was trying to keep me for himself. Zambalí asked Duralí to hand me over for the Grand Lord [Grand Turk]. It was nightfall when he arrived. Duralí said he didn't want to give me up. Zambalí responded, "Look here, Duralí, I see clearly that you are drunk and that it is the wine that is talking, not you. However, *gu-Allah* and *vi-Allah*—which means by God and for God—and by the head of the Grand Lord, if by tomorrow you do not give him to me, I will bring you to Tunis by dragging

you tied to the tail of my horse!" Morning came. They ordered me to get ready to leave for Tunis. I didn't have anything to pack except an old breviary that was given me in the *baño* of Duralí; a *barragán listado,* which is like a striped mantilla [short cape] of various colors with which I covered myself; a poor habit of old sackcloth that rubbed against my flesh, which since the time we were in the galley was already raw from the roughness of the cloth; and a little blue cap that covered half my head. Those then were the vestments of the wretched archbishop.

HOW HE PRAYED WITHOUT A BREVIARY

27. **Cyril:** *So, until they gave you a breviary in the* baño, *you hadn't prayed the Hours from the time they captured you? How did you fulfill the obligation of the Divine Office?*

28. **Anastasius:** I used to say some of the psalms I knew from memory and Our Fathers and Hail Marys in the amount that seemed to me enough for Matins, Prime, and the other Hours in the eyes of a good man.

29. Finally, they put me on a packhorse that was loaded with containers of water carrying fish. I was taken from Bizerte to the pasha, well accompanied by lancers and harquebusiers to guard the *Papaz.*

CROSSING A RIVER BY SWIMMING THE HORSE; WORDS OF THE MOOR WHO WAS LEADING

30. We arrived at a river called the Fiumara of Bizerte, which was rising on account of the rains. It could not be forded. It is usual for the Turks to cross by stripping naked, carrying their clothes on top of their heads, and swimming the horses.[25] They commanded me to do the same. As something new for me, I could not help being afraid of the water. But Zambalí, who had gone first, ordered a Moor to switch horses with me, his horse being a good one on which I could cross more easily. He climbed onto my horse and led the horse I was on by the reins. Upon entering the water, the Moor said to me, "Papaz, hold tightly to the horse's mane and look at the sky, not the water. Don't be afraid. This way you will not fall." I kept these words in my heart for many other

situations because they gave me life. When a man does what he can, thinking about the things of heaven, turning his eyes away from the troubles he is in, and losing his fear through confidence in God, he does not lose heart.

THEY ARRIVE AT TUNIS

31. We arrived at Tunis. They brought me before the pasha at his *alcazaba* or palace and made me kneel in front of him. He began to ask me at length for detailed news about the king and the affairs of Spain, which was the last thing I desired to speak about, thinking that we were to talk about my rescue and liberty. From there, they brought me to the *compaña*—which is his storeroom—where the first thing I heard was the great moaning of a sorrowful Christian named Juan Casaz, who had just been given eight hundred blows with a stick; not a single bone was left uninjured. I stayed there that night and another day, and during that time, the *casacas* came to visit me. This is what they call the clean-shaven youths whom they keep as "girlfriends" for their abominable entertainments—dressed up, with makeup and perfume, to suit the needs of such an evil business. They keep them as sheltered and enclosed as others do their mistresses.

GONZALO MACIIUCA, SLAVE OF ABRAHIM AGA

32. One of these, Abrahim Aga, had a Christian slave named Gonzalo Machuca from Córdoba to whom he said, "Machuca, look at your Papaz. Go and kiss his hand." "I will gladly do so," said Machuca, and coming to me, he knelt down. I gave him my hand and a very well-made blessing as if I really were his archbishop. He told me secretly, "Father, don't waste your time thinking about negotiating your rescue or speaking of it, even though they might speak of it to you. Rather, say that you will have to die here and that you have no one in the land of the Christians who remembers you, because there is no other way to freedom." This was news to me, for at each moment I desired that the pasha call me to discuss my rescue, and I had no other thought than to see myself quickly freed from that

country. Since the *rengil* Abrahim—*rengiles* or *casacas* are what the Turks call those who serve in that evil business—saw that Machuca was talking to me in secret, he said in a loud, angry voice, "What are you talking about, dog? Are you persuading him not to become a Moor?" I laughed to myself, or—to say it better—I lamented, seeing that God had brought me to such a state where someone would think it necessary for Machuca to keep me in the faith. Although he was a good enough fellow, he was certainly not one of the most spiritual in the *baño*.

THEY BRING HIM TO THE BAÑO AND PUT HIS FEET IN SHACKLES

33. In spite of all this, I was still hoping that the pasha would call me to talk about my redemption,[26] but it did not happen. Instead, they brought me to the *baño* with the other Christian captives and shackled me as a Christian being held for ransom.

WHAT IS THE BAÑO?

34. **Cyril:** *What do they mean by* baño, *and what is it like to live there?*

35. **Anastasius:** The *baño* is the prison of the Christian captives. It is also called a dungeon or *sagena,* which is the same thing. It is underground with just a small opening, like a well, for light and air. The door, which is very strong and has many locks, opens onto a small courtyard where the armed guards are. Another well-locked door there closes off this most guarded area of the *alcazaba* or fortress of Tunis, and they keep such great vigilance that no Christians are able to escape. The door is closed at sunset, when the Christians are rounded up, and opened right at sunup so that they can go out to work. The *baño* is a very narrow and tight place. In order to make room for six hundred Christians, as we were, we were put on cots—which they call *camaradas* [comrades]—one on top of the other, like the wattle used to raise silkworms. At the bottom, we made a space that served as a church, with two altars, where I and my companion, Don Luis, canon of Lipari in Sicily, slept. He had been bought by the pasha from another Moor who had captured him so that he could say Mass for the Christians.

THEY LET THE CHRISTIANS HEAR MASS; HE PREACHES TO THE CHRISTIAN CAPTIVES

36. **Cyril:** *Well, good heavens! They permitted you to say Mass?*

WORDS OF THE PASHA

37. **Anastasius:** Yes, and with such willingness that when my rescue was discussed, the pasha, my patron, said, "I do not want to give up my Papaz for any money because he makes my Christians good." He said this because I preached to them every night after they had been rounded up and had eaten supper. For a pulpit, I sat on a galley barrel at the door of our church where I could be heard throughout the whole *baño*. We also celebrated our Vespers at this hour with a lot of music—guitar and similar instruments—and all the Christians singing out without caring much about being on pitch. And since every time I preached I would speak badly about Muhammad and his sect, in order to sustain the faith of some weak Christians who were on the verge of apostatizing, a Turkish guard—some were stationed inside the *baño*—went to the pasha and complained that the Papaz was speaking badly about their holy prophet Muhammad. Whereupon the pasha reprimanded him, saying, "Dog, who told you to listen to the Papaz preach? Do you perhaps want to become a Christian? Leave them alone. Are they not inside their own doors? Do you want them to speak well of Muhammad?"

THE DISCOMFORT OF THE BAÑO

38. Because the *baño* was so narrow and held six hundred Christians, most of them in chains, there was a great amount of noise and stench, and an infinity of bed bugs and lice, which are the enemy of bodily rest. I can only tell you that the worst Christian dungeon is a garden of delights in comparison to what this was like. The food is two pieces of black bread, worse than barley bread and not very big either. The captives have only water to drink, and it is necessary to be alert when the camels are coming, each one taking his jug to the courtyard of the guards where the camels are brought.

39. **Cyril:** *For this reason they would not be sorry to be brought out for work.*

CRIBETE OR BED OF THE CAPTIVES; CUSTOM OF PRAYING STRETCHED OUT

40. **Anastasius:** I never had the good fortune since, with twenty or thirty other captives, old and worn out or otherwise weighed down with iron chains (as I was), I always remained inside. I was usually stretched out on my *cribete*—a bed the Christians made from thistle canes—with a *barragán*—a blanket that also served as mattress and sheet—because I was not able to bear the *traviesas,* which are the irons they put on me. I did not stand, sit, or kneel except when I said Mass, which was very difficult. Stretched out this way, I became accustomed to praying and studying better than in any other way. These shackles were put on me when I first entered the *baño* and were not removed until they were exchanged for *magiarescas,* which I will tell you about later [PA 7.7]. I was not free of them except for two days when one foot was freed so that I could go and hear the confession of a Lutheran whom they had stabbed. God did me the mercy of giving me that soul, although with much persuasion.[27] In all, my misery lasted, as God knows, from the middle of November until Christmas [1593], the eve on which I received a great gift from our Lord, which I will soon recount for you [PA 6.45–47]. It would have been a perfect joy if my sins and the avarice of the pasha, my patron, had not impeded it.

WHAT HE DID IN THE BAÑO

41. I heard the confessions of my fellow Christian captives; I corrected them; I consoled them after they were caned; I settled their disputes; and I visited them when they were sick. And if the Moors wanted to cut off their ears or noses, I was able to gain their pardon with money, which those same Christians had given me with great obedience; I served as a depository for their money so they would not gamble it away. Even the Turks who were ill and went to the Christian *barberos* for cures gave their money to me instead of to them, saying,[28]

WORDS OF THE TURKS WHO WERE ILL

42. "Papaz, take these ten ducats. If Master Peter is able to cure me within so many days, give them to him. If not, give them back to me since we are not so foolish as those of your country that we give money to a doctor when he does not cure us." I also served as an oracle in cases of theft because when a Moor was missing something that might have been stolen by the Christians, they would come to me for my judgment and give me some money.[29] And I served as a secretary to the renegades who came to me to write their letters of information about important matters, which they gave to the viceroys of Naples or Sicily.

SALVADOR DE LA CRUZ, A PORTUGUESE CLERIC WHO WAS BURNED ALIVE BECAUSE HE WROTE FOR THE RENEGADES THEIR LETTERS OF INFORMATION FOR CHRISTENDOM

43. This was a dangerous office because, a little while after I was rescued, a friend of mine, Salvador de la Cruz, a Portuguese priest, was burned alive in Algiers for doing the same thing. I also made certificates for them—as if I really were an archbishop—written in Latin and slipped into some *nóminas* that the Muslims use,[30] so that if one were able to flee to a Christian country, it certified for the courts of the Inquisition and the archbishops that the renegade came of his own free will. With this, they would be pardoned and given a private penance and made to abjure *de vehementi*,[31] which many were able to do—glory be to God—and for which being named "archbishop" served me well. I also wrote for them letters for other renegades who were elsewhere.

SOME RENEGADES CAME TO CHRISTIAN LANDS ON ACCOUNT OF GRACIÁN

44. I was busy arranging the rescue of Christians. With money that came to me for my ransom and with my credit as an "archbishop," God did me the mercy of gaining freedom for those who were more in danger of renouncing the faith than others.[32] I exercised the office of pastor, offering Mass throughout the week with my companion, Don Luis. One of

us said Mass before sunrise for the six hundred Christians in the *baño* who had to go out to work. The other said Mass after daybreak for the Christians who were slaves of the janissaries and of other individuals.[33] There were more than sixteen hundred slaves in Tunis. Masses were said secretly for the Christian women of the *cerraje*[34] and for many male and female renegades with the intention that God grant them a way to return to the faith (daily rations were never lacking for whoever said Mass). In the end, I had a consoling life like that of a little bishop because—as I will tell you later—gifts and money were not lacking and I was exercising my talents in the service of needy people, with visible fruit.

THE SERMON "PAPARETA" GAVE TO GRACIÁN

45. But returning to our Christmas Vespers of the year 1593. . . . There was a Portuguese Christian whom I used to reprimand for swearing. The Turks called him "Papareta"—meaning little goose—because he was very small in body. They always gave nicknames to the Christians, except for me whom they never called anything but "Papazquivir," meaning great priest. Papareta came to me that evening, before the *baño* was closed for the night. Kneeling before me and taking my hands, he began kissing them and crying and preaching to me with great effect that I remain firm in the faith, that I look to Jesus Christ and the Virgin Mary, that I fix my eyes on the blessedness of heaven, and similar things.

THE NEWS HE WAS GIVEN THAT THEY WERE GOING TO BURN HIM ALIVE

46. I was disturbed and said to myself, what is happening that Papareta is preaching to me? I asked him, "Brother, why are you saying this to me?" He replied, "Don't you know, Father? I wouldn't want to be the first one to tell you the news." He wanted to draw back without telling me, but I insisted that for the love of God he should tell me. He replied,

> 47. You should know that the janissaries have held an *aduana*—which is what they call their meetings; there are more than four

thousand of these soldiers of the Grand Turk guarding this country—and they have sent a message to the pasha saying that they know Your Reverence is an inquisitor and that you have burned more than fifty renegades in the land of the Christians. They demand that you be handed over to them to be burned alive. Thus, you can prepare yourself for the morning, Christmas Day at eight o'clock, because the pasha will not dare to challenge the janissaries.

FRAY JUAN VANEGAS

48. I was already aware of the insolence of the janissaries against the pasha and that Fray Juan Vanegas, a Calced Carmelite, native of Toledo, was burned alive in Algiers just because he was said to be the cousin of an inquisitor. This was recounted to me by his companion, Fray Juan Ruiz, a Carmelite, who was with me then in the same *baño*. They were taken captive together on their way to Rome.

49. I believed the news; I swallowed death. Instantly my nerves shrunk, my throat tightened, and my blood, which was soon to burn in the fire, froze. Completely shaken and unable to say a word, nature went through its accustomed agony; indeed, it didn't even pardon Christ in the garden.

50. The rest of the Christians came in from work, and the doors of the *baño* were shut. They all came to me crying, to console me, verifying the news about the fire. I began to make acts of martyrdom, since I was dying for the faith because of hatred for the Inquisition by which Christendom is conserved. I brought back to memory many resolutions that I had made in prayer to die for Christ, especially the ones I made two days earlier when they had stoned alive a Jew for only saying, "Have a bad journey, Muhammad!" Although I was sad that he was dying a Jew, I had a great envy of him for having died, desiring as I did a similar end in order to reach glory, leave so much misery, and be finished with trials and persecutions. But all these thoughts did not keep me from feeling afflicted, since I feared my weakness and lack of virtue and whether I would have the courage for such a cruel death. They

build the fire around the Christian so that he is roasted little by little. I made a general confession to Father Luis and said my three Masses that night with as much fervor as I could, and the fear passed.[35] Morning came. The hour approached, and every noise I heard made my blood stir, imagining that they were coming for me. Instead, at that hour, a Christian captive named Montilla came to console me, asking me to congratulate him for some good news he was bringing me. He had arranged with a renegade friend of his that when he saw me tied to the stake to be burned, he would sneak up and give me a thrust of the knife in the heart. For this good deed, he would give his friend ten *escudos*. I consoled myself with the news that I would die more quickly without so much suffering. Midday passed. They made me eat even though I had no appetite, for it is one thing to make acts of martyrdom *en seco* and another to look death in the eye.[36] Some days passed. Each morning I awaited the execution of this sentence without knowing what was going on. But I was well prepared by then and didn't feel much fear. Besides, with the many acts of resignation and contrition I had made, the delay annoyed me.

THE REASON THEY WANTED TO BURN HIM AT THE STAKE

51. **Cyril:** *What made the janissaries think you were an inquisitor, and how were you relieved of this anguish?*

52. **Anastasius:** When they captured me, I was in a frigate of the Inquisition that was going from Naples to Rome to pick up galley prisoners of the Holy Office. Dividing up the spoils they took from us, the Turks found the chains and shackles that the captain, Antonio de Leiva, was carrying. From this, they realized that the frigate belonged to the Inquisition and was on its way to pick up the galley prisoners. I alone appeared to be a person of some account since all the others were sailors or poor people. They deduced that I was an inquisitor who was traveling with those chains to get the prisoners, because such work did not seem like any other than that of an inquisitor.

WORDS OF THE PASHA TO THE JANISSARIES BY WHICH GRACIÁN WAS SPARED BEING BURNED ALIVE

53. The pasha's reply to the janissaries, and his avarice, took from me my crown of passing through the fire to eternal delights, for I had already passed through the dangers of water. He said, "Tell those gentlemen that with pleasure I will give them my Papaz so that they can burn him and all my Christians if they wish and even my very person. But I beseech them to consider two things: One, my Papaz is not a man of such little fortune or lowly estate as that of an inquisitor. Rather, he is a great archbishop who is going to Rome to be a cardinal, and within a few days of that he will become the pope. Also, as they already know, the Grand Lord sent a command to me to obtain the release of Bey Amatarráez,[37] who is held prisoner in the fortress of Naples, and Captain Asán, who is sailing around in the galleys of Spain. They will give me these two for this Papaz, and at least thirty thousand *escudos* for his ransom, and this money is for your salaries. But all the same, find out whether he really is an inquisitor and burn him whenever you want."

54. With this reply, the fury of the janissaries was restrained for the time being, and the days passed with them going about seeking information on whether I was an inquisitor while I was battling in my heart with the fire. And so the matter remained without it being spoken of again, because once the first fury of the Turk passes, everything gets better.

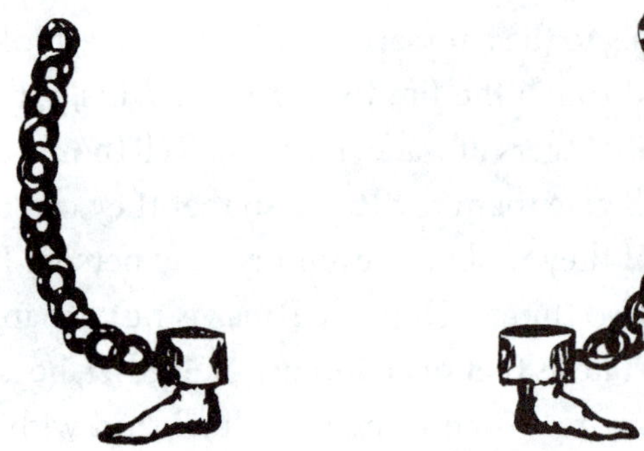

Seventh Dialogue: Freedom

Gracián continues recounting the afflictions he suffered in captivity: his fear of being burned alive for returning Mami[1] to the faith and some false testimonies that were then raised against him; how he was ransomed and, suffering hardships and poverty, came to Rome where Pope Clement VIII commanded him to join the Calced Carmelites; how, having served in the office of theologian to Cardinal [Pedro] Deza, protector of Spain, His Holiness sent him with a commission to Africa, which he fulfilled; and how, on returning to give an account of his commission to the pope, the pope having died, he stayed in the kingdom of Valencia. With this, he finishes explaining the chains of the hieroglyph.

THE CONVERSION OF THE RENEGADE MAMI

1. **Anastasius:** I remained then,[2] continuing the spiritual exercises I had with my brother captives until the end of Lent that year [1594]. Shortly after Easter, another calamity came to me, similar to the one before. A

renegade named Mami, who was a native of Salamanca, was brought as a prisoner to the *baño* because he was accused of murdering his patron. I wanted to learn to write Arabic, which he knew. I got him to teach it to me, and while he gave me lessons, I persuaded him to return to our faith. He resolved to do just that, so I heard his confession. But in order to absolve him, it was necessary for him to publicly, before Moors and Christians, confess the Catholic faith as true and the faith of Muhammad as false. It was obvious that in doing this he would be burned alive or cut to pieces with the scimitar, which is the punishment given to renegades who return to the faith. He was determined to suffer this martyrdom to save his soul.

WORDS OF ZALIMAMET

2. Accompanied by some brave Christians, he went to the courtyard of the guards where he made this confession. Then he reentered the *baño* to receive absolution and await his martyrdom for his confession. Meanwhile, I awaited the punishment that would surely be given to me for persuading him to return to the faith. When a renegade named Zalimamet, who was the head jailor of the Christians, heard Mami's confession of faith, he said, "How can you say that? Have you not professed *Allah illa Allah, Mohamed rasul Allah*?" (This means "There is but one God, and Muhammad is his messenger." These are the words used by one who professes their sect.) "Well, who has deceived you now?" And turning to the many Christians who were there, he said with much anger, "Does this Papaz of yours think that he is going to make Christians of all of us? Well, he will soon see what happens!" And in a great commotion, he and some other Turks went to tell the pasha.

WHAT THE CHRISTIAN CAPTIVES SAID AGAINST GRACIÁN

3. The Christians rose up against me with much anger saying, "Father, who got you into this tight spot? Not long ago, God saved you from the fire. You should have let this dog go to hell so that they would not burn both of you. God will be showing you much mercy if you only get

five hundred blows with the stick, from which we know you will die. If the Turks call you and order your shackles removed, then it is certain they will take you away immediately and burn you without further ado." Since I was already well prepared from the time before, it didn't bother me now. I responded, "Leave us be. Let us gain one soul for God, come what may."

4. Within two hours of Mami's public confession of the faith and I absolving him and naming him Alonso de la Cruz, as he was called before he became a renegade, we heard loud voices coming from the door of the *baño* saying, "Papazquivir and Mami, come out here!" The jailors usually called out that way when they were going to take someone from the dungeon for execution. We went out together hand in hand to a small room of the courtyard where there was an iron forge. There we saw six or seven very grave and well-dressed Turks. As we presented ourselves before them, I was reminded of some pictures or canvases I had seen where the martyrs are depicted appearing before tyrants.

THE PAIN CAUSED BY THE IRON SHACKLES, ESPECIALLY WHEN THEY WERE PUT ON OR TAKEN OFF

5. We ourselves did not say a word. One of the Turks very calmly said, "Take the shackles off the Papaz." Great pain is felt in the shins by the hammerblows required to put on and take off the shackles. They are usually more painful to wear than two pairs of shackles used in Christian prisons. The fact that I saw my feet set free gave me some comfort, because I had been desiring to see a day when I would be free of those irons just so that I could cross one foot over the other (for my aspirations only came to this much at that time).

HE WAS TROUBLED, THINKING THEY WANTED TO BURN HIM

6. But remembering what the Christians had said about the fire, my nerves immediately contracted, my throat became knotted, and I was swallowing saliva, thinking that from there we were going directly to

the bonfire without even a chance to confess except to God (although I had just said Mass and had given Communion to Alonso de la Cruz). It is one thing to think of death and make acts of accepting it and quite another to look death in the eye. They ordered that my shackles be put on Mami, my converted son. With that, my blood returned a little to my body, and I thought to myself, "If they were going to burn us, why did they put the shackles on him, and for what reason would they burn me and let him live, since according to them he committed a greater offense?" I did not see them draw their scimitars as they usually do; but if they had, I certainly would be dead.

THE MAGYARIAN SHACKLES

7. They finished putting the shackles on him, and the Turk who seemed to be in charge of the others said, "Take out the Magyarian shackles." These irons, which are twisted and heavy, with hooks fastened on the ends by large, clinched nails, are used by the Magyars[3]—a race of people who make war on the Turks—on their captives. In all of Barbary, it was the only set of this type of irons, and they put them on me. They had been brought from Constantinople for Captain Juan Valiente, whose deeds were like his name.[4] No little time was expended, nor did they give just a few hammerblows in riveting the nails; nor did I feel just a little pain in my shins. This done, without them or us speaking any words, they turned their backs on us and left us alone. Then the Christian captives came to our aid. Some were very happy that they did not take us away to be burned or beat us with sticks. Others reproached me because I had put myself in that danger by converting a renegade.[5] Still others consoled me, saying that God would give me strength to endure those shackles as I had endured the first ones. I could hardly move about with them on. They laid me in my bed, or *cribete,* and ordered that leather *gamberes*[6] be made so that I could stand up to say Mass. These were like a pair of boots pieced together with a large round pad at the bottom, on which the irons rested.[7]

WHY THEY DID NOT BURN GRACIÁN THEN; WORDS OF THE PASHA

8. A little later, I learned what the pasha had said when they gave him the news of the conversion of Alonso de la Cruz:

> 9. I wish that many renegades like Alonso, who belong to other owners, would turn Christian again so that I could use them in my galleys, as I will do with Mami. It is punishment enough, which he will have to endure for the rest of his life. Everyone take care not to say anything about this to the mufti (who is like the bishop of the city) or to the *cadí* (who is like the magistrate) so that they do not burn our Papaz, for I will cut off the head of anyone who says anything; nothing else matters.

10. **Cyril:** *This pasha really valued your life.*

THEY TOLD GRACIÁN THEY WOULD TRADE HIM FOR BEY AMATARRÁEZ, THE MAIN HELMSMAN OF THE GRAND TURK, WHO WAS BEING HELD PRISONER IN A CASTLE OF NAPLES, AND THE OTHER CAPTAIN WHO WAS SAILING IN THE GALLEYS OF SPAIN[8]

11. **Anastasius:** He only valued me for the thirty thousand ducats he thought he could get for my ransom or for the release of the two captains, which the Grand Turk wanted him to get. That is why he talked with me shortly before the janissaries wanted to burn me, asking that I write to the land of the Christians that they give him those two Turks in exchange for me. I told him I would write but that, according to what the Christians told me, the king would not hand them over for any amount of money. I added that even if he were to hand them over, I should never consent that they be set free because it was they who could cause the greatest harm to Christendom since they knew best the ways in and out of our ports. It would be better for me to lose my life than to be the cause of so many others losing their liberty.

A DANGER CAUSED BY A RENEGADE WHO, FOR MONEY, WANTED TO MAKE HIM FLEE

12. A little while after this incident, a renegade came to me asking that I give him five hundred ducats and he would find a way for me to escape from prison. I told him that he should go with God [i.e., get lost], that I did not have the money to give him nor would anyone take me at such a poor price. Besides, my legs were not so light that I could flee from where I was. I knew there were many Christians who were free to go about the city without chains, who knew the language and the ports, and for many years had been planning to flee but still had not managed to do so.

MANZUR, THE SPECIAL GUARD OF GRACIÁN

13. A rumor that the Papaz wanted to escape began to grow, so they patrolled at night above the *baño* where the windows and vents were. In addition to the common guards for all the Christians, they assigned a particular guard to me, named Manzur, who checked my irons each night to make sure I was not filing them. He did other things to vex me, making insolent threats and such, so that it was necessary to give him some *reales* to leave me alone.

THE COMPASSION AND GIFTS OF THE MARABOUTS

14. Among the Moors, I acquired the name and fame of a great priest who was very holy, so that many marabouts came to visit and console me.[9] They gave me many presents and cried when they saw the irons, saying, "May fire burn this traitor of a pasha! Look at what heavy irons they put on this servant of God, as if he were going to escape!"

FALSE TESTIMONY RAISED AGAINST HIM BY A CAPTIVE

15. At that time, they brought in a captive priest, the son of a Spaniard and a Neapolitan, who came to me for consolation. He revealed to me that he had twenty-five gold *escudos* to help with his ransom and that they would ransom him for forty (because he was old and decrepit and they did not know he was a priest). I told him that I would help him

with the fifteen *escudos* he needed in order to be ransomed. He repaid my good deed by telling others that I was a sodomite and it was for this reason—so he said—that I was being carried in the pope's galleys when the Turks captured me. Although many other false testimonies had been made about my person, this was the first of its kind. The fact is, the Christians did not believe it, and whether or not the Turks believed it made no difference since with them that sort of thing was not defaming.

16. **Cyril:** *For what reason did he make this libel, and what did you do to him?*

THE UNHAPPY DEATH OF THIS CAPTIVE PRIEST

17. **Anastasius:** I don't know except that there are some men who have a twisted disposition, such as this one. A few days later, he persuaded two renegades of his master to flee to the land of the Christians. As they were preparing for the flight, he accused them to their master of intending to escape. For this, they smothered him one night. He was found dead the next morning without anyone knowing how it happened except me, since a Christian companion of his told me. This companion was astonished by his strange behavior and begged me to say Mass for his soul.

FALSE TESTIMONY RAISED AGAINST HIM BY A MERCHANT FROM TRAPANI

18. Just when final arrangements were nearly made for my release (in a trade for two Turks who were in Sicily and whom the countess of Olivares, the vicereine of Sicily, was willing to hand over), a merchant from Trapani came to Tunis with merchandise. He said that he knew me and that the countess could give at least six thousand *escudos* outright. Consequently, my rescue was upset for the time being.

WORDS OF THE MERCHANT OF TRAPANI

19. I could not imagine why the merchant treated me so badly, but he was heard saying in the plaza, "So the Parrino"—this is what priests are called by the Sicilians—"thought he was now going to go free to his

country? Well, let him burst his chains! He is Spanish, and these Spaniards have made us subjects in our own country of Sicily!"

RAMADÁN HOLDAX DEFENDS GRACIÁN

20. Hearing these words, a renegade named Ramadán Holdax said to him, "You dog, heretic, devil, and evil Christian! What has that poor Papaz done to you that you deprived him of his liberty? I swear, if it were not for the fact that he would suffer on account of it, I would knife you here and now!" This merchant of Trapani was the brother of a renegade who was the *chaya* or head steward of the pasha, my patron, which explains why he had come there with merchandise.

21. Many other things happened to me in the nearly two years of my captivity [October 11, 1593, to April 11, 1595]. What I have recounted for you is enough. We would never finish if I were to tell you everything.

22. **Cyril:** *Tell me how you were rescued, for I want to know.*

23. **Anastasius:** I want to take the story back a little so that God will be glorified.

HE FREED ABRAHAM GEBRE, A JEW, FROM DEATH

24. When I was in Lisbon, I freed a Jew named Abraham Gebre from death—for some soldiers were going to kill him—by settling certain differences between the prince of Morocco, who was afterward baptized, and Cid Albucarín, the alcaide.[10] They were in Lisbon, having fled from Fez [in Morocco], on account of the wars of King Sebastián, which is a long story.[11] It is enough to say that the Jew did not die, and he was no longer afraid on account of the peace I made between those two Moors. He thanked me for this good deed by wanting to give me thirty ducats, but I said that I didn't do good to anyone for money and that I hoped God would pay me better than he could by the hands of another Jew.[12]

SIMÓN ESCANASI OF TUNIS

25. Well, it so happened that a rich Jew from Tunis, named Simón Escanasi,[13] had gone with merchandise to Naples. Upon his arrival at the

port of Gaeta, he was arrested and his property was seized. Some relatives of mine in Gaeta, learning that this Jew was rich and powerful in Tunis, helped him and obtained his release and that of his possessions.

DAMIÁN PALAVESINO OF NAPLES GAVE SIX HUNDRED ESCUDOS ON LOAN

26. They begged him to try to have me rescued and gave him six hundred *escudos* to take to me for this purpose; these were borrowed from a Genoese-Neapolitan whose name was Damián Palavesino. Full of gratitude, Escanasi took the money to the Genoese who reside in Tabarka, next to Tunis. They are called the Lomellinis and have an alliance and business contracts with the Turks.[14] Their fortress is that of Tabarka.

27. One month when the pasha was supposed to pay the janissaries, he didn't have enough money. These soldiers, who are so exacting and insolent, said to the pasha, "Give us our pay or give us your head." If he didn't pay them on the given day, they would beat him up and kill him. Seeing himself in this tight situation, the pasha asked the Jew, Escanasi, to loan him money so that he could pay the soldiers.

WORDS OF ESCANASI TO THE PASHA

28. He said, "Do you want these janissaries to kill me?" Escanasi responded,

> 29. I have no money. But what better solution do you have than to ransom this Papaz in order to get enough money to pay the janissaries? If you wait any longer to negotiate his ransom, you will not get anything more for him than a sack of bones. I have come from his country, and I bring six hundred *escudos* for his rescue. I spoke with his relatives who informed me of who he is. Although he is very much a servant of God and a preacher and a religious, his order will give nothing for him, nor does he have any title or income other than that of a poor friar. As for the rest, you have been deceived.

FREEDOM OF GRACIÁN

30. The pasha was persuaded, and he told Escanasi to talk to me and to arrange the price. The Jew talked to me,[15] saying that if that day passed and the pasha found somewhere else to get the money he needed, I had no hope of rescue. I said to him that I had nothing except the six hundred ducats[16] that he told me he had brought to Tabarka and that I had no reason to trick him or anyone else. He replied, "Let us take these irons off you now. As for what happens after that . . . God is great!" I said in my heart, "If this Jew says God is great, am I to say God is little?" I begged him to take care of this business. He sought to borrow thirteen hundred *escudos* of gold, the price at which he arranged the ransom, and he got it at once from among the Moors and the Jews. Due to Escanasi's diligence, the letter of ransom was signed and my irons were removed,[17] though with more than enough blows. The pasha was paid his money, and he was able to pay his soldiers.

THE PASHA REGRETS HAVING GIVEN UP GRACIÁN FOR SUCH A SMALL RANSOM

31. Escanasi took me away and hid me, foreseeing—perspicacious as he was—what could happen and did happen. The next day, after the pasha saw himself free of his janissaries, he regretted taking the ransom, saying he had been tricked and that I should have given him at least six thousand ducats. They went in search of me in order to bring me back to prison. Escanasi approached the *cadí* and the mufti and showed them the ransom receipts and the documents of liberation. There was much turmoil on account of the pasha's evil wrath, and I was trembling for fear they would return me to the *baño* once again.

FELIPE PENA, FRENCH CONSUL IN TUNIS

32. Finally the Jew won his case and took me to the home of the French consul where I stayed one month until I was brought to Tabarka. There Stéfano Salinier, the Lomellini agent who was then the alcalde of that fortress,[18] gave Escanasi the six hundred ducats he had deposited there

for me. He also gave him seven hundred ducats for which I was to be held in Tabarka with a companion whom I ransomed, a priest named Master Utiel, until the bill of security came from Genoa.

THEY ARRIVE IN ROME

33. Thus I left there and arrived in Genoa [August 18, 1595] and went from there to Rome, very hungry and begging alms. I asked for the habit from the general of the Augustinians, showing him the memorial I had when I was captured. He did not want to give it to me because I had a debt of two thousand ducats, which is what my ransom came to with interest.

THE POPE ORDERS HIM TO JOIN THE CALCED CARMELITES

34. I threw myself at the feet of the pope. He drew up a brief so that I could beg money to pay off the debt from my ransom as do other captives.[19] I asked him to give me a state of life in which to live. He ordered me to join the Calced Carmelites despite the fact that the sentence of the *consulta* stated I could not return to the Calced or the Discalced. For a little while, I was with the Calced at San Martín in Montibus.[20]

THEY MAKE HIM THEOLOGIAN TO CARDINAL DEZA

35. From there, the protector of my order [Cardinal Pinelli] sent me to the house of Cardinal [Pedro] Deza, protector of Spain. I served him for five years in the office of theologian, writing and printing books.

THE POPE SENDS HIM TO AFRICA WITH AN HONORABLE COMMISSION

36. As a result of the memorials I had given to the pope, he and the cardinals of the Congregation of the Propagation of the Faith[21] thought I should return to Africa with a commission, which they gave me, to go and announce the holy year jubilee to the Christians of those parts.[22] I went to the king for letters that would grant me safe conduct by the captains on the frontiers.[23] Thus, I was able to be with my mother when she died.[24]

HE GOES TO TÉTOUAN

37. I went to Ceuta and from there to Tétouan.[25] I completed my commission and returned with an order to negotiate peace between our king and the sharif, which did not work out.[26] I went to the monastery of Madrid.[27] From there I went to Valencia and Alicante in order to return to Rome and give an account to Pope Clement VIII, but God took him.[28] I stayed in Valencia preaching and printing my books. I was sent to Pamplona to preach during Lent.[29] From there I came to Flanders.[30]

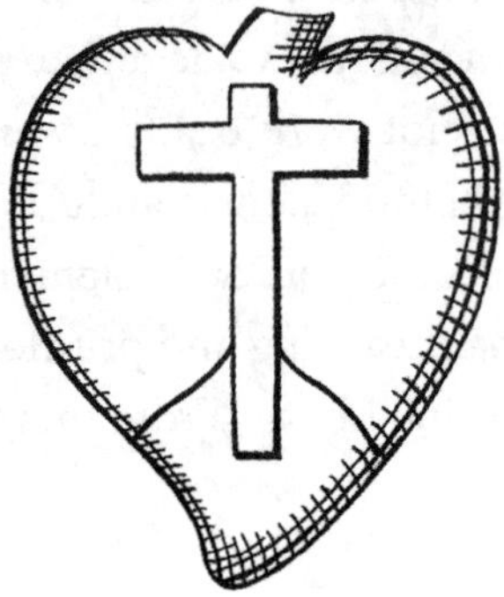

Eighth Dialogue: AFFLICTIONS

THIS DIALOGUE DEALS WITH INTERIOR AFFLICTIONS AND TRIBULATIONS, BY WHICH THE CROSS INSIDE THE HEART IS EXPLAINED, AND DEBATES WHETHER IT IS GOOD TO ASK FOR TRIALS IN PRAYER.[1] GRACIÁN RECOUNTS SOME OF HIS INTERIOR TRIBULATIONS: INTERIOR FOG,[2] FEAR, SCRUPLES, DISTRUST, SUSPENSION, COMPELLING ZEAL, ABANDONMENT OF THE SOUL, TEMPTATIONS, MELANCHOLY, AND OPPRESSION OF THE HEART. HE EXPLAINS ALL THESE ALONG WITH SOME THINGS THAT HAPPENED TO HIM DURING THE TIME OF HIS PEREGRINATIONS AND EXTERIOR LABORS.

1. **Cyril:** *I am satisfied with your explanation regarding the unshod feet and the chains, by which I have come to know about the travails of the order and your captivity. But what does the cross inside the heart signify?*[3]

GRACIÁN ASKED FOR THE NAKED CROSS

2. **Anastasius:** It reminds me of two things. One is the desire I have had to suffer. From the time I began to pray, when I was twenty years old, I have asked God for crosses and labors. With great purpose, I asked our Lord that in this life I not be led by the road of riches, honor, or

esteem—temporal or spiritual—which would give me dignities permissible to persons as the reward of their learning, nor by the road of visions, revelations, or miracles, for which men are regarded as holy. In place of these, I asked for the naked and shameful cross, because it was represented to me as the straight and sure road to heaven.

3. **Cyril:** *You did not pray before the age of twenty?*

HE GIVES AN ACCOUNT OF HIS LIFE BEFORE HE WAS TWENTY

4. **Anastasius:** I am leaving out my childhood from the time I was born in Valladolid in the year 1545 until I was eight years old, when I began to go to confession to a priest named Martínez of the Company.[4] I began studying grammar and rhetoric at the age of ten. At fifteen, I began the arts, and I received the master of arts at nineteen. This was a time of innocence because studies keep the mind occupied and it cannot take in much more, except for a little vocal prayer.

DEBATES WHETHER IT IS GOOD TO ASK FOR TRIALS; REASONS IT IS NOT GOOD TO ASK

5. **Cyril:** *It doesn't seem to me that it was right to ask God for trials, nor do I approve of that petition, for several reasons. One, in the best prayer in the world, which was the prayer of Christ in the garden, the Lord did not ask for the chalice but rather, "If it be possible, take this chalice from me" [Mt 26:39], although He was resigned to the divine will. Two, nowhere in the whole missal or breviary will you find a prayer in which we ask for trials, whereas you will see many in which we ask the Lord to free us from them. Three, among the petitions of the Our Father, which is the norm of all prayers, we ask God to deliver us from evil—evil of body and soul, according to the doctors [of the church]—and to keep us from falling into temptation. What greater temptation is there than persecutions wherein one's patience is sorely tried? Four, "If you go sailing," says St. John Chrysostom, "in the middle of winter with contrary winds, should you be surprised that there are storms and tribulations? You took them upon yourself." It seems there is no lack of arrogance or presumption on your part in thinking you are so brave*

for wanting to run into battle. I could give you many other reasons I don't think your petition was very sensible.

WHAT WE MAY RIGHTLY ASK OF GOD

6. **Anastasius:** I have considered this point many times. Certainly, we must ask God for patience in trials and tribulations, which are never lacking in one way or another. Second, we must ask that God's will be done and that He give us conformity with His will, whether in rejoicing or in suffering.

CONDITIONS WITH WHICH ONE MAY ASK FOR TRIALS

7. To ask for ease and for favors contrary to the will of God is not good. But, presuming that it is the will of God and with the condition that it is for His greater glory and the good of the soul, I do not think it is wrong to ask for tribulations. St. Augustine says, "Lord, give me cuts and burns here in this world so that you may pardon me in eternity." Habakkuk prays, "Lord, let decay invade my bones so that I may go up joined to our people."[5] Trials are profitable for gaining pardon for sins, since they are penances, and a soul strapped with mortification does not go astray with the good things of life. Our Lord called St. John and St. James foolish because they asked for rest and He was offering them the chalice [see Mt 20:22; Mk 10:38]; thus, they would have been wise to ask for it. "If I see," says St. Macarius, "a bag that is rotten and foul-smelling and I know it is full of rubies and diamonds, I would not be wrong to ask my friend for it, even suffering the revulsion it would cause me to hold it against my breast, knowing the riches I would possess."

THE BLESSINGS CONTAINED IN AFFLICTIONS

8. Who is able to count the riches and pearls contained in the cross that is placed in the heart? Although Sacred Scripture is full of evidence of this and natural reason persuades us of it, it is another thing to see it by experience. Someone who is sick does not do wrong in requesting and paying for purgatives, medicinal syrups, or bleedings,

knowing that these are the means of regaining health. What means are clearer for attaining eternal life than tribulations, through which humility and patience are gained? St. Paul glories in them when he says, "We boast of our afflictions! We know that affliction makes for endurance and endurance for tested virtue, and tested virtue for hope, and hope does not disappoint" [Rom 5:3–5]. If you were to see a gold cross full of precious stones, wouldn't you ask for it and place it on your heart, since it is a sign of the cross consecrated by Christ's body and adorned with his members like pearls? Well, tell me, which of these is a greater sign of the cross of Christ: tribulations or the gold cross? Who doubts that the best prayer we can make is to ask for the imitation of Christ? What do you find in Christ to imitate? Is it honors, rest, contentment, and the like, or insults, injuries, and death on the cross? If I were to see two roads, one wide and leading to perdition, the other narrow and rocky by which one walks to life, which of these two would it be right to ask for? Well then, tell me, where does one go, generally speaking, by the road of honors, possessions, rest, and contentment? Is it not clear that it leads to perdition, as we see in worldly people who follow it, and that all the saints go by the rough and narrow way to eternal life? God is most wise, and He loves us most wisely. We see that to whomever asks for afflictions, He gives them most liberally; and very often to the person who asks for rest, He gives afflictions. Therefore, it is better to ask for what He is more pleased to give. There cannot be a fixed rule about this since a sick and weak person, knowing it is necessary to eat in order to live, asks the doctor for tasty and nourishing food, whereas someone who feels himself full of bad humors that need to be removed asks for special diets, bleedings, and purgatives.

RESOLUTION OF THE DOUBT

9. I don't want to debate this anymore with you or respond to your arguments, which are very strong. I saw that I was inclined to ambition and pride, for which reason the purgative of insults was healthier than

the honor of titles. Therefore, although I could have had titles in the world since I had a brother who was a private secretary of the king and I had studied as much as anyone,[6] I chose a strict religious order that was starting a reform, knowing that I would not be lacking tribulations and affronts. I do not repent of having asked for them because from experience I can say, "It was good for me to be humiliated, so I could learn your ways" [Ps 119(118):71].[7]

GRACIÁN RECOUNTS THE AFFLICTIONS OF HIS YOUTH BEFORE BECOMING A RELIGIOUS

10. Soon after making my petition, I began to realize that God was doing me the favor I asked of Him by giving me afflictions. My master [i.e., teacher or professor] was invited to be a candidate for the chair of first theology. Prior to that, I was friendly with the college students who supported a candidate competing against him; these friends were much given to the service of God, and we all confessed to Father Master Deza of the Company.[8] Even when the time for voting came, I did not stop my accustomed friendship with them. After having voted, I avoided entering the university and did all the other things that are mandated, which we swore to observe, for fear of offending God if I broke my word. Because of this, some of my fellow students formed a bad opinion of me, thinking I had voted against my master, especially since I was still friends with the opposing students and did not go around soliciting votes for him as they did.

DANGER FOR HAVING VOTED WITH RECTITUDE

11. A great storm rose up against me to the extent that one of them came to speak to me with much insolence and foul language. He carried a dagger in case, entering into a serious argument, he would have occasion to use it on me.

HE HATES THE PRETENSIONS OF UNIVERSITY CHAIRS

12. The Lord freed me from this danger and rewarded me with a loathing of all the pretensions of schools and with the determination

to never think about a teaching position nor to seek one and thus avoid the dangers of conscience into which many candidates fall, even though they be religious.[9]

HE DID NOT WANT TO BE A STUDENT AT THE COLLEGE OF CUENCA IN SALAMANCA

13. Thus, I was weaned from the milk of the university that inebriates many, so that even though I was invited to Salamanca with a scholarship from the major College of Cuenca, I did not want to accept it. I was also motivated by a certain point of honor, for it seemed to me that I would be taking a step backward if I were to break the series of acts I was making, which are nine, in order to obtain the doctorate of theology at Alcalá, a career that is very difficult.[10]

HIS MANY LECTURES IN ALCALÁ

14. Although I distanced myself from professorships, the Lord did not let me put aside teaching. I taught almost the whole course of arts, substituting for Dr. Ortiz, and I taught metaphysics to all of Ocáriz's and Laxa's students. There are some great men who took my course who to this day keep and greatly appreciate my notes. For a few months, I taught Sacred Scripture for Dr. Don Alonso de Mendoza, who held the chair of Sacred Scripture in Alcalá.

15. Then I was ordained to the priesthood [March 25, 1570], being twenty-four years old, and began hearing confessions; I had been preaching since the age of twenty-three. There was a *beata* named María de Medina who was a great servant of God (she and another woman, the wife of a silversmith, exposed the Lutherans at the time of Cazalla[11]). She once wrested a wanton woman from the grip of a cleric who was living with her and brought her to my confessional. I heard her confession and put her on the road to salvation, hiding her from him with whom she had been living in sin.

THE FALSE TESTIMONY RAISED AGAINST GRACIÁN THAT HE WAS LIVING WITH HER

16. This cleric accused me of living with that woman and said that María de Medina was the go-between. This gossip went all around the university. I was as though half dead because this was the first time that false testimony of this type was made against me. Since I was preaching then—with much success and a good reputation—I thought this was the end of the world. With a dagger in his belt, the cleric came to speak with me in order to find an excuse from my words to run me through.

WORDS OF MARÍA DE MEDINA

17. The Lord freed me, and I complained to María de Medina for having involved me in this entanglement. Smiling, she said to me like a prophetess, "You are complaining about that? The time will come when you will see so many affronts that you will esteem this one as nothing."

18. I have related these two incidents in order to explain how liberal God is in giving affronts and contradictions to whoever asks for them and how quickly He executes them.

CONCERNING THE INTERIOR TRIBULATIONS HE HAS SUFFERED

19. The symbol of the cross in the heart also signifies the interior crosses—tribulations of soul and afflictions of spirit—that have been my companions, together with exterior persecutions. To the degree that the soul is superior to and more delicate than the body, crosses of the heart are greater, subtler, livelier, stronger, and more painful than crosses of the flesh.

20. **Cyril:** *I would like you to discuss this doctrine with me slowly, as you are obliged to do since the apostle says, "If we are afflicted, it is for your encouragement and salvation"* [*2 Cor 1:6, NAB*]. *The exterior tribulations you have recounted serve only to make me feel sorrow and compassion, and such cases are too rare to have experience of them. As for interior tribulations, which many souls experience however restful their lives appear on the surface, it is*

necessary to know and understand them in their roots, and there is no better surgeon than one who has been under the knife.

THE BOOK OF INTERIOR TRIBULATIONS, AND CONSOLATIONS OF THE HEART THAT PERSECUTED SOULS EXPERIENCE

21. **Anastasius:** I have already written of them in a large book about the Apocalypse of St. John, where I describe consolations and desolations found in the afflicted heart. You can read about them there.[12]

22. **Cyril:** *How do I know whether that book will be printed and see the light of day? If it is very big, I don't ask you to tell me everything that is in it. Instead, in just a few words, give me light about some of the interior crosses you have experienced, and, if you don't mind, please name them for me.*

23. **Anastasius:** I have experienced an interior fog that torments, fears that intimidate, desperation that depresses, indecisiveness that smothers the soul, unceasing zeal that gnaws at the heart, exterior and interior abandonment, strong temptations, dryness, and many other crosses. Let these be enough for you, and don't ask me any more questions, for it is hard to have one's heart exposed for all to see.

24. **Cyril:** *I will not stop bothering you until you at least say a few words about each one.*

INTERIOR FOG

25. **Anastasius:** Fog is an obscurity and dryness that comes to the soul when she forgets all the things that console her and give her light. She remains in a dreadful oblivion. Since she does not see the fruit of her labors or anything else consoling, every flea seems like an elephant, just as for one who goes out at night every mosquito seems gigantic. Even when something is not serious but is in fact quite small, this fog turns it into a great cross.

FEAR AND PUSILLANIMITY

26. This fog gives rise to fear that, besides enlarging any and every danger and causing the heart uneasiness, makes it seem as if all the

bad things that can happen will happen. It is as if the soul were experiencing them already, and she doesn't know how to handle so much misfortune. She cowers with fear of any adversary or rival, yielding to all with an incredible pusillanimity and dejection. When I am tormented with this cross, if I happen to see a water carrier or a slave, I have a great envy of their state and the blessedness of their life because they do not have contradictions with holy friars as I do. This dejection is a greater pain in a generous soul, as it is for one who has been rich to become poor.

SCRUPLES

27. As everyone knows, scruples cause much distress, especially when there is a great desire for salvation and the matter is very serious. It is no consolation to say, "This is childish"—which can be said to the scrupulous person who is distressed for breaking a devotional fast—when, by the light of wisdom and experience, incidents of grave sins are clearly seen. I saw that many were murmuring about such holy persons as my Discalced brethren, judging them to be impassioned, and it seemed to me that I alone was the cause of these murmurs and sins and that I was worse than a killer or a highwayman.

28. Isn't it true that when scruples are encountered one after another, whatever is done is done with remorse of conscience?[13] Here's the problem: If I responded truthfully and defended myself, a scruple sprang up that I was discrediting the order and impeding the good that was able to be done in the church of God by such a perfect and exemplary order. If I stayed quiet and did not defend myself, I had a scruple that I was consenting to the lie of the false testimony raised against me and holy persons—my accomplices—who were the Discalced Carmelite nuns. In addition to this, it gave me a great scruple to see that they greatly exaggerated those faults that I did not think were faults or that, at most, were light and venial. I had a scruple as to whether my past confessions were good since I had not been aware of these things, or whether I was deceived by a crass ignorance and my soul would be condemned.

Adding these scruples and fears to the exterior afflictions I suffered made for a mixture of crosses intolerable to bear.

DISTRUST REGARDING SALVATION

29. Desperation and distrust regarding one's salvation is no less a heavy cross. I recalled that God is accustomed to begin the pains of hell in this life for some reprobates, such as Cain who went about exiled and trembling, King Antiochus, and others. And since I experienced so many persecutions and had been rejected and expelled by His servants who were indebted to me,[14] I wondered whether I was a reprobate destined for hell and already let out of the hand of God and deprived of grace, with no remedy for salvation. This cross is so heavy, I don't know how to explain it in words.

SUSPENSION

30. The interior cross that tormented me most often was indecisiveness and indetermination. It is like gallows on which the soul hangs, swaying back and forth in the air. I don't know what to call this cross, but I will explain it here. I greatly desired to succeed in doing the will of God on very serious occasions. Placing my business in the balance of whether to do one thing or another, it seemed that either God permitted or the devil arranged that the reasons on one side weighed the same as those on the other side. Of those I consulted, some said one thing and others the opposite thing. I did not know where to put my head or my feet, and I remained in an insufferable suspension, seeing inconveniences on one side as well as on the other. Many times, the side I chose was the worst, resulting in greater harms and inconveniences, and my heart would be crushed with remorse. I would say to myself, "It is my fault. If I had done the opposite, such and such difficulties would not have come my way."

31. I want to give you an example. When I went from Portugal to the *consulta*, I had a thought—one that tormented me—to go directly to Rome, since I had permission from the cardinal protector [Domenico

Pinelli], and many had advised me to go. But I determined instead to go to Madrid and place myself in the hands of the fathers, confident of my innocence and in the power that usually accompanies humility, submission, and obedience such that even lions become calm when they see their opponent surrendered at their feet. Consequently, from my not having escaped them by going to Rome, the scandal you know of spread through all of Spain and even Christendom, with countless temerarious judgments, as you have seen. Afterward, I was distressed—and am still distressed—to be the cause of all that harm, all because I had imprudently deceived myself with the title of virtue. This cross is always tormenting in this way: before one side is chosen, it torments with a war of contrary reasons; and after the choice is executed, it torments with the harm that follows.

COMPELLING ZEAL

32. It seems that God goes about seeking ways to torment the heart, shooting arrows where it hurts most. Not the least sharp is zeal, which gnaws and eats away the insides with no relief. A desire is put in the soul for the greater glory of God, the good of the church, and the salvation of souls. This desire is so strong that you would give a thousand lives to counsel your neighbors about the road to heaven. Blind with this impetus, you hurl yourself at them, speaking right to their faces.

33. I will give you an example that will amaze you. When I was in Rome wearing the habit of an infamous evildoer[15] and feared that the pope would send me to the galley, I went to prayer. There it was put into my heart that I should go straight to the pope without fear and tell him certain things pertinent to his salvation and the good of the church. I resisted those thoughts, saying that I was in no state to be so bold and was doing well just to stay alive, but they seemed to reproach me. They indicated that I had such little love of God, that my spirit was false—since I was afraid—and that God did not need the honor or authority of men in order to send His messages. I was unable to find consolation in my spirit unless I went to the pope [Clement

VIII]. In the end, the pressure was so great that I went at once to the feet of the pontiff and said I don't know what things but giving him some secret messages that were said to me in prayer. I was resigned that from there I would be sent to either the galleys or the gallows. I don't know if the messages that were given to me were true or false, from God or from the devil, but I know that the pope turned the color of scarlet and looked at me from head to toe without saying a word except, "Very well, you can go in peace." Since then, I began to feel more kindness from him, for he had been told so many abominable things about me that he was like a lion.

INTERIOR AND EXTERIOR ABANDONMENT TOGETHER

34. I have experienced interior and exterior abandonment together. As for the exterior, when all the persons who were able to console me saw my rivals persecuting me, those who did not know me gave credit to them and my friends turned their backs on me. When I spoke to them, seeking consolation or counsel, they shrugged their shoulders. One of the oldest and holiest persons I knew said to me, "You have no other remedy than to go to a mountain or a desert where people will never see you again."

35. Interior abandonment is a much greater pain and an intolerable cross of the heart. Sometimes I would have such clear light and an efficacious desire about something, with so much clarity that I would swear to it and give a thousand lives for it, convinced that it was the will of God, and then I would be left so alone in that apprehension because all human reasons and all the opinions of learned and experienced men and my friends would be against it. And if I was inclined to carry it out, it would be with intolerable repugnance, feeling that I was motivated by self-love and going against the will of God. Yet, if I wanted to ignore my own opinion and follow the viewpoint of others and natural reason, I would feel such a great interior reprimand from Christ and His mother that I would have preferred a thousand deaths rather than experience such abandonment.

36. I will recount something for you so that you will understand this cross. The pope sent me the brief that I was to enter the Discalced Augustinians. The permission of that order to receive me arrived, along with an order to found the monastery of Saints Peter and Marcellinus in Rome and another in Naples.[16] I also received many letters from friends congratulating me that my afflictions were now at an end and my honor restored, since having been expelled from the Discalced Carmelites they were making me a founder of Discalced Augustinians, and that such a renowned order was as great as the other. I had here the express will of the pope, vicar of God, the favorable opinion of all my friends, and the dictate of natural reason. I should have been very content and happy, but my spirit was resisting all this with such force that it seemed the Virgin was visibly saying to me:

INTERIOR WORDS OF THE VIRGIN MARY THAT HE NOT LEAVE HER ORDER OF CARMEL

37. "So now you want to leave me? Do you not know what I have done for you? What about your vocation to my order? Don't you know that all this is the result of persecution and that if the pope and the others incline you to leave Carmel, it is on account of the negotiations of your rivals? That is not my will, and on that road I will leave you and you will be lost." She added similar things. Nevertheless, I closed my ears to these words and this light, and the anguish of this interior battle—the greatest I have ever had—passed. But my determination did not last more than three or four hours, for then I saw myself stripped naked and in the power of the Turks.[17] It was the greatest joy I have ever had—as I will tell you later[18]—to see clearly the will of God in my new habit of Adam and that neither my will was done, which was to persevere in the habit of Carmel, nor that of my rivals, which was to take it from me.

TEMPTATIONS OF THE FLESH AND DESPAIR

38. It is amazing to see the ways of God when He wants to afflict a heart, and how He attacks it on all sides! My exterior persecutions and

the interior crosses I have recounted were not enough. God permitted Lucifer—from whom I had freed someone of a diabolical relationship long ago, as I have recounted[19]—to attack me with such terrible sensual temptations and occasions to act on them that I don't know how to describe them. These temptations and occasions are normal for anyone who travels around different countries, lives outside the cloister, doesn't lack money, and believes he is already a lost soul. I couldn't stop thinking that since I was surely going to hell for having ruined such a holy order as the Discalced, there was no longer any reason to abstain from the pleasures of the flesh that were at hand. He suggested similar reasons, as is his wont. But if the details of these interior temptations and exterior dangerous occasions were to be explained, it would be necessary to spend much time on them, and this is a matter so putrid that it is better not to stir that mucky pond.

DRYNESS, AFFLICTIONS, SPIRIT OF BLASPHEMY, OPPRESSION OF SOUL, "FORETASTE OF HELL"

39. Dryness of spirit, afflictions of the heart, oppression that seems to squeeze the heart between two rocks, a spirit of blasphemy, and what St. Mark the hermit calls *praegustatio gehenae,* which means a foretaste of hell, have not been lacking to me. The foretaste of hell can be likened to a little sip that someone takes from a pot to check its flavor, and to me this little sip seems to be the peak of sadness or melancholy. On this point, I could write more from what I have learned by reading my own conscience than from what I have studied in books or seen from experience, which has been a lot. I have not neglected books of devotion or theology on this topic, nor Hippocrates and Galeno or their commentators in what they have written on the subject of the melancholic humor. Despite all that Mother Teresa of Jesus had taught me so that I could be of help to the souls of nuns and friars, and what I learned from the experiences of melancholic and deluded souls whom I examined in Jaén, Evora, and Lisbon, nothing could have helped me more regarding the matter than what has happened to me and what I know from my own experience.[20]

40. Blessed be the Lord for I can say, in imitation of Him and to His glory, I can sympathize with the infirmities of my brothers, since I have been tempted in everything. As St. Paul said, speaking of Christ, "We do not have a high priest who is unable to sympathize with our weakness, but one who was tempted in every way that we are" [Heb 4:15, NAB]. I can say this part of the verse but not what follows—"like us in all things but without sin"—since I have committed innumerable offenses against God. May He pardon me and receive—in reparation for my many errors and faults and the bad example I have given to my brothers—my persecutions, signified by the unshod feet; hardships of captivity, which are understood by the chains; and interior tribulations, which are represented hieroglyphically by the cross inside the heart.

Ninth Dialogue: Calced

In the ninth dialogue, Gracián explains the shield of the Order of Carmel and its stars. He recounts the desire he has always had to persevere in this order until death; the persistence of his superiors to have him removed him from the order, eventually expelling him so he could never return to it; how, having obtained a brief in order to return to the Discalced, they did not want to admit him and Pope Clement VIII ordered him to enter the Calced; and the good reception the Calced gave him, making him a master of the order with the seniority he would have had among them if he had professed with them from the beginning.

1. **Anastasius:** The three stars inside the shield and the twelve above the crown—being the coat of arms of the Order of Carmel—signify the perseverance I have had in this order in honor and love of the Virgin Mary, and the plotting of the devil to remove me from it.

2. **Cyril:** *Why does the order have this coat of arms?*

THE COAT OF ARMS OF THE ORDER OF CARMEL

3. **Anastasius:** The three stars signify the three stages that this order has had: the first star—which is placed in a cave[1]—is the period of the prophets, from Elijah, who gave the order its beginning in his cave, until St. John the Baptist; the second star is the second stage, from St. John the Baptist until the first general of the Latins, named Berthold;[2] and the third star is the third stage, from Berthold until the end of the world.

TWELVE POINTS OF THE RULE; "FLORES CARMELI," *DISCIPLINA REGULAR,* AND *DILUCIDARIO DEL VERDADERO ESPÍRITU*

4. The twelve stars of the crown signify the title of the order, which is of our Lady, the Virgin Mary, of whom St. John speaks in the Apocalypse in the figure of the woman clothed with the sun, who has a crown of twelve stars over her head [see Rev 12:1].[3] They also signify the twelve points of the Rule, which are obedience, chastity, poverty, recollection, mental prayer, Divine Office, chapter, abstinence from meat, manual labor, silence, humility, and supererogation.[4] You can read about this in two large books that I have written. One is called "Flores Carmeli" [Flowers of Carmel], which is not yet published, and the other is *Disciplina regular* [Regular discipline], which is printed in Italian.[5] These stars remind me of the spirit and devotion of this order's principal saints, a spirit and devotion I desire. The three stars—purity, light, and love—are a summary of everything spiritual, as I stated in the book called *Dilucidario del verdadero espíritu* [Elucidation of the true spirit].[6]

SAINTS OF THE ORDER FOR WHOM GRACIÁN HAS THE MOST DEVOTION

5. The twelve stars represent the twelve saints I desired to have a great devotion to. Four are from the first stage of the prophets: Elijah, Elisha, St. John the Baptist, and Agabus. It is said of Agabus that he was very much in love with the Virgin Mary and made a great effort to win her in marriage. Not being able to do so, he retired to Mount Carmel where he made a vow of chastity and later became one of Christ's

disciples.[7] From the second stage: the Magdalene, St. Jerome—for whom I am named—St. Basil, and St. Febronia, a Carmelite religious who suffered an extraordinary martyrdom. From the third stage: St. Angelus, St. Albert, St. Simon Stock, who received the scapular, and St. Euphrasia, a Carmelite whose life inspires me with devotion.[8] But there is no need for us to be detained any longer in this. Let's get on with our purpose.

GRACIÁN WANTED TO JOIN THE COMPANY OF JESUS

6. Before entering the order, I was at the point of joining the Company of Jesus and had already agreed to do so, having been accepted by their provincial, Father Gil González.[9] Arrangements were made by Father Pedro García, who later went to India, and my entrance was delayed until I received my bachelor's degree, which needed little time; after this degree I was hoping to get my master's. My desire to enter the Company grew cold, and I don't know if my sins or God hindered it, since these are secret judgments.[10]

7. I entered the order without the counsel, help, or opinion of any creature or confessor but only with an impetus of love for our Lady, who—as I said[11]—called me to labor in these beginnings. During the year of my novitiate, I had strong and terrible thoughts about leaving the order, foreseeing the dangers and hardships I would have to suffer in it, but our Lady stopped me. When I made my profession,[12] I endured with much contentment the fatigue of governing and the tribulations and hardships that I told you about,[13] without ever having regretted my profession or, for my part, ever having felt discontentment or the least inclination to leave the order.

8. At the time of my greatest persecutions, my rivals, in order to prevent the division that eventually occurred, made a cunning attempt to get me out of the order.[14] Thus, some mutual friends of ours went to my mother—I always thought they went of their own accord—saying that I wanted to leave the Discalced Carmelites; that I would be better off getting away from conflicts with my own superiors and from troubles and

persecutions; that the other orders were as holy and as important as the Carmelites; that I would be held in the esteem I deserved; and similar reasons. Perhaps their intention was that my mother, moved by love for her own flesh and blood, would be the first to propose this to me and beg me to leave the order; then they would come to me and encourage me to agree with this. My mother responded that she knew nothing of this and would speak with me. She sent for me and spoke these words: "They have told me that you want to leave the order of our Lady. If such a thing has crossed your mind, don't ever speak or write to me again, or even call me mother. I do not want a son who has so little courage that persecution makes him leave such a mother as the Blessed Virgin Mary and turn his back on her order, he who gave himself to her wholeheartedly and whom I afterward also entrusted to her." I was greatly disturbed by these words because I could tell where this plot came from and that they would not stop there. What they were not able to do by this skillful trick they would do by force, as did happen. I had my hands full in trying to placate my mother and to persuade her that none of this was true. After I convinced her, she consoled me and encouraged me by saying that our Lord and the Virgin were better served by constancy in tribulations than by more restful and consoling services.

THE DILIGENCE THEY HAD IN MAKING SURE THAT AFTER GRACIÁN WAS EXPELLED, HE WOULD NOT RETURN TO THE ORDER

9. They took the habit from me, as I said,[15] using all the authority possible through excommunications and seeking favors from the king, the pope, and the cardinals so that I would never be able to return to the Calced or the Discalced. They made every effort imaginable to ensure that I would remain in the status of a secular or join some other order, because they knew that once I entered another order, I—not being a man of duplicity—would not try to come back to the Order of Carmel. I have already recounted the negotiations that took place until finally it was decided that I should join the Discalced Augustinians,[16] when I was taken captive. Although everyone felt sorry on account of my captivity,

I don't know that some weren't glad of it to be sure that I would never again return to the order. Even after I was freed, they tried to hinder me from returning to the order.

THE DEATHS OF THOSE WHO WANTED TO EXPEL GRACIÁN FROM THE ORDER

10. Believe it or not, in the first year of my captivity, God carried off to heaven almost all the judges who expelled me and most of those who sought to have me ousted from the order; by now they will have rendered an account of it to God.[17] Those who remained were not without fear on account of a rumor of the secular people that the deaths were a just judgment of God. In the hereafter, we will all go before His tribunal, where what is hidden in our hearts will be made manifest.

THE DECREE OF THE CARDINALS AND THE POPE THAT GRACIÁN RETURN TO THE DISCALCED CARMELITES

11. When I returned to Rome in the habit of a captive, I asked the general of the Augustinians, as I have said,[18] to give me the habit of their order, since it had been granted to me before my captivity. He did not want to give it to me. This was in God's providence because had he given it to me, I would not die wearing the white mantle.[19] I asked the pope for a religious order in which to live, without specifying any in particular. He sent me to the Congregation for Religious. Revoking the sentence and expulsion, they decreed that I return to the Discalced Carmelites. Although the procurator of the Discalced Carmelites objected to this, the cardinals responded that even if I were guilty of the most insolent faults in the world, I had suffered enough. The decree went to the pope. Monsignor [Barbiano] Vestrio drew up the brief and sent it to Spain to the Discalced Carmelites. They were to obey it. Those who were then governing did not want to obey, since they were cut from the same cloth as those who gave the sentence of expulsion. Word went around that they did not want to obey Rome. We approached the auditor of the Apostolic Camera in the hope that he might give censures

against this rebelliousness.[20] He gave them, and we went round and round in this battle.[21]

12. **Cyril:** *Good heavens! You had a brief for your return to the Discalced?*

13. **Anastasius:** I have it here if you want to read it. I have always kept these authentic copies in order to enlighten those (or some of them) who believed it was my choice not to return to the order to die in the habit, and so that all my friends would know of the effort I made to come back. Although many Discalced nuns say they have had revelations that I will return to the order, it is God who says what will be.

14. **Cyril:** *How was this imbroglio settled, and how did you come to join the Calced, since the sentence also expelled you from the Calced?*

15. **Anastasius:** The Discalced saw that they were caught in a tight spot: either I return to them or they are accused of disobedience to the papal brief. In order to free themselves from both dangers, they sent a long memorial to His Holiness containing two points: first, why it was not right for me to return to the Discalced, citing the grounds for the sentence and stating my main faults with severe and loaded words; second, that I had obtained a surreptitious brief.

WORDS OF VESTRIO TO THE POPE

16. This second point gave me back my life because in Rome to call a brief "surreptitious" makes a big impression. The pope, having kept the memorial in his possession because he did not want to turn it over to the secretary in charge of memorials—as is done with others—called Monsignor Vestrio, his secretary, and said to him, "Read this memorial." Having read it, Monsignor Vestrio responded, "Most Holy Father, whether this friar Gracián is good or bad, or whether these faults spoken of are true or false, I do not know. But I do know that I am not untruthful with Your Holiness, nor do I make false and surreptitious briefs." In order to free himself from this lie imputed to him, he brought and showed to the pope the decree of the congregation. I do not know what happened or what the pope said in my favor, but I did learn that

Vestrio called for the procurator of the Discalced Carmelites and sternly rebuked him.

HOW AND WHY GRACIÁN JOINED THE CALCED

17. Vestrio sent for me and placed the memorial in my hands so that I could read it. He said to me, "It seems to His Holiness and to me and to everyone that even if these fathers were to desire it, you should not return to them. Instead, you should join the Calced. See what sort of brief you want and I will give it to you, written with the most honorable words and authorizing your person with whatever you desire, because His Holiness has commanded me to do this."

18. Thus I joined the Calced, because I was resigned to do whatever the pope commanded me to do. The pope must have spoken to the protector of the order because with much favor he sent me to the monastery of San Martín in Montibus, ordering them to give me the general's cell.[22] I was in it only a short time before they sent me to the house of Cardinal Deza with the office of theologian, as I said,[23] preaching in Rome and attending to very serious and honorable business as well as to grave matters of the Inquisition since my patron, Cardinal Deza, was a senior member of the congregation of the Holy Office and the protector of Spain.

REASONS WHY IT WAS GOOD FOR GRACIÁN TO JOIN THE CALCED CARMELITES

19. At first, I felt a little sorry seeing myself in the habit of the Calced. But after I considered it carefully and spoke about it with our Lord in prayer and with some discreet and experienced friends, I realized it was most suitable for me for many reasons. For one thing, I was returning directly to my profession, since the general [Father Juan Bautista Rubeo (Rossi) de Ravena] was Calced when I made my vows. It was many years later that the Discalced elected their own general,[24] and to a new [Discalced] general it would have been necessary to make a new profession. The Rule, in which consists the essence of the order, is the

same for both Calced and Discalced. The constitutions that were in place when I received the habit and made my profession, in the first years of the Discalced, were changed, with the addition of the laws of the new government of the *consulta,* to which I never consented. To bind oneself to keep laws to which the heart is not inclined is a clear danger to one's soul.

THE LAWS OF THE CONSULTA

20. **Cyril:** *Will you not tell me what these laws of the* consulta *were and why they were so offensive to you?*

21. **Anastasius:** That is a new topic far from what we are talking about. It is enough to say that they ordained that the superiors, that is, the provincials as well as the vicar general and even the general himself, were not to have a consultative and decisive vote in the ordinary government. Instead, they were only to gather information and send cases to the *consulta* and everything would be determined there. This is how it is done in the republics of Genoa and Venice, as well as in religious orders during the eight days of the provincial chapter when neither the provincial nor the priors do anything on their own; rather, everything is done by the whole definitory which sees and adjudicates all proceedings. Although this kind of government must be good for those republics and for very serious cases—thanks be to God there were no such cases among the Discalced Carmelites at that time—it was very harmful in regard to insignificant things and little faults, and consolations or desolations to which the provincial needed to attend when he made visitations. The friars were uneasy and fearful, with sadness and bitterness of heart, while waiting to know how their cases would end; after a long time, when the remedy of the *consulta* arrived, the case that had been long forgotten would be renewed and a wound reopened. The provincials were looked down on when they made visits because their subjects knew they could do nothing more than a commissary or a scribe who gathers information. To sum up, it is not necessary to give multiple reasons that I opposed the *consulta*; too many have already been written

and printed by both sides. It is enough to tell you that, from the time the church of God began until then, in no order, including this one, was this mode of government ever seen; thus, all the other orders laughed at it. And it was not surprising that everyone was going the wrong way and only two or three got it right because, although they might have been holy and learned, they had been professed only a short time.

22. But let us continue with the reasons I acquiesced in putting on the habit of the Calced. If the habit on the outside was more delicate, on the inside I could clothe myself as I wished. In order to attend to serious business in the service of God—for which it was frequently necessary to travel in a coach—the habit of a Discalced was not so suitable, since it was the coarse dress of the desert. I would either have given offense to others in wearing it or have had to give up very important occupations that were for the good of souls. I consoled myself with the thought that many times the hunter dresses in dull brown or green—the color of the fields—and uses quail decoys to hunt in the fields. Though the life of the Calced is not as severe in food, fasting, disciplines, and all the rest as the Discalced, I was able to take whatever I wanted of them, as can any layperson. There are many who appear to live comfortably but interiorly do very good penance. I also consoled myself with the fact that I was now older and worn out from past labors, and my strength was diminished. What the Discalced would have had to gradually grant me by dispensation from their laws, I was granted by Christ and His vicar the pope all at once. I was put in the habit and state of life in which, with the mitigation of Eugene IV—who granted a plenary indulgence to whomever follows it—I was able to conserve my health and strength to serve God more. I saw clearly that perfection, which I so much desired, does not consist only in exterior roughness of life. As St. Paul says, "If I hand over my body to be burned [and I have not charity, it avails me nothing]" [1 Cor 13:3]. When he then names some of the signs of charity, saying, "love is patient, love is kind" [1 Cor 13:4], he does not include exterior mortification among them. The twelve he does name can be

attained with the habit of the Calced, as is practiced by other orders although they do not go about barefoot.

23. The mortification, confusion, and reproach I felt at seeing myself in a delicate habit after always having worn a coarse one—which makes a greater impression on the hearts of those who see it in the pulpit and sows I do not know what scent of good desires when it passes through the street—was bearable, seeing that I was unworthy of such a great blessing. And I realized that I was doing some mortification in going out on the street, as when religious go out with their heads covered with ashes and so forth.

THE DIVERSE CLOTHES OF GRACIÁN

24. I now learned what true mortification is. It is not only to go to the refectory with a rope around the neck or a cross on the back; it is to change into more clothes than an actor: from the cassock and mantle of a learned doctor to the coarse woolen habit, patched and worn, of the Discalced Carmelite; from this most blessed habit to the handsome cassock and mantle that was put on me when I was expelled; from this to the habit of a hermit with a large hat and friar's tonsure with which I went about in Rome; and from that to a habit of black wool and a hoodless cloak of the same color that I had on when I was captured, for I was on the verge of entering the Discalced Augustinians. After this one, God put me in the habit in which He created me for I saw myself practically naked except for some loin cloth; then I found myself in a ragged skirt and a blue cap and shoes full of holes. When I was taken to Tunis, I wore a *barragán* [cape] of blue and red stripes;[25] soon after my arrival, I was clothed entirely in white, with a small scapular and boots with *gamberes* to support my chains,[26] and a black round cap on my head such as the Jews wear. When I was ransomed, I wore a habit of white *barragán*, a dark gray cloak of the galley slaves, a hat, and, as a sign of my liberty, a cross around my neck. On the roads, I wore an *almaizar* of black and white stripes that I had taken with me from Barbary.[27] When at last I went about Rome doing my negotiating, I wore a cassock and

cape made of black-dyed *barragán,* as is fitting for a priest freed from the land of the Turks; and just as I was planning to put on my habit of the Discalced Carmelites—as I had the brief—I was put in the habit of the Calced, which had clothed many holy and learned men of this order, and thus I had no reason to go about mortified.

THEY DID NOT WANT TO ACCEPT THE BRIEF GIVEN TO GRACIÁN

25. My friends congratulated me upon seeing me in the Calced habit and consoled me by saying that God had done me a great mercy in not returning me to the Discalced. Those who were then governing were of the same mind as those who had trampled on me, and if they were to see me among themselves, they would thrash me anew.

IT IS HARD TO BEAR THOSE WHO WANT TO PROMOTE THE HONOR OF ONE'S PERSECUTORS

26. It is hard for a religious not to have the benevolence of his superiors, especially for me who had begun to see the horns of the bull when they did not want to accept the brief of my return to them. I knew they were zealous for the order and had to safeguard the honor of their predecessors. In order to silence those who said they were acting from passion, they had to dig up new reasons I deserved to be expelled, or at least, why they should hide me away in some little monastery in the middle of nowhere where I could do nothing more than confess some *beata* and go to choir. I also knew that God did not want the lamp to be put under a bushel basket but rather on a lampstand in order to enlighten many religious toward greater freedom and more generous obedience [see Mt 5:15], as I later experienced. But this is enough for now about the habit and the stars of the shield of the order. We can talk at greater length another day.

27. **Cyril:** *Won't you tell me now before I forget: do you have a papal brief to be among the Calced?*

28. **Anastasius:** I have no other brief than the one revoking the sentence and allowing me to return to the Discalced, nor do I want any

other brief. Monsignor Vestrio offered to draw up for me a very favorable one with honorable terms, since after the conflict I told you about regarding the memorial we remained good friends.

29. **Cyril:** *Well, how do the Calced have you among them with this point in doubt?*

HOW GRACIÁN IS AMONG THE CALCED AND WITH WHAT FACULTY; PATENT OF THE PROTECTOR

30. When they saw the brief I had for the Discalced, they approached Cardinal [Domenico] Pinelli, protector of all the Carmelites. He went to Pope Clement VIII, who *vivae vocis oraculo* said that it was his will that I be among the Calced.[28] On the strength of these words from the pope, the protector signed and sealed a patent and sent it to the general, Enrico Silvio. With it, they were reassured, for they doubted at first whether they could receive me, although they wanted to. Thus, they showed great pleasure to see me in their habit. Then the general made me a master of the order, giving me the seniority I would have had, had I professed with them from the time I professed with the Discalced. They have always respected this, which is no little thing to be thankful for.

Tenth Dialogue: CONSOLATIONS

GRACIÁN RECOUNTS THE GREAT GIFTS, CONSOLATIONS, AND EXTERIOR BENEFITS THAT HE RECEIVED FROM OUR LORD MIXED TOGETHER WITH ALL HIS TRIALS AND TRIBULATIONS, FROM THE TIME HE BEGAN TO SUFFER IN HIS YOUTH UNTIL HE WAS FREED FROM CAPTIVITY. THESE WERE LIKE SOFT PADS THAT GOD PLACED ON HIS SHOULDERS SO THAT THE WEIGHT OF THE CROSS HE GAVE HIM WOULD NOT HURT HIM; GRACIÁN THUS EXPLAINS THE INTERMINGLING OF THE CROWN OF THORNS WITH THE CROWN OF PRECIOUS JEWELS IN THE HIEROGLYPH.

1. **Cyril:** *Let's proceed to the explanation of the two crowns, a mixture of thorns, gold, and precious stones woven together, which surely contains some mystery.*

WHAT THE TWO CROWNS SIGNIFY; ARISTEAS; EMBLEM OF KING SOLOMON

2. **Anastasius:** Some modern authors say—I say modern because although I have searched with much diligence among the ancients, I have found only Aristeas,[1] a member of the royal council of Ptolemy Philadelphus, king of Egypt, who went as an ambassador to the high priest of Jerusalem in order to bring back the Bible and its seventy translators. He wrote about his commission in a little book, and there he mentions a crown of precious stones that was kept on the table of

proposition, which was all in gold. Some modern authors say that the most wise King Solomon devised an emblem of a crown made of jewels intermixed with thorns, with the words "victory of love" in the middle. Surrounding it were six hieroglyphic letters: *A, C, F, R, I,* and *C*. Desiring to understand the meaning of this hieroglyph, his vassals begged the queen of Sheba—who was then in Jerusalem and, according to what they say, so much loved by the king that she carried a son in her womb as a pledge of his love—to ask him to explain this enigma and the meaning of the six letters [see 1 Kings 10:1–13].

EXPLANATION OF THE SIX LETTERS

3. Solomon interprets them in three ways:

4. First: *Aurea Corona Fortissimus Regnat In Coelis* [With a golden crown, the strongest one reigns in the heavens], signifying that the mighty Christ reigns in heaven with a glorious crown of gold.

5. Second: *Aspera Corona Filius Dei Redimitus Inferiora Calcat* [The Son of God, crowned with a bitter crown, conquers the lower realms], signifying that the Son of God was crowned with a sharp crown of thorns, and in virtue of this crown subjected the demons and put all created things under His feet.

A MIXTURE OF TRIBULATIONS WITH DELIGHTS

6. Third: *Amoris Cognita Fortitudo Regalium Insigniorum Copulatio* [The strength of love is known when it unites regal insignia], as if to say that the strength of love, born of knowledge and contemplation, is what joins these royal insignia of Christ: thorns with pearls, labors with rest, persecutions with favors, and so on. He told the queen of Sheba that in times to come, Christ and His followers, uniting hardships with delights, would show the strength that love possesses.

7. Many other things are said regarding this. Without going into whether this history is true or not, what it means to me is that God has a great and strong love for souls, even souls of sinners like me, the greatest

sinner in the world. Not only does He give them the reward of their labors in the next life, and spiritual riches in this life, some of which I will recount, but during times of suffering, He interweaves such pearls of great succor, support, and consolation that, although it seems the thorns wound, the precious stones that are united and mixed with the thorns enrich the soul with strength and encouragement.

PSALM [89(88):2]: THE MERCIES OF THE LORD I WILL SING IN ETERNITY[2]

8. I wish I had the words for what I am now going to say concerning my experiences of the benignity, mercy, and goodness of God. You should at least help me give thanks and be amazed at my ingratitude since I do not go about like a madman proclaiming and singing the mercies of God.

9. I do not wish to speak now about the spiritual graces I have received; I will say something about that later when I explain the names of Jesus and Mary.[3] Instead, I shall speak of the mixture that God makes of good events, comforts, and temporal gifts, commingled and interwoven with the thorns of afflictions. When a man is knocked down or is about to fall, God places His hand underneath him so that he does not hurt himself on the rock, according to the words of David: "Though he fall, he does not lie prostrate, for the hand of the Lord sustains him" [Ps 37:24, NAB]. Or He sends His angels to carry him in their arms when they see him falling from the cliff, fulfilling the words: "He has commanded His angels to watch over all your ways. Upon their hands, they shall bear you up lest you dash your foot against a stone" [Ps 91(90):11–12]. I would like to explain this whole psalm to you, drawing on what I have experienced.

10. But in order to give you a better understanding of the mixture of my successes and misfortunes—which are the jewels with the thorns of the crown—and of the way God held me in His hand when I was about to be wounded and lost in the interior and exterior trials I have had, signified by the cross and the chains on the unshod feet as I have already

explained, I want to tell you what happened in Evora on Pentecost in the year 1590.

THE VISION AND WORDS OF ANA MARTÍNEZ IN EVORA

11. I had said Mass and had given Communion to a *beata* named Ana Martínez, a great servant of God. From her childhood, she was given to prayer and penance until her present age of seventy. She came to me after Communion, saying to me in her Portuguese language, "What is the matter, son, what is the matter?" I responded that nothing was the matter and insisted that she tell me why she was asking me this. She said that at the time of the elevation of the Blessed Sacrament during Mass, she had visibly seen our Lord place a heavy cross on my shoulders, but with cushions so that I did not feel it much, neither did it wound or hurt me much. I thought the cross meant that [the friars] were going to elect me vicar general of the Discalced (at that very time they were holding the chapter and elected Father Nicolás Doria). But it was very much the reverse because at that chapter they enacted the laws of the *consulta* and the new government.[4] I did not understand what this cross was until I experienced it later, as I have already told you.

12. Now I will tell you about the cushions that protected me so that the weight of the cross would not wound my shoulders so much. I will follow with my afflictions in the same order, interweaving the jewels with the thorns.

THE HONOR OF LETTERS AND ESTEEM AT ALCALÁ

13. Before entering religious life, I had the two frights I mentioned earlier: the one with my classmates because of the votes; and the other, the false testimony about María de Medina.[5] Yet the Lord had given me much honor on account of my taking first place in the licentiate among all my classmates, which is the greatest honor the university can bestow. I came through the lessons, the acts, and the defense of my thesis with as much applause and esteem as any of those who attended that school in my time. I was thus offered a fellowship from Salamanca [University] with the

major College of Cuenca, which I scorned as I have already said.[6] I even had a reputation for virtue, which I did not merit, for the eyes of many were deceived by me.

HIS HEALTH DURING THE TIME OF NOVITIATE

14. I joined the order. Just when I thought I would die of the cold and the austerity, the pains that I usually had in my back, head, and stomach disappeared, especially when my cork slippers were taken from me. I remained with such strength and health that walking on the snow without shoes seemed like walking on roses. I don't know how to express this except in the way that books of chivalry talk about knights-errant: that in times of their greatest wounds, fairies brought them to magical fountains from which they emerged healed and more valiant than ever so that they could no longer be wounded, like Orlando.[7]

15. **Cyril:** *Such a "fairy" as the Virgin Mary was involved in this!*

PLEASURE OF FOOD IN THE REFECTORY

16. **Anastasius:** Well, as for the food, I don't know how to explain how tasty it was and how the turnips, cabbage, and gruel of the refectory fattened me up, since before then such food would have bloated and killed my stomach.

17. **Cyril:** *That seems like a great miracle.*

WHEN THE SPIRIT IS CENTERED, EVERYTHING TASTES GOOD AND FATTENS

18. **Anastasius:** Don't believe in miracles so easily. It is only natural that when the spirit is centered, the harmony redounds to the body's health and pleasure. When the spirit is not centered, even chicken and pheasant become poison, and sugar, jelly, and syrup become as bitter as aloes, as happened to me when I was in the house of Andrés de Bobadilla struggling with my vocation.[8] This is because taste is not in the dishes but in the palate where the organ of taste is found. We know well what the philosophers say: "The imagination produces the

effect." St. Bernard says, "To the healthy palate sugar is sweet, but to the sick it is bitter."

CONSIDERATION OF THE VIRGIN

19. Being in the house of the Virgin and in her service, I could easily imagine that the Virgin Mary was placing the morsels in my mouth with her very beautiful hand. See if there wasn't reason for the food to taste good, even if it were morsels of nettles, given that it was from the hand of so beautiful and dear a Lady.

FRAY MIGUEL DE LA VIRGEN

20. We had among us a novice from Navarre a little older than I. When he drank a little red wine, or more precisely, *zupia,*[9] which was given to the monastery as alms, he imagined that he was putting his mouth to the wound in the side of Christ and drinking that blood. It had such an extraordinarily good taste to him that sometimes he lost his senses and remained enraptured while drinking it.

FRAY BENITO DE JESÚS Y LA VIRGEN

21. And what shall I say about Fray Benito,[10] who never slept more than three hours a night and ate only bread and water? He was fat and content and had rosy cheeks. When, as his superior, I made him eat meat and sleep for twelve hours, he became as skinny as a stick in two days. This is because a regular routine and diet bring about much strength and health, as you see in the galley slaves who don't eat or drink anything but fetid water and black biscuits.

ISABEL DE SANTO DOMINGO CONSOLES HIM

22. In the afflictions I suffered in the novitiate, which I already told you about,[11] God gave me Mother Isabel de Santo Domingo for my consolation when I wanted to leave. She was the prioress of the Discalced Carmelite nuns in Pastrana at that time and afterward the foundress of the monasteries in Segovia and Zaragoza. Although she was only listening to me and not saying anything, in speaking with her and telling her

of my thoughts and temptations, the clouds of my heart took flight, the sky of my spirit became serene, and the sun and light of my usual happiness came out.

HOW HARMFUL IT IS TO CONCEAL THOUGHTS AND TEMPTATIONS

23. I hold it to be a tactic of the devil to get people to conceal their thoughts and temptations. By means of deceptive pride or despair, he keeps them from speaking up, with the result that their interior putrifies. With the rotten vapors that emerge and go to the imagination, many souls have been destroyed.

THE MORTIFICATION OF A NUN WHO CONCEALED HER THOUGHTS

24. You might bare your soul only to a cat, as I experienced in the case of a Discalced Carmelite nun who had many interior afflictions but kept quiet about them. I ordered her to tell all her thoughts to the cat each day; this was no little trouble because the cat was surly and often scratched. She humbled herself and obeyed. In this way, God calmed her interior, and she became one of the most spiritual nuns in the community.

25. I have related these things to explain the "cushions" I had during the year of my novitiate.

26. After my profession, in all the labors of my governing and the persecutions that I told you about, I had Mother Teresa of Jesus—until God took her—for my support, consolation, and relief. She consoled me with her sweet and holy words when she was present and with her letters when she was absent. Even now, I receive her consolation from the letters I saved, which are sown together in a book four fingers high.[12] You will learn who Mother Teresa of Jesus was—her spirit, her natural and supernatural graces, and her gentleness, discretion, and prudence—by reading her books and the books written about her life by Father Ribera and by other fathers under the authorship of the bishop of Tarazona.[13] Therefore, on this point I do not intend to say anything, because I could write another book larger than those already written if

I were to relate what I learned from her mouth: how she loved me, the gifts of soul and body she made to me, what we went through together on the roads when we made foundations, and, finally, what I know of her in particular, which probably no other ears have heard.

27. In order to see for yourself whether she would reveal her secrets to me and console and advise me in my afflictions, read this paper written in her hand that she left. She instructed that it should be given to me, saying, "For some day he will need this."

> 28. The second day of Pentecost,[14] after having made this resolution,[15] on our way to Seville, we heard Mass in a hermitage in Ecija and stayed there for siesta. My companions were in the hermitage, and I was alone in the sacristy there when I began to think about the great favors the Holy Spirit had once shown me on the vigil of Pentecost. I had great desires to do some signal service for Him, and I could not think of anything I had not already done, or at least promised, for to say all was done is surely incorrect. I remembered that although I had made a vow of obedience, it was not made in such a way as to be perfect obedience. I thought to myself that it would be pleasing to the Holy Spirit to promise what I proposed in regard to Father Fray Jerome. On the one hand, this seemed like nothing special. On the other hand, it was to do something very difficult, considering that you don't reveal your interior state to superiors; that if you don't get along with one superior, there is finally a change and another one comes along; and that I would be without interior and exterior liberty for the rest of my life. I found myself hesitating a little, even a lot, to make such a vow. This resistance of my will displeased me because it seemed there was something here that I had not yet done for God, which was to offer myself completely, something I had always avoided doing. In this case, the difficulty pressured me in such a way that it seemed I had never done anything so difficult in my life, not even making my religious profession, which caused me so much resistance, other than when I left my father's house to become a nun.

For this reason, I did not consider how much I loved him [Father Gracián] but instead thought of him as a stranger, nor did I consider his capabilities; I only considered whether it would be good to do this for the Holy Spirit. The doubts that came to mind as to whether it would serve God or not were all that held me back. After battling within myself for some time, the Lord gave me great confidence. And reminding myself that our Lord Jesus Christ had given him to me,[16] it seemed that I should make this promise for the Holy Spirit, thus obliging the Holy Spirit to give him light for my sake. With this, I went down on my knees and promised to do all that he might ask for the rest of my life as long as it was not against God and those superiors to whom I owed obedience. I meant this only in regard to serious matters, in order to remove any scruples, so that if I asked him about something that he told me not to speak of anymore, or something regarding his comfort or mine, which are trifles, it didn't mean that I no longer wanted to obey him. Concerning my faults or sins, I would not knowingly hide anything, which is also more than we owe our superiors. In sum, I resolved to hold him in the place of God, interiorly and exteriorly. I don't know if I did something meritorious, but it seemed to me that I had done a great thing for the Holy Spirit, at least as far as I understood. Thus I remained with great satisfaction and happiness, which I still have. Thinking that I would be restricted, I have instead found more freedom and am very confident that our Lord will grant him [Father Gracián] new mercies on account of this service I have rendered Him, so that some of these mercies will reach me and that he will give me light in everything. Blessed be He who created a person who satisfies me in such a way that I would dare do this.

29. **Cyril:** *Good heavens, what a rare document! It clearly shows what love, reverence, and familiarity Mother had with you when she was still alive, after making her promise, and the joy she had from your comfort and consolation. As she says,*[17] *Christ Himself took your right hand and*

hers and joined them together, commanding her to hold you in His place while she lived, and she made this novel vow of obedience to you for the rest of her life. How is it possible that those who considered Mother Teresa to be a saint, in seeing this document, denigrated you, as you told me, as being full of faults regarding the Discalced nuns? Didn't they realize that neither Mother nor her nuns would have trusted you so much unless she were pleased with you? For what purpose did she write this for you in her own hand?

30. **Anastasius:** That I do not know, but she left two copies. I carry one with me, and the other is in the possession of a nun who is my blood sister at the Discalced Carmelite monastery of Consuegra.[18] [Mother Teresa] said that when she died, they were to be given to me because the time would come when I would need them. There are many other things she left in writing and told me herself regarding the future, things that would astonish you if you heard them. I don't know whether those who denigrated me ever saw this document or believed it to be Mother's if they did. Nor did it seem good to me and my reputation to go about showing or divulging private things of mine that have the scent of honor, since this is not what I asked God for when I began to live a life of prayer.

31. Only once did I make use of it for my benefit, for it seemed necessary to do so. I showed it to the patriarch in Valencia when they took my deposition for the canonization of the holy Ignatius of Loyola, founder of the Company of Jesus.[19] I was questioned by the Rota whether I had ever been sentenced or my honor tarnished, because those who are in disgrace aren't able to be witnesses in a case for canonization. I replied yes, that I had been sentenced. But, so that I might still testify, I presented to them the brief that Pope Clement VIII gave me when he sent me to Africa to be an apostolic preacher, which showed my qualifications, and the document written by Mother Teresa of Jesus in her own hand, to see whether these two things made any difference. The brief was copied by the scribe to go with the record of my deposition. As for the other document, the

patriarch kissed it many times with tears, recognizing the handwriting of Mother Teresa because he had some of her letters. And thus they accepted my deposition.[20] In regard to this matter and what Mother said or left in writing about me, don't ask me anything more.

32. **Cyril:** *When did the event recorded in this document take place?*

33. **Anastasius:** A little after my profession, when I came to Beas and met Mother for the first time. I then sent her to Seville to make a foundation, despite the fact that she wanted to go to Madrid [to make a foundation there]. It seemed to me that to found a Carmelite monastery in Madrid would bring into question our sincerity of purpose. I don't know who would defend the contrary; all I know is that one who passed through this history knows it better.[21]

ANTONIO GRACIÁN, HIS BROTHER, SECRETARY OF THE KING

34. In these difficulties, I also had the help of my brother, Antonio Gracián, secretary of the king, through whose hands passed all that we needed for the good of our order.

DOÑA JUANA DANTISCO, HIS MOTHER

35. I also had my mother who consoled and encouraged me greatly in these trials. After Mother Teresa of Jesus, I loved her more than any creature on earth, not only because she gave birth to me—for that is the lesser thing—but also because she always helped me in the things of God and virtue.

THE LOVE THE DISCALCED HAD FOR HIM; THE INCREASE OF THE ORDER IN HOUSES AND MEMBERS

36. I had several great consolations and cushions for carrying the cross: the immense love the Discalced friars and nuns had for me, for they held me more as an idol than a superior; the contentment I had from seeing the order grow, with the many foundations made and the good subjects who entered during the nine or ten years that I governed as visitator and provincial; the honor I received from many laypeople as the superior of

so holy an order; and many other things that I won't mention. For just as the sun outshines the stars, so it seems that what I said about Mother Teresa of Jesus consoling, counseling, and encouraging me is enough to leave the other things in silence.

37. In my troubles with the nuncio Sega and the dangers and fears in which I saw myself, I had the encouragement and consolation that Mother Teresa of Jesus gave me with her letters when she was absent; I received new ones every day. I also had the consolation of my mother, who was present. Not as a mother of the flesh but as a mother of the spirit did she clear away the storm clouds and encourage me to suffer a thousand deaths for the Virgin and her order.

THE FAVOR OF KING DON PHILIP II

38. I also had the favor of the king, Don Philip II, who knew about all these things. He knew what had provoked the indignation of the nuncio and that he himself was the cause of it for having sent a request to Rome that the pope cancel the jurisdiction of the nuncios over religious orders. Since he was so prudent and powerful, I knew very well that he would bring me to peace and safety, for it was he who put me in this battle in the first place. And so he did, for he had always taken care to shelter me when I was in a difficult position. Until the king received the brief in which His Holiness Gregory XIII commanded that the nuncio Sega accede to the king of Spain in everything and be guided by all that he said—that is, until the nuncio's hands were tied—he hid me in the house of a member of his royal council so that the nuncio wouldn't trample me underfoot.

39. Afterward, when I allowed myself to be seen and the nuncio apprehended me, wanting to avenge himself for the offense he had received—as it appeared to him—by the curtailing of his jurisdiction, he told the king that he was punishing me not for having followed the king's orders but rather for the insolence and excesses of which I was accused by the friars of Andalusia. In order to show that he was not moved by passion, he asked that other judges join him to look at my case.

THE JUDGES THAT THE KING SENT TO ASSIST THE NUNCIO

40. The king took him at his word and so named as assistants Don Luis Manrique, his principal almoner, and Master Fray Villavicencio, a most serious and learned man of the Order of St. Augustine, both of whom went to calm down the nuncio. Don Luis, who spoke with the king every day, declared these accusations of the Andalusians to be calumnies. He and the other assistant planned to collect all the necessary information and make a report in order to obtain a papal brief for the separation of the province. To this end, they used all possible diligence and care, for which the Discalced are much indebted to them.

41. When they saw that the nuncio was resolved not to deal with the question of the province or the general well-being of our congregation until he had first sentenced me, they came and told me that, in conformity with their conscience, there was no way they could sentence me with any punishment without new information and that while they delayed in getting it, the plans for the province would fall apart; but if I, as a religious, were willing to accept some usual monastic punishment as mortification, then they, with my consent and in no other way, would agree to that sentence. And thus, as I have already said,[22] the sentence was given, the king being informed of it. When the king saw that the nuncio was placated, he made sure that the sentence was revoked, as it in fact was.

THE DUKE OF ALBA, DON FERNANDO DE TOLEDO, IMPRISONED IN UCEDA

42. At that time, it was a "cushion" and no small consolation to hear the confession of the duke of Alba, Don Fernando de Toledo, and to attend to him when he was imprisoned in Uceda on account of the affairs of his son, Don Fadrique. He consoled and comforted me in my troubles, in keeping with the courtesies of a duke, and I comforted him and the duchess in their imprisonment. It is a great consolation to hear the confession of such a man and a great soldier,[23] one whom the world believed to be so cruel, for if someone took a handful of wheat

contrary to his orders when they marched through Christian lands, he would hang him. And he was supposedly so full of pride for using "*vos*" in addressing persons with titles whom others always addressed as "*señoría*."[24] He was hated by many for this. On the other hand, examining the reasons he had for acting this way and putting my hand in his soul, so to speak, I found a conscience so pure and humble that, desiring to suffer a thousand deaths and affronts for Christ and His church, he was determined to lose his life, honor, and home before committing a mortal sin. I am not the only one who thinks this. All his confessors are of the same opinion, especially Father Fray Luis de Granada who would say when he was going to hear his confession in Lisbon, "I am going to confess that holy soul of the duke," at which the Portuguese got a good laugh because they trembled before him as if he were Nero.[25]

43. **Cyril:** *How dangerous it is to judge someone! I would really like to know more about this holy duke.*

44. **Anastasius:** It is not a good idea to interrupt the matter at hand because I have to continue with the consolations I had and recount the "cushions" with which God softened the heavy cross I received when the Discalced expelled me from their congregation, for it seemed to me I would never be consoled.

45. A great commotion was made by those who were saying they were impassioned. They accused them of being ungrateful for all I had done for the province and of being imprudent for wanting to defame me by throwing into the public square the faults of one who had always governed them. It was being said that even if I had committed the worst excesses in the world, they should have put all this in a well, and me too, rather than bring discredit to the order, because people would judge from this case what the Discalced must really be like, since the one they held to be most saintly and who governed them a long time was discovered to be so evil. Because of the insinuating words of the charges and the sentence, which they showed to everyone to justify themselves,

some seculars and friars of other religious orders imagined some very bad and awful faults.

MARÍA DE SAN JOSÉ, PRIORESS OF SEVILLE

46. Among other things, they said that a sister of mine who is a Discalced nun in Seville, named Juliana de la Madre de Dios, was my daughter by the prioress (who later was also greatly persecuted because she sent a petition to Pope Sixtus V to have the constitutions of Mother Teresa of Jesus confirmed so that the superiors of the order could in no way alter them).[26] When my mother heard the rumors, she responded, "They didn't suffer what I did in giving birth to her!"

FAVORABLE OPINION OF HIS OPPONENTS

47. Well, when the fathers who sentenced me heard these things, touched by fear or scruple for having caused such defamation by putting those insinuating words in the sentence, they said and affirmed by oath that they did not find a grave fault in me but only some venial carelessness and that they had wanted to punish me in this way for the perfection and good of the whole congregation. By this they meant that I was impeding the government of the *consulta,* in which they thought the whole good of the congregation consisted, moved as they were by the zeal of which I have already spoken.[27] However, this reason did not satisfy many. My friends and I didn't say anything. We were satisfied with the honor that my judges were willing to swear that I had not committed a grave fault (although what moved them was not a grave fault either but rather perfection) and that I tried to preserve my order from the bad government of the *consulta* by such lawful means as appealing to the pope. Never did I excuse myself nor will I excuse myself from carelessness and venial sins because the Holy Spirit says, "The just man falls seven times a day" [Prov 24:16]. This indicates that he who wants to defend his innocence so much that he won't keep silent when accused of venial sins is not just, nor is he prudent.

48. It is true there are some venial things so contrary to perfection that they are the root cause of much harm. But the difficulty lies in what perfection consists: whether it is to observe so rigorous a retirement, cloister, penance, and abstinence that charity is undermined—holding it to be a fault to eat in the house of a secular when one goes there to assist in a happy death, or to preach in some village outside the city far from the monastery—or whether it is more perfect to save souls as Christ did, setting aside the law and not holding it to be a sin, even venial, to eat in the house of Zacchaeus or to let the Magdalene wash his feet. Well then, seeing that we live in weak, mortal flesh, one who preaches, hears confessions, and assists the dying is not able to be as zealous in religious observance and the common life as others who have no other work than to come and go to the choir and the refectory. And this debate is so contentious, and always has been: many who place perfection in rigorous austerity refrain from helping souls to avoid endangering their chastity, but those who place perfection in charity would condescend to the weaknesses of the flesh, licit according to natural and divine law, in order not to fail to help souls or hide the talent God gave them.[28]

49. **Cyril:** *How much I would like for us to investigate this point because I see that the Carthusians and Capuchins, who are so holy, do not hear confessions, help the dying, or even leave their monasteries. And the fathers of the Company of Jesus and other orders, although they wear shirts and go out and eat, and so forth, are no less fruitful in the church. I would like to know which is better.*

50. **Anastasius:** What is best is that each one follows his vocation. It seems to me that the vocation of the Discalced Carmelites is not like that of the Carthusians or Capuchins. Nor is it their vocation, unlike that of the Company, to wear a delicate habit, eat meat, or use linen, and so on. The vocation of the Discalced Carmelites, while keeping their austerity as much as possible, is to assist souls, as did their predecessors. It would be something novel indeed to be like the Carthusians and

Capuchins in not going out or assisting the dying. Nor is their vocation like that of the Company or other orders. So whoever would want to introduce one way or the other, going to extremes, would be doing wrong. But let us continue now with our consolations.

JOAQUÍN ZAFONTE ACCOMPANIES GRACIÁN TO ROME AND SERVES HIM ON THE WAY

51. When I came in view of the sea, alone and afflicted, God provided me with a companion in the form of a servant, the son of the innkeeper of the place where I was staying in Alicante. His name was Joaquín Zafonte. He was of such good grace, so capable, so good a scribe, and very experienced about the roads; at another time he had gone to Rome with a bishop. He was also so faithful and virtuous, so clean-cut and attractive, so loving, and as diligent as anyone I could imagine. God put into the mind of his mother that, by his going with me, I would be able to get him ordained a priest, as in fact I was able to do. This young man accompanied me, consoled me, and counseled and served me with such solicitude and diligence from the time we left Alicante until I was captured—he was ordained shortly before that happened—that I never had to worry about my person, living very carefree and unconcerned about temporal things. I held him to be like the angel Raphael for he saved me from the danger of the ship that sank, which I told you about,[29] making sure that I embarked on the galleys. And if I hadn't sent him back to Spain an ordained priest—with much regret on his part because he did not want to leave me in all my tribulations—I believe without a doubt that the Turks would never have taken me prisoner.

PEDRO CEREZO PARDO SENDS FIVE HUNDRED DUCATS TO HIM IN ROME

52. When we arrived in Rome, just when I ran out of money, a certificate of exchange for five hundred gold *escudos* came from Seville sent by Pedro Cerezo Pardo (God reward him). I was annoyed to find myself with so much money, but four hundred were to later serve

toward my rescue; and if it had not been available, I would have lost my chance to be freed. The rest I used for travel expenses, until I was taken captive.

CARDINAL DEZA SEATS HIM AT HIS TABLE

53. When I thought I was going to go without eating, before this credit arrived, Cardinal Deza, seeing me without money at the Urso Inn in Rome, inquired about me and brought me to his table, which was as splendid as that of any other cardinal. I noticed that God took care of my hunger with such abundance.

DON ANTONIO DE SOTOMAYOR HELPS HIM AND CONSOLES HIM IN ROME

54. A little while later, when I saw myself without honor and the procurators of the Discalced, who were against me, going around Rome telling people about the case and showing the sentence, God permitted that Monsignor Don Antonio de Sotomayor, officer of Grace and Justice, who was the advocate of the Discalced and handled all their cases and business, wanted to talk to me.[30] He did so in a skillful and cautious manner in order to learn how best to refute me so that he could better fulfill his office. I spoke with openness and sincerity, baring my heart and giving him an account of all my intentions (because he was a great servant of God and I did not know that he was the procurator of the opposing party). He was moved to favor me in such a way that he immediately returned all the documents to the Discalced and told them to never enter through his doors again, and he took my side as if it were his own affair.[31] He took me, as I wore the habit of a pilgrim, in his coach to see all the sights of Rome and gave me his hand in friendship without my being able to refuse him.

FATHER TRIGOSO, CAPUCHIN

55. [Sotomayor] and Father Trigoso,[32] a Capuchin who was formerly a member of the Society of Jesus and who wrote commentaries on St. Bonaventure, tried to reconcile me with the Discalced so that I could

return to them in peace, but they were not able to come to an understanding with them.

THE DUCHESS OF SESSA AND HER HUSBAND, THE AMBASSADOR TO ROME, FAVORED, LOVED, AND CONSOLED HIM

56. During this time, the duchess of Sessa, who was the ambassador's wife,[33] without knowing me beforehand, took pity on me. She had a great desire to see me on account of what my adversaries were saying and the great lengths to which they were going in order to defame me. I saw her; she spoke to me about spiritual matters, and I gave her some devotions and information about Mother Teresa of Jesus. She took such a liking to me that from then until now, she has always confided all her secrets to me. The ambassador showed me the letter of the king and advised me what would be best to do.[34]

NO ACCOUNT IS TAKEN IN ROME OF THE BAD THINGS SAID ABOUT FRIARS

57. Most Romans, when they heard the offensive things said about me, paid no attention. Rather, they said, "*cose fratesche!*" since they considered—as they did then—the ignominy and persecution of friars as a laughing matter.[35] Actually, in a certain way, they honor a persecuted friar because, as everyone knows, Sixtus V came to Rome to be free of persecutions of friars and he rose to be pope.

DON ANTONIO MIERES

58. Finally, seeing myself at the table of such a cardinal; going regularly to the house of the ambassador; enjoying the good opinion of Monsignor Sotomayor and others, such as Don Antonio Mieres, the empress's principal chaplain who was then attending her in Rome and to whom important people in Spain had written to look for me and treat me well; going about in a pilgrim's habit and always having a well-dressed servant to accompany me; and being available to console and hear the confessions of important courtiers of Rome, I thus saw myself, at the time of my greatest affronts, with the greatest honor I have ever had.

Many of my Roman friends tried to persuade me not to return to the friars, insisting that I take the clerical habit and apply for a position, for surely I would be given a dispensation and an important office. But God would never want the pretensions of worldly honor to be the cause of my going backward spiritually. However, when God gives worldly honor, there is no reason to reject it.

THE COUNTESS OF OLIVARES, VICE REGENT OF SICILY

59. When I went to Naples and Sicily in order to avoid using corrupt means and false information to join another order—as I have said[36]—I was not lacking favors and consolations. The countess of Olivares, vice regent of Sicily,[37] received me with great love and ordered that I be lodged and provided for at the Spanish Hospital of St. James in Palermo. There in the hospital I was given rooms on the ground floor, with awnings, as if I were an Armenian bishop.[38]

SIMÓN, MAJORDOMO OF THE HOSPITAL OF PALERMO

60. I was also provided with an attendant from the same hospital, named Simón, who had been a servant of my father. He regaled me so much that I scolded him for what he was spending. He said that because the hospital was giving me much less than what the viceroy and his wife ordered, he was spending his own money; thus, he ate and dined with me.

SOLDIERS AND CAPTAINS

61. No less did the captains and soldiers cherish me greatly, because I preached to them, heard their confessions, and dealt with their affairs. All in all, I had a very quiet and good life there. I even wrote a book about the order called "Flores Carmeli" [Flowers of Carmel].[39]

DON PEDRO DE LEIVA

62. Returning to Rome, I sailed to Messina on the flagship of Don Pedro de Leiva, with quarters in the stern and eating with him at his table. And from Messina to Naples, I sailed on the flagship of the galleys of the pope, enjoying the same life as the general who was sailing on it.

RELATIVES IN GAETA

63. I arrived in Gaeta where I was treated very well by my relatives.

RELICS AND SIGHTS THAT HE SEES

64. Finally, throughout this pilgrimage of Italy, I enjoyed visiting holy relics and holy places and seeing many sights such as the caves of Sybil, the antiquities of Pozzuoli, the ruins of Rome, the Trinity of Gaeta, and other things. If I had gone to Italy only to see these things, it was worth it, regardless of the trials or affronts.

65. **Cyril:** *I'm picturing you at the prison of the Turks! I expect that was a blow without relief, an affliction without consolation, a life without rest, or to say it better, death and no life.*

66. **Anastasius:** Does it seem to you that God has His hands so tied that He cannot catch one who is falling down on so hard a rock, or that He is lacking cushions to put beneath so heavy a cross? When did Daniel, Ezekiel, Tobias, Joseph, and other captive slaves have greater consolations and delights than in their captivity? I have already told you that I escaped from that intolerable nightmare of whether or not to join the Discalced Augustinians.[40] God clearly manifested His will by placing me in that state of captivity, bypassing the channels of my desires and the intentions of my adversaries.

REST FROM INTERIOR TRIALS DURING CAPTIVITY

67. The joy my spirit received at seeing myself stripped of all things, separated from all creatures, and placed in the hands of God was so great that I don't know how to explain it to you. But let's not talk about interior gifts and consolations—these will be addressed later and more slowly[41]—but about sensible and exterior consolations, which we have called "cushions."

68. Never did I have better health, never did I see myself fatter, never did I sleep with greater ease or have quieter sleep, and never did I eat with greater pleasure or drink with greater gusto.

THE GOOD TASTE OF SOME GARLIC BULBS

69. After I boarded the galley, one day I took—with the slyness of a slave—two heads of garlic from the basket of a Turk when his head was turned. I kept them to eat, little by little, with the black biscuits, feeling great pity for the kings who lack such delicate and tasty delights as raw garlic eaten right down to the fingertips and who drink precious wine but have never tasted the green water from the puddles of which the Turks let us have our fill when they took us to the Island of Ventotene near Naples.

PLEASURE IN SEEING NEW THINGS

70. It seemed as if I was watching an entertaining play put on by the Turks and the Christian captives. I enjoyed seeing these novel things. Although I had to change my clothes, I was delighted to have my part in it.

FRUIT IN NEEDY SOULS

71. I am leaving aside the satisfaction it was to hear the confessions of the afflicted who came to me crying as if I were their father or mother; to prevent the weak from denying the faith; and to convert some renegades who [afterward] went to Christian lands with certificates I secretly gave them so that they could present them to the Inquisition.

THE CONVERSION AND DEATH OF MASTER WILLIAM, A LUTHERAN

72. Even if the only satisfaction I received was hearing the confession of, giving the last rites to, and burying a Lutheran, this favor would be enough to console me for all my troubles. He converted at my bidding and died in my arms, just as I finished giving him the sacraments. I had brought him the Blessed Sacrament, which I had hidden under my cloak as I went along the streets of Túnez (for which the pasha had one of the shackles removed from my feet).[42]

HEARING CONFESSIONS OF CAPTIVES AND TAKING CARE OF THE SICK

73. And what shall I tell you about the satisfaction it was to hear the confessions of captives who had gone years without confessing, drawing them out of the greatest sins? Or assisting the sick among them, those who would have died had I not instructed the Christian barbers to make some remedies that I knew about from philosophy and experience.

WORDS OF THE CHRISTIAN CAPTIVES WHEN I ENTERED THE *BAÑO*

74. I recall that when I arrived at the *baño* with my recently acquired shackles, dying of hunger, and my body badly blistered from the sackcloth and the crammed quarters of the *galeota,* the leading Christian captives came and reasoned with me thus: "How very sorry we are, Father, to see you in this state, which is the unhappiest in this life. But who knows whether God brought you to us for the salvation of the sixteen hundred souls here who are lacking Christian instruction?[43] And if God brought you here, as we believe, be concerned with our salvation. You won't have to worry about taking care of yourself."

GIFTS OF THE CAPTIVES

75. One of them gave me twelve *reales* in case I wanted to buy something I liked. Another gave me a cotton shirt. The Christian women of the seraglio—although I found out afterward that it was by order of the sultana, who was a renegade—sent me by way of a captive who was their servant (whom they called Diego) a shirt they wear there made of linen cloth, like the ones worn in Holland. Then the Christians clothed me in a white *barragán,* made to my liking, and invited me to eat with them. They put nine roasted partridges on a stone bench along the wall to be shared among the very few [captives] that were there. No Christian brought anything tasty that was not gained either from their work (they go out to work) or with their itchy fingers (which is commonly done there because they are in extreme necessity and are not able to get things in any other way; taking it from the Turks who possess

their persons and their labors unjustly is held in that land to be not theft but rather *reintegratio rei propriae* [occult compensation]).[44] They divided their food with me, often complaining that they were offended because I was reluctant to take it. The breadmaker who made the bread for the table of the pasha, which was the whitest and tastiest I have ever seen, sent me a loaf every day; the breadmaker for the janissaries—all the breadmakers were Christians—would send me six loaves of white bread; and from the seraglio—the place where the women are—the Christians and renegades sent me bread that the sultanas ate and many other gifts.

GIFTS OF THE RENEGADES

76. The renegades in particular secretly brought me gifts. They came and played music for me, entertained me, and informed me of things they wrote to the viceroys and to Christendom. I welcomed them because by not shunning them, some were converted.

THE BOOK *VICTORIA DE LA FE* [VICTORY OF FAITH]

77. When I sent for the old and sick Christians who stayed in the *baño,* they would come and tell me stories of things of that land, from which afterward I was able to write a book called *Victoria de la fe* [Victory of faith]. The Turks who came to the *baño* to eat lunch and drink *aguardiente*[45] made by the Christians would invite me to join them. Sometimes, when they persisted, I could not excuse myself unless I told them I had not yet said Mass.

OFFERINGS OF THE CHRISTIAN CAPTIVES

78. I had money in abundance because when we said Mass on Sundays and feasts, the Christians gave offerings. This collection was shared among the priests—we were two—and used for supplying the church with candles, wine, and vestments.[46] We received forty or even fifty ásperos each week. With just seven, we could eat abundantly because things are so cheap in that land.

SMALL OFFERINGS FOR MASSES AND CONFESSIONS

79. Besides this, small offerings were never lacking for the Masses requested by the Christians and by the renegades who secretly asked for Masses that God would convert them. They gave five ásperos for each Mass; there, this money is worth more than four of our *reales*. And when the Christians went to confession, they usually gave us alms.

THE DEPOSIT OF FOUR HUNDRED ESCUDOS OF DIEGO THE SILVERSMITH

80. Others left their coins with me for fear that the Turks would take them. One of them loaned me money—four hundred *escudos* of gold in doubloons of two and four pieces—so that I could use it for my rescue. If we were to return to Christian lands, I would repay him then. In sum, I had an abundance of everything. But the best and greatest satisfaction was that nothing was wasted because the bread, the food, and the money that came to me from one side or another sustained the sick and afflicted of the *baño* who were dying of hunger. And the four hundred *escudos* were very well used, since I ransomed a dozen Christians with them and other money secretly given to me by some renegades in order to rescue their relatives. Some of them would have denied the faith if they were not rescued. There is no greater satisfaction on earth than to do works of mercy for the most miserable and to have the means to do it. My companion, the priest canon of Lipari, had one hundred *escudos* in his "girdle," which is what we called the purses of the Christians because they wore a pouch around their waist next to their skin and fastened to their pants. He kept it for his ransom and, with a little more, he would have been freed had God not taken him away from life in that land. He was taken to Algiers with eleven or twelve other priests and friars who were captured shortly before I was ransomed, leaving me alone in the *baño*.[47]

THE PASSING OF TIME TOOK AWAY THE STENCH AND THE PAINFUL DIN

81. By the end of eight or ten days, the stench no longer bothers you. That is what happens to those who work in hospitals or jails. When the ears get used to the continuous clanging of the chains, sleep is not hindered. That is what happens to the dogs of a blacksmith. The weight of the chains and not being able to move was easy to bear since I was always lying on my cot, except when I said Mass or went out to eat my meals on the stone bench.

PLACE OF PRAYER AND REFLECTION

82. Although my body could not get around easily, my thoughts had much space in which to fly and wander about many parts of the world, such as the regions of speculative study and lectures on prayer. This I did during the twenty-four hours of the day and night, except for the time I spent in recreation with some Christians who came to see me when I wished and the few hours I spent sleeping; I did not sleep much [see PA 10.77]. If God put me in danger of being burned alive twice and of drowning six times,[48] look at me here alive. His divine hand freed me from it all—roasting in fire or drowning in water—like the egg of the divine hen that, extending its wings on the cross, wants to "gather her chicks" [Mt 23:37] and shelter beneath her wings those who seek to defend themselves from the snares of the devil.

83. I could recount so many pleasant events and such enjoyable pastimes during that time of captivity that you would say God sent me there in order to give me delights in this life. The Christians I ransomed and the many works to which I gave myself obstructed my rescue because, seeing them, the Turks were convinced that I was an archbishop and that money was being given to me in secret. But God remedied this by means of the Jew, Simón Escanasi, who ransomed me. As for the troubles I suffered after being rescued, the great delight that came from being free was enough of a relief without mentioning the other honors and contentment that came to me, which I might say something about later.

84. **Cyril:** *I am satisfied with the compensations that God made for your exterior crosses, for it helps me to understand the verse "who framed mischief by statute" [Ps 94(93):20]. I don't know how else to explain this verse without calling God a deceiver and a feigner, except by saying that, although there are trials in His service, He hides delights and gifts in them.*

85. **Anastasius:** The compensations for interior crosses are much greater than those I have just recounted, as much as the soul is greater than the body, but let's leave that for now. I will tell you something about it in greater detail when I explain the six letters above the crown and the "Jesus Mary" of the heart.[49]

A C F R I C

Eleventh Dialogue: Succor

Gracián explains twelve interior helps of the afflicted soul that keep her from falling into despair, impatience, vengeance, and any other sin during times of tribulation, as contained in the six letters above the crown: A: love of one's enemies and contempt of self; C: contrition and penance, and confidence in God alone; F: a living faith, and fortitude with silence and hope; R: resignation to the will of God and renunciation of all created things; I: judgment and justice, and imitation of Christ; and C: consideration and counsel.[1]

1. **Anastasius:** Rightly does the prophet Isaiah call Christ our good teacher and captain [see Isa 55:4], since as teacher He instructs and as captain He gives weapons to the afflicted who confide in Him. And from the tower of Mt. Lebanon on the frontier of Damascus, where hang a thousand shields and all the weapons of the strong [see Song 4:4], He takes down shields and arms for the soul to use in her defense against blows. The fight is against the devil, and the soul is able to batter and wound him, her adversary. The devil is not an enemy made of flesh and blood but the prince of darkness [see Eph 6:12]. When he attacks in a great persecution, natural strength is not enough against him. But if the soul shields and protects herself with the armor that Christ gives

and uses His sword to break the snares of the enemy while taking cover under the wings of the cross, which is the protection given by God, the soul avoids being wounded while wounding her enemy. Using God's defenses makes this spiritual combat sweet-tasting and delightful.

SPIRITUAL DEFENSES TO AVOID FALTERING IN TRIALS

2. Of the thousand, even innumerable, shields that are on this tower, I want to tell you about twelve. This number is apropos for acquiring knowledge, seeing that Christ was twelve years old when He debated with the doctors in the temple [see Lk 2:41–47]. The twelve shields are signified by the six letters of the crown, which I'll explain. Two shields are represented in each letter: in the *A*, love of one's enemies and contempt of self; in the *C*, contrition for sins, and meditation and prayer; in the *F*, living faith and firmness of purpose; in the *R*, renunciation of all created things and resignation to the will of God; in the *I*, universal justice and final judgment; and in the *C*, counsel of good friends and silence.

3. I have heard these twelve doctrines and counsels, among many others, from the mouth of the Lord. They have been a defense for me and have given me courage and consolation in my interior and exterior trials and tribulations. I want to tell you about them so that with these shields and weapons you can defend yourself when you see yourself attacked. I also want to fulfill the words of the apostle who says that if God consoles us in our tribulations, it is so that we can console all those who are distressed "with the consolation with which we ourselves are consoled by God" [2 Cor 1:4].

4. **Cyril:** *Before you go on, I want to ask how, from the mouth of God, you heard these consolations and the doctrines you plan to tell me about. In what manner have you seen Him? And so that I will be assured of the teaching you wish to give me, how do you know that what you have heard are the words of God?*

5. **Anastasius:** You have questioned well. I will tell you of my manner of visions and revelations at length further on [PA 15], but so that you

will be satisfied now and believe me, you should know that there are two kinds of visions and revelations. What is seen with the bodily eyes or the eyes of the soul, I call vision. Revelation is what is heard either interiorly or exteriorly. And these occur in two ways: First, when Christ is seen exteriorly and visibly and He speaks some words of particular consolation to someone who is suffering, as He did to St. Anthony after his skirmishes,[2] appearing so beautifully and saying, "Here I am. Do not fear." Although this kind of vision is much esteemed by many, I give it less value than the second kind I will tell you about because the devil is accustomed to changing himself into an angel of light, as we know by faith; thus, an exterior vision is less reliable [see 2 Cor 11:14]. Also, the heart remains ever troubled with the question of whether it was God who consoled him or the devil in order to deceive him, and whether those words are true or false.

6. The second kind of visions and revelations are those that are seen with the interior eyes of faith and the words heard are the same as those that the Holy Spirit has spoken in Sacred Scripture. With these words, He teaches, encourages, and defends the soul. This way is more certain and sure, and since the heart is quieted, it doesn't bring any of the inconveniences of the first. By this second way, God has spoken to, taught, consoled, and encouraged me. And the consolation He has given me can benefit you and whoever is troubled. So I do not refuse to tell you of my consolations nor am I ashamed because, as the apostle says, "I am not ashamed of the Gospel" [Rom 1:16, NAB].

7. **Cyril:** *So, really, what you are telling me is that your consolations are nothing other than taking the Bible and reading the verses that are most relevant to the doctrine of patience and that I can do as much for myself, as can anyone, without there being anything novel about God having consoled you.*

8. **Anastasius:** There is more to it than that. Although there is no one who does not know the word *God* and have it on his lips, at times this word comes to the heart with such light, force, and efficacy that there are no words to explain the strength given to the soul when God places

that weight and brightness in it. A spark of fire is the same whether it falls into a river or into a storehouse of gunpowder, but look at how different the effects are: in the water it is extinguished, and in the gunpowder the fort of the enemy blows up, however fortified it is. This has happened to me with some words of Scripture that have come to my heart in times of trial. Although they are common and well known, the battery of the adversary goes flying, his towers crumble, and the soul remains content and secure. Thus, in the doctrines that I will give you, I will always use the very words of the Holy Spirit and tell you of the strength they have given me.

A: LOVE OF ENEMIES AND CONTEMPT OF SELF

Love of Enemies

WHAT LOVE OF ENEMIES MEANS

9. "Love your enemies" [Mt 5:44; Lk 6:27, 35, NAB]. Many times—when I was suffering most acutely—the Lord gave me to understand that in this love consists my well-being, consolation, and profit.

10. **Cyril:** *How is it possible for me to love and wish someone well who takes away my honor and exiles me from my country? It is enough to have patience.*

11. **Anastasius:** Notice that the Lord does not say *"amate"* your enemies.[3] Many times I was given to understand that *amare* has to do with the appetite and pleasure, while *diligere* has only to do with the will,[4] even though the appetite and pleasure might be contrary to it. *Diligere* is the same as *ex duobus eligere,* meaning to choose between two things. Let's say I have a very bad fever and am dying of thirst, and I have before me two glasses. One is made of crystal, full of clear, cool, and fine water. The other glass is dirty and contains a purgative of an abominable color, a terrible stench, and an intolerable bitterness. The doctor, who I know is learned and wants me to get well, tells me, "Take this purgative because it

will save your life, and don't drink that water for it will kill you." I believe the doctor, close my eyes, hold my nose, and with my stomach turning inside out, force myself to suffer my "punishment" and drink the purgative. Although my eyes, appetite, and taste want to go after the water, my reason comprehends the good that is in the purgative and my will makes the effort to follow the reasons given me by the doctor for taking the purgative.

CONSIDERATIONS ABOUT ONE'S ENEMY IN ORDER TO LOVE HIM

12. I considered my adversaries as the living image of Christ, which neither Zeuxis nor Apeles would have known how to paint so well.[5] If a painting falls from the wall and hits me on the head, the blow will hurt me, and I will tend to the wound and be careful that it doesn't happen again. But I would not spit on the painting or despise it; that would be ignorant. Rather, I would appreciate it as before, cleaning off the dirt and returning it to its place. The persecutions pained me. I tried to apply an easy remedy to my affronts by fleeing from the occasions where they could dishonor me again. My adversaries were powerful and to harm them was to harm myself.

13. If the Blessed Sacrament is enclosed in a poorly made tabernacle, I don't for that reason fail to adore and reverence it even though I might prefer to see it enclosed in gold and precious material. I know that by His essence, presence, and power, God dwells in the one who persecutes me. I might very much wish that the "tabernacle" were more pleasing, but I close my eyes to the exterior and not to what is inside.

14. If a mother has a deranged son who turns against her and spits in her face, she will blame the madness, and have pity on her son and love him as much as she did before he became sick. For me, the new government of the *consulta* was madness but my sons to whom I gave the habit and brought up in the order were without fault. I bore the affronts, which I felt, and I desired to see my sons with light and all the good that could come to them.

15. If a father could not recognize his son due to some spell that made the son appear to be an enemy and he knifes him, believing that in killing him he would save the lives of his other sons, then the son who is knifed, knowing that his father is under a spell, defends himself by wounding him only slightly, without ever drawing the sword—for he does not wish to kill or do harm—and he flees if he can, beseeching God to undo the spell.

16. One of the greatest trials I have suffered in this bloody battle was always having to go about making peace and not daring to give a cutting wound, although many times I could have done so. The wounds of my fathers pained me doubly due to the great love I had for them and the scruple I had against harming them, and the pain received in prayer when we go to God and find Him angry because we did not believe His words.

17. "Love your enemies" [Mt 5:44, NAB]. Do I have to hate those whom I interiorly see are making me a crown of glory for the next life, and of honor and spiritual good in this life? As I later experienced—which I will soon tell you about—and hope to enjoy when God takes me from this life, I knew very well that God chastised me with His own hand like a father, saying, "Whoever is dear to me, I reprove and chastise" [Rev 3:19, NAB]. Should I not kiss the discipline[6]—which my adversaries were—hoping for the sweet confections of the spirit that I have enjoyed? Such is the mother who, having spanked her son, says to him, "Come here, kiss little Martin,[7] and I will give you sweets and you will be my son."

WE MUST BE THANKFUL FOR A GOOD WILL EVEN THOUGH THE UNDERSTANDING ERRS

18. "This will prove that you are sons of your heavenly Father" [Mt 5:45, NAB]. I knew that they were not my enemies, nor did they wish me evil; their will was to succeed in what seemed to them was best. I was grateful for their will and excused their understanding, which was not at fault, since to merit or demerit pertains only to the will.[8] Of no little account to me were the words I heard from Cid Albucarín,

a very prudent Moor who lived in Lisbon. In trying to persuade him to become a Christian and giving him many reasons for this, I said to him, "Do not be annoyed, Your Lordship, that I speak to you and try to persuade you in this way." He responded, "It certainly doesn't annoy me. On the contrary, I am grateful to you, and I love and esteem you because I see your will is to serve God, which I appreciate very much. You are in error, but your understanding is not guilty." It was he who was erring in his Muhammadan sect, but the reason he gave me helped me to understand that although my adversaries were wrong in their obstinacy regarding their *consulta*, they desired the service of God and the good of the order. For this I was grateful to them, and it was the cause of my loving them well.

19. "Do good to those who hate you" [Lk 6:27, NAB]. I did for them the good that I was able to do because "deeds are love." I could tell you how, even after my troubles with them, I did very good deeds for the Discalced, such as:[9]

20. I helped with the foundation of the monastery of the Discalced nuns in Rome. We settled on the price of the house of St. Joseph the same day I arrived there from captivity. Father Soto, the pope's cantor, and I had arranged this foundation to be like those of the other Discalced Carmelite nuns.[10]

21. I wrote the countess of Castellar, who had consulted me about how best to use certain monies, and I told her to use it to found the monastery of San José of the Discalced Carmelite nuns of Alcalá.[11]

22. And I can say that I was the occasion for the foundation of the Discalced Carmelite friars in Rome.[12] Let me explain why I say that I was the occasion. I understood how important it was that there should be a monastery of this order in that city, where the head of the church is. There was not one there, whereas there are four monasteries of the Calced Carmelites: Transpontina, St. Martin, St. Chrisologos, and St. Julian. At that time, I was in the house of Cardinal Deza in Rome with some favor and friends, and Fray Pedro

de la Madre de Dios and the prior of the Discalced Carmelites in Genoa came there. I told them to found a monastery in Rome and that if they didn't, I would found one. And I said they should look at what an "honor" it would be for them that one who had been expelled from their congregation for bad conduct was their founder in Rome. These words greatly astonished them. And since they took me for an audacious person and saw how much favor I enjoyed in Rome, they made the effort to make the foundation. I gave many thanks to God to see this monastery made.

23. "Whether by occasion [or by truth],"[13] I have persuaded many to found monasteries of this order and to make them properly; at least my conscience doesn't reproach me of having harmed the Discalced or of having spoken ill of them, but rather of having done much good. Some people, not understanding the situation, think that the friars, because of what they did to me, lost much credibility, invited misfortune, and have been the cause of great scandal. But this scandal has been passive, not active, on my part, since I have suffered so much. Likewise, being crucified by the Jews did not make Christ responsible for the afflictions that befell Jerusalem.

24. "Pray for those who calumniate and persecute you" [see Mt 5:44]. There is one thing the Lord has given me to understand that I want you and everyone to remember: that you always begin your prayer praying for your adversaries before yourself. You will see from experience what you gain, for it is good to take God at His word when He tells us to say, "Forgive us," and so forth: "Lord, I now forgive my enemies, and I pray for them that You give them such and such blessings and glory. Forgive me my sins and grant what I ask. Do You not tell us that with the measure we measure with, we will be measured [see Mt 7:2]? I wish my adversaries well. Please look lovingly on me," and so on. If I were to explain all the good that comes from loving your enemies and the great fruits that the soul gains in this way, it would be necessary to write a big book. Let's proceed to the second help also contained in the letter *A*.

LOATHING AND ABASEMENT OF SELF[14]

25. When the soul sees herself loathed and abased by all and believes they are right, and that it is more likely that she is deceived with the blindness of self-love than that they are mistaken, she also loathes and abases herself, desiring not to have honor or contentment in the world, nor that anyone remember her.

26. Because of this loathing and contempt, seeing that Christ Jesus was loathed and despised by men, the soul enters the number of His disciples, recalling these words of the Lord: "Whoever comes to Me and does not hate his father and his mother and his own self, cannot be My disciple" [Lk 14:26]. This is the true origin of humility and the summit of the edifice of Jerusalem that, as St. Augustine said, "begins with the love of God and reaches to hatred of self, just as Babylon begins with self-love and ends with hatred of God." It is a great satisfaction for the soul to see herself already fallen so that she does not have to fear they will knock her down; she rests calmly in her center and, like a root in dry earth, does not feel the impetus of the winds of the world that combat with the tall cedars. It is marvelous to see how, from this loathing and abasement of self, a person rises to an interior greatness and excellence that he feels within himself. He would not want to change places with any prince or king of the earth for this; instead, he has them all under his feet because now he has nothing to fear or hope for from men. Just as when a ball hits a rock with great impetus, with greater force it rises, so did Christ, who "humbled Himself, becoming obedient unto death, even death on a cross, for which God exalted Him, giving Him a name above every other name" [Phil 2:8–9]. Truly, it is a great mistake for a religious who professes to imitate Christ to seek fame and honor. When he goes about fighting for the restitution of his honor, he instead gains the reputation of one who is ambitious and proud, which is a great dishonor. But if he keeps quiet and lowly, he has the name of a good religious and humble servant of God, as has happened to me. Many persons who had never met me, hearing shameful things being said about me while I remained silent, sought me out as if I were somebody.

27. I conclude this matter then by saying, "It is good that You humbled me so that I may learn Your ways" [Ps 119(118):71].[15] God has done me a great mercy in knocking me down in order to teach me something I did not know before, namely, the justification and other great riches that are enclosed in abasement.

C: CONTRITION AND CONFIDENCE

Contrition and Penance for Past Sins

REMEMBRANCE OF SINS WHEN THERE ARE SORROWS

28. When sadness is already afoot, with tears in the eyes and grief in the heart due to the humiliations received—which are fully felt since otherwise they would not be a cross—the soul remembers her sins and adds this memory to her sorrow. From this churning river, she catches the good fish of true contrition and true repentance.[16] She considers how much more she, who has so offended God, deserves to suffer, and that even if she were to suffer the torments and pains of hell, these would be light in comparison to the gravity of her sins. With this in mind, the sorrow she suffers dissolves like salt in this water of tears. Thus, due to the contrition she has gained from this hidden spring, she remains with great interior contentment.

SORROWS ARE TAKEN FOR PENANCE

29. One who weeps heartily for his sins finds joy in the austerity and penance of the hair shirt, the discipline, and the fasts, because it seems to him that he is making satisfaction for his sins in this life and avoiding eternal punishment.[17] Thus, by accepting humiliations, contempt, and tribulations as penance for the sins of his past life—and even having his confessor give them as penance, naming them in particular, when he gives absolution—he experiences great relief, and the sorrow and bitterness of heart that they have caused is taken away. This verse is apropos: "Before I was humbled I went astray, but now I keep your words"

[Ps 119(118):67]. In other words, I was already a sinner when they knocked me down, and thus, to reform my life, I sought to keep the commandments of God.

MEDITATE ON THE MISERERE PSALM IN TIMES OF AFFLICTION

30. The psalm, *Miserere Mei,*[18] is a great consolation in times of trial fortified with penance. To tell the truth, there is no one so just and holy who doesn't have some faults and failures, from which his adversaries take occasion to persecute and humiliate him. And these faults, however little they might be, are magnified and give him pain, seeing that they are the root cause of his sorrows. From this is born the desire for purity of soul and other ineffable delights, gifts, and spiritual goods.

True Confidence in God Alone

NO CONFIDENCE IN MEN

31. In my tribulations, I have experienced being forsaken by all my relatives and friends. Some persuaded themselves that what was said about me was true, holding it to be more likely that I had been negligent and was at fault—if not in everything, at least in part—before condemning as partisan such holy men as those who persecuted me. Others shrugged their shoulders and abandoned me, not daring to take my part in order to avoid becoming my accomplices. And many who had received good deeds from me, forgetting these benefits, which is no small sorrow, supported whoever won.

FROM THE LOSS OF CONFIDENCE IN CREATURES IS BORN CONFIDENCE IN GOD

32. As a result, I experienced a loss of confidence in all mortals, however powerful they were, according to these words: "Put no trust in princes, nor in a son of man, in whom there is no salvation" [Ps 146(145):3] and "Cursed is the man who trusts in man, who seeks his strength in flesh" [Jer 17:5]. I raised my eyes to God since, being infinite, all powerful, good, wise, and merciful, He alone was enough to help me

and draw me out of snares and dangers. He alone was able to pardon my sins from which I understood all these sorrows and troubles came. And thus I consoled myself with this verse: "In You, O Lord, I have hoped; let me never be put to confusion" [Ps 31(30):2; 71(70):1], and I remembered a lovely book written by my father called *Speravi, sive de falsa et vera spe* [I have hoped, or concerning false and true hope], which deals with this subject.[19]

F: LIVING FAITH AND FORTITUDE

Living Faith

33. There are so many places in Sacred Scripture, as well as in the words God has given to the saints who have suffered and in those interior words He gives to suffering souls, in which He promises glory, grace, virtue, spirit, consolations, and spiritual blessings to those who bear their troubles patiently. If the sufferer is unbelieving, he would think that these words of God are not true; but if he has faith, however little it might be, he would think that the heavens and the earth would fail before the words of God would fail, and he would have to be very happy and content, seeing that God is leading him by the sure road of the cross. "Narrow is the way that leads to life" [Mt 7:14] and although it is narrow and rocky, it has eternal life for its destination.[20]

THE BOOK OF JOB IS OF GREAT CONSOLATION

34. It is thus a great help and relief in times of trial to read books, especially the book of Job and its commentaries and many others that deal with this subject. In them, as in a mirror, the soul sees her tribulations, both exterior and interior. So it is that when someone asks God for His word, if he wants to be just and true in his request and that no one judge him otherwise, he prays God to give it according to these words: "You are just when You pass sentence on me, vindicated when You give judgment" [Ps 51(50):6].

Strength in Silence and Hope

35. Not in vain is it said, "In silence and hope will be your strength" [Is 30:15]. There is no better help in tribulations than to keep quiet, according to these words of David: "Dumb and silent before the wicked, I refrained from any speech; but my sorrow increased" [Ps 39(38):3]. As one who says, "When they persecuted me, I put a lock on my tongue and like a mute I said nothing," I humbled myself and did not go around telling people I was innocent, and I renewed my sorrow for past sins.[21]

36. If the persecution is real, especially if those who are persecuting are holy and known to be motivated by zeal, it is not possible to say anything. If you wish to excuse them by saying they have a reason for what they do, deceiving yourself with a false humility that says, "I am not greatly injured," then you defame yourself. To defame a public man with a lie is not without guilt. This is what David seems to mean in these words: "Had Your law not been my delight, I should have perished in my afflictions" [Ps 119(118):92]. That is to say, "Lord, had I not meditated on Your law in order to keep it, I would be lost in my humility," or, rather, in what I thought was humility. If, on the other hand, you were to speak on your own behalf and say that false testimony was raised against you, you would remain full of scruples that you had defamed your brothers and that they would be held by others to be prejudiced and malicious. Thus, there is nothing more honorable than to keep quiet, dissimulate, and not desire to discuss the matter with your friends but turn conversation to other things. With the ones who persecute you, there is nothing better than to keep quiet, because if you say they are right, you give them a chance to persecute you more. If you want to defend and excuse yourself with more arguments (how easily wounded souls are angered), you might end up saying something more severe from which nothing good would follow but only more harm. Thus, if my father were to come at me with a drawn sword, there is no greater defense than to turn my back on him and flee. If I strike him, I strike my own father. If I let him strike me, I am wounded. Likewise, when a persecutor attacks me with words,

there is no better recourse than to keep quiet and turn away, and even to leave the place where they live and flee to a place where there is no occasion to argue about the matter.

37. When my persecutions were most acute, it was a great relief to see myself in Barbary [Tunis and environs] and, after I came back from there, to stay in other places where there was no one to argue with me about these things, hoping only in God in whom is my strength.

R: RESIGNATION AND RENUNCIATION

Resignation to the Will of God

PURPOSE OF PRAYER

38. The purpose of all prayer and spiritual exercises is to conform the soul to the divine will, to love what God loves and to hate what God hates. And in nothing else is this resignation tested so much as in afflictions and persecutions, especially those that are very serious and most contrary to our own will.

WORDS OF RESIGNATION

39. And so, when sorrows oppress, contradictions torment, and the heart becomes embittered, there is no better remedy than to say to the Lord, "Your will be done" [Mt 26:42, NAB]. Although you might feel the cross very much and it seems you do not have the patience to bear such a great persecution, say as best as you can, "Lord, if it is possible, let me not drink this bitter chalice, yet not my will but Yours be done" [Mt 26:39].

40. Sometimes a person is so afflicted, disconsolate, impatient, and angry that all interior and exterior doors are closed to any consolation. This is because the feelings rebel and the will is in opposition. And, what afflicts most, the understanding is so blind, the spirit so disturbed, and the memory so forgetful of God and of the reasons that could give some consolation that no comfort is to be found. Thus, insofar as you

are able, you must make an effort, and even though it seems you say it only with your mouth, you must repeat often: "Your will be done."

41. One night, when my most serious troubles began, I saw the design of the whole cloth that was to be woven over many years. Unable to sleep because of the anguish this caused, I put my hand out like a shield and repeated this verse: "Glory to the Father and to the Son and to the Holy Spirit," and made an act of resignation. Since then, I have been accustomed to say the same verse in times of great difficulties, with the result that in a short time I would find myself free of anxiety and with ineffable light and consolation. What seemed like a serpent to me was turned into a staff, and I knew it was best for my well-being because it was the will of God. It was a consolation for me to see that even before that tribulation came,[22] God had planned and ordained it for my good, just as the tribulations of Job were ordained by God and planned with Satan in the tribunal of heaven [see Job 1:6–12]. When a sick person is told to take a purgative for his good, knowing that the doctor is competent and loves him and has consulted with other excellent doctors so that there is no chance of making a mistake, he consoles himself and endures the bitterness. Likewise, when tribulations come, ordained by the will of God as decided in the divine consistory of the Father, the Son, and the Holy Spirit, and you say, "Glory to the Father and to the Son and to the Holy Spirit," you console yourself, seeing that the divine will is being fulfilled.

WORDS OF CONSOLATION WHEN THE FRUIT OF TALENTS IS TAKEN AWAY

42. It is true that sometimes it doesn't seem to be the will of God but rather a scheme of the devil when a man who has a wealth of learning, a good reputation, and so forth for winning souls for God and is in the best years of his life, can be defamed, stuck in a corner, and deprived of the fruit he could produce for the church. But it is a consolation to know that everything comes from God, that He wills it, and that He knows why such fruit is impeded.[23] I would console myself with the retort of

a stubborn servant who, when her master was whipping her, would say, "Have at it. You are spending from your own house!" In sum, there is nothing so afflictive as to see the labor of many years of study, undertaken to be able to do some good, go to waste. How well this will be seen on the Day of Judgment, when this sentiment will be manifested by those who had great constancy. "Then shall the just one with great assurance confront his oppressors who set at naught his labors"[Wis 5.1, NAB].

CONSOLATION IS IN THE EXERCISE OF LOVE ALONE

43. It is also a consolation for a person in this situation to resolve not to make any other exercise than the love of God, knowing that if he were to spend the whole day occupied in such love and contemplation, with no time given to preaching or confessing, nothing would be lost. On the contrary, he would gain, whereas in exterior exercises, he would lose.[24] For what profit would there be to gain the whole world if your soul were to suffer the loss of love? It is clearly seen, when the Lord gives light after some struggle, that nothing gives God more pleasure than for the soul to suffer trials and carry the cross with patience. Charity, as the apostle says, does not consist in speaking in tongues of men or angels, in having visions, revelations, or prophecies, in performing miracles, in giving many alms, or in doing great penances, even though you might give your body to be burned; really, all this is nothing and worth nothing without charity. Rather, charity consists in having patience and benignity, and not becoming irritated with those who persecute you. "Charity is patient, charity is kind. It is not jealous, it is not pompous," and so on [1 Cor 13:4].

WORDS OF A SERVANT OF GOD WHO DESIRED THE CROSS

44. I recall a great servant of God who on one occasion, desirous of giving much pleasure to His Divine Majesty, said to Him, "Lord, I know well that in nothing could I give You greater pleasure than to suffer for You. Give me some work in which I can suffer." And He gave

her the most extraordinary and insufferable bodily pains that you can imagine. The doctors were unable to understand the illness in order to cure her because it was given by the hand of God. Another religious of ours, whom I will not name because I do not know if she is deceased yet, had the same desire to suffer, so Jesus Christ (whom she saw visibly going through the cloister) placed the crown of thorns on her head, pressing it down with His most blessed hands. It left her with an incredible pain in the head but with so much consolation, knowing that it was from the hand of God, that she was disconsolate when she was without it.[25]

Renunciation of All the Goods of This World

45. Let's say a rich man has a cupboard of Venetian glass. Some of the pieces that he greatly valued break, and he feels their loss very much. Seeing that all the glassware is fragile and that some breaking every day would cause him grief, he throws them all away. From then on, he uses vessels of gold and silver instead of glassware. Likewise, a person who sees he has lost his honor, which at best is a glass cup that can be esteemed only in this life, throws away all the temporal things that could give pleasure, holding them as dung and trash compared to the spiritual and eternal riches that Christ gives [see Phil 3:8]. He is truly determined not to make any account of the benevolence of friends, human favors, honors, esteem, dignities, and so forth, but to place all his attention on the love of God and on the virtues, which are like vessels of gold and silver and are eternally durable. Thus, what formerly gave him pleasure—like seeing himself esteemed and praised or given some ecclesiastical dignity—after experiencing how little it is worth and how quickly it ends, now annoys, disgusts, and bores him, and he remains consoled with what he has within his heart, which no one can take from him.

I: JUSTICE AND JUDGMENT, AND IMITATION OF CHRIST

Justice and Judgment

46. "I have done judgment and justice; give me not up to them that slander me," says David [Ps 119(118):121], as if to say, "Lord, may I not be given over to the hands of those who calumniate me, whether they be devils, who by means of persecutions want to take away the peace and quiet of my soul, or men acting under the cover of zeal or, rather, who want to slander me because I render judgment and justice."

47. Rendering judgment, to be precise, is to examine your conscience with as much rigor and care as the Eternal King will examine it on the Day of Judgment. According to what the prophet Micah says, "What is good has been explained to you, O man; this is what the Lord asks of you, only this: to act justly, to love tenderly, and to walk humbly with your God" [Mic 6:8], three things please God very much: to render justice, to love mercy, and to walk with attentiveness in the divine presence. When the winds of tribulation blow, it is easy for a person to fall into some faults, especially anger, impatience, rash judgment, and other similar things, that, with the blindness of passion, do not let him see. But in considering and examining them, he does justice to himself when he chastises those same offenses with the pain of the tribulation he suffers; this is an admirable defense for suffering it well.

48. Justice is to pay what is owed. It is just that whoever has become proud pays by being brought low; whoever has slandered others pays by being slandered; and finally, whoever has followed his appetites and desires has to pay with afflictions and persecutions. Thus, just as one who pays his debts is relieved—although it might be difficult to hand over the money—so one who suffers interior and exterior crosses in this life is relieved because he is paying something of what he owes to God, to his neighbor, and to himself.

Imitation of Christ

49. What troubles and sorrows can we have that Christ has not suffered much more and to a much higher degree? Our whole consolation is Christ, since as high priest He was tried and afflicted in every way and thus sympathizes with our adversities [see Heb 4:15]. Therefore, when we suffer, let us fix our eyes on our Captain and on His wounds suffered for our sake, and let us continue to deny ourselves and take up our cross, since in order to be healed of the bites of the poisonous serpents that torment us, there is no better remedy than to look at the bronze serpent, which is Christ crucified [see Num 21:6–9; Jn 3:14].

DESIRE FOR MARTYRDOM

50. In pondering this, I have experienced in my soul such a great urge and desire to suffer and die for Christ that, if the desire were not tempered with the difficulties I was already suffering, this urge alone would have been enough to cause me to die. But with the consolation of suffering something for Christ by means of these persecutions, with which the urge to suffer was alleviated, a great help was given in my tribulations. What before were thorns and thistles become flowers and apples, with which the soul, fainting with love and the desire to suffer for Christ, is sustained [see Song 2:5].

C: CONSIDERATION AND COUNSEL

Considerations

51. Reflection, meditation, reading good books, and the consolation of good friends are a great comfort and support against the harm that tribulations can cause.[26] The most important things to consider are these:

SUFFERINGS OF THE SAINTS

52. Consider the extent to which the saints suffered and the torments they endured so as to be sure of receiving the palm of martyrdom, and

that we have not shed blood as they shed blood: "In your struggles you have not yet resisted to the point of shedding blood" [Heb 12:4].

REMEMBRANCE OF DEATH

53. The remembrance of death is of great importance because when trials are most difficult, the soul, oppressed and realizing that everything finally ends with death, feels strengthened by having suffered and having learned to suffer.

JUDGMENT

54. In the face of calumnies and false testimonies, since here on earth the rights and views of the persecuted are not heard, the soul is consoled that on the Day of Judgment the truth will be manifested before the whole world, and her adversaries will be summoned before the Supreme Judge. For this reason, she is not afflicted at seeing that men judge contrary to the truth.

GLORY

55. The consideration of glory [heaven] is no less fruitful, considering that "what we suffer in this life can never be compared with the glory as yet unrevealed" [Rom 8:18]. Knowing that no one will be crowned except one who has fought fairly [see 2 Tim 2:5], the soul is encouraged to fight in times of trial and not yield to impatience. As the laborer likes to sweat, the soldier to fight, and the merchant to sail and brave the storms, each with the hope for the fruit, the victory, or the riches that he seeks, so those who are persecuted and suffering like afflictions and troubles, hoping that for such a brief little thing, there will be a great eternal reward. A bride is not aggravated by the labor of bathing and changing her clothes so that she will be clean and beautifully attired for the wedding. Likewise, knowing that nothing defiled will enter the city of the celestial Jerusalem, the soul bears the reproaches of men and other tribulations with patience [see Rev 21:27]. With a clean and purified conscience, the soul, being of fine

gold and silver, is carried as a vessel of honor to the great table of the wedding feast of the celestial Lamb.

HELL

56. I have experienced that reflecting on the pains of hell and purgatory is very important for being fortified in adverse events. The Lord permitted that at the time I was captured and stripped naked in a Turkish *galeota*,[27] condemned I thought to perpetual rowing, one of the captives rowing there gave me a book by Denis the Carthusian (which describes the Four Last Things [*The Imitation of Christ*]), which he took from a Turk who had robbed it with many other books from a Christian vessel. Opening it, the first thing that appeared and that I read was about the pains of hell. I continued reading as the ship sailed along, meditating slowly on what was written there. From this meditation, the life I was then suffering did not seem so difficult, seeing how different captivity and the galley are from hell.

57. There are many other considerations that are helpful, but these are the main ones.

Counsel

THE SOUL IN TRIBULATION IS BLIND

58. When the soul is undergoing a real tribulation, the greatest harm is blindness because it seems that the reason is clouded and the understanding lacks light. With the blows of affliction come impulses for vengeance and for doing things so contrary to what is appropriate that if the soul were to carry out what she wishes, she would find herself very deceived and either falling into sin or suffering greater persecutions.

59. What I have experienced to be a great help is that a person should not trust himself but be determined to do nothing according to his own counsel or pleasure. The reasons for vengeance—made

more acute by passion—are so compelling that he thinks no one else will have the light in that affair as he himself has, whose honor and very being are at stake; however, it is better to forbear the urge for revenge. Choose three friends with whom to take counsel about what to do (I am speaking of serious things), and do not make up your mind without the advice of all three. One of these friends should be the holiest you can find, whom you put in charge of dealing with God about your affair to see what might be most pleasing to His Divine Majesty; the second should be learned so that he can advise you in accordance with sound learning; and the third should be a man of discretion and experience. If you follow the opinion and advice of these three friends, God will help you, and your affairs will turn out well.

60. **Cyril:** *I'm glad to have heard about these twelve aids, shields, and defenses of the soul in times of tribulation from the mouth of a surgeon who has been so cut up himself.*[28] *But I wish you would tell me more about the aids, even if they don't begin with the six letters of the shield. Suffering is so common that such aids and defenses are among the most important things to know about in this life.*

SACRED SCRIPTURE, A GREAT PROTECTION

61. **Anastasius:** I don't find any shield better than the words of the divine letters, which are sharp arrows of the all-powerful God to liberate the soul from evil lips and lying tongues [see Ps 120(119):2, 4]. If I were to tell you all the places in the divine Scriptures that have benefited me, I would have to write a big book. But without leaving these same six letters of the shield, I want to remind you of six psalms of David. If you meditate on them slowly, you will find a great refuge in times of tribulation. And take my advice: when you see yourself afflicted, say them with attentiveness. They are as follows:

Psalms of David for Times of Tribulation

62. **A** = "I cried to the Lord in my distress and He heard me . . ." [*Ad Dominum cum tribularer clamavi, (et) exaudivit me*] [Ps 120(119)].[29]

C = "When I called, God heard me . . ." [*Cum invocarem exaudivit me Deus*] [Ps 4].

F = "His foundations upon the holy mountains . . ." [*Fundamenta eius in montibus sanctis*] [Ps 87(86)].

R = "Be good to Your servant, that I may live . . ." [*Retribue servo tuo, vivifica me*] [Ps 119(118):17].

I = "In You, Lord, I place my hope . . ." [*In te, Domine, speravi*] [Ps 7].

C = "Give thanks to the Lord for He is good . . ." [*Confitemini Domino quoniam bonus*] [Ps 106(105)] or "I will praise You, God, with all my heart . . ." [*Confitebor tibi, Deus, in toto corde meo*] [Ps 9].

63. If you meditate on them very well, you will find the fruit you seek. Not in vain does St. Cyprian say that in this world we would miss the psalms of David more than the sun that shines upon us. Just as the light of the visible sun is such a consolation and relief for the afflicted, so the light of the psalter is of no less benefit to those experiencing tribulations.

Twelfth Dialogue: Writings

Gracián recounts his studies from the time he began them and tells of the books he has written, those that have been printed or are ready to be printed and those that can easily be finished, and the great number of other things he has already written for the benefit of souls. He explains why he wrote this devotional material and what the twelve stars of the shield mean.

1. **Cyril:** *I would like to know the significance of the twelve stars that are above the six letters you have just explained.*

2. **Anastasius:** In addition to being a part of the shield of Carmel, for there are twelve stars on the crown of the Virgin Mary of whom St. John speaks in the Apocalypse [see Rev 12:1],[1] they remind me of some books I have written: twelve principal ones that I have had printed, a few others that could soon be printed, and an equal number begun that can easily be finished.

3. **Cyril:** *I'd like to know about your studies and writings and the light you have given by your learning, starting from the beginning.*

Gracián gives an account of his studies

4. **Anastasius:** I began to study at ten years of age. I completed grammar, rhetoric, and Greek at fifteen. At nineteen, I received my master's

degree, having heard the four subjects of the arts, and then took theology until I was twenty-three. I spent the four remaining years, until I was twenty-seven, studying theology and making the nine acts that are required in Alcalá for the doctorate.[2] That same year, I entered religious life. Because of the many things I had to do in founding and governing monasteries and the continual preaching, confessing, and other ministries, I could study but little. But never, little or much, did I leave off studying.

MOTIVE FOR WRITING SPIRITUAL BOOKS; FRAY FRANCISCO DE JESÚS

5. One day when I was in Seville and wondering whether I should write something for the benefit of souls and the light of the Church, Fray Francisco de Jesús, "el Indigno,"[3] a man of great spirituality as I will later relate,[4] was coming out of mental prayer. With great fervor and his face ablaze, he said to me, "Our Lord Jesus Christ told me to tell you for Him that you should write books for the good of souls," or something along those lines. Not paying as much attention to his revelation as to my own desire to write and not hide the talent that the Lord had given to me, I made up my mind to write.

6. Going over in my mind and with the Lord which teachings would be more fruitful for souls and more pleasing to Christ the Master who is our good, I thought that writing on scholastic theology did not suit me, although I had attended many classes on it, had done well, and had many papers on it. It is better for those who write such books to be actually studying and discussing it in the schools, and at that time works of very learned scholastics were being published. It also didn't seem necessary to write about positive theology or commentaries on Sacred Scripture because whoever might be occupied in reading my books would use their time and intelligence better by reading those of the sacred doctors.

TRUE SERMONS

7. It was never my intention to write or print sermons; although I have some folders of them, they are not polished. In my opinion, a true sermon comes from the desire to benefit others and is given according to the time and the persons to whom you preach. I never cared for sermons printed in the vernacular; any worth reading are those written by the saints. To write biographies and historical narrations as others have done didn't seem like a good use of my time. As for logic and metaphysics, I had some good papers from past studies, but it seemed I would be going backward to occupy myself in that.

8. I decided to write about mystical theology and things of devotion and prayer and the interior dealings between the soul and God because this material would be of greater benefit to my own soul. Due to my practice of mental prayer, my dealings with the spirit of Mother Teresa of Jesus, and having examined many spiritual souls, I had more experience in this area. I had also read some books on it.

BOOKS PRINTED UP TO THE YEAR 1610

9. Thus, up to now, I have printed the following books:[5]

- *Lámpara encendida* [*The Burning Lamp*],[6] which deals with perfection and vocal and mental prayer. I first printed it in Pamplona and later in Naples in Spanish and Italian. Finally, with additions and corrections, it was printed in Brussels.
- *Josefina* [Joseph],[7] concerning the excellent characteristics of the glorious St. Joseph, printed in Rome in Spanish and Italian, and later in Barcelona, Madrid, and Brussels. This book has done much good for souls because it explains the spirit of this saint in order to increase devotion to him, and because many preachers have found material in it for preaching his praises.
- *Tratado del Jubileo del Año Santo* [Treatise for the jubilee of the holy year], in Italian. Printed in Rome in the year 1599, it was

useful at that time because it dealt with the matter of indulgences, and so forth.

- *De la disciplina regular* [Concerning the regular discipline]. This is printed in Italian and has been very useful because it is read in the refectory of many monasteries in Italy. My purpose in explaining the Carmelite Rule of St. Albert was to give light on how to keep the rules of all religious orders with spirit.
- *Dilucidario del verdadero espíritu* [Elucidation of the true spirit]. This was printed in Madrid and later in Brussels, although I wrote it in Rome, with the intention of explaining the true nature of prayer and the deceptions that come from false spirits, and taking the opportunity to defend the doctrine of Mother Teresa of Jesus.

10. These books are somewhat large, but those that follow are not so voluminous.

- *Arbol prodigioso* [The prodigious tree], about twelve ways to pray the rosary. I printed it in Florence in the Italian language. *Cerco espiritual* [Spiritual fortification], a little book about the forty temptations of the world, the devil, and the flesh, printed in Rome in Spanish.
- *Estímulo o celo de la propagación de la fe* [Stimulus or zeal for the propagation of the faith], which is meant to give fervor to those who go to convert gentiles and heretics. I first printed it in Seville. Later it was printed in Naples and finally in Brussels for a congregation that Monsignor Vives began in Rome.[8]
- *Redención de cautivos* [Redemption of captives]. Printed in Rome to be given to Pope Clement VIII and to inspire the devout faithful to undertake works of mercy on behalf of captives.
- *Mística teología* [Mystical theology], a collection of the writings of St. Bonaventure, with an *Itinerario de la perfección* [Itinerary of perfection], which I added to help explain his doctrine. It was first printed in Madrid and later in Brussels.

- *Vida en Cristo* [Life in Christ], concerning the true perfection of a soul in divine union. This was written against a perverse doctrine regarding union that was causing harm in Flanders and France.
- *El devoto peregrino* [The devout pilgrim], a little book on how to gain the indulgence of the Jubilee of the holy year, with material about confession and Communion.
- A table called *Reloj de Acab* [The clock of Acab], and another, *Suma de los siete ángeles príncipes* [Summa of the seven angel princes], and other tables and little works that were able to be included. It was printed in Rome and in Flanders, in the city of Brussels.

11. Books that are ready to be printed:

- "Jubileo del Año Santo" [Jubilee of the Holy Year], in Spanish, which will not be printed because the time of the jubilee has passed. It is enough to have printed it in Italian.
- "Disciplina regular" [Regular discipline], written in Spanish. It has three parts and would be of great fruit in Spain if it were printed, as is the Italian edition in Italy.
- "Flores Carmeli" [Flowers of Carmel], which is a compendium of the origin and antiquity of the Carmelite Order and the foundation of the Discalced.
- "Consuelos y desconsuelos interiores de las almas atribuladas" [Interior consolations and desolations of souls in tribulation], which explains the teaching of the Apocalypse of St. John. This is a book written from personal experience, which can give much light to souls who suffer tribulations.
- "Sufragio de las ánimas de purgatorio" [Suffrage concerning souls in purgatory]. This is with the printer, and it would be necessary to polish it up a little for it to bear fruit in Spain, as the Italian version has done in Italy.
- "Opúsculos" [Minor works], which includes "De la Guerra, Cifra y Anatomía" [Concerning war, codes, and anatomy], and some

"Cartas a príncipes y señores" [Letters to princes and lords], and other things.

- "Excelencia y valor de nuestra santa fe católica" [Excellence and value of our holy Catholic faith], divided into three parts. These are dialogues about things that happened in Barbary, written in the same dialect spoken by the slaves. Although it would be entertaining, it won't be printed because of its less than serious style.
- "El soldado católico" [The Catholic soldier].[9] This book is made up of twenty colloquies that deal with the excellence of our holy faith and the abomination of the Lutheran heresy, and explains that it is not good to dispute with heretics.
- "De la ceguedad de Babilonia" [Concerning the blindness of Babylon], written against the most recent heresy of our times, namely, heretical hypocrisy. It would be very beneficial if it were printed.
- "De potestate Papae" [Concerning the authority of the pope], written against the book of Don Fernando de las Infantas.

12. Other books that are handwritten and could easily be finished and prepared for printing (they should not be printed otherwise):

- "Vida y doctrina de Nuestra Señora" [Life and teaching of our Lady], in Spanish and Latin, a collection of the words spoken by the most holy Virgin that are found in books of revelations she has made to her devotees.
- A book comprised of diverse minor works about the Order of Carmel, such as "Antiquitas Carmelitana" [Carmelite antiquities], "Suma del Libro de Juan patriarca cuarenta y cuatro de Jerusalén" [Summa of the book of John, the forty-fourth patriarch of Jerusalem], "Exposición de la Regla por Juan Soret" [Exposition of the Rule by John Soreth], "Sermón del título de la Religión" [Sermon on the title of the order], "Cronología Carmelitana" [Carmelite chronology], and "Reforma de Religiones" [Reform of religious orders].

- Another book of minor works that could be printed is a collection of "Los cinco talentos" [The five talents], "La hipocresía contra las hijas del amor proprio" [Hypocrisy of the daughters of self-love], "Consejos breves" [Brief counsels], "Sumario de devociones" [Summary of devotions], "Alas de águila" [Wings of the eagle], "Jeroglífica sacra" [Sacred hieroglyphy], "Discurso de la disciplina de bondad" [Discourse on the practice of goodness], *Arbol prodigioso* [The prodigious tree], "Pater noster" [The Our Father], and so forth. All of these are in a folder entitled number 14.
- There is also a folder, number 15, from which these could be taken out and printed: "Vida de san Angel carmelita" [The life of the Carmelite St. Angelus], "[Vida] de san Andrés" [The life of St. Andrew], "Remedio de tribulaciones" [Remedy for tribulations], and "Copias de cartas" [Copies of letters]. All of these books are written on folio paper.
- And in notebooks, there are others that can be printed after polishing a few things, including the minor works called "Collationes Patrum" [Collations of the fathers], "Corona de doce estrellas" [Crown of twelve stars], "Altar de Elías" [Altar of Elijah], "Arado de Eliseo" [Plough of Elisha], "Matrimonio espiritual entre el libre albedrío y su pasión" [Spiritual marriage between free will and its passion], "Pastor bueno" [The Good Shepherd], and "Torre de fortaleza de Sión" [The fortified tower of Zion], which deals with the state of religious orders. All of these are in the notebook marked number 8.
- In number 9 there are "Lugares comunes de Concilios" [Common themes of councils], "Noviciado de los Carmelitas Descalzos" [Novitiate of the Discalced Carmelites], "Tratado de la melancolía" [*Treatise on Melancholy*], also known as "el Cerro" [The hill],[10] "Octavas" [Octaves], "Rimas de la Orden" [Rhymes of the order], and other similar things.

- In number 10: "Diálogos entre Anastasio y Eliseo" [Dialogues between Anastasius and Elisha], concerning perfection, "Tratado de la oración mental" [Treatise on mental prayer], "Tronos excelsos" [Thrones on high], "Carro de Elías" [Elijah's chariot], "Tratado del relajado contra el Cerro" [Treatise on laxity against the hill], "Diálogos entre Angela y Eliseo" [Dialogues between Angela and Elisha];[11] "Examen de espíritus" [Examination of spirits], which is divided into three parts and can easily be finished and printed, "Recopilación de los Estatutos de la Orden por lugares comunes" [Compilation of the statutes of the order according to common themes].

Thirteenth Dialogue: FOUNDATIONS

GRACIÁN BEGINS TO RECOUNT THE FRUIT OF HIS LABORS AND TELLS OF THE FOUNDATIONS OF THE MONASTERIES OF THE DISCALCED CARMELITES THAT HE DEALT WITH WHILE HE WAS THE SUPERIOR OF THAT ORDER AS WELL AS AFTER HE LEFT IT. HE REFERS BRIEFLY TO MANY PARTICULAR THINGS THAT HAPPENED AT THE TIME OF THESE FOUNDATIONS AND NAMES SOME OF THE PRINCIPAL PERSONS WHO HELPED IN THEM AS WELL AS SOME OF THE MOST CELEBRATED NUNS AND FRIARS OF THOSE BEGINNINGS.

1. **Cyril:** *Truthful is the Lord and His words, which say that "if the grain of wheat falls to the ground and dies, it will give much fruit" [Jn 12:24]. I wish to know what fruit and good works have followed the many trials, contradictions, tribulations, and affronts that befell you and divested you of the honor, reputation, peace, and status of your person.*

2. **Anastasius:** The words of the same Lord are also true when He says, "A bad tree cannot give good fruit" [Mt 7:18]. Well then, what good works do you expect from a soul as bad as mine, of whom can be said what the Lord says about His vineyard through Isaiah: "He hoped it might give grapes, but it gave only wild grapes" [Is 5:2, 4]. These grapes that do not ripen are called dog grapes and are not good for eating or for wine. Of what use is the salt that has lost its flavor, as I have, except to be thrown out and expelled from a perfect order and trampled underfoot by the entire world? [see Mt 5:13].

GOOD FRUIT IS OF GOD

3. **Cyril:** *We know very well that the Holy Scriptures also say that our good works are done in us by God and that He alone is the help of Israel, being of itself perdition. Of ourselves, we do not give good fruit—as a council of the Church says—but only sin and falsehood. I am now asking you what good works and fruit God has brought forth in using you as an instrument. What I mean is, in what have you occupied yourself during your lifetime? In recounting these good works to me, three good fruits or ends will follow.*

THREE GOOD ENDS IN RECOUNTING GOOD WORKS

4. *The first is the glory of God, because His power, wisdom, and goodness are brought into view in His use of so vile, impertinent, and bad an instrument as you are to do such great, good, and profitable things, and because "he delights not in the strength of horses or the fleetness of men" [Ps 147(146):10]. God does not need your strength, wisdom, or goodness for His good works.*

5. *The second is to give encouragement to miserable sinners so that they do not feel frightened, discouraged, or crushed in the service of God, knowing that by such despicable and lowly men He can do great works. And it will be a great pleasure for me and many others to know the journey of your life and the good you have done in the church. Since I have been distressed hearing of your troubles, it is not good for you to keep quiet about the good works and mercy of God; rather, you should sing of them eternally, as David says.*[1] *If you die, there will not be anyone to ask about the many things you can tell me now. If you keep silent, you will carry them with you to the grave.*

6. *The third and principal end is for your own humiliation, so that you can confess that if God had given the means for work to another man and had placed him in the affairs in which you have been placed, how much he would have accomplished, whereas you, like a bad steward, have ruined the house of your Lord.*

OCCUPATIONS IS A BETTER NAME FOR GOOD WORKS

7. **Anastasius:** You have convinced me that I should recount them but with the understanding that we call them not good works or fruits but rather occupations.

BOOK OF THE FOUNDATIONS OF THE DISCALCED

8. I could tell you about them in three ways: The first way is going in the order of the years, months, and days in which they occurred. Although this would be somewhat interesting, it would be too hard on my memory. I have already written a large book, *Fundaciones de los Carmelitas Descalzos* [Foundations of the Discalced Carmelite Friars],[2] which you can read, where I proceed chronologically.

9. I could also proceed by dividing my life into three ages: the first, from the time I received the habit of the Discalced until the death of St. Teresa of Jesus; the second, from her death until I saw myself without the habit; and third, from then until now. I say three ages because from the time I was born until I was twenty-seven, when I finished my studies and entered the order, although there are some things to tell, they are not so much to our purpose here.

10. It seems to me that it would be better to follow this order: first, to recount briefly what I remember about the foundations of the monasteries of the Discalced friars in which I was occupied, in case that book doesn't come into your hands; second, a few of the foundations and reforms of other orders in which I helped; and third, serious and important business affairs that have come my way since I entered the order until now.

CONCERNING THE ORIGINS OF THE FOUNDATIONS OF THE DISCALCED CARMELITE MONASTERIES OF MANCERA, PASTRANA, ALCALÁ, AND ALTOMIRA, AND SOME OF THE RELIGIOUS OF THAT TIME

11. The first monastery I founded was that of Seville, for when I entered the order, the monasteries of Mancera, Pastrana, Altomira and the College of Alcalá were already founded.[3]

12. **Cyril:** *Tell me, I beg you, so that we can proceed on a more solid foundation, how did these four monasteries begin, even though you did not found them yourself?*

MOTHER TERESA OF JESUS, FOUNDRESS

13. Mother Teresa of Jesus—rightly called foundress of the Discalced friars and nuns[4]—having founded some monasteries of nuns, thought they would not go forward if there were not Discalced friars of the same order to assist them. Therefore, she obtained permission from General Fray Juan Bautista de Ravena to found two monasteries of friars.[5]

FRAY ANTONIO DE JESÚS, THE FIRST DISCALCED; FRAY JOHN OF THE CROSS

14. She persuaded two of the holiest and most spiritual Calced fathers to become Discalced: Fray Antonio de Jesús Heredia, who entered religious life very young and was a sincere and good religious all his life, and Fray John of the Cross. John of the Cross's perfection and spirit was very great, as is seen from the brief of Pope Clement VIII granting permission to transfer his body from Granada to Segovia, which is practically a beatification.[6]

DURUELO, FIRST FOUNDATION OF THE DISCALCED FRIARS

15. She showed them the way to live, following the prayer, recollection, austerity, and so on, that the nuns followed. And she negotiated with a widow of Salamanca to donate in her little town, called Duruelo, an old house that served as a hay barn. Here they made a church, a choir, and an office as best they could. This was the flowing spring and origin of all the Discalced Carmelite friars.

16. **Cyril:** *The birth of this order in a stable is not lacking in mystery. St. Francis was born in a stable,*[7] *and the founder of the Christian religion, Jesus Christ, was born in a poor stable, lying in a manger among the animals.*

MANCERA AND THE MIRACULOUS WELL

17. **Anastasius:** Later, Don Luis de Toledo gave them a hermitage—which had a beautiful image of our Lady—in his town of Mancera so that the monastery of Duruelo could be moved there. Since the lack of water was a serious concern for the religious, God showed where it was when He directed Father Fray Antonio to dig a well, a spring of very good water. The monastery of Mancera continued for a long time, and many good subjects received the habit there.

18. Prince Ruy Gómez de Silva wanted to establish a monastery of Discalced Carmelite nuns in the town of Pastrana.[8] Mother Teresa went to Madrid in order to go there and make this foundation. She was staying in the [Franciscan] monastery of Los Ángeles in the company of Doña Leonor Mascareñas—a very holy woman who had once been the governess of King Philip II[9]—when two hermits, Ambrosio Mariano and Juan de la Miseria, came to talk to her there.

FRAY AMBROSIO MARIANO, THE FIRST DISCALCED THAT HAD NEVER BEEN A CALCED; THE HERMITS OF TARDÓN

19. Father Mariano told her of their plans to go to Rome to ask the pope to confirm an eremitical style of life that some servants of God were following in the mountains of Tardón, next to Córdoba, where they observed much prayer, fasting, and austerity, and lived by the work of their hands. Mother Teresa told him that, if he liked, she would show him that same manner of life, confirmed by many popes; then she gave him the Primitive Rule of Carmel to read, which she carried in her breviary. Reading it, the father understood that this was the same kind of life for which he wanted to go to Rome. So, she revealed to him her plans for a foundation of Discalced Carmelite friars and persuaded him to go to Pastrana to found a monastery of friars, since she was going there herself to found a monastery of nuns.

SAN PEDRO

20. In this way, with Prince Ruy Gómez helping with the temporal needs, the second monastery was founded. Pastrana is, and has been, the principal seminary of the order.[10] For the site, Father Mariano chose a hill or mountain away from the town, where there was a hermitage called San Pedro. The place, being very austere and spiritual, gave the sense of the eremitical life.

VISION OF JUAN JIMÉNEZ

21. This foundation was not lacking in mystery. More than forty years before it was made, a laborer of the town, named Juan Jiménez de Pedro Corona, had a spirit of prophecy. This was verified in many ways and was told to me by his nephew who was more than ninety years old. Juan once saw a procession of barefoot friars coming from the mouth of a cave that was in the hill of San Pedro. They were wearing coarse brown habits and white mantles, and, with lighted candles in their hands, were processing around the hill. Since he told this vision to many in the town, God permitted it to become the common refrain for someone who was drunk: they would say that he had seen the barefoot friars coming from the mouth of the cave of San Pedro. But when they later saw the monastery founded and that from the mouth of the cave—which was the front gate—there were friars coming out in procession to surround the hermitage, they understood that the vision of Juan Jiménez had been mysterious.

22. **Cyril:** *Tell me, I beg you, who were these two fathers who were the first Discalced of the order without having first been Calced Carmelites?*

23. **Anastasius:** Father Mariano was a doctor of law, very learned and clever, of the Azaros nobility of Naples. He came to Spain on business for the prince of Sulmona, but he grew disgusted with the entanglements of the world. To save himself, he left everything and went to Tardón in the company of Father Matheus, who directed the hermits there. After Father Mariano became a Discalced Carmelite

friar, he labored and bore much fruit in the foundations and business of the order.

FRAY JUAN DE LA MISERIA, FIRST DISCALCED LAY BROTHER

24. Brother Juan was the son of a carder of Abruzzo in the kingdom of Naples. He entered a monastery of Discalced Franciscans called Fontecolombo. But because the devils maltreated him by roaring and causing a ruckus, the friars threw him out with only a brown sackcloth on his back. Without anything on his head or his feet, he came to Spain. As he told me, there was always a voice sounding in his ear that said, "Go to Spain, to Spain." He walked like that toward France until he came to a hermitage; I believe it was in the kingdom of Murcia. Because there was no holy image there, he asked a carpenter to lend him a hammer and chisel. From the figure of the dove, which is an image of our Lady in the monastery of Fontecolombo and which he carried deeply impressed in his imagination and soul, he made a similar one from wood, which he called "the Dove." This image worked miracles in that hermitage. Since it seemed to him that he was recognized and esteemed in that country, he fled from there to Tardón and stayed with Father Mariano a long time as a hermit and a friar. There is much that could be told about his spirit and prayer, and miraculous things.

FOUNDATION OF THE COLLEGE OF ST. CYRIL OF ALCALÁ

25. Some of the fathers from the monastery of Pastrana founded the College of St. Cyril of Alcalá. This was the principal nursery of the whole order because the students of that prestigious university came there to inquire about the order and apply to enter. From there, they were sent to Pastrana. Those who entered in those first beginnings via the college were the ones who later gave the most light to the order.

FRAY AMBROSIO DE SAN PEDRO, FRAY GABRIEL DE LA ASUNCIÓN

26. For this foundation, much is owed to two cousins, both natives of Pastrana, whose names are Fray Ambrosio de San Pedro and Fray

Gabriel de la Asunción. Although they did not have degrees, their great prudence, virtue, and spirit made up for this, and they helped much to promote learning in the order.

FOUNDATION OF ALTOMIRA

27. On a mountain near Illana and Almonacil was a hermitage called Our Lady of Altomira, where a priest, a great servant of God, resided. He managed to get Discalced friars from Pastrana to found a monastery there.

FRAY FRANCISCO DE JESÚS

28. One of the first was Fray Francisco de Jesús [Gomez (not "el Indigno")] who had formerly been a Calced. He was a man of much uprightness and spirit and very good in the confessional, although he was not learned. Once I said to one of the most important and learned men in all of Spain, who was later president of the Indies and bishop of Córdoba (and who was going to confession to this Father Fray Francisco, prior of the monastery in Granada), "Sir, why does your Grace go to confession to Fray Francisco, you being responsible for such serious matters?" (He was the judicial vicar of the chancery.) "Don't you know how little learning he has?" He replied to me, "I would go many leagues for confession with him. Going to confession to him, I find myself a new man. He has enough learning to know the Ten Commandments and understand them with his good judgment. And when there is some doubtful point being raised by our tribunal, he asks me what I think, or else he asks me to communicate about the case with someone who understands it. And if it turns out poorly, he reproaches me so much that I don't dare be careless again.

FRAY ELÍAS DE SAN MARTÍN, FRAY FRANCISCO

29. In this monastery of Altomira, Father Fray Elías de San Martín entered as a lay brother. He was later the general of the order and one of the most distinguished members of it,[11] and the first superior and

founder of the Discalced Trinitarians.[12] He was clothed the same day, month, and year that I received the habit in Pastrana.[13] And because his vocation was special and exemplary, I want to tell you about it.

30. A rich widow of the town of Illana had two sons. The younger one, who was a student in Alcalá, entered in Pastrana. The older one was one of the most mischievous, restless, and combative youths in that part of the country. For the day of his brother Fray Francisco's profession, he brought food to the monastery.[14] When he saw that the friars got up at midnight and took the discipline, fasted, prayed, and did other exercises of religion, he had a change of heart. He said to himself, "These friars get up at midnight and spend the night keeping watch in the service of God, while I often pass entire nights without sleeping and getting into fights, risking my life and the loss of my soul in order to serve the devil. What will become of me? I want to look after my soul." With this determination, he received the habit in Altomira as a lay brother because he only knew how to read. During the whole time of his novitiate, he went up and down that sierra many times—sometimes in snow—always barefooted, carrying bread, beans, vegetables, and charcoal that were given to him as alms for the monastery. Those who had been his companions in mischief looked at him with tears of confusion. One day in this same year of his novitiate, the prior, Fray Francisco de Jesús, said to him, "Look, Fray Elías, see if you can study this book of grammar." He took the book in his hands and read, studied, and memorized it by himself that year with the result that shortly after his profession they sent him to study arts and theology at Alcalá. There he became a great man of learning and turned out to be one of the best preachers of the order. He governed the college and its studies as rector for a long time. He was so restless, irascible, and combative before he was a friar that just to have an occasion to fight and wield his knife, he would go to other towns and hamstring the bulls that were run. It is marvelous that, since joining the order, along with his other virtues, he possesses an admirable meekness.[15]

31. This, in sum, is what touches on the foundations of the first four monasteries before I entered the order.

FOUNDATIONS HE MADE WHEN HE WAS PRELATE

FOUNDATION OF THE MONASTERY OF LOS REMEDIOS IN SEVILLE

32. The first monastery that I founded as a religious was that of Seville, which—as I already said[16]—Father Mariano and I took the occasion to found in order to absent ourselves from some turmoil that might have come to the order due to the princess of Éboli joining it. We also went there to close the monastery of Discalced friars in San Juan del Puerto.

FRAY FRANCISCO DE VARGAS, APOSTOLIC VISITATOR OF ANDALUSIA

33. We went to Seville where Father Fray Francisco de Vargas, provincial of the Dominicans and visitator of the Calced Carmelites, gave me his authority, handing over to me the same original brief of visitator that he had from Pius V.[17] With this authority, we dissolved the monastery of San Juan del Puerto and founded one in Seville in the hermitage of Nuestra Señora de los Remedios,[18] which the archbishop gave to us. But we had a lot of opposition from our Calced fathers who claimed that we did not have the authority to found monasteries of the Discalced without permission from the Calced general. We also had an argument with some clerics who alleged that the archbishop was not able to give us that hermitage because it had certain trees that were providing income for an ecclesiastical benefice of a cleric who claimed it for himself. The Minim friars of St. Francis of Paola also argued with us over property boundaries.

DON CRISTÓBAL DE ROJAS Y SANDOVAL, ARCHBISHOP OF SEVILLE; RESULTS OF CONFIDENCE IN GOD

34. All this was overcome with God's help and with that of the archbishop of Seville, Don Cristóbal de Rojas, who favored us. In gratitude

for this good deed, Father Mariano tried to help him get out of debt, for he had many debts. You can see what confidence in God does: we had nothing to eat; we entered that monastery with only eighteen *reales*; we were ten or twelve, counting the novices we received there and those that came from San Juan del Puerto; and here we were trying to get the archbishop out of debt, and he owed more than one hundred thousand ducats!

THE VOCATION OF FRAY NICOLÁS DE JESÚS MARÍA, THE ONE WHO EXPELLED HIM

35. God did it through the good intentions of Mariano, who had his great friend in Seville, a Genoese businessman named Nicolao Doria, take charge of the collection and administration of the rents of the archbishopric in order to reduce the debt. Thus, he got the archbishop out of debt. Due to the communication that Nicolao Doria had with us, and his own good desires, he left the secular state and was ordained a priest. He studied theology at a college in Seville under the direction of Master Rodrigo. Desiring greater perfection, he left all worldly things and received the habit of the Discalced, which I myself gave him in our monastery of Los Remedios.[19] Later, this great father became the first vicar general and one of the most important friars of the order, of whom I could recount many great things that others have probably already written about. But in case they have forgotten to recount it, I will say here that in order not to have any scruple about restitution regarding his business affairs—although according to sound ethics he certainly had nothing to worry about—he paid back more than thirty thousand ducats. He had the keenest ingenuity and was one of the greatest experts of his time with regard to currency exchanges and other business contracts, especially those of the Genoese. Studying the matter very carefully, with his good zeal and spirit, and much prayer, he was able to enlighten the king, Don Philip II, who then issued a decree that—it is said—freed Spain from the oppressive burden of the Genoese bankers. If the damage had not been stopped, the king would not have had the

money to pay his many debts, which were increasing due to currency exchanges and contracts that were difficult to understand. This deed alone was enough to have Doria canonized a saint, and the king would have given him whatever bishopric or archbishopric in Spain he wished to receive.[20] But having much humility and perfection, he sought rewards not on earth but in heaven, and he brought to the order the zeal of Elijah and rigorous observance.[21]

OTHER EFFECTS OF CONFIDENCE IN THAT FOUNDATION

36. It is a great thing for the poor to have confidence in God! Once, at the beginning of this foundation, the friars had absolutely nothing to eat and it was already midday.

OCCUPATIONS AT THAT TIME

37. Father Mariano saw that I was somewhat distressed when I told him to help me search for a little oil or bread for the monastery. I was seeing how many things I had to do—I usually preached; heard confessions of the people; governed my monastery; took care of the business of the order; fought with adversaries, who were not just a few; and gave public lectures in the afternoon on Sacred Scripture in the main church, which required more study than preparing two sermons. So he said to me, "Now that we have nothing, this is a good time to begin work on a room for the house. Come, let's begin making the hypogea [i.e., the catacombs] of Rome." And with half an old spade that was lying around, he called a poor fellow at the door, named Rodrigo, and we began to dig the hypogea, which is a structure of underground arches that serves as a foundation. We did this during mealtime because we had no reason to go to the refectory since there was nothing to eat. I laughed to myself, seeing that we were losing our minds with hunger and here we were working to build the hypogea! But after eight months, a lovely room was made that is worth many ducats.

38. Since I mentioned the poor man at the door, and I am still dealing here with the subject of confidence, let me add that we were feeding

many poor people who were coming to the door. We made pots of vegetables from the garden and shared with them the little bread that we had received as alms. Once, when some friends, prudent with human wisdom, scolded me, questioning how I could feed the poor when I and my brethren had nothing to eat, I replied that I fed them by making this deal with God: "Lord, I feed You in Your poor; and You feed me and my brethren, for we too are poor." The day we lack poor people at our door, we ourselves will die of hunger. One day a woman with a patched coat came to me. I thought she came to ask for alms, but with much humility she asked me to pardon her and take the little bit of alms she had to give. It was a certificate of exchange for a thousand ducats, which could be cashed at the auction house of Seville. With this check, God knew how to compensate for the cabbages we had given out at the door! Some merchants treated us very well in those beginnings. Among others, one of the main ones was Pedro Cerezo Pardo, who spent a great sum of money from then on to help the order grow.

DIEGO EVANGELISTA, BASILIO, AND ANTONIO THE PORTUGUESE

39. At this time, the habit was received by many friars who became great lights in the order, such as Fray Diego Evangelista, who became a great preacher, Fray Basilio, and others. I must tell you about a mortification performed by a Portuguese friar named Antonio. One day, in order to test him to see if his vocation was founded in humility, I commanded him to strip from his waist up and, with a rope around his neck, go up into the pulpit of the refectory while the friars were eating and recount to them all the sins he had committed during his whole life, beginning with the ugliest and the biggest. Without any objection he began to do it. Just as he was about to tell his sins, I told him to keep silent and to come down from the pulpit. I was so impressed by this example of mortification performed by one who was still a layman that I gave him the habit of the order that very day. A little while later, we sent him to the monastery of Almodóvar del Campo for his studies; he succeeded very well at them.

FOUNDATION OF THE MONASTERY OF ALMODÓVAR DEL CAMPO

40. This monastery was founded, and the friars taught the students of the town reading and writing; with alms and the money that was customarily given to a tutor, it was well maintained. One of the people who helped us most was a married lady, the niece of Father Master Ávila.[22] Her prayer, spirit, and virtue amazed me. Two hours before sunrise each day, she made very good mental prayer next to the bed of her husband. Afterward, she started on her chores, which were numerous because she made provisions for her husband's shepherds, and he had many shepherds as well as a lot of livestock. If some friar—there were few—lacked his primary schooling, we sent him to study at this monastery. I say there were few because at that time we did not give the habit to someone destined for the priesthood if he did not already know at least how to read and write.[23] And there were so many who asked for the habit that we were able to choose those who had already studied arts and theology. As for the lay brothers, we chose those who knew some trade by which they could support the monastery, just as Pastrana had supported itself for some time by weaving silks called *anafayas*.

FRAY BENITO DE JESÚS Y LA VIRGEN; FRAY JUAN DE JESÚS ROCA; THE DISCALCED CARMELITE NUNS OF ALCALÁ FOUNDED BY MARÍA DE JESÚS AND NOT BY MOTHER TERESA

41. One who became very accomplished in this craft was Fray Benito de Jesús y la Virgen, whom I must tell you about. He had studied grammar at Alcalá and was the servant of Master Roca, who was later known as Fray Juan de Jesús. By the way, Master Roca received the habit in Pastrana half a year before me [January 1, 1572], being moved by a sermon he heard me preach to the Discalced Carmelite nuns in Alcalá where I spoke about the antiquity of the order. His entrance into the order was not without mystery because the rooms he had lived in collapsed the day after he left to join the order. He would have lost his life if he had been inside and had not gone in

search of religious life. The order owes much to this saint because, in addition to his continuous religious exercises, he worked hard in Rome together with Fray Diego de la Trinidad to obtain the Brief of Separation of the province.

42. But to get back to his servant Fray Benito, he worked at his loom with such spirit and prayer and a continuous act of love for God and our Lady that each time he threw the shuttle of the loom, he would say, "Praised be Jesus, praised be the Virgin." At the end of the week, he would confess the number of times he threw the shuttle without making that act of praise. With this continual love of God and our Lady, he became so simple and spiritual that he forgot all he knew, including the name of his father and where he came from. He slept only three hours a night. The rest of the time, he was in the presence of God in continual prayer or working at his loom or before the Blessed Sacrament, which he called his treasure. I could recount miracles and other stupendous things that I know about this saint if I weren't in a hurry to tell you about the foundation of the monastery of La Roda.

THE FOUNDATION OF THE MONASTERY OF LA RODA; DOÑA CATALINA DE CARDONA

43. In Naples, a daughter was born to a captain—a relative of the lords of Cardona—and she was named Doña Catalina de Cardona. This lady, after she was widowed, came to Spain in the company of the duchess of Calabria. When the duchess returned to Italy, Catalina remained in the service of the princess of Éboli. One day, after going with some other maidservants of the princess to hear a sermon of Dr. Agustín de Cazalla—considered one of the best preachers in Spain at that time—she said to her companions, "Ladies, let's not come to hear this preacher again because they're going to burn him at the stake for heresy." Scandalized, they asked her why she said that. She answered that she had seen a great flame of fire coming from his head and that the Lord had given her to understand why. Thus it came to pass, for I saw him burned at the stake in Valladolid.[24]

THE AUSTERE LIFE OF DOÑA CATALINA DE CARDONA

44. Later, after speaking with a hermit named Father Piña, who lived in the hermitage of Vera Cruz in Alcalá de Henares, this lady left the household of Ruy Gómez. Under Father Piña's guidance, she went to a desert near La Roda (a town of La Mancha), and there she dug herself a cave. She used a rock for a bed and a stone for a pillow, wore only sackcloth, and took the discipline every day with great severity. Without eating more than a small tortilla, which she prepared from a little wheat that was given to her every three days, and drinking water from the Júcar River—on which banks was her cave—she spent most of the day and night in prayer. Her life was one of the most austere and mysterious we have seen in Spain in our time, with the admiration of all the people of the surrounding towns. They called her "the good woman." She went to confession and received Holy Communion regularly at the monastery of the Mercedarians, two leagues from her cave.

THE MIRACLE OF CURING A MADMAN

45. Once there was a furious madman of great strength who was kept tied up. Breaking free of his chains, he went to the cave of the good woman. It was midnight. Breaking through the door, he told her to go with him because he was God the Father and he wanted to bless all the water in the Júcar River so that it would not be necessary to bless water every day. The servant of God went with him, and he carried her almost the whole night along the banks of the river in that madness. Afterward, they returned to the cave, and he fell asleep at the door. She went in and persevered in prayer, taking the discipline for that crazy man. In the morning, he woke up fully sane and was never crazy again.

SHE DRIVES AWAY THE DEVILS

46. Many times a devil would enter her cave, sometimes in the form of a fierce animal, such as a wolf or lion. One time she found the demon in the form of a large and frightening frog under her head. Without any fear, she would said, "Get out of here, you scoundrel, for I will whip

you!" And then she would take some chains and lash her thin little body of seventy years. She would bleed so much that her clothes were always stuck to her, emitting a great fragrance of sweet odor, as I myself was amazed to experience. With those lashes, the devil would disappear.

VISION

47. This servant of God once saw our Lord Jesus Christ in a coarse brown habit and a white mantle of rough wool, and He was barefoot. He told her it was His will that she dress in that manner. She went about making inquiries and asked the friars to whom she went to confession what order that habit was from. They did not know what to say. One day, Father Mariano happened to pass by there; if I remember correctly, he was on his way to make the foundation in La Peñuela. She saw the habit he wore, recognized it, and spoke to Father about it. Then she went to Madrid, where many ladies gave her an abundance of silks, relics, and money.[25] With these she returned to her cave, above which Father Mariano founded the monastery of La Roda, and he clothed this Mother Doña Catalina de Cardona in the habit of a Discalced Carmelite friar, with a little mantle of a lay brother. She persevered like this in a hermitage made for her near the monastery until she died. She is buried in a side chapel of the church. When Mother Teresa of Jesus was on her way to make a foundation in Villanueva de la Jara, she went into this very chapel to pray. The saint appeared to her and spoke at length about things that stayed in Mother Teresa's heart.[26]

48. I made mention of La Peñuela, which was founded in a desert next to the Sierra Morena. So much silence, recollection, austerity, and prayer are observed there that we can say it is the first spring of all the deserts that were founded later.[27] Lay brothers of great holiness were clothed in the habit here, like Fray García and another, Basilio, who had been a shepherd in Sierra Morena.

49. La Peñuela is not very far from the city of Granada, where the monastery of Los Mártires was founded in a hermitage located in front of the Alhambra, next to the dungeons where the Moors used to hold their

Christian captives.[28] Because it had no water, the count of Tendilla,[29] alcaide of the Alhambra, gave us a fountain for our monastery. We were digging in the field, where the garden was later made, in order to build the tank, and came across some tombs of the Moors. These were identifiable because they contained little jugs with raisins. In a tomb carved out of stone were found some very white bones, solid and heavy, without a skull. Among the bones was a small silver cross, which I devoutly kept along with the bones. When a friar came down with a bad case of malarial fever, I asked him to say devoutly an Our Father and a Hail Mary. Then I placed the bones upon his head, and the fever left him. Father Fray Bartolomé de Jesús placed the cross on the bad eyes of a woman, and she was healed. I hold as certain that these were the bones of the holy bishop Don Gonzalo who was taken captive in the time of the Moors.[30] He used the money that was raised for his ransom in Jaén, where he was the bishop, to buy the freedom of other Christian captives whom he saw were weak in the faith. I was confirmed in this opinion because when I told the archbishop of Granada, Don Pedro Guerrero, about the discovery of the bones, he told me that he had a skull given to him by a priest, who was a hermit in the hermitage of Los Mártires. This hermit told the archbishop that the holy bishop Don Gonzalo had appeared to him, telling him to dig in such and such a place and he would find the head and that the body was buried nearby because he was beheaded by the Moors. And so it was that near where the head was found, we found the body.

50. Many things happened in the foundation of this monastery of Granada, but since they are not very relevant to the order, I will leave them out of this account. I will also touch quickly on foundations of other monasteries that were made in my time and with my intervention and license, such as the monastery of Daimiel. It is located three leagues from Almodóvar del Campo, a region from which some very good members of the order have come because the people of that town are very devout. Among these I cannot forget to mention Fray Miguel who came to Pastrana to ask to be accepted as a lay brother. Having just

been elected provincial and not having a lay servant to accompany me in making visitations of the monasteries, I asked him to serve me in that capacity, for he seemed suitable for this. He willingly accepted and gave me ninety *reales* that he was carrying for his habit and some other things. He accompanied me for four years,[31] serving me with much love and giving me the example of a perfect life. When we arrived at an inn, he would buy food for me and my companion; he used to get up two hours before sunrise to pray; on the road, he was almost always in the presence of God; he slept on a cloak on the floor next to my bed; and he endured much fatigue in the foundations. I gave him the habit of a lay brother in Valladolid, full of regret to lose such company, which I esteemed as if he were the angel Raphael. He died shortly after he was professed, and there was a great crowd of prominant people who came to his burial. They took pieces of his habit for relics, as from a holy body.

51. Another monastery was founded in La Manchuela, next to Jaén. It was very edifying and notable to see many of the farmwomen coming to the church to listen to the friars reading the meditation points for their mental prayer. They attended the entire hour of prayer as if they were nuns. After their plowing, the young men came to the church in the afternoon to make their hour of mental prayer. Since it was already getting dark, they took the discipline while a friar sang the *Miserere mei* for them.[32] This spiritual exercise was also done with the students at Alcalá, who were in the care of Father Fray Blas de San Alberto, a great servant of God.

52. Since I mentioned our students, it would be good to speak briefly about the foundation of the College of Baeza, which brought great fruit to that city on account of the fervor and austerity that our order professes. It is true that the region was well disposed, thanks to a college—founded by Father Master Ávila—of very holy priests who went about preaching and hearing confessions in those towns and living an apostolic life. They would lecture to the secular students, teaching them knowledge, prayerfulness, and mortification as if they were friars. In this town, there is great spirituality, in both men and women. Great crowds of people

frequently receive the sacraments in all the parish churches, which is the usual case at monasteries, where those seeking perfection tend to go for the sacraments.

53. I knew two noteworthy women there. One was named Teresa de Ibros, a countrywoman and wife of a shepherd, in whom I saw so much prayer and spirituality, raptures, visions, and other true and perfect supernatural things that I was amazed. I could write a big book about her. No less notable was Doña María Flores. She was one of the most beautiful young ladies in the city and was much sought after for marriage because she was rich, but God was calling her to perfection. One day, she put hemp sandals on her feet, sackcloth over her skin, and a brown toque of poor raw silk material on her head; and with a sewing needle in hand and a great cross upon her shoulders, she went out into the plaza shouting to everyone, "Long live the poverty of Jesus Christ!" She gave her house to the poor and retired to live in poverty and perfection with her older sister, a *beata*. From this came the beginning of the foundation of the monastery of Discalced Franciscan nuns of that city.

54. Because weevils are found among the good wheat and impurities among the gold, there were also in Baeza some deluded and deceived spirits, bold and imprudent. Father Fray Eliseo de los Mártires, who was most prudent, upright, and spiritual, cured many of this malady. Afterward, he governed the monasteries of the West Indies.[33]

55. To give you an example of this for your instruction, I want to tell you what happened to a *beata* named Juana Calancha, who had the reputation of being holy and enriched with miracles, revelations, and raptures. To tell you the truth, I never trusted that woman. But condescending on account of the requests and opinions of other friars, I gave permission for her to be received as a lay sister in the monastery of Beas. Shortly after she arrived, she began to have raptures. But Mother Ana de Jesús—who was then the prioress—seeing that on account of her raptures she was failing in her work assignments, said to her on one occasion, "Sister, here we have no need of your raptures but that you wash

the dishes well." She wasn't in the monastery but a week when, around eleven at night, Sister Catalina de Jesús—of whose life much could be written[34]—heard a voice that said, "Keep watch, for it is good to keep watch." Being attentive, around midnight she heard some strange voices, like those of the Moors or people from another country, at the window where that nun was sleeping. With a small lamp, she went to where this nun was, and even though there were only ten steps from one place to the other, it took her a quarter of an hour to get there. It seemed as if she had chains on. She entered the cell and smelled a stench so horrible she thought she would die. She found the nun uncovered in a most disconcerting posture and was told by the nun that she was there with Jesus Christ. Catalina de Jesús said to her with great fervor and prophetic spirit, "Oh, sister, it is the devil that has fooled you and has not let you confess the truth to your confessor." The novice declared to her that ever since she was seven years old, she went about in the company of a lovely boy her same age who grew as she grew. When they reached the age of thirteen or fourteen, the boy said he wanted to marry her, and the marriage was made. He persuaded her to have carnal union with him and not to tell of it to anyone nor to reveal it to her confessor, because he was Jesus Christ. As a sign of this, he gave her visions, raptures, and apparent miracles. This woman persisted in this abominable sin for many years. God willed that she be delivered, bringing her to the Inquisition in Murcia where they made her undergo the auto-de-fé with a black candle in her hand.[35] Having given her a hundred lashes in the public square, they ordered her not to return to that sin under pain of being burned at the stake as a relapsed sinner.

56. What great harm is done by illusions, such as those of Magdalena de la Cruz in Córdoba. A monastery of Discalced Carmelite friars had just been founded in that illustrious city, and a lady, who was the sister of Doña Sancha de Guzmán, would come there for confession with me. She told me about these things concerning Magdalena de la Cruz and how her sister had exposed them. I will not relate the whole story for it is very long. Besides, a father of the Company has written a big book

about Doña Sancha and the rigorous life she led ever since God called her. In summary, however, it is this:

57. One morning Doña Sancha desired to put on a brocade dress in order to attend Queen Isabel as a lady-in-waiting. Jesus Christ appeared to her with His cross on His back and said to her: "Sanchica, for you." From that moment on, she wore a hair shirt under her dress of black taffeta, which she usually wore when she dressed casually without ceremony. She fasted and prayed continuously, never leaving the dais in her house that looked out upon the church. Father Master Ávila, among others, went there to hear her confession and bring her Communion up to the day she died. Well, one day, the bishop of Córdoba went to visit with her and he told her about the marvels of this Magdalena de la Cruz. She said to him, "Oh, my Lord, look carefully into these things, for they are illusions of the devil." Thus was the nefarious affair discovered. This lady, Doña Sancha, was the aunt of Don Andrés de Córdoba, to whom our order owes a great deal for the foundation in Salamanca, and I in particular for the way he, as auditor of the Rota, helped me in Rome. They are of the lineage of the Córdobas, lords of Guadalcázar. A monastery of Discalced Carmelite friars was founded in that town, and another was founded near Córdoba in the town called Bujalance. Both monasteries have formed good Carmelites and have been spiritually beneficial to the laypeople.

58. A monastery called Fuensanta, near Iznatorafe in the district of Baeza, has also been spiritually fruitful. It is in a place where there used to be a church with four towers and a fountain gushing up below the main altar. Because the origin of this monastery is noteworthy, I want to briefly tell about it here.

59. When the Moors were in control of Spain, the Moorish king of Iznatorafe had a very beautiful wife. She became a Christian by the persuasive teaching of one of her Christian captives. When her husband the king found out, he ordered that she be taken down to the dense woods near the town. Her hands and feet were cut off, according to his orders,

and she was left there to die. Seeing herself in that condition, this lady and queen called on the Virgin Mary, Queen of Heaven, to whom she was greatly devoted. The Virgin Mary carried her to a fountain nearby and, washing her in that water, restored her hands and feet. When the news reached her husband, the Moorish king, he had himself baptized and built a palace there, with four towers and a church. The altar was placed over the fountain, which was called holy because many have been cured by its water.[36]

60. A great servant of God named Teresa, who lived in Iznatorafe, used to go to this monastery to confess to Father Fray Simón Stock, who with his great voice was very effective in his preaching. He governed that house for a long time. I cannot keep quiet about the time there was a great pestilence in Seville. With tears he begged me, his superior, to give him permission to go there to die administering the sacraments in a hospital for the victims. Although he was struck with the pestilence, he was cured. He served for a long time in that monastery to the great satisfaction of the magistrates and rulers of Seville who held him to be a saint.

61. But leaving behind the monastery of Fuensanta and another monastery that was founded nearby, called El Calvario, where the friars have farmlands, let me tell you about the foundation of the monastery of Málaga, which was made shortly after the time of the pestilence.

62. In the monastery of the Discalced Carmelites of Granada, there was an old and gouty friar who had been a Calced, named Fray Gabriel de la Peñuela, a servant of God and of good lineage. He once happened to go to Málaga on business. The *percheles*—which is what they call the fishermen—offered him a hermitage they had, dedicated to St. Andrew, so that a monastery of Discalced Carmelites could be founded there. The foundation was opposed by the Dominican friars because their monastery was nearby, and the bishop of Málaga, Don Juan Pacheco, did not want to give his permission for it. Fray Gabriel wrote to me in Granada that I should get a decree from the court of equity against the

Dominican friars and the bishop in order to make that foundation. It seemed to me that the monastery would be very good and render great service to God; however, it was better to make it not by a legal action but rather with humility and good will. I commended the matter to God. I walked to Málaga and went straight to the bishop. With much sincerity and humility, I told him that I had been asked to take forceful legal action against His Lordship. But the decree that I had in hand was to entreat him—if it was for the service of God and his good pleasure—to found a monastery of Discalced Carmelites at San Andrés of the Percheles,[37] considering that, of those who died of the pestilence in Málaga, more than four thousand bodies were buried in that area and dogs and other animals were pulling out pieces of flesh from the graves. Thus, I said, it would be good if a monastery were there to fence in that field, take account of the bodies, and commend their souls to God. More than fifteen hundred were children who died before they reached the age of reason and were in heaven; it was only right that their holy relics should not be eaten by animals. Also, many people of the Percheles, including the *jábega*[38]—which is how they refer to the uncatechized people there—would have someone to go to for confession and to say Mass for them. In the end, however, I said I would abide by whatever His Lordship commanded. He looked at me from head to toe and made no reply just then, except to say that I should come another day to eat with him and preach in the main church on the first Sunday. I did so. When I returned afterward to discuss the business of the foundation, he said these words to me: "I and my priests are fond of the Dominicans, and we will hold them in favor against you in any lawsuit. But just keep quiet and do what seems to be for the greater service of God, for He will help you." With these words, which I well understood, I took a vacant house in the barrio there, for there were many of them on account of the plague. I had the entrance hall of the house set up as a church with an altar, and I took up residence there with my friars. With the faculty given to us by the bull of the Crusades, I asked permission from the bishop to say Mass there, without using a bell. Within a short time, I was given many good vestments as alms. The bishop smoothed things out with the Dominican fathers to the extent that they led us in procession with the Blessed Sacrament from their house to our church of St. Andrew. The first work undertaken was to close up the tombs and graves in the field where those who had died from the plague were buried. Then work began on the house. The city gave us a tower with a big bell that was used in former times to sound the alarm when the Moors came.

63. To expand an order, there is no better way than by establishing houses of studies near public universities because good vocations enter there, as I experienced in the monasteries of Alcalá, Baeza, Seville, and Granada, where there are universities. I wanted to make foundations in Salamanca, Toledo, and Valladolid, which also have universities. Although I was invited to make foundations in many towns, it was always my opinion that there should be few monasteries of select persons and in principal places, particularly where there are universities, in order to expand this order of the Most Holy Virgin Mary throughout the world for the good of souls, just as the Company of Jesus had expanded.

64. Thus I founded the monastery of friars in Valladolid, despite much opposition from the Calced fathers. One night they tried to arrest the friars and have us tear down the work. They succeeded in getting the abbot provisor of Valladolid to impede the foundation with censures and excommunications, for which reason we petitioned the court of equity to intervene on our behalf against their forceful dissolution of our monastery.[39] Finally, a servant of God gave us a garden with a hermitage dedicated to St. Alexis. Her father, a gardener named Fernando de Cabria, had worked in the name of this saint who had suffered greatly and lived under a staircase for many years. In a short time, however, the monastery was moved from there to a better site. Doña María de Mendoza, a lady from Cobos, and her brother, Don Alvaro de Mendoza, bishop of Palencia, favored this foundation very much, and many good friars were formed there.

65. One morning, I went from my monastery to that of the nuns with my companion, Fray Tomás de la Ascensión. I was speaking with the Discalced prioress, María Bautista—niece of Mother Teresa of Jesus and a woman of great perfection with a rare and acute ingenuity—when a merchant named Jerónimo de Carvajal from Salamanca came to the monastery. He asked the prioress if she had any messages she wanted to send to the nuns in Salamanca, since he was on his way there in a coach by himself. I said to my companion, "This is a good opportunity to go and found a college in Salamanca. Let's get in the coach trusting in God, for the Virgin Mary has no need of anything for her foundations other than the three *reales* you are carrying," which he brought from the monastery to buy I don't know what. Because we had to pass through the length of the town and it seemed improper to us that Discalced Carmelite friars travel by coach, we put on some empty sacks to hide our habits until we were out in the open country where no one could see us.

66. Upon arriving at Salamanca, we went to visit the bishop, Don Jerónimo Manrique, who was then making a visitation of a town called Vitigudino. We told him what we had in mind. He gave us a license to make the foundation and sent us to his vicar general, who at that time was Don Andrés de Córdoba, chaplain of San Bartolomé, who I said helped us in Rome and in the foundation of Guadalcázar.[40] Don Andrés gave us a large church, on the other side of the bridge, that had been founded by the commander of the Magdalene and was named San Lázaro.[41] It had altars and very good statues. There were also vestments, but they were in poor condition because there was no one to clean and repair them. The church had also been a hospital for lepers. We founded our college there with the help of this chaplain of San Bartolomé—who gave us bread each week—and other important people of the city, like Doña Catalina de Aguilera and her relatives. She was the sister of the judge of the royal council of Aguilera and a holy woman. Although it was a little arduous for our friars to cross the bridge each day to attend class at the university, since they had so little protection for their feet and clothes and it gets very cold in that city—for which reason lectures

were later held at our college—those beginnings were nevertheless very fruitful. San Lázaro was next to a house of prostitution. Many students who used to frequent the place stopped going there because they had to pass by the monastery and felt shame on account of the friars. Many sins were thus prevented. The greatest benefit was to that poor neighborhood, which had been a den of iniquity.[42] It had houses to conceal persons who, with the excuse that they were going to relax in the gardens, went to them in order to sin. No other part of the city was such a receptacle of so many adulteries and sacrileges as that neighborhood. Well, it came to pass that a rich innkeeper of that area—who for many years had been a witness of the things that went on in the neighborhood of San Lázaro and how it improved afterward—often went to confession with me; I heard her confession when she was close to dying. In our conversations, she would tell me about all the brothels and mesdames that were in the neighborhood. I told the bishop and the magistrate what was going on and, with the innkeeper informing us as to how to investigate and gather evidence, the mesdames were sent away and punished, the area was cleaned up, and innumerable mortal sins were avoided. May the Lord be blessed forever.

67. For a long time, the Discalced nuns in Toledo wanted a monastery of friars to be founded in their city. This foundation came about as follows: I went there one Lent to preach and stayed in a house vacated by the nuns when they moved to a better one. While I was there, I worked on founding a monastery for the friars. The city gave us a house, with towers, located in front of the one in which I was staying. We lived there until we moved to a place near the Castle of St. Cervantes outside the city. We sold the house to the Bernardine nuns, whose foundation—as I will say later[43]—cost me much time.

68. I cannot fail to speak of what happened before this monastery was founded. A lay brother named Fray Francisco, who accompanied me, had excellent penmanship and was helping me write my books. My brother Luis Gracián taught him to write. This lay brother fell ill with

erysipelas.[44] Visiting him one evening, he seemed to me depressed. He gave me a letter to read in which he asked for my permission to go to the native people of Guinea with the desire to be eaten by them in honor of Christ. I gave him permission, thinking to myself that if he died of the erysipelas, this good desire would help him on the way to the next life; if he lived, I had it within my power to withdraw the permission or do whatever I thought best. He received this permission with great fervor, gratitude, and acts of love for God and of martyrdom. It seemed to me he was drawing his last breath of life. I sent for my companion, Fray Cristóbal de San Alberto—a very devout man and diligent in taking care of all the traveling arrangements for the visitations we were making—and he wasn't long in bringing extreme unction. Since it was necessary to anoint the sick brother quickly, we did not have time to say the psalms and other prayers that normally go with the anointing but only had time to say the words that are the form of the sacrament. Just as I finished the last rites, he expired. His face was so beautiful, and his bed—which had smelled bad on account of the many medicinal ointments he received—had such a sweet fragrance that could be smelled throughout the house. I was amazed. Although young boys usually flee from dead bodies, my brother Luis stayed the night keeping vigil at the body and kissing the hands as though it were truly the body of a saint. Without a doubt, I believe he was. He had taken the habit with great fervor and still had the milk of the novitiate since he had been professed for only eight months. I saw to it myself that he was buried with special care. Preaching in a church the next day, I begged for alms to help me bury my companion. Four parishes with their four processional crosses came to the funeral, with a great accompaniment of clergy and principal men of the city, as if he were a great lord. We carried him through the streets of Toledo with his face uncovered, his head crowned with flowers, and his body covered with a brown, rough woolen mantle. Many people hung out their windows to see him. He was buried in the monastery of the Calced with a solemn high Mass and a sermon praising God, who honors His poor in life and in death.

69. Since the death of this saint awakens my memory, I will say something about Fray Juan del Espíritu Santo, who died in Pastrana with no less admiration at his holy death. He was a very good student. With the time of his ordination coming, I asked him to prepare himself for the subdiaconate. He smiled at me, saying, "I for minor orders, Father? I'll be ordained for the baking!" He said this because he had a special gift for making bread. (At that time, the friars made all the bread in the monastery, everyone helping to knead the dough.) I took this as coming from someone who was humble and said nothing. But as the time for ordination was soon approaching, I returned to him to speak about it. Smiling, he said, "Your Reverence will see that I will not be ordained, that I am not fit for such an elevated ministry." The next day, he suddenly came down with a fever. The doctor came to visit him and ordered that he immediately be given the sacraments and also extreme unction. After he was anointed, he sat up in bed and gave the friars a reflection, encouraging them in the perfect observance of the Rule and the true spirit of obedience. He did this with such elevated doctrine that we were all amazed. When he finished his reflection, he turned his head to the side and said, "Ay! What do you want here, traitor?" Saying this, he extended his arms and raised them high with these words: "Is it time now, Lord, for me to go? Let us go in this good hour!" Then he breathed his last, looking radiant. The friars did not know what else to do but sing the Te Deum. Then they brought in many roses, making a crown for him and scattering them all around his room, holding it for certain that the Virgin had crowned him in heaven.

70. I have related this in connection with the foundation of Toledo. I also founded a monastery in the city of Úbeda, receiving a house and much help for it at the beginning from a councillor named Pedro de Segura. The relatives of Secretary Juan Vázquez de Molina, who were numerous in that city where he was from, favored the foundation. At the beginning of the foundation of this monastery, I gave the habit to Francisco Hernández, who was afterward named Fray Francisco de Jesús el Indigno.[45] He was raised from childhood in the house of Father

Master Ávila with the good milk of prayer, generosity, fervor, and zeal that this saint had sown in Andalusia. For this, Father Master Ávila was called by many the apostle of that region. I would write at great length about him if his life hadn't already been written in a very good book by Father Fray Luis de Granada.[46] Well, his disciple Francisco became so fervent and devout, especially with regard to the Blessed Sacrament—whose servant he was in a great way—that on the day the feast of Corpus Christi was celebrated, it seemed that he was out of his mind with pure fervor and devotion. On one occasion, going before the procession praising the Lord, he leaped up and his body went flying through the air a great distance. He fell on some rocks but without hurting himself, at which all the people were amazed and thought it was a miracle. He would join the processions dressed up like King David in the company of the boys who were singing the praises of God. Ever since he left the household of Master Ávila, he dedicated himself to teaching Christian doctrine to the boys. He was so well instructed that he knew the catechism in both prose and rhyme, in the way that schoolchildren are taught, and this catechism was enough for him to preach a long time with good results. It was the same for him, though with miracles, among the people of the Congo, where I sent him with other companions, as I will say further on.[47]

71. Near Úbeda is Jaén. By command of the bishop [Francisco Sarmiento de Mendoza], I went there on some important business—as I will afterward relate[48]—and a canon named [Don Juan Pérez de] Godoy gave me a good site where I founded the monastery of the Discalced Carmelite friars of Jaén. A short time later, the friars from there founded the monastery of Nuestra Señora de la Cabeza near Andújar, although afterward, for good reason, it did not continue.

72. I sent Father Mariano to Lisbon. There, near the section of Alcántara called Pampulla, he found a very good site for the foundation of the Discalced Carmelite monastery of San Felipe, which was the cradle of the other monasteries in Portugal. Many Portuguese entered there, and they

turned out to be admirable religious because the people of that country are devout and generous. The friars of San Felipe were a great help to the military when Drake came with Don Antonio, as I will relate later.[49]

73. I also sent Father Fray Nicolao Doria to Genoa. He founded a monastery in that city, which turned out very well and bore much fruit. It is the origin of the foundations in Italy, and many good religious have been formed in it. Among its first members was Fray Pedro de la Madre de Dios of Aragon, whom the archbishop of Genoa sent to preach in some of the towns of his archbishopric. He lost his fear of speaking Italian because they were country people with whom it was not necessary to have a polished language but only to be understood. Although he spoke broken Italian at first, he became so proficient in the Tuscan language that, when by chance preaching in Rome, he was as well understood by everyone as any other good preacher. Pope Clement VIII especially held Fray Pedro in such esteem that he was very near to making him a cardinal because of his preaching and his virtues. He had done this for Father Toledo and Father Bellarmine of the Company of Jesus and another priest who was a Capuchin. But God willed to spare Fray Pedro this charge so that he could help begin the congregation of the Discalced Carmelites in Italy. Although it is the same order as the one in Spain, they have different prelates and, in some sense, a different spirit because they zealously commit themselves to the conversion of souls; this can be seen by those who went to Persia. Those of Spain, on the other hand, strive to perfect themselves in recollection and the eremitical life, founding hermitages where the life of the ancient fathers shines forth with great ardor and austerity.[50]

74. Having gone to Pamplona for the foundation of the Discalced Carmelite nuns, I spoke with Father Fray Martín Cruzat, who was an important councillor and nobleman of that city, and gave him the habit. Desiring to serve God with greater perfection, he left his estate to his daughter, Doña Margarita, a great servant of God, and built a hermitage in Oriz—his hometown, which is two leagues from Pamplona—where

he lived an exemplary life with great perfection. After I gave the habit to this servant of God, I sent him back to his city where he founded the monastery of the Discalced Carmelite friars of Pamplona, which is one of the best and holiest monasteries the order has.

75. When my time as provincial was at an end, a chapter was held and we elected Father Fray Nicolás Doria de Jesús María as provincial. Because he was absent, being in Genoa for the foundation there, I remained first definitor of that chapter, governing the province until he returned. In the definitory, I named twelve religious who seemed most suitable to send to the West Indies. They founded a monastery in Mexico, which was the origin of all the monasteries that have been founded in the Indies. It bore much fruit and is still bearing fruit in those places. And it was God who permitted them to go at that moment because, if it had passed, they never would have gone to the Indies, considering the events I later experienced.[51]

76. These are the monasteries that I remember having founded while I was with the Discalced Carmelites. If I were to tell of the many things that took place, it would be necessary to compose a big book or to refer to the one I already wrote called *Fundaciones de los Carmelitas Descalzos* [Foundations of the Discalced Carmelites].[52]

FOUNDATIONS OF MONASTERIES OF THE DISCALCED CARMELITE NUNS

77. **Cyril:** *How I would like to read this book of the* Foundations, *or that you had expanded more in referring to the particulars that must have occurred in them. But now tell me which foundations of the Discalced Carmelite nuns you were involved in or were made with your commission.*

78. **Anastasius:** Concerning the foundations of nuns, Mother Teresa of Jesus has written a book, and Dr. Ribera[53] and the bishop of Tarazona have written at length in their books about the life of Mother Teresa.[54] There is no reason for me to tire myself with this now. It is enough to

say in summary that with my license and commission as superior, the monasteries of the Discalced Carmelite nuns of Beas, Caravaca, Seville, Granada, Soria, Palencia, Burgos, Lisbon, and Pamplona were founded.

79. **Cyril:** *Tell me something that Mother Teresa and those authors have left unwritten.*

80. **Anastasius:** Mother Teresa was going to make the foundation in Beas with the patent of the general. But then she realized that the town—in what concerns religious orders—is under the jurisdiction not of Castile but rather of Andalusia, and Mother Teresa did not have a patent to found outside of Castile. Thus it was necessary that I give her a license in virtue of the commission I had from Fray Francisco de Vargas, visitator of the Order of Carmel in Andalusia. With that very commission, she became my subject and I ordered her to found monasteries in Andalusia. We were together in the monastery of Beas for more than a month in the spring of the year 1575. I hadn't seen her before in person but had only communicated with her by letter. The whole time I was there, she communicated her spirit to me without hiding anything. I likewise told her everything about my interior life. There we agreed to always be in conformity in all affairs. She, in addition to her religious vows, made a particular vow to obey me all her life according to a particular revelation she had.[55]

81. At this time a priest, who was a great servant of God, came there, and I gave him the habit of the Discalced Carmelites in the speak room of the nuns.[56] His name was Fray Gregorio Nacianceno, who later was a provincial. You have heard many very good things said about him. Because this is a good place, I want to tell you a funny story of what happened at that time. Mother Teresa brought in her company Father Julián de Ávila as a confessor. He was an elderly holy priest, devout, recollected, and humble, the brother of one of the first Carmelite nuns to be clothed in the habit at San José in Ávila.[57] This servant of God asked me if I would give him the scapular of the order as a brother, in order to receive the graces and indulgences gained by

our devotees. Desiring to make it a special event, I wanted to give it to him with solemnity. So, one day, I ordered the nuns to come after dinner to the grille in the speak room wearing their mantles and, with lighted candles in their hands, singing the "Veni Creator Spiritus," as is customary when someone is given the habit.

82. They opened a wicker chest and took out a large habit that they wanted to have blessed for a nun. In the same chest was the scapular made for Father Julián de Ávila. I ordered him to kneel and began very slowly to make a long discourse in praise of the order and religious life, which lasted one hour. During this time, the nuns were so happy and amazed that Father Julián wanted to become a friar, and Mother Teresa was no less surprised that he had never mentioned it to her. But Father Julián, as he told me later, was in the greatest affliction of spirit because of the battle going on with his warring thoughts. On the one hand, he said to himself, "How can I be a friar since I never had, nor do I have now, such a desire, nor has the thought ever crossed my mind?" He was thinking of the obligation he had to take care of his sisters and all the other inconveniences of being a friar. On the other hand, he thought it was a revelation of Mother Teresa of Jesus that he become a friar, so what else could he do? He was changing colors and sweating and feeling afflicted until I finished the talk by saying that for all the work he had done for the order and accompanying Mother Teresa, I was giving him the brotherhood with all the graces gained by those who wear the scapular. With that, he was relieved of the distress he felt. To the great laughter of everyone, he told us what was going on in his heart during that hour.

83. From there, he went in company with Antonio Gaitán—a gentleman of Ávila and a great servant of God who also accompanied Mother Teresa—to look into making the foundation of the Discalced Carmelite nuns in Caravaca. This foundation was very well made and bore much fruit in that town. After a few days, Mother Teresa traveled from Beas—where she left Mother Ana de Jesús as prioress—to Seville to found the

monastery there. She took Mother María de San José with her in order to make her prioress. Later the foundress of Lisbon, this nun was one of the most pure, holy, courageous, prudent, and discreet women I have ever known in the order, after Mother Teresa. And she was the one who suffered the most trials and contradictions for standing firm that the laws ordained and left by Mother Teresa not be changed.[58]

84. While Mother Teresa was at the foundation in Seville, her brother Lorenzo de Cepeda came from the Indies with his two sons and his little daughter Teresita. She was put in the monastery there, and we called her "Teresica."[59] This servant of God, Lorenzo, was a big help in meeting the temporal needs of the foundation of that monastery and also a spiritual comfort and support. The nuns had a great cross on account of a melancholic cleric who denounced them to the Inquisition, as if they were heretics. I suffered no less because important people berated me for bringing the Discalced nuns to Seville. When I tried to console myself with Mother Teresa, she pained me more because she laughed at these things and took pleasure in suffering, saying, "Would that we were all burned at the stake for Christ, dear Father! But, thanks be to God, there is no fear that in matters of the faith we will be found remiss. We would first die a thousand deaths."

85. **Cyril:** *Will you not tell me what they were accused of to the Inquisition?*

86. **Anastasius:** It was said that they went to confession to one another. They did this according to the rule given by Mother Teresa: that the nuns are to give the prioress an account of their spirit.[60] When the inquisitors came to examine the case, they questioned Mother Isabel de San Jerónimo whether the Discalced nuns revealed their consciences to the superiors. She responded that it was so. They questioned her further on whether at times they told their sins. She answered, "Yes, my lord, but the prioress to whom we speak does not absolve us," at which the inquisitor laughed heartily. The calumny was discovered, and the cleric was reprimanded. They held Mother Teresa and her nuns in great esteem, having very carefully examined her life and customs and her

way of doing things. The same was done by the archbishop and by the prior of the Carthusians and other important people of the city, who began to give them alms.[61]

87. In this monastery, I ordered Mother Teresa to do two things that mortified her very much, because she asked me to mortify her. I was looking for ways to mortify her that she would really feel, not the ordinary mortifications such as going to the refectory with a cross on your back, which was a pleasing recreation to her. So I told her to prepare herself for a general confession and to recall all the sins of her whole life, which I wanted her to confess in a general way. I knew that nothing caused this servant of God as much sorrow as remembering her faults. I let her go around greatly afflicted with the sins in her mouth, putting off her confession day after day for very light reasons until finally I said I did not want to hear her confession. She felt this mortification very much.[62]

88. On another occasion, when Fray Juan de la Miseria was painting inside the cloister, I ordered him to paint her portrait. She was to stay in a pose and let herself be painted. She felt this very much because she was very humble. She did not feel discomfort or unpleasantness in the position in which Fray Juan painted her—he made her sit without moving her head or looking up for a long time—as much as that there would remain a memory and likeness of her in the world. In the end, he painted her poorly because, although he was a painter, he wasn't a painter of the first rank. So Mother Teresa said with much grace: "God forgive you, Fray Juan, for now that you have painted me, you have painted me ugly and bleary-eyed."[63] This is the painting we now have of Mother Teresa, which I wish were truer to life because she had a most gracious look that moved you to devotion.

89. From this monastery, by order of the general, Mother Teresa went to Toledo without engaging in more foundations until the storm clouds had passed. She sent me to find a site and to scope out the lay of the land because it was not so easy to found a monastery without learning

beforehand what was there. I went to Palencia. Some canons of the cathedral discouraged me by telling me of the great poverty of the city and that the nuns would not be able to support themselves. I therefore concluded that the foundation should not be made. But, by chance, I met a very important man named Suero de Vega, son of Juan de Vega, who was president of the royal council. He was very devout and spiritual. He and his wife, Doña Elvira de Mendoza, daughter of the count of Osorno, fasted two days a week, had their hours of mental prayer, received Holy Communion weekly, and gave much in alms. This gentleman encouraged me and afterward supported the monastery very much.[64]

90. Mother Teresa sent Mother Ana de Jesús to make the foundation of the monastery in Granada,[65] which turned out very well. After having gone personally to make the foundation of Soria, Mother Teresa returned to Ávila where I appointed her prioress.[66] Soon afterward, she said to me that it would be of service to God to found a monastery in Burgos. I asked her if she had a license from the archbishop. She showed me an old letter in which the archbishop told her that he would be pleased to have a monastery of Discalced Carmelite nuns in that city. I told her that wasn't good enough, that it was necessary to have explicit permission. She already knew how exacting the archbishop of Burgos [Don Cristóbal Vela] was and that it would not be good to find ourselves in a fix after we got there. She responded to me in these words: "Look, Father, the things of God do not require so much human prudence and discretion. I know that the nuns will be very fruitful in Burgos. Forget about your reasons, and let's go there." I replied, "Let's go then, with Godspeed." Although she was sick and the weather was very harsh, being cold, wet, and muddy—it was Christmastime[67]—we traveled by way of Valladolid, with much difficulty.

91. The abbot of Valladolid came to speak to her about founding a school for girls in a room attached to a monastery of Discalced Carmelite nuns. It would have a door and a large window opening out to the school from where the nuns would be able to teach reading, needlework, prayer,

and good conduct to the young ladies. Three nuns could go out to govern them with the offices of principal, teacher, and porter, similar to the schools for girls founded in Alcalá and Toledo. Interestingly enough, this kind of foundation appealed to Mother Teresa because she said that the young ladies would be formed in a spiritual atmosphere of prayer. And when they later married, they would serve God in their husbands and children, which would be a great good for the Christian republic.[68]

92. We continued on our way to Burgos with much difficulty because of the great cold and all the mud and water. As I was passing by a large pool of water, one of the nuns turned around to look back—the coach of Mother Teresa was in the lead—and saw the mule I was riding bend down to drink. Thinking that I had fallen into the water, she began to yell, at which Mother Teresa and the nuns were frightened until I came up to the coach. On another day, however, the Lord repaid me for this fright I gave them. At a bad place in the road, the driver fell, and the wheels passed on both sides of his body without harming him, yet I imagined—either God permitted it or the devil caused it—that Mother Teresa had fallen and the wheels had struck her on the head. This image was so strong that I lost feeling in my hands and dropped the reins. But the good Lord willed that the mule go quickly up to the coach, and I came to my senses and saw that Mother was alive. I gave thanks to our Lord who gives us what we need to suffer and frees us from danger.

93. Making the foundation was no small undertaking. The archbishop did not want to give the license, just as I had told Mother Teresa. There was nothing that could be done. With much displeasure, I had to return to Valladolid to preach during Lent, which was approaching, and to continue with the visitation of my monasteries. Eventually, however, the monastery of Burgos was very well made. This was the last foundation I undertook in the company of Mother because, returning from Burgos, the Lord took her during the month of October in the year 1582.[69]

94. Without her, I founded two other monasteries of nuns: One was in Lisbon, called San Alberto out of devotion to Cardinal Archduke Albert

who was then governing.[70] He favored—and even today favors—the nuns with alms. I took for foundress Mother María de San José along with other nuns from Seville. Shortly before this, Mother Isabel de San Francisco and some nuns left Seville with my commission to found the monastery of Sanlúcar de Alpechín. Accompanying the nuns [to Lisbon] were four friars: Father Fray Antonio de Jesús, Father Fray Mariano, a lay brother named Fray Juan, and myself, along with Pedro Cerezo Pardo and other seculars. As we approached Olivenza, in Portugal, a large rabid dog came upon us on the road and attacked Father Fray Antonio and his companion, Fray Juan, and bit two mules. If Pedro Cerezo had not killed it, it could have greatly harmed us. As it was, the two mules that were bitten died of rabies, and a healer of Olivenza treated all of us. This must have been a sign that the devil was rabid about the foundation because, while their monastery was being built, the nuns stayed at the Annunciation Convent of the Dominicans, where the deception of the false wounds of the prioress was discovered, as I will tell you about later.[71] Many other good things resulted from this foundation, such as the conversion of souls and the assistance of the nuns' prayers when the fighting against Drake and Don Antonio took place there.[72]

95. After this monastery was founded, I went to found the monastery of the nuns in Pamplona. I took for foundress Mother Catalina de Cristo, a great saint, as was evident in her holy death and miracles. This is the same nun whom Mother Teresa wanted to take to be prioress of the monastery in Soria, from where the foundation of Pamplona came. I remember saying to her, "Mother, why do you want to make her prioress, since she does not know how to read or write very well?" Mother Teresa responded, "She knows how to be a saint, and that is enough."

96. Accompanying this Mother and the other nuns for the foundation in Pamplona was Mother Leonor de la Misericordia.[73] Her vocation, life, and virtues were so rare that I want to say something in more detail. This lady was the sister of Don Jerónimo de Ayanz, famous for his great

strength, and Don Francés de Ayanz, head huntsman of Navarre. She was married to an important gentleman. Although she was very beautiful and elegant, she lived such an austere and holy life when she was a secular that, when her husband was away, she would sleep on a stairway, suffering the discomfort of the steps, for it seemed too indulgent to her to sleep on a smooth and level bed. Mother Teresa had come to Soria to make a foundation at the insistence of Doña Beatriz de Beamonte, aunt of Doña Leonor de Ayanz. Doña Beatriz, by the way, who also later became a nun of our order, always said that the spirit of a man named Pirula, held to be a prophet in Spain and who was later punished in Toledo as a fraud, was a false spirit. When Doña Leonor came to speak with Mother Teresa, she embraced her with much love, saying, "Mother, if only it were possible for me to be a Discalced nun." Holy Mother, with a prophetic spirit, responded, "Be on your way, daughter. Within a year you will be one." As it turned out, they were able to arrange things favorably. The bishop of Soria dissolved her marriage, and she was able to become a Discalced nun. Although she had been married for eight years, she proved to be a virgin and to have suffered the burden of an illegitimate marriage with such patience and holiness that for this alone the crown of a virgin martyr could be placed on her.[74] A large book could be written about her, especially if we mention her great prudence, valor, and natural graces such as writing, painting, and other talents of women and the manner with which she governed the monasteries of Pamplona and Barcelona where she was prioress. Not even her brothers Don Jerónimo and Don Francés exceeded her in manly spirit, or any Carmelite nun in modesty, good spirit, and perfection.

97. The nuns arrived in Pamplona during the month of December, accompanied by the lord of Oriz,[75] who was a hermit at that time. I had been waiting for them in the city for some days, preaching with good effect to the people there. Some women who knew not Castilian but only Basque came to hear me, and they said they understood my words. Doña Catalina Xavier, niece of Father Francisco Xavier of the Company and wife of Don Francés de Ayanz, helped us greatly with this

foundation.[76] She had the nuns in her house for a few days while the monastery was being built.

98. These, then, are the monasteries of the friars and the nuns in whose foundations I was occupied while I still had the habit of a Discalced friar, before my great persecutions began.

99. **Cyril:** *I would like to know if you helped found some monasteries of the Discalced Carmelites after you left the order, or what works you did that could be considered the fruit of the great tribulations and affronts you suffered in your expulsion and captivity in Barbary.*

100. **Anastasius:** So that you will give thanks to God and everyone will know that God is able to do His works by means of an evil and dishonorable man, I will recount for you the very serious and important affairs in the service of the Lord in which I found myself after having been stripped of the habit as someone disreputable and incorrigible. You will also understand how good was my resolve not to seek to recover my honor, nor to fight with my brothers about revoking the sentence and declaring it unjust, but instead to suffer in silence and throw myself into the hands of God.

101. I had a great concern whether it was an offense to God for a public man to let his honor be lost, because with it he can help souls and his brothers. This scruple was taken from me by very important, learned, and holy persons when, having been informed of the case, they advised me that I was not obliged to pursue litigation. Besides, I saw myself in such a fallen state that whatever diligence I put forth in the matter would be like kicking against the goad. But, even more, I was reassured by the events I later experienced in the state of my humiliating and unhappy misfortune. Recounting the foundations of the Discalced friars and nuns, I will tell you things that will surprise you.

102. The very day I arrived in Rome, having been rescued from captivity, Father Soto[77]—cantor of the pope and a great servant of God—was planning to buy a house for the foundation of a monastery of Discalced Carmelite nuns in Rome. This father knew me from long before, and

he conferred with me about it. We bought a house near Montecavallo and fixed it up, adapting all the rooms in the way that Mother Teresa arranged her monasteries. I spoke with six or seven young ladies that Father Soto had approved to become the first Discalced Carmelite nuns. He gathered them together in a private home, and there I taught them the ceremonies of the Discalced, reading the Rule to them and making sure they did what the nuns do. In this way, they were prepared without a Discalced foundress. Father Soto had felt how difficult it was to found a monastery of Discalced Carmelite nuns without having someone to show them how to put the Rule and constitutions into practice. The monastery of Discalced nuns in Genoa did not want to give any nuns for the foundation, nor did the monasteries in Spain want to help. Although they wanted to get an Augustinian nun from the convent of St. Martha for a foundress and teacher, later it seemed that she might do harm in teaching them the customs of her own order, which was relaxed. Thus the monastery was very well founded, much to the pleasure of Pope Clement VIII. He favored the nuns with good government by placing them directly under the jurisdiction of the Apostolic See. In his name, they were governed by Cardinal César Baronio[78]—who afterward placed his own niece there—and were given money for the foundation. Since childhood, these young ladies had been formed in prayer and spirituality and possessed the sincerity of angels. They had been instructed by two saintly Roman ladies whom I met in that city: Lady Olimpia Ursina, duchess of Aquasparta, and her aunt, the marquise of Rangona. Both ladies favored the foundation on account of the support of the spiritual men of Rome who often gathered in their homes.

103. One day, when I was at the house of the marquise of Rangona and feeling very afflicted by the many troubles I had at that time, I met an old holy priest, Father Filippo. He was the founder of the Congregation of the Oratory of Our Lady of Vallicella. This saint, seeing me thus, placed his hand on my face, saying, “Brother, do not doubt,” as if he understood the desolation I then felt. From that touch of affection and the words he spoke, I felt such great consolation and peace descend

into my heart, greater than any I have ever had in my life. May God be blessed, who gives so much grace to His servants that they can console the afflicted![79]

104. Returning, then, to our monastery . . . Cardinal César Baronio governed it in the name of His Holiness. Whenever he was going to give the habit to someone or have a profession, I often went to assist him, having the book in hand in order to advise him how the ceremonies are done in our order. The nuns of this monastery once brought a little relic into the church. The relic was of the body of Mother Teresa, and it gave off a very sweet fragrance. When His Holiness heard of it, he granted them permission to place the portrait of Holy Mother on the altar, which is a type of beatification. He took great care to do everything necessary, giving the briefs and commissions, in order to have her canonized.

105. Shortly after this foundation was made, Father Pedro de la Madre de Dios and his companions came to Rome from their monastery in Genoa. At that time I was staying in the house of Cardinal Deza as his theologian, in the habit of a Calced Carmelite. I told them that they should found a monastery in Rome where the head of the church is and that if they didn't, I would. When they saw I had already founded a monastery of nuns, that I held the office of theologian of the cardinal, and that I was favored by many cardinals and the ambassador of Spain, they feared my determination and daring. They did not want it said that someone expelled from the order was founding a monastery in Rome, so they came quickly and founded the monastery of Nuestra Señora de la Scala.[80] This monastery has done, is doing, and will do much good.

106. From this foundation came the beginnings of the congregation of the Discalced [Carmelites] of Italy. As I have said [PA 13.73], although they follow the same Rule and norms as the Discalced of Spain, the Spaniards strive more to perfect themselves by withdrawal, while those of Italy strive to win souls for God by apostolic zeal. Thus they have made foundations in Poland and have sent friars to Persia. And if Father Fray Tomás de Jesús, desirous of peace, obedience, and humility, hadn't managed to

put a stop to the Congregation of St. Paul for the conversion of infidels and gentiles, Pope Paul V would have instituted it within the Discalced Carmelites of Italy by now.[81] I have a printed copy of the brief for its founding in my possession. It was later founded by Monsignor Juan Bautista Vives, officer of Grace and Justice.[82]

107. From Flanders, I corresponded with Father Fray Tomás. One day on my way from Brussels to Antwerp, the bishop of Antwerp [Jean Le Mire] and other important persons discussed with me whether the Discalced Carmelite friars would make foundations in these States of Flanders. They offered to give them a college in Antwerp and an income for them to teach courses of scholastic theology on the material in which there is controversy with the heretics. The city of Antwerp borders Holland, from which so many of them come to dispute with the Catholics. It seemed to them—and it seemed to me also—that this order would do much good with the learning and zeal they profess and the austere and rigorous way in which they live and minister. Although the fathers of the Company of Jesus—who have done a lot of good and still do as we see—profess learning and zeal, they have nothing about them that is austere in appearance. The Capuchins—who are esteemed here for their austerity and rigor—do not profess learning, nor do they hear confessions, but only live a penitential life withdrawn from the world. I wrote of these things to Father Fray Tomás, and he communicated them to the vicar general of the order and the other fathers. They decided to send six friars for these foundations. Although they were a little afraid that Ana de Jesús, who wanted to bring Discalced friars from Spain, would hinder their growth, their concern ceased when the fathers of Spain resolved not to come to Flanders. The friars from Italy received letters and money from the archduke [Cardinal Albert] for them to come.

108. Mother Ana de Jesús and the other sisters came from Paris, and so far they have founded the monasteries of Brussels, Louvain, and Mons de Henao. If they had more sisters, they would have founded

many others. I want to say something about how they came from Spain to Paris, since God granted me the favor to have some part in these foundations.

109. A long time ago in Seville, I met Juan de Quintanadueñas Brétigny.[83] He was a native of Rouen though his father was Spanish. When I was in Rome, he discussed with me by letter how much a monastery of Discalced Carmelite nuns was desired in Rouen and that there were ways to found one. Cardinal Joyosa [François de Joyeuse] would favor them, and some wealthy ladies—relatives of Dr. Quesada and good servants of God—wanted to begin. Since there was no way to proceed because the Discalced Carmelite fathers did not want to permit nuns to make foundations in France, we agreed, also by letter, that the king and queen of France should write to the king and queen of Spain, asking that the nuns be sent. We even obtained a brief from His Holiness for this. This same Monsignor Brétigny went to Spain with Monsignor Don Pierre de Bérulle[84]—a holy, learned, and zealous priest—to negotiate. María de San José, the prioress at Lisbon whom they had wanted to be foundress, was deceased, so Ana de Jesús, as foundress, and her companion sisters went to make the foundation. Arriving in Paris to get the consent of the king in order to make the foundation in Rouen, the monastery was founded in Paris instead, through the support of the duchess of Longueville[85] and other important persons.[86] From there they made foundations in Amiens, Dijon, Tours, and other places. These nuns are greatly esteemed and sought after because of the great good they do by their good life, to the confusion of the heretics and the edification of the Catholics.

110. During my time in Rome, I was also in correspondence with Doña Beatriz de Mendoza, the countess of Castellar. She once wrote me that she desired to do some deed pleasing to the Lord. I advised her to found a monastery of Discalced Carmelite nuns of Mother Teresa of Jesus in Alcalá de Henares. There is a monastery there of the same order called La Concepción, founded by a *beata* named María de Jesús and under

the jurisdiction of the ordinary. I used to preach and hear confessions there when I was a secular priest, and, in fact, it was the reason I entered religious life, but they did not follow the same observance in all things as did the nuns of Mother Teresa.[87]

111. **Cyril:** *I wish to know whether you have founded any monastery of the Calced Carmelites, friars or nuns.*

112. **Anastasius:** No, because I am of the opinion that only the monasteries of reformed orders should be increased in the church. Although it is true that the general of the Calced, Fray Enrico Silvio Enríquez,[88] and other servants of God of the same order have invited me to help them make foundations of reformed Calced—so that a third type of order can be made between the Calced and the Discalced, like the Franciscan Recollects—I did not agree with this type of foundation. It seemed to me that the Discalced were enough for the reform of Carmel, since their original purpose was for this reformation.[89] However, a priest named Fray Francisco Potel, a true servant of God, was provincial of the Calced in Flanders and wanted to reform the monasteries of his province by removing some of the abuses that were in them, beginning with the monastery of Arras. When this servant of God came to Brussels, I confess that I accompanied him to speak to the archduke so that he would be well received, and to the nuncio [Guido Bentivoglio], so that the nuncio would give Fray Francisco a brief (which he was given). Beg the Lord that some good comes of it.

Fourteenth Dialogue: FRUITS

GRACIÁN CONTINUES WITH THE SAME SUBJECT REGARDING THE FRUIT OF HIS LABORS. HE RECOUNTS SOME OF THE REFORMATIONS OF THIS ORDER OF CARMEL AND OTHER ORDERS AND CONGREGATIONS IN WHICH HE HAS ASSISTED, AND SOME DIFFICULT DEALINGS AND CONFLICTS HE HAS HAD WITH SINNERS AND HERETICS. THESE FRUITS ARE SIGNIFIED BY THE JEWELS IN THE CROWN ON THE SHIELD.

1. **Cyril:** *You have told me about all the foundations of the Discalced Carmelite friars and nuns in which you had a part when you were their superior as well as afterward when you were no longer with them. Now, since we have mentioned reformed orders, I would like you to tell me about other reforms in which you were involved and the most important affairs that have occupied you.*

2. **Anastasius:** In order to proceed with greater order and clarity, you should know that ever since I was of a tender age, our Lord impressed upon my soul five very fervent and most efficacious desires: First, that all the orders of Christianity reform themselves and that religious return to following the life and customs of their first founders, for I was given to understand that they are the bones and nerves of the Christian republic; if they were corrupt and lax, this mystical body would not be able to stay healthy. Second, that the gentiles, infidels, and heretics be

converted to faith in Christ so that His divine blood, which was shed for so many thousands of souls, will not have been shed in vain since these souls are condemned for being outside the Catholic Church.[1] Third, that the sins of the world be hindered, that Christians be saved, and that those who have faith attain grace. Fourth, that persons of prayer and spirituality ascertain the most secure, beneficial, and meritorious way and avoid illusions, useless business of little spiritual significance, and other imperfections with which the devil tries to hinder their increase of charity. The fifth and last desire was to employ myself in great works in the service of God because, this Lord being infinite, it seemed it would have been too ungenerous of me to occupy myself in small works.

3. For the fulfillment of these five desires, our Lord has placed me in occupations, opportunities, and affairs that, had He given them to someone who was not as evil as myself, would have brought forth much fruit. So that you will give great thanks to God, you will see from the unfolding of this history that the most serious occupations were offered to me after I no longer wore the habit of the Discalced.

4. The fact is, I had no sooner made my profession in Pastrana when I was entrusted with the visitation and reform of the Calced Carmelites in Andalusia.[2] I was occupied in this for more than four or five years, even though my main intention was to promote and advance the foundations of the Discalced; the Calced were opposing us and it was easier to defend ourselves by having them as subjects rather than superiors. Still, its reformation was not without fruit. Although many advised me to proceed with rigor—punishing faults and taking their monasteries for the Discalced—it always seemed to me that a better method was to put the young ones in studies. Besides keeping them busy, learning is a good means toward virtue. Thus, I arranged for classes to be given in Granada, where I sent Fray Jerónimo Ferrer, a very learned servant of God. I established houses of studies in Seville and Castro del Río, from which many friars later came forth whose learning and virtue

contributed to the honor of the order in that province. I made the best ones superiors, rewarded and praised the good ones, and marginalized and demoted the ones who were not good. And I was patient with all, treating them with kindness and respect, for which I hope in God there was some benefit.[3]

5. When Drake and Don Antonio attacked Lisbon, it was believed that six thousand harquebuses were hidden in the Calced monastery of the Carmen and that the revolt was going to start from there by which Lisbon and perhaps all of Portugal would be lost, with much harm to the faith.[4] Cardinal Archduke Albert sent me to enter the Carmen with the patent of visitator and reformer of all the Calced Carmelites of Portugal. At first, it was a great offense to have someone who was Castilian, Discalced, and younger than they enter for the purpose of reform, especially since that province was the most reformed of the order; but afterward, they saw that my intention was only to defend their honor and make the Castilians realize that our friars were not treasonous. The suspicion based on this false testimony was so strong that the artillery of the castle was aimed at the Carmen, and companies of soldiers stealthily surrounded the monastery at night. Seeing that I disabused the Castilians of their bad opinion, the friars rejoiced and thanked me very much. I sent some friars—those who might have become restless because of their great devotion to the cause of Don Antonio—away from Lisbon to other monasteries, not as a punishment but as a reward and an honor. Thus was the order reformed, at least with regard to that unrest, which was not just a little. At that time, one of the principal masters had stirred up a lot of trouble,[5] wanting to prove that he was a legitimate heir of Don Antonio. Other friars, who had been captains and soldiers in the militia, also sided with this Don Antonio. I didn't go too much into their other customs because, as I said, they were capable of reforming other provinces.

6. When I was the theologian of Cardinal Deza, in the habit of the Calced, Fray Miguel Garro and his companion, Fray Juan, Discalced

Augustinians, came to Rome to secure and establish the reform of their order, which was then beginning in Spain. They had much opposition from their [cardinal] protector and from the Augustinian fathers of the Observance. Among other things, it was believed that they were without a rule and constitutions and that they were governed only by the whim and brains of four ignorant friars. The two friars approached me and I obtained for them the favor of the ambassador of Spain and that of many cardinals. Since my patron was the protector of the Spanish, they overcame the opposition. Taking constitutions that were followed by some of the reformed [Augustinian] friars of Italy, such as those of the Church of Nostra Señora del Popolo,[6] and changing them slightly—with some additions from the way of life of the Discalced Carmelites—they presented them to the pontiff, Clement VIII. Their constitutions pleased him, and he issued an apostolic brief for the friars to erect a province and to found monasteries of Discalced Augustinians.

7. A short time later, a Discalced Trinitarian, Fray Juan Bautista [de la Concepción], came to me. He had serious opposition from the same man who had promised to help him take care of his business but was actually undermining it. Eventually, with the same favor I mentioned above regarding the brief obtained by the Discalced Augustinians, a brief of His Holiness was drawn up, much to the encouragement of Father Fray Juan Bautista. It authorized Father Fray Elías de San Martín, general of the Discalced Carmelites, to preside over, govern, and found monasteries of Discalced Trinitarians until they had a sufficient number of monasteries to make a province and elect a provincial from among themselves.[7]

8. After that, when I was commissioned to go to Africa and was in Madrid to procure letters of safe conduct from the king, the sacristan of the monastery of the Mercedarians, Fray Juan, came to speak with the countess of Castellar. He wanted to begin the reformation of the Order of La Merced, and he asked her for help. The countess sent for me and we agreed to confide in his own general and ask him for permission to found houses of Discalced Mercedarians. She herself offered to found

two houses in two of her towns. I read their rule, which is that of St. Augustine, and their constitutions. Adding relevant parts from the constitutions of the Discalced Carmelites, Trinitarians, and Augustinians, reformed constitutions were drawn up, and the beginning of the Discalced Mercedarians was thus made.[8]

9. When I was in Rome without the habit of any order at the time of my greatest sufferings, Cardinal Alejandrino[9]—nephew of Pius V and head of the Congregation for Religious—wanted to send me to Naples to join some reformed Dominicans who had their monastery in Chiaia so that I might help with that reform. But as God did not want me to leave the order of His Virgin Mother and willed that I still have some merit in the reformation of the order of the glorious St. Dominic, He ordained that upon my return from Africa the second time, in my Calced habit, Doña María of Toledo, duchess of Alba and wife of Duke Don Fadrique, sent for me from Villafranca. She wanted me to help in the reformation of the Discalced Dominican nuns that was begun in a monastery she founded named La Laura. So I stayed in her house that whole summer in the company of Father Master Fray Diego de Yanguas, a Dominican. I gave talks to the nuns each day, teaching them about the reformation of Mother Teresa of Jesus; helped put in order the constitutions that Doña María drafted in virtue of a brief she obtained from Pope Clement VIII; and persuaded her to relocate the community from the monastery of La Laura in Villafranca, which is in Galicia, to Valladolid. In order that these Discalced Dominican nuns might increase, I went to Toledo to speak with Doña Juana de Castilla, who had founded a monastery of Discalced Dominicans in that city, and gave talks to her nuns, showing them how to build upon their foundation. We arranged with a Dominican nun, the sister of the lord of Valdemoro, to make a foundation of Discalced Dominicans in his town, thus executing his wife's will. When the lady was dying, she arranged with her husband that a foundation of Discalced Carmelite nuns be made, but when the will was actually drawn up, she wanted to say Discalced Dominicans instead, and she left rent for this. Later, I went to Valencia

and spoke with other Dominican nuns about founding monasteries of this reformation of their order in that kingdom.

10. When the court moved to Valladolid, my brother was given an apartment adjacent to a monastery of Discalced Bernardine nuns, which was founded as a daughter house of Las Huelgas of Burgos. The whole time I was in that city—which was a considerable amount of time—I gave talks to them each day, teaching them the ways of the Discalced Carmelite nuns and what Mother Teresa observed in her reforms. The nuns wrote down these talks. With this and with meeting regularly with their confessor, Fray Juan, great good was done. Fray Juan, of the Order of St. Bernard [the Cistercians], was a great servant of God who began the reformation [of that monastery] and used to listen to my talks. Now, Don Juan de Alarcón, lord of a town called Bonache, would come to this monastery to say Mass and hear confessions. He had been a gallant and dashing gentleman when he was married; when his wife died, he was ordained a priest. He led such a rigorous life, with such a fervent spirit, that he went to Rome to obtain permission for the reformation of all the nuns of Spain. When he returned with letters of His Holiness for the Catholic king and his ministers, His Majesty sent him to reform the monastery of Las Huelgas of Burgos and all its daughter houses. Great good might have come of this reform, using the method we both discussed, if the nuns of Las Huelgas had not been ladies of high standing, desirous of keeping their old customs. It was his intention that these Discalced Bernardine nuns increase and found more monasteries. I went to Toledo and arranged to buy a house left vacant by the Discalced Carmelite fathers when they moved to the other side of the bridge. The second monastery of Discalced Bernardines was founded in that house.[10]

11. While I was in the city of Toledo, I applied to the archbishop and his council for a license for the countess of Castellar to found her monastery of Corpus Christi in Madrid, from which began the reformation of the Discalced Jeronimites; she and I had previously discussed introducing the way of Mother Teresa into that order.[11] There was no

little opposition to this idea. The Jeronimite friars and nuns live with great observance and seclusion and made every effort that there not be reformed or Discalced Jeronimite nuns, lest it be said afterward that there was something to reform in the Jeronimites or that there had been some relaxation.

12. Also, when preaching in Madrid, I went to the church of the Caballero de Gracia many times.[12] He was disappointed by some reformed clerics who tried to make a foundation there. When that foundation fell apart, he asked me to get the Franciscan nuns of Concepción Monastery, who would live with a greater spirit of reformation, to come. A nun of much prudence, the daughter of the marquis of Auñón, whose name was Doña Baltasara, came from the monastery of Santa Clara to join the reforming nuns.

13. After this, I went to Alicante, which was on my way to Rome where I was going in order to give an account to Pope Clement VIII of my commission to Africa. Because of my preaching there that Lent [1605], it was arranged with Dean Zaragoza, a great servant of God, and Captain Ballibrera and other important men of the town that a monastery of reformed nuns be founded in the city. Although the bishop of Orihuela, a Dominican friar to whom they were to be subject, wanted them to be Dominicans while I wanted Discalced Carmelites, neither of us could win over the civil authorities. They didn't want mendicant orders but only wanted the canonesses of the monastery of San Cristóbal of Valencia. They said they already had Discalced Franciscans in the monastery of La Verónica, and they did not want nuns who were subject to friars. I went to Valencia and discussed this case with the cardinal. He gave us two nuns most desirous of reformation. I returned with them to Alicante in the company of Master Cristóbal Colón, the archbishop's visitator—who at one time was the confessor of Mother Teresa of Jesus [13]—and the monastery of reformed Augustinian canonesses was founded.

14. From Alicante, I boarded a galley in order to go to Barcelona to arrange for the printing of my books, but the ship and others sailing

with it were ordered to return to Alicante, where I disembarked. Desiring to make the journey by land, I passed through Valencia. There I was detained by Cardinal Don Juan de Ribera, archbishop of Valencia. He commissioned me to conduct a visitation of the monasteries of the Discalced Augustinian canonesses, who have a claim on Mother Teresa of Jesus since they follow her constitutions in conjunction with the rule of St. Augustine. The holy cardinal instituted this order because the Discalced Carmelite friars did not want Carmelite nuns to be subject to the bishop.[14] In the beginning, it was necessary to visit and instruct them, in the same way that I used to visit the Carmelite nuns in the time of Mother Teresa. When I began this visitation, I found that the monasteries of Valencia, Alcoy, and Denia were well established, although the house of Denia was built more to my liking, as was the monastery of Santa Ursula in Valencia. When I finished the visitation, I made arrangements for the foundation of two more monasteries of the same order. One was in the town called Ollería, which is in the jurisdiction of Valencia, and the other was in Almansa, which is of the diocese of Cartagena.[15] I was glad to leave when that visitation was over because they were asking for many more monasteries of that order and the Discalced Carmelite nuns were not increasing much in that region.

15. Before leaving Valencia, I discussed with Dean Frígola and other stewards of the hospital about having the Brothers of Obregón come in order to improve the service given to the poor by that distinguished hospital.[16] Long before, when I was in Portugal, a hospital for soldiers, located in the Castle of Lisbon, was reformed this way. Its ministry was entrusted to me by the marquis of Santa Cruz, who was the general, and Don Gabriel Niño, field marshal of the soldiers who were treated and healed there. Since those brothers did so much good, they were brought from Lisbon to the Hospital of the Misericordia, and they got others from the court hospital in Madrid to join them. In this manner, the Misericordia was successfully reformed.

16. No less good was done for some monasteries in Flanders, especially those of the Carmelite Order. The provincial, Father Fray Hernando de San Vitores, with counsel and support, was able to establish enclosure in his monasteries; previously, they had no enclosure and women came in whenever they liked.[17] And the provincial from Arras of the Flemish province, Fray Francisco Potel, procured the reformation of the monasteries of his province. After discussing the situation with me, he and I spoke about it to Archduke Albert and to the nuncio of Flanders, who issued a brief by which some good was done by way of reformation.

17. One of the best fruits of these occupations is the salvation of souls and the conversion of gentiles, infidels, and heretics. Regarding these conversions, I can give much thanks to God for having provided me with very good opportunities throughout the time of my pilgrimage.

18. At the beginning of the foundation in Seville, a great servant of God called Licentiate Padilla came to our monastery of Los Remedios.[18] He had brought a certain quantity of beads, strings, and rosaries to be distributed to the people in the kingdom of the Congo where he was planning to go for their conversion, but since these things were stolen from the inn where he was staying, he came to lodge in our monastery. He inspired in me and in the first friars who were there a desire for the conversion of those people. I spoke with him about the need in the church for the reformation of religious orders so they could provide sufficient ministers for the conversion of the gentiles and for the benefit and perfection of Catholics. This servant of God, being so fervent and zealous, was moved to work for these reforms. Therefore, with letters from the archbishop of Seville, Don Cristóbal de Rojas, he went to the king, Don Philip II, and stirred up desires for the reforms and their promotion, which had grown lukewarm since the death of Pius V. At the solicitation of this servant of God, the nuncio Ormaneto gave his authorization to continue the reforms.

19. In the monastery of Seville, in these beginnings, the concord or brotherhood was made between the Discalced Franciscans and us

Discalced Carmelites to go and convert the gentiles. The superiors of both groups signed a written document.[19] Many of the Franciscans who were awaiting passage to the Far East at that time were crucified in Japan, as is written about in a history by Father Osorio, a Discalced Franciscan.[20] I then wrote and had printed a little book called *Estímulo de la propagación de la fe* [Stimulus for the propagation of the faith], which has been and still is very fruitful, although to some of our own friars, who were not led by God in this spirit of zeal, it did not seem good.[21] It was later reprinted by the Congregation for the Propagation of the Faith, which Monsignor Vives has instituted in Rome.

20. Countless souls were converted to the faith by Father Fray Francisco de Jesús, called el Indigno, and his companions, whom I sent to the kingdom of the Congo. I persisted in sending our friars for the conversion of the people there, even though the first group drowned and another group I then sent was captured by heretics. Although some people were discouraged on account of these losses, it caused me to have more determination, seeing that the devil was so openly trying to impede us. That is what I told King Don Philip II when he learned about the loss of those we sent on the two previous occasions. He commanded us to send a third group. Of the fruit that was brought forth with miracles in those lands, I have written at length.[22]

21. Also, when I finished my term as provincial and remained president of the chapter as first definitor, in the absence of the newly elected provincial, Father Fray Nicolás Doria, I sent twelve religious of ours to the West Indies [Mexico]. There they founded a monastery and afterward went on multiplying. They have done and are doing a great deal of good in the conversion of the gentiles of those Indies.[23]

22. The hardship that I thought would bear the least fruit was my captivity. I thought I would end my life and works dying in those lands or occupied with rowing in the galleys of the Turks. But the Lord gathered very good roses from those thorns because many of the captive Christians who were set on denying the faith persevered in the faith

on account of the talks, admonitions, and sermons I gave in the prison. The Lord gave me some credibility with the Turks and the means by which to rescue some of the weaker Christians who were on the verge of denying the faith. He also granted that I persuade many renegades and Moors to return to the holy Catholic faith and help them flee to Christian lands. For this purpose, I gave them testimonial letters written in Latin. In order to keep the Turks from finding them, I hid them in some *nóminas,* which the Moors were accustomed to carry in leather pouches around their necks. When the Christians went to the Inquisition and presented these testimonials, they were reconciled with a moderate secret penance. I later met in Christian lands many of those who had come from Barbary.

23. What I hope in the Lord has done notable good in the cause of these conversions are the many memorials I gave to Pope Clement VIII when I returned to Rome after my captivity. One of them is circulating in a little book I published called *De redención de cautivos* [Concerning the redemption of captives]. I pleaded with His Holiness to have compassion for the many souls who suffer in those places from not having ministers to help them in the practice of the faith. In large part, it was due to these memorials and my continual solicitude in speaking to the cardinals of Rome about this situation that His Holiness erected and instituted a new congregation of cardinals called "*Propaganda Fide*" [Propagation of the Faith], making Cardinal Santa Severina its head. He summoned me one day with regard to my memorials, asking me to help the congregation carry out what they proposed.[24]

24. This congregation ordered me to return to Barbary with a brief of His Holiness, authorizing me to preach the holy year of 1600 in the company of Father Fray Ambrosio de Soncino, a very holy and fervent man of the Capuchin Order.[25] Before becoming a religious, he was the marquis of Soncino in the state of Milan. He and his companions went to Algiers, because the Capuchins have safe conduct to go to those parts, while I went to the court of the king of Spain to get letters of

introduction for the governors of the frontiers and for the sharif, king of Morocco and Fez, so that they would grant me safe conduct to enter their states.[26]

25. Thus, in the year 1601, I went to Ceuta.[27] I gave letters of the king to the marquis of Villarreal, the governor of that frontier. He obtained safe conduct for me from the alcaide of Tétouan.[28] While passing through there, I did some good for the captives and renegades of that city. Much more might have been accomplished if what I discussed with the alcaide and what he wrote from Tétouan to the sharif in Morocco had been put into effect; namely, that it would be good if peace were made between the sharif and the king of Spain,[29] and that the sharif cede the Al-Arache River to the king of Spain. The alcaide believed that such an important negotiation like this could only be done according to points of protocol. Since neither the sharif nor the king of Spain was willing to send a man of importance and authority as ambassador to ask for this peace accord, he thought there was no better means of making this agreement than through the mediation of a religious who did not profess points of honor. When he saw that I was carrying letters from the king for the sharif as well as a papal bull, he wanted me to negotiate the peace. So he wrote to Morocco. I saw the good that such a peace might bring and I did not want to disappoint him. I left to speak about this with the marquis of Villarreal in Ceuta, the duke of Medina Sidonia in Sanlúcar,[30] and the governor of Castile in San Juan del Puerto. To them it seemed like something heaven sent. They wrote about it to the king and the duke of Lerma.[31] I waited in Ceuta for the reply, preaching there during Lent, and as I saw they were delaying, I went to Aranjuez to speak to His Majesty, his confessor, and the duke of Lerma, telling them that if they wanted me to return to Morocco, they should send for me at my monastery in Toledo where I would be waiting.[32] I wish to God that I had returned to Morocco—though I imagined I would never again return to Christian lands—for if the peace had been made, the Al-Arache River would have been ours and the armada would not have been lost in the year 1607.[33]

26. Another fruit of these kinds of conversions resulted from the labors I recounted to you. Having written many letters of instruction to Monsignor Vives in Rome for the foundation of a congregation that is now called Propagation of the Faith, it was established and at first was to be made up of Discalced Carmelites. His Holiness issued the brief and named Father Fray Tomás de Jesús as its vicar general.[34] I corresponded with Father Tomás about the work of conversions, especially regarding the mission to Persia.[35] He and Father Fray Pablo Simón de Jesús María, who had just returned from Persia, arranged with Pope Paul V that I go there with the title of bishop of Armenia for the conversion of Persia.[36] That mission has cooled off a bit, but our Carmelites in Kraków are still talking about conversions there and the great benefit that can be done for the kingdom of the Muscovites, recently made subject to the king of Poland.[37] I have written to them about this and have sent them books from here in Flanders by way of Frankfurt and Cologne.

27. I was preaching in Valencia and Pamplona in the year 1607 when the marquis of Guadaleste was named the ambassador for Flanders. He asked me if I wanted to go to that country with him. I responded that I would comply with whatever obedience asked of me. He took me at my word and got a patent from the nuncio of Spain for me to accompany him.[38] Since there are so many heresies in this region, the ministry of the ambassador of Spain is very important in the business of combating them. I hope in God that the things I have dealt with him about and the sermons, disputations, and books I have written against heresies have done some good in support of the faith against the Lutheran and Calvinist heresies.

28. Turning now to other conversions, particularly those of sinners, the Lord has been merciful in rewarding my labors on their behalf in that many offenses against God have been thwarted. A house was set up in Seville for wayward girls. The problem was great in that city because there was no place to gather and teach the many girls who became sinners when they got older; they were already starting to be so at a young age. Some lay people who were servants of God discussed doing this

good work, such as a certain Castro and his companions. In their company was a very fervent, dark African,[39] a slave named Juanillo. He was a young man, about twenty years old. So great was the opposition of the monastery of Las Recogidas del Nombre de Jesús and their patrons—the duke of Medina and others—that there was no more talk about doing this good work. The fathers of the Company and everyone else dealing with this project were also lukewarm about it. Juanillo came to me one day, saying, "Well, how is it, Father, that such a holy work can be left undone for fear of men? So that you may see who God is, I alone, an uneducated African slave, will have to do it in spite of all the opposition of hell. Sign this paper for me, in which you recommend this as a good work." I signed it for him, and within fifteen days he was getting a house and teachers for the instruction of the girls. This was the beginning of a very important work in that city.

29. When I was in Lisbon for the foundation of the monastery of the Discalced Carmelite nuns, a very good woman named Contreras came to the city and lodged in the house of a woman of ill repute named Isabel Pulida. When Contreras reproached her for the bad life she was living, Isabel replied that she and other Castilian women would gladly change their ways, but there were no houses in that city where repentant women could be received. Contreras shared this with Doña Inés de Ayala, the wife of Don Juan de Ayala, majordomo of Cardinal Archduke Albert. They informed me of the situation and entrusted me with the task of founding a monastery for repentant women in Lisbon. I spoke with the captain of the artillery, Céspedes, a great servant of God, and he helped me considerably. We placed three or four of these women in a private residence and provided for them. I asked the archbishop for a license to found a monastery for them. He referred me to the cardinal, and I obtained the license. I rented a house that had been a monastery of Flemish nuns, called Nuestra Señora de Gloria, and placed three or four of the repentant women there. When word got around about such a monastery, many women converted. For its support and government, an association of leading noblemen of that kingdom was established;

Count Merino-mor Don Duarte de Castelo Branco and Francisco Barreto, majordomo of His Highness, were among them. These gentlemen bought them the house and provided means for its sustenance. Each year when the ships sailed for the Indies, they sent some of the more beautiful women to marry there. Many married exceedingly well; with this enticement, many women converted. A very pleasing work was done in Lisbon for our Lord.

30. When I was in Naples in the year 1598, I happened to go to the hospital for incurables in the company of the marquise of La Valle. A Spanish woman, who had been brought to this hospital where they took in repentant prostitutes, spoke to me. She said that if there was a house for wayward Spanish women in Naples, it would be a great benefit and many sins would be avoided in that city. I discussed the matter with Father Iñigo de Mendoza of the Company of Jesus, son of Don Alvaro de Mendoza, governor of the principal castle of Naples. We arranged for the founding of a house for repentant women and rented one in the Spanish quarter next to Santa Ana. I used some of the money that had been given in alms in Naples for my rescue to buy beds, tables, and odds and ends for the new house and persuaded some of these women to come and live there. They greatly enlightened me about the witchcraft and other abominations being practiced among the Spanish in Naples. Concerned that something be done about it, I spoke with Cardinal Gesualdo who was then the archbishop of Naples and a member of the Congregation of the Holy Office in Rome. If the Italians had been more courageous in dealing with the Spanish there, much good could have been done in this matter. Enlightened about these things, I discussed them with the confessor of the king and other persons when I was in Spain, wanting them to realize that when these Spaniards and wayward Spanish women go to Italy and then return to Spain, they ignite the fire of sorcery and commit abominable sins. Although there were great difficulties in the beginning, the convent of repentant women in Naples went forward with the help of the count and countess of Lemos, who were the vice regents of Naples. The countess smoothed out the

difficulties, and the convent of repentant women was set up.[40] The convent called Soledad was instituted not for wayward women but for poor girls who were the daughters of soldiers.[41] I went there many times to preach and hear confessions.

31. In this ministry of the conversion of prostitutes in different parts of Spain and Italy, our Lord has shown me much favor. I could count many women who, being helped with Christian education and alms, have turned away from a bad life, especially in Seville.

32. Also, in this matter of conversion of sinners, I owe much to our Lord for those who were converted in Barbary during the time I was a slave. I was able to do good to their souls by constantly sharing the Word of God; many of those who had gone a long time without going to confession came to me repentent and changed their lives. After I returned to Rome, many apostate friars and a few apostate nuns who were fugitives from their orders came to me. This was during the five years I was there in the habit of a Calced Carmelite in the office of theologian of Cardinal Deza. With the favor God had given me with the cardinals and my acquaintance with the superiors of the orders, most of whom were my friends, and the experience I had of religious life—since all things are useful in their time—the Lord was served in that those nuns and friars were enabled to return to their religious profession. It would take too long if I were to say in detail what has taken place in this matter. Even if God had brought me to Rome and permitted all my troubles for no other reason than to help reconcile apostate friars and nuns, I would consider it all worthwhile.

33. For many years, I dealt with Mother Teresa of Jesus and her daughters and other persons of great prayer who had many unusual spiritual experiences. These included Sister Ursula in Naples, who was examined by Sixtus V; Sister Isabela and many *beatas* of Baeza and Jaén; Father Fray Melchor Cano, a Dominican who was sometimes enraptured for sixteen hours;[42] and many Franciscan nuns, like the one from St. Clare of Carrión. With this experience and having read many books about

spiritual experiences and having studied carefully the subject of authentic and illusionary spirits, the Lord gave me much light for discernment of spirits, judgment of illusions, and deceptions of the devil in order to give some help.

34. In Lisbon, I was in contact with Father Fray Luis de Granada.[43] We discussed very particularly the spirit of María de la Visitación, prioress of the Annunciation, who said she had the stigmata, and that of Ana Rodríguez, a *beata,* who said she had a crucifix imprinted on her chest. I also discussed these things with María de San José, prioress of the Discalced Carmelites in Lisbon. With the written testimony of her opinion and the report I gave to the king at El Escorial, the Inquisition intervened to investigate the wounds. They were discovered to be fake. I realized that by means of this deception and others in Lisbon, the people were becoming restless to such an extent that the entire kingdom of Portugal could have been lost.[44] Because of the enemies I had made on account of this case, I was forced to flee from Portugal lest they kill me.

35. I was also brought to Evora by the archbishop, Don Teutonio de Braganza, to examine persons who, under the pretext of receiving revelations, were disquieting the souls of the Portuguese.[45] Much harm could have been done if God did not remedy the situation. Here I met women of very unusual spirits. Among them was a poor bricklayer's wife. She told me that God had revealed to her a few years earlier all that afterward happened in France with the death of King Henry III, who was killed by the Dominican friar.[46] Similarly, in Seville, I examined a woman who spoke many languages. She told me that she had spoken in a prophetic spirit with Queen Mary of England, who was the wife of King Don Philip II.[47] She appeared to her—she was already deceased a few years—and told her many grave things that would happen in the region of Flanders and the Spanish domains, as did indeed happen years later.[48]

36. Before getting involved with these spirits in Portugal, I was brought by the bishop of Jaén, Don Francisco Sarmiento, to his city and house.

For more than half a year, he had me examine the extraordinary spirits of some *beatas*. The Lord was served because some deceptive teachings were uprooted, which a priest named Gaspar Lucas had sown.[49] I wrote a book about it titled *Higuera loca* [Crazy fig tree], dealing with the deceptions woven by the devil by way of sensuality. Many *beatas* are indeed holy, and I have guided others to become holy, like one in Granada named Doña Lussía Dermana de San Jerónimo, who afterward got others to follow her example. But among the *beatas*, I have also found many false spirits, especially spirits held bound by scruples and baseless fears. To help these souls, it is more important to teach the true spirit of the love of God, purity, and humility than to simply tell them not to fool around with illusions and dealings with the devil.

37. In Brussels, there was a married man who was held to be very spiritual and who had written many books of lofty spiritual doctrine. He went around conversing with Carthusian and Capuchin fathers and many nuns and persuaded them of a teaching that had the appearance of great perfection because it led them to immediate union with God. But his teaching gave the impression that there was less perfection in vocal prayers, veneration of images, and making pilgrimages, and that these should be left in order to come to what is more perfect, namely, the prayer of immediate union. This teaching greatly disposes one for the Lutheran heresy. I sometimes met him in the company of the prior of the Carthusians and other servants of God. I wrote an *Apología* [Defense] against him and, apropos of this, a book titled *Vida del alma y verdadera imitación de Cristo* [Life of the soul and true imitation of Christ]. I hope to God there has been and will be some beneficial results.[50]

38. In the year 1609, I went to see the Discalced Carmelite nuns in Mons de Henao. They informed me that a cleric named Carlos Fevre had visited them and told them great things. He prophesied a great reform of the church and that the House of Austria was going to lose the empire. He was saying many other things of this nature to many Carthusian and

Capuchin fathers, nuns, other servants of God, and important ladies. I told him we had to talk. I examined him for three days. Although he was well read and injected Sacred Scripture into almost everything he said, in the end I understood that he was crazy and had lost his judgment because of too much prayer and penance. I brought him to the nuncio, who was in Flanders, and arranged that he be locked up so that he could not say Mass or disquiet the souls of sincere people to whom he spoke. I also gave the nuncio my opinion about some revelations of a prioress of the Bridgetines of Tournai, revelations that were communicated to me by order of Monsignor de Venesi. Thus was this cleric's way of reformation brought to an end.[51]

39. The Lord has placed in my hands very important business in His service, besides what I have recounted, such as dealing with the soldiers and rebels of Lisbon and hearing the confessions of those imprisoned by Don Antonio, since they did not trust confessing to any Portuguese. The cessation of rebellions and restlessness of that kingdom was procured because things were communicated to me in confession for the purpose of discussing them in secret with Cardinal Archduke Albert. By this means, much good was done. Likewise, much good was done among the Spanish soldiers, restoring peace to their souls and preventing revolts.

40. Once, while I was in the monastery of the Discalced Carmelites in Alcalá, a very grave man, one of the richest and most illustrious men of the court, came to me. Not wanting anyone to see or know anything, he took me with him to Madrid during the night and put me up in a principal house of the city. I was hidden for two days, occupied with a matter of great importance with the result that many sins and much turmoil that might have occurred were prevented. Since it was a secret, I will not tell you what it was.[52]

41. In Rome, in my office as theologian of the cardinal [Deza] of one of the oldest congregations, that of the Holy Office, I was given very serious responsibilities in the service of God. My patron [Cardinal

Deza] used to send me to deliver secret messages, like the one I once carried to the cardinal of Florence, who was later Pope Leo XI,[53] messages that could not be communicated or confided to secular servants.

42. Finally, in all these hardships that I have suffered, I have never stopped studying, writing, printing books, preaching, hearing confessions, governing monasteries, and being occupied in works of the active life, such as visiting and consoling the sick and sometimes teaching and lecturing. For instance, I once lectured in Sacred Scripture in Seville for Dr. Molina at a time when I was very busy with the foundation of the monasteries there.[54]

Fifteenth Dialogue: Prayer

Gracián gives an account of his spirit and method of prayer and explains his teaching according to the twelve ways of proceeding [in the spirit]; in each of these ways, he refers to something that has happened to him. This material corresponds to the name of Jesus, which is in the middle of the shield.[1]

1. **Cyril:** *I want you to state and explain for me your spirit and prayer, especially what God has given you after your hardships and persecutions.*

2. **Anastasius:** I told you at the beginning that I would rather tell you my sins than my virtues, and to have *espíritu* [spirit] and prayer is virtue. I only agreed to recount some of the hardships I suffered and the mercies I received.

3. **Cyril:** *You are wrong, because the spirit is a mercy of God toward souls and a gift from above, from the Father of lights [see Jas 1:17]. It is a talent to profit from and a good that the steward receives from his Lord to make use of and trade with.*[2] *If I were to ask a steward how much money he was given by his master in order to go shopping in the market, he doesn't have to act proud if it is a lot or be sad if it is little. He has only to be confounded, seeing how badly he used the talents he had received for gaining a profit and what an unfaithful steward he has been, according to the saying of St. Paul: "The first requirement of an administrator is that he be found trustworthy"*

[1 Cor 4:2]. St. Augustine reveals his spirit in the book of his Meditations*, St. Jerome reveals some of his revelations, St. Paul writes of his raptures, and Hermas, his disciple, writes of his visions in a book called* The Shepherd*. Fray Roberto, Fray Huguentino Amadeo, and other very spiritual men write in the same way. St. Mechtilde, St. Isabel Escomagensa, St. Bridget, St. Catherine of Siena, St. Catherine of Genoa, St. Angela di Foligno, and blessed Mother Teresa of Jesus write entire books about their visions, revelations, and spirit. St. Hildegard wrote a large book of her visions called* Scivias.[3] *As the Holy Spirit says, "Who knows a man's innermost self but the man's own spirit within him?" [1 Cor 2:11]. Who is going to tell us by what spirit God has led you unless you tell us? You are obliged, as St. Paul says [see 2 Cor 1:4], to console and instruct us if you have received consolation, light, and doctrine in your spirit since "God does not light a lamp in order to hide it under a bushel basket, but rather puts it on a lampstand so that it may give light to all in the house. Thus, let your light shine before men so that they may glorify your Eternal Father in heaven" [Mt 5:15–16].*

4. **Anastasius:** How is it possible to tell you what has gone on in my spirit in the fifty years that I have been praying, whether poorly or well? For sometimes, in the blink of an eye, abundant light and so many concepts come to me that I could write many books just on that brief flash of resplendent light.

5. **Cyril:** *I am not asking you about all the concepts that have come to you in prayer, for I already see that these are beyond numbering; and neither is there memory for all that, nor tongue or pen to speak and write of them. I am asking you about your method of prayer and the way God has led your spirit. According to what I know and have read in the saints, there are twelve principal ways of the spirit. These ways are like twelve interior windows through which good desires enter and light is given to the free will, or like the twelve gates of the city of Jerusalem, or the twelve precious stones that are on the breastplate of Aaron the priest [see Rev 21:10–13; Ex 28:29].*

- *6. The first is vocal prayer and the reading of good books;*

- *the second, meditation and study;*
- *the third, contemplation;*
- *the fourth, exterior vision with the bodily eyes;*
- *the fifth, interior or imaginative vision;*
- *the sixth, intellectual vision;*
- *the seventh, to hear exterior words with the bodily ears;*
- *the eighth, words formed interiorly that are heard in the heart;*
- *the ninth, unformed interior concepts and words, which are like the writing of God in the soul and which seem to be signs of the divine will;*
- *the tenth, dreams that come to a person while asleep, like those of Pharaoh or Nebuchadnezzar;*
- *the eleventh, interior attention, which is when the soul is not completely absorbed or enraptured but awake, yet with the senses so impeded and occupied that she is not aware of anything exterior;*
- *the twelfth and last, ecstasies and raptures, when the exterior and interior powers are completely absorbed and elevated.*

Tell me, according to these ways, how it goes with you, and give me something that will serve as an example I can learn from.

7. **Anastasius:** With sincerity and truth, I will tell you something of what I have experienced and what I think will most benefit you for the glory of God and the good of your soul. This is what moves me to write this account of my spirit, even though I would much rather tell you about my faults and failings since I have had so many that I could recount and write about.

VOCAL PRAYER AND READING

8. My vocal prayer has not amounted to much more than a third part of the rosary of our Lady, a few devotions, the Divine Office, and Mass, nothing else.

9. My reading and study of good books has been habitual since the time I was ten years old, when I began to study, until now, though primarily ever since I began theology, which is my profession. Many times our Lord has given me to understand that since He gives light to the learned in the ordinary way of their study, it is not necessary that He give it to them by special revelations and visions, as He does with women and uneducated persons. On the other hand, when speculative concepts and things of learning come during prayer, the soul resists them so that the prayer doesn't turn into study, for God is all wise. If I read St. Thomas or other authors about the doctrine of the Holy Trinity and I understand something of that mystery through the examples found in those books or from what my professors taught, it is not necessary that God reveal these things to me in prayer. The fact is, the spirit cannot so easily escape the light of wisdom. On the contrary, after a few prayers, when a person goes to the books, he understands the teachings found in them with much more clarity than before. What's more, doctrine gained from books and study is not so dry that it fails to move the will. I once heard a lecture on grace that was worth more to me than much prayer I might have made because the professor so persuaded me regarding the greatness and excellence of grace that I was inspired to obtain it.[4]

10. I have derived much benefit from the vocal prayers that are called ejaculations, especially from the words of the Our Father. I have spent many hours repeating with my lips "*sanctificetur nomen tuum*" [hallowed be Thy name], having in my heart the desire for what is contained in those words. I think it is a big mistake in many persons to set a task of completing a great number of vocal prayers and devotions they have, for they are saying them without attention. I would desire more, as St. Paul says, to say five words with meaning than ten thousand with only the tongue [see 1 Cor 14:19].[5]

11. **Cyril:** *It would please me if you told me what devotions you have, apart from the canonical hours.*

12. **Anastasius:** A third part of the rosary; three Hail Marys to the Immaculate Conception for chastity; three Creeds to the Holy Trinity in order to keep the faith until death; and for a good death, five Our Fathers and five Hail Marys to the five holy wounds, and nine to the nine choirs of angels.[6] I do these more or less according to time, occupation, and spiritual desire.

MEDITATION AND STUDY

13. My prayer began when I was still a boy. I read books on prayer and meditation by Father Fray Luis de Granada and studied his teaching. I tried to put it into practice according to the days of the week, taking from his morning and evening meditations the virtues most necessary for my growth.

14. **Cyril:** I would like to know which meditations were most beneficial and which virtues you most liked to exercise.

15. **Anastasius:** I already wrote at length about that in *Lámpara encendida* [*The Burning Lamp*]. You can read about it there. In summary, beginning with the Saturday evening meditation on heaven and the Sunday morning meditation on the resurrection of Christ, the virtue exercised on Sunday was love of God; on Monday, the virtue exercised was humility, having considered blessings received and Christ's washing of the disciples' feet; on Tuesday, penance, from the meditations on sin and Christ's prayer in the garden; on Wednesday, poverty and despising the world, from the meditations on the miseries of life and the scourging of Christ; on Thursday, fear of God, from the meditations on death and the Ecce Homo; on Friday, love of neighbor and zeal for souls, which was born of the meditations on the judgment and Christ crucified; and on Saturday, devotion to our Lady, which was born of the meditations on the pains of hell and Christ's descent from the cross. These meditations and the exercise of these virtues—which are the most important ones—served me well for a long time and did me a lot of good.[7]

16. I have also benefited from meditations on the commandments of God and those of the church, the precepts of the Rule, and other obligations of my state. I considered very carefully the manner in which they are to be understood; the way they are to be kept; the imperfections and faults I was committing in each one; and the hindrances, impediments, and temptations that were coming to me in their observance. I also considered the state of my soul and her powers, examining very carefully what was taking place in my conscience and comparing my thoughts, words, and deeds with the thoughts, words, and deeds of Christ and the saints. From these meditations, I have experienced great benefits, for not in vain does the Holy Spirit say, "Do not let the book of the law of God depart from your mouth, and meditate on it day and night" [Josh 1:8].

17. With meditation on the Blessed Sacrament and the wonders contained in it, I have experienced the enkindling of the fire of divine love, according to the verse, "In my meditations a fire blazed forth" [Ps 39(38):4].

18. It is amazing to see what variation there is in the diverse modes of meditation at different times. Sometimes I have spent days, months, and years without being able to leave off meditating on the Our Father, finding in it such ineffable spiritual treasures; if I were to write about them, many reams of paper would be required. I have also experienced remaining in meditation on just one point, such as the cross of Christ, and being unable to finish even after a long time as I would find in it all that I could desire. Many times I was given to understand that the best way to meditate is not to keep any set order but to follow and reflect upon the point that best suits the soul. It is just ignorance that some people, in order to keep the rules written in books, leave off following the way that does them the most good. If I place myself in prayer and it comes to mind to meditate on Christ crucified and this causes me great fervor and benefit, I do not have to stop and meditate on hell because it is Friday evening. Although it is good to have

rules and order in these things, they are for beginners who have to be taught from scratch. The Spirit of the Lord blows as it wills and where it wills [Jn 3:8]; we do not have to close the door on it in order to keep the precepts and rules of men.

CONTEMPLATION

19. Contemplation is detained thought, when the soul is engaged in a concept with attention and quietude. It is different from meditation, which goes from one thought to another. It is like someone who enters a painter's studio, where there are many paintings. Seeing a painting that pleases him, his eyes and gaze remain fixed on it with attention for a time without looking at other paintings. As has happened to me in the single word "God," considering His divinity, omnipotence, and so forth, the soul finds such great expansion and satisfaction that she does not desire nor is able to turn to other thoughts. She wrestles with this thought alone until she gains the blessing, as Jacob did with the angel [see Gen 32:25–31], persisting in it for many hours. The spirit, detained in that one thought, suspects that a great treasure and a rich mine are to be found in it if she perseveres in digging, and she is not content to give just a few strikes with the shovel; rather, she stays there repeating them many times.

20. **Cyril:** I wish to know what this mine or treasure is that is born of contemplation and whether contemplation is a work only of the understanding or if it also embraces the desires of the will.

21. **Anastasius:** Clearly, the fruit of a good thought detained in contemplation is a good desire, which comes to rest and abide in the will. This desire is for heroic virtues such as humility, martyrdom, purity of soul, and so forth. I was once given to understand that, since all virtues are born from love of God and neighbor and have this same love as their end, I should employ all my desires in the love of God; thus I experienced that "all good things together came to me in her company" [Wis

7:11, NAB]. When this queen leads and the maidens of the other virtues follow, the soul takes the straight road, but when the other virtues are exercised dryly, that is, without charity, she is not free of bitterness of heart, restlessness, and other worms that are often found in souls who practice prayer.

22. **Cyril:** *Since we have arrived at this point concerning contemplation and charity, tell me, what effects of charity have you experienced most particularly? I have read that there are twelve principal ones, among others, that are useful to know: jubilation, joy of heart, inebriation of the spirit, fervor of the heart, a tender conscience, devotion, impetus, fire of the love of God, dying of love, fainting of love, union with Christ, and zeal for souls.*

23. **Anastasius:** I told you at the start that I will not tell you of any virtue of mine—because there is none in me—but only of my sins and lies. If I were to say I had love of God and that I have felt in me some of those twelve effects, I believe they would not be genuine in me, since I am bad. Also, the devil is accustomed to putting into the heart stones that appear to be precious gems. Although I might have experienced something of these effects of love, how do I know whether they are true or false? Since I cannot know whether I am in the grace of God, neither can I know whether I have charity—which is the firstborn of grace—or the effects born of charity.[8] Thus, there is no reason to deal anymore about this matter or for you to tire yourself asking me about it.

24. **Cyril:** *I know well that the Council of Orange says that man produces nothing but sins and lies,[9] but do you want to tie the hands of God? Can He not turn stones into sons of Abraham and in one moment snatch up to the third heaven a persecutor of the church [see Mt 3:9; 2 Cor 12:2]? I am not asking you now whether the diamonds and rubies that I have identified in you—enameled in your spirit—are true or false, genuine or deceptive. Tell me sincerely what you have felt, and let us leave it to God, who is the good lapidary, to judge these precious stones.*

25. **Anastasius:** You sure are persistent. Many things have occurred that seem like these effects, which would take too long to recount, especially the zeal and union, the impetus, peace, and spiritual joy, and so on; and since I believe them to be fake stones in me, I do not want to speak of them.

26. **Cyril:** *It displeases me that you do not want to say anything. I already know that you act this way because of the scruple you have: since you believe these pearls in your crown are false—inasmuch as they are enclosed in your soul—you do not want me to take them for real and thereby make you a deceiver. Well then, so that my spirit can benefit from this doctrine and teach it to others, tell me in a few words what these effects of love are. Explain how they are born in the soul and how they can benefit us when we have them. At least you can tell me about the doctrine you have learned or have come to know from experience.*

27. **Anastasius:** I have already written about it at length in *Lámpara encendida* [*The Burning Lamp*] and *Dilucidario del verdadero espíritu* [Elucidation of the true spirit], and particularly in a book entitled "Corona de doce estrellas" [Crown of twelve stars], which is not yet printed. But, so that you will stop pestering me, I will sum up in as few words as possible what the true effects of love are, in whom they are found, and how they are born.

28. They are found in pure souls who live with security of conscience; I call it "security of conscience" when a person is not aware of having a mortal sin that he has not confessed. They are born of love of God and neighbor. Properly speaking, the Lord gives them as gracious gifts to whomever He wishes when He wishes, and He normally communicates them to those who have suffered for Him. Just as the rose comes forth among thorns, ambergris is the disgusting vomit of a whale,[10] musk perfume is extracted from the filthy parts of a civet cat, the carbuncle is said to be found in the head of a toad, honey is made by bees that inflict pain with their stingers, and silk is spun by ugly worms, likewise,

these delightful, precious, and divine effects of the love of God are found in souls vomited from the world, harried, and persecuted.

29. *Jubilation* is an interior rejoicing of the spirit, which the soul feels with the exercise of divine things. It is something like a smile of the heart. *Contentment* is when holy things are found to give pleasure. *Spiritual joy* is interior serenity born of peace of the soul when, not fearing the troubles of this life, she casts out bitterness of heart and receives whatever happens, like David, from the hand of God. *Inebriation of the spirit* is when this joy increases so much that it makes one forget all created things, and the soul, filled with the divine wine of the Spirit, desires only to please the Lord. *Fervor* is the continuous desire to please God; the soul cannot rest in anything that is not for the service of God. *Dying of love* is the renunciation of self and all creatures in order to live only in the will of God. *Fire of love* is the burning of the heart that, seeing what God deserves, burns within to serve Him. *Fainting of love* is when the heart is overwhelmed by the impetuous desire to serve God and the soul lacks strength to withstand the violence that is suffered supernaturally. *Impetus* is the force that the will puts into loving God. *Devotion* is an interior feeling that the soul has when making vocal and mental prayer. *Union* is the exchange the soul makes with God when she entrusts to Him all her powers and receives in their place those of Christ in order to work with them. *Zeal for souls* is the efficacious desire to benefit the souls of our neighbors in order to save them, seeing that Christ hung on the cross for their sake.

30. With these few words, you will understand something of these effects. I don't want to delay any longer on this doctrine.

REVELATIONS AND EXTERIOR VISIONS

31. **Cyril:** *I would like to know what revelations and visions you have experienced, what they are like, and how the soul feels when she sees a vision with the eyes of the body.*

32. **Anastasius:** I can say very little about this because only a few times have I seen a vision with my bodily eyes. Once was when I saw that animal, a figure of a goat, which I recounted earlier,[11] and another occasion was when I saw Mother Teresa of Jesus six months after her death. The truth is, I neither esteem nor appreciate such visions. On the contrary, I hold it as a great mercy of God that my spirit has not been guided by this road of sensible revelations, ecstasies, raptures, miracles, or other extraordinary things that are usually so esteemed by the world. I wanted my glory within my heart, my spirit hidden, my embers underneath the ashes, and that no one know what goes on in my soul.

33. I want to give you the reasons for this. First, since we know that Satan can transform himself into an angel of light, appearing in a good figure in order to deceive, who do you think is going to put me in danger of illusions? Second, St. Paul says that while we are in this life we walk by faith and not by sight, and the just man—says the prophet—lives by faith, which is the evidence for what is unseen [see 2 Cor 5:7; Hab 2:4; and Heb 11:1], so why should I want to see anything? Third, those who have visions waste much time in trying to learn whether they are true or false, from God or the devil, and they go about full of fear that they will be deceived. Well then, why do I want visions when I can go by the level and secure road? Finally, revelations have two benefits: one, they give light to the understanding regarding hidden things, as when an image is covered with a veil and whoever removes the veil reveals a picture; second, they move the will to adore Christ more efficaciously if He is seen in this way. In order to save my soul and please God, it is enough for me to have the light of faith revealed in Sacred Scripture to the prophets and holy evangelists who wrote it down and to the sacred teachers who interpreted it; it is not necessary that I have a new particular light revealed to me. If I adore the Blessed Sacrament—which I know for certain is Christ—why would I want to go and look for a vision of Christ, since I wouldn't know whether it is Christ or the demon transfigured into an angel of light? To tell you the truth, I am not comfortable with

those people who go around telling of their revelations or those who follow after them. I believe there is great deception in this.[12]

34. **Cyril:** *Well, good heavens, is it not of the Catholic faith that there have been exterior revelations, like Moses's vision of the burning bush and the three angels seen by Abraham [see Ex 3:2; Gen 18:1–2]? And in order to canonize the saints, do they not investigate whether their revelations are divine and supernatural? Do you not esteem them? Isn't prophecy one of the graces "freely given"? Did not St. Paul and many others recount their visions? Thus he says, "I will go on to visions and revelations: I saw Jesus Christ" [2 Cor 12:1–2], and so forth. How then can you despise and hold as of little worth mercies so high, so divine and supernatural, and esteemed by all those who have written lives of the saints?*

35. **Anastasius:** I am not speaking against revelations and visions as such, nor do I deny them. I am only saying that I do not want them for myself. Just as a delicious and hearty dish is sweet, beneficial, and tasty for a body that is healthy and robust, if you give it to someone who is sick, it will not do him any good. Likewise, visions and revelations, miracles and raptures, and so forth, are good for souls who are humble but not for me who am proud. Instead, let me frankly and truthfully tell you a secret. When I went about in the dress and habit of austerity and exterior lowliness, as the Discalced do, I did not have as much security and contentment of soul—seeing that people were impressed by such an exterior and took me for a good man—as when I saw myself in a more common and delicate [Calced] habit, with a life, conduct, and manner of a lax religious, having fallen from the high reputation I formerly had. Just as there is danger of ambition and pride in a good appearance, from which religious who wear the garb of austerity and lowliness flee, there is, likewise, the same danger—and much greater—of ambition, vainglory, and self-esteem in proud souls like mine when seen in the exterior habit of holiness.

36. I know by faith—and sacred theology teaches me—that charity is above all the virtues and thus conserves faith and humility; revelations

and exterior visions are not necessary. Many times I was given to understand by a very clear light that what would be done with a visibly revealed Christ is to be done with the Blessed Sacrament and with a painted image. I understood further that I will profit more in this because, in addition to the adoration—which is more certain in regard to the sacrament than to some special revelation—the merit of faith is increased, which is very pleasing to God in these times when heretics deny the presence of Christ in the sacrament and oppose the adoration of images. I remember one day in particular when, standing before an image of the Ecce Homo, I was given to understand, "See here your certain, secure, and continuous revelation. What you do with this image and what it teaches you is more certain than what you do with Christ if He were to visibly reveal Himself to you, because there is a mystical relation between the image and the person represented by the image."

37. **Cyril:** *Tell me what "mystical relation" means, for I do not understand this very well.*

38. **Anastasius:** These are terms of logic and metaphysics. This is the way I understand the matter, having studied them. It is not necessary for you to understand them, nor shall I take time here to explain; an example will suffice so that you will be able to understand something. A bride, aware that her husband is present although she does not see him, is speaking to his portrait that is painted on a wood tablet she is holding in her hands, and she knows that this demonstration of love and the sweet things she says to the portrait are heard by the husband. He is happy. He receives more love than if she were to say the same things in his presence, since she shows more affection in that adoration where there is not as much appearance of grandeur as there is in the living husband. It is clear that the bride doesn't say the sweet things to the piece of wood but rather to the husband whom she holds as present in the image. Also, the husband delights in hearing these expressions of love by means of the image much more than if she were to say them to some actual man who looked like him. This is because the painted

tablet of wood is not able to deceive, whereas another man, if he says that he is her husband, might fool her by dressing himself in the clothes and appearance of her husband. But this is enough now about exterior visions.

39. **Cyril:** *Still, tell me, I beg you, since you say you have seen Mother Teresa of Jesus, when did you see her and in what light? What did she look like when you saw her, and what did you feel in that revelation?*

40. **Anastasius:** Since it is printed in some books, I will tell you. The first Sunday of Lent within the year in which she died, I was saying Matins in my room at eleven at night. I was very tired from having preached two sermons that day in the main church of Seville. I raised my eyes and saw a clear light, whiter, subtler, and more delicate than the light of a candle or even of the sun. On the contrary, those lights are very gross compared to the light I saw. The light of the sun or a candle does not pass through the eyes to the interior, but that clear light, I tell you, penetrated to the intimate recesses of my heart. It did not flash, hurt, or dazzle. Rather, it penetrated sweetly, softly, and consolingly. In this light, I saw her face very resplendent and beautiful, not as old as when she died, but as if she were forty years old. Interiorly, not with the exterior ears of the body, I heard these words: "We of heaven and you of earth are to be one and the same in purity and love: we rejoicing and you suffering. And what we do here with the Divine Essence, you must do there with the Blessed Sacrament. Tell this to all my daughters."[13]

41. This vision happened in an instant. I remained fearful, thinking it was an illusion of the devil, especially since I had preached that day against illusions. Four desires were impressed in my heart: for purity of heart, for love of God and neighbor, for suffering trials for Christ, and for adoration of the Blessed Sacrament. I later found great benefit in these four desires. Since I saw that what I was told was good and that it conformed to the faith and to Sacred Scripture, I did not place any more care in examining whether it was an illusion or a true revelation.

I have experienced the great good that has come to me from these four exercises, and all that is good is from God, however it comes.[14]

42. **Cyril:** *Have you ever seen demons or souls that are in hell, purgatory, or heaven, or similar things, as has happened to Mother Teresa and to other persons?*

43. **Anastasius:** No, glory to God, for I am such a coward that I have not wanted the Lord to give me that cross. On the contrary, I have severely reprimanded persons who have said they have seen souls in hell or in heaven, for what follows or can follow is that the living cease making suffrages and Mass offerings for them. This is a trick of the devil in order to impede such a good thing or to defame some deceased person by saying that his soul is in eternal punishment. The truth is, sometimes being alone at night or walking in scary places I have seen what appeared to be shadows that have surprised and frightened me, but none of them had a figure, nor did I take any of them to be true. It was only my fear that placed the interior phantoms before my eyes and made me look at them, except for the time—as I said—I saw that billy goat of pitch, spotted with flames, although I suspect that this too was one of these phantoms fabricated by my fear.[15]

INTERIOR REVELATIONS OR IMAGINATIVE VISIONS

44. Just as in the exterior vision an image is put visibly before the eyes of the body with clear light more delicate than sunlight, giving concepts to the understanding and moving the will—as I said above—so also an image is sometimes placed interiorly in the imagination and fantasy, with interior light. This image works more efficaciously in the will and the understanding than does the natural imagination using discourse. In the same way, St. John saw the visions of the Apocalypse, which he calls visions of the spirit. St. Hildegard had many of these visions and wrote them down in her book called *Scivias,* which teaches a very profitable and necessary doctrine for the good of souls.

45. This vision and the image that is seen differ from what is fabricated by the imagination and fantasy, in the same way that the sun seen in a mirror differs from the sun painted with brush and colors. The image fabricated by the imagination in meditation—as when you think of Christ crucified by fabricating an interior image—takes longer to produce and requires more effort of the imaginative power, which is sluggish when it comes to forming interior images. Sometimes the body is of such a humor that however much a person works with the imagination—closing the eyes, gritting the teeth, and making mental effort—it is not able to fabricate an image. But this interior vision comes in an instant, like a flash of lightning. When it is good, it brings many good concepts with a very clear interior light and moves the will to good desires. Sometimes these concepts and desires come together with the vision. Other times, after the vision has passed, they come when the soul realizes what that interior image means. I have had many of these visions at different times, but it would take too long to relate them and the truths that I was given to understand by them.

46. **Cyril:** *Give me one example so that I can understand the basis of this teaching.*

47. **Anastasius:** One time when I was quite distracted and paying little attention to anything in particular, I saw the figure of a lady, like an empress with an imperial crown. Her face was so beautiful, so lively, and so delicate that however many paintings I have seen of beautiful women since then, they seem ugly and gross to me compared to the figure I saw. It caused in me great devotion to our Lady, and I wondered whether this figure was similar to the beauty of the heavenly Virgin. My affection and devotion lasted a long time. When I want to return to it in my memory and make it present, I am not able to fabricate so lively and perfect an image as I saw then. Yet from the glimmer of the face that has remained in my memory, there has come a great strength for resisting bad thoughts and undertaking good works for love of the most holy Virgin Mary.

48. Many other times, I have seen in the interior of my imagination beautiful and resplendent faces of persons I did not know, but I was given to understand that they are saints who are in heaven.[16] One time, in this kind of vision, I saw a burning city and all its streets full of burning logs. Walking through that city, it was necessary to look carefully where I put my feet to avoid getting burned. I was given to understand that in the world there are a great many dangers, snares, traps, and temptations of every kind—which were represented to me in that instant—and that it is necessary to go with much care and vigilance if I am to save myself.

INTELLECTUAL VISION

49. I have received many mercies from the Lord in this type of vision; it encompasses almost all my spirit. I am very thankful to God for having led me by this road because these visions are more secure and beneficial than exterior and imaginative visions, and the devil has less chance to meddle in them. Although many persons think these communications of God are less desirable, in my judgment they are more secure than sensible and exterior communications, since God is invisible and souls are immaterial.

50. **Cyril:** *Aren't they the same, intellectual vision and contemplation, which you spoke about above?*

51. **Anastasius:** No, because in contemplation when the soul is attentively and slowly considering a concept, she is working with the understanding; it is less profound and of less light and efficacy. But an intellectual vision is given from on high and is brought to the understanding; it contains within itself more concepts and gives more strength to the spirit than contemplation.

52. Let us look at some examples. A man is in a bedroom looking through the window to a living room of his house,[17] but when another window is opened for him and he is brought to it, he sees a plaza and a great multitude of persons and houses. Or say a person climbs up a

hill, looking carefully at the plants and rocks that are along the road, but when he gets to the top of the hill, in the blink of an eye, he sees innumerable meadows, fields, springs, rivers, and woods, all visible from that height and about which there is much to tell. In the same way, the soul is contemplating a particular concept and then—often when not thinking of anything—something like a window is opened inside the spirit. The soul is transported there to see innumerable concepts with just one look or a single concept very much higher than the soul could possibly attain on her own. This is because she is raised up to a certain summit of knowledge where she discovers great, excellent, and innumerable verities with a single glance.

53. St. Hildegard says that this is how the Lord gave her an explanation of all Sacred Scripture when at prayer on one occasion in the year 1141, when she was forty-two years old. This does not mean that in one instant she was able to put in her memory all the chapters and verses of the Bible with their interpretations (which is impossible because that would require many years). Rather, she was given a certain light, an interior ability, a new clarity, and an "I don't know what" that she calls this explanation of Sacred Scripture,[18] with which, when she afterward read the Bible, she understood it in such a good and correct way, it was as if the best theologian in the world had explained it to her.

54. In this vision, there are no colors or images as in exterior and imaginative visions but rather doctrine and concepts. These concepts and principles are of two kinds. One is when the understanding perceives many of them at once; and although they all come at once, it knows them distinctly, one from the other. If one were to stop to write them down, many books could be written from just one glance through this window. Sometimes all or most of these concepts are forgotten; other times, they are firmly kept in the memory in order to enrich the understanding and the will for the benefit of one's own soul and the souls of others. Sometimes in this intellectual vision a single concept is given to the soul, but it is quite pregnant and full of

many more concepts within it. When a person slowly reflects on such a concept, innumerable verities are discovered that could be written about afterward if there was time. It is as if a pouch of jewels, precious stones, and pearls—too numerous to count, look at, or admire—is thrown through a window that has been opened into the interior. This is enough now about this point.

55. **Cyril:** *I will not be satisfied unless you tell me in particular about some of the meadows you have seen when arriving at the peak, or some of the riches you have received in one of those pouches that has been thrown to you through the window of an intellectual vision.*

56. **Anastasius:** How is it possible to relate what has happened in the fifty years of my exercise of prayer, having already said that this is my usual way of proceeding in the spirit? I have had many of these visions concerning matters related to studies, speculative science, interpretation of Sacred Scripture, sermons I have preached, confessions I have heard, business—whether my own or others—and, primarily, prayer and my spirit.

57. **Cyril:** *I'm not asking you to tell me everything, only something that will serve as an example of what you have touched upon, because I do not understand these high teachings very well unless they are made concrete and described in detail.*

58. **Anastasius:** You are so persistent that I will have to give in for the greater glory and honor of God, for the good of your soul, and to my own confusion. May you know that if someone else had received as much light—even if he were the most rustic Ethiopian of Africa—how much he would have benefited and how backward I have remained with no improvement.

59. In regard to study, I remember that when I was a captive in Tunis, in darkness and chains and prostrate on a cot, my mind would wander leisurely through all parts of the world. One day, in an instant—in an intellectual vision—the *five worlds* were placed before me: the natural

world; the little world or microcosm, which is man; the rational world, which is of all concepts and quiddities or essences of logic and metaphysics; the moral world, of all virtues and vices; and the intellectual or scientific world, of all the practical and speculative arts and sciences. Each one of these worlds has *twenty orbs*, just as the natural world has twenty,[19] four of which are below the earth, commonly known as hell, purgatory, limbo, and the bosom of Abraham. The natural world also has four elements: earth, water, air, and fire; seven heavenly planets: the Moon, Mercury, Venus, the sun, Mars, Jupiter, and Saturn;[20] and four major heavens, which are called the starry heaven, the heaven of the first movable, the crystalline heaven, and the empyrean heaven. All these make nineteen, and over all of them is the twentieth orb, which is God, who comprehends and encloses within Himself all the rest. In each one of these twenty orbs, *twelve signs* were made known to me. In the same way that I saw this natural world divided into twenty orbs and each one of the twenty into twelve signs, so were each of the four other worlds divided into twenty orbs and each orb into twelve. Each orb in one world corresponded to an orb in another world, and each sign had its corresponding sign in another world. It seemed to me that I had arrived at the encyclopedia so named by Aristotle and so much desired by the philosophers, for it is the divine circle of the sciences, where some sciences are entered into through others. Thus, I proposed to write a book called "Pentecosmia," which means "the five worlds" or universal encyclopedia, and I made notes in a little book, but nothing came of it because it would have been necessary to write too much. There the matter rested.[21]

INTELLECTUAL VISION IN REGARD TO SACRED SCRIPTURE

60. Many times with regard to Sacred Scripture some matter or doctrine was given to me by this light of an intellectual vision, so that I understood many verses and chapters of the divine writings. I especially

remember an occasion when, reading the Song of Solomon, one of these visions enlightened me about the intimate loving relationship between God and the soul. With this understanding, I could have written extensively on it.

SERMONS

61. As for sermons, often when reading the gospel passage on which I have to preach and reflecting on it a bit, the plan and all the doctrine of the sermon that I have to deliver comes to me in this kind of vision so that, without needing to see more books, I am prepared to go into the pulpit; at the most, I would read in a few places of the Bible where it seemed to me I could draw out the doctrine. From these intellectual visions and outlines of sermons, I made some tables of universal doctrine that I could use for many different sermons I was then preaching. I have them written in three large notebooks. No one would understand what I have written but, since I remember their plan and the doctrine noted therein, I am able to make use of them for a lot of writing, both of sermons and of moral and spiritual doctrine. When there is no new vision of the kind I am speaking about, it is enough for me to look over some of these tables I have made. This is why preaching is not difficult for me, even if I preach every day; I only suffer from the physical labor of preaching. To others, it seems impossible to preach a good sermon without studying for a week.[22]

62. In the confessional—and this has happened to me countless times—when listening attentively to a penitent, the Lord gives me light so that I am able to know his conscience and tell him some of the sins that for shame he is silent about. They are greatly amazed that I know the secrets of their hearts. In like manner, examining some spiritual persons, I am able to tell them what is necessary for their progress, including some secret failings they have that keep them from going forward. The truth is, from theology itself and the particular things mentioned by the penitent, the confessor is able to obtain much interior light if he

has learning, experience, and intelligence; it is not necessary to have an intellectual vision.

63. In serious business—both my own and that of others, and both general business of the realm and of particular persons and families—light would often come to me about events that were to take place. This light would be so clear and efficacious that although the causes [of such events] were hidden, the event that was placed before me could not be doubted. I could give you many examples of this, but it is enough to relate one regarding my vocation: although my friends and natural reasons persuaded me that I should enter another order, I persevered in this order of our Lady by means of one of these lights, seeing from the beginning all the things that afterward happened and things that I believe will yet happen.

64. I have received in this kind of intellectual vision many doctrines regarding things of the spirit and prayer, about which I could write a great many treatises. You will find many of them in my book *Dilucidario [del verdadero espíritu* (Elucidation of the true spirit)] and in other books I have written. I want to tell you of one in particular. Thinking one day about a teaching disseminated by some spiritual men—that perfection consists in immediate union with God without any interior or exterior act—a light came to me in one of these intellectual visions: that true perfection consists in the imitation of Christ. And, as if all the mysteries of our Lord were put before me, as well as the way in which the soul is to imitate Him, there came to my mind all the doctrines that are now written in the book I published entitled *Vida del alma [y verdadera imitación de Cristo* (Life of the soul and true imitation of Christ)]. Some of the teachings in that book came from what I remembered of this vision, and some came from new visions, as you can read in the book.

EXTERIOR WORDS

65. When the Lord called Samuel—who went to Eli thinking he had called him—it was with words that Samuel heard exteriorly with his bodily ears. In the same way, an angel spoke to St. Methodius, by which he composed his book of revelations. I already told you what happened in the time of the persecutions with the nuncio Sega: Father Mariano and I and all the people in the house heard those voices as if many were complaining.[23] All of us were frightened because it could not have been natural. Sometimes, being asleep or inattentive, I have heard noises interiorly, such as sounds and knocks that have awakened me from sleep and aroused my spirit to pray. More likely, they were natural noises and sounds but I would not know where they came from because at night sometimes a little mouse makes as much knocking and noise as if it were a horse.

WORDS FORMED INTERIORLY

66. I often hear within my soul "formed" words that do not sound in the ear. Instead, it is as if they were written inside my imagination, and I read them within myself. These words are of many kinds. Some seem to come from the mouth of God, apt sayings to the soul according to what she is meditating on, such as "Love me"; "Pay no heed to persecutions"; "Exercise humility"; "Have devotion to the Blessed Sacrament of the altar and the Virgin Mary"; and so on. If I were to tell you the many words I remember, it would be necessary to write a big book. I believe that the divine treatise *Contemptus mundi* [Contempt for the world] is made from interior words like these gathered at different times by the soul who wrote it;[24] that is why it makes such sweet and agreeable consonance in the good spirit that, wherever you open it to read, it seems to speak to you, saying what you are most in need of hearing. In ancient times, the holy hermits wrote down these words, or some of them, in order to remember what God spoke to them in their heart. They called

them *nóminas* and carried them with them for reading in times of temptation. From this practice arose the abuse of carrying *nóminas* and written words to combat certain sicknesses.

67. There are other kinds of interior words that are not new but rather already known. When they come to the interior, they give so much light to the understanding and move the will so forcefully that it seems as though a hidden treasure is enclosed in them.

68. I want to give you an example by which you will understand this better. Once, three words were spoken to me interiorly: "Jesus, Mary, Joseph." In "Jesus," I was made to understand that I was to glorify, adore, serve, love, and give thanks, and that I should desire—if it were up to me—all these things regarding God: that God be God; that He be infinite, omnipotent, immense, and eternal, with all the other attributes He has; and that He have all the essential glory there is among the three Divine Persons. Second, that Christ have God's being; that He be united with the divinity of the Word; and that He have all the grace that the Eternal Father has given Him and all the glory that He possesses in heaven. Third, that the Virgin Mary be the Mother of God and have all the virtues, grace, and glory that she has. Fourth, that all the angels rejoice in God and have the grace and glory that is in them. Fifth, that all the saints see God, that they served Him as they did, and that they enjoy all the glory they have.

69. In "Mary," an efficacious desire was given to me that all peoples of the world be saved: that gentiles and infidels be baptized; that heretics return to the church; that sinners be converted; that all ecclesiastical and secular princes govern as they should; that all religious orders be reformed; that noblemen and important people give good example; that all confessors and preachers fulfill their office well; that all relatives, friends, and those commended to me be saved; and that the souls in purgatory be granted eternal rest.

70. In "Joseph," I desired that my own soul, for the honor and glory of the Eternal Father, be kept in perfect purity, rectitude, and firmness,

with all the virtues by which these three things are attained, that is, purity by means of penance, mortification, and modesty; rectitude by means of observance of the commandments of God, truthfulness in words, and good intention in works; and firmness by means of perseverance, patience, and constancy. In honor of the Son of God, I desired three other principal perfections: living faith, true interior and exterior light, and perfect vocal and mental prayer, with the virtues that correspond to these perfections. In honor of the Holy Spirit, I desired love of God, love of neighbor, and perfection and union in Christ.

71. It seemed to me that no prayer or petition could fill up and satisfy the soul as this one, which I was given to understand was to be called the "prayer of plenitude." In this way of "fullness," I persevered a long time without wanting to ask for or desire anything less than all that is contained in these three names, "Jesus, Mary, Joseph." And since in prayer you deal with God who is infinite, and whatever thing you ask for or desire is little for such a great Lord, I was sorry for having wasted time in other particular prayers and desires. The concepts contained in these three words come to the soul in two ways: first, they come together all at once, bringing great benefit to the soul; and second, the soul lingers in the prayer, spending three or four hours singling out the many things that are contained in it, without being bored or tired with the prayer. When I go to prayer and find myself dry, just by pronouncing with the lips these three words, "Jesus, Mary, Joseph," and repeating them a few times, the fire of devotion springs up and my soul remains content with its habitual prayer of plenitude. I cannot tell you how this is because there are not words to adequately explain what the soul feels, just as an interior image seen in an imaginative vision cannot be painted.

72. There are other words. Those that most ordinarily come to me and on which I have spent the most time in prayer are the very words of Sacred Scripture. I find within them a hidden treasure and manna. You cannot know what this is like unless you receive it. I want to give you an example. These words written by St. Paul came to me one time and

have greatly benefited me: "For from Him and in Him and through Him, all things are. To Him be honor and glory forever and ever, amen" [Rom 11:36]. To help you understand this way of prayer, you ought to know that *pan* [bread] in Greek means "all." This "all" is the bread of the Blessed Sacrament, which contains within it all that is good, that is, God, Christ, the Virgin, the angels, and the saints. They are the five loaves or parts of the whole bread with which the baskets were filled, as St. John says [see Jn 6:13].

73. With this teaching in mind, the soul goes to prayer. Desires, thoughts, and petitions come forth "from Him," meaning from the bread of the Blessed Sacrament, as though the soul herself is annihilated and the Blessed Sacrament is praying in her place. And because nothing whatsoever will be denied of what the Lord asks, the soul enters into this prayer with great confidence and banishes all fear and pusillanimity of asking great things of God—which normally intimidates her, seeing that she is so base and of such little merit—because now the prayer is coming not from the soul but rather "from Him." It is the same with praying "in Him," because He to whom the prayer is directed and with whom the soul speaks is the same Bread who asks, speaks, and desires; from this, confidence and fervor increase greatly. To pray "through Him" is to have the Lord as both the means and the reason for the soul's obtaining what she asks for, considering who God is, the passion and death of Christ, and the merits of the Virgin Mary, the angels, and the saints. Since the soul has such good support and reason to obtain what she asks, she knows that nothing will be denied her. Thus, she does not ask little but "all," which is to say, all that is the will of God and for the honor and glory of Christ, His Mother, the angels, and the saints. The end that moves the soul to this prayer is "to Him be honor and glory," the same glory and honor of God. I don't know how to describe this way of prayer except as "circular." Thus were the words, "Jerusalem is built as a city with compact unity" [Ps 122(121):3], explained to me: the soul goes from God to God through God for God. With this circular prayer, which has lasted a long time with me, I have found and continue

to find great benefit. The same thing happens in it as in the plenitude of "Jesus, Mary, Joseph," namely, that when I find myself dry and I say the words "from Him," and so on, my spirit is renewed.

74. I have experienced no less benefit in praying the Our Father, lingering on it for many hours, days, months, and even years, not knowing any other way to pray it than by repeating one phrase of the Our Father, such as "hallowed be Thy name." When God gives prayer in this interior way of which I am speaking, innumerable desires and concepts come with each word. Once, having a great desire to attain true prayer and not be fooled by illusions or lose time in poor prayer, the words "hallowed be Thy name" of the Our Father came to me with this light: that if, when the disciples asked Christ, the best spiritual master in the world, to teach them how to pray, He responded, "When you pray, say: Our Father" [Lk 11:2; Mt 6:9], and so forth, then—as I was given to understand—the most essential and surest prayer a person can have is contained in the Our Father. Although I have written many things in explanation of the Our Father, with this light, I could write much more.

75. These words also came to me: "Friend, lend me three loaves" [Lk 11:5, NAB]. In these three loaves of bread, I understand that the soul is asking for three "all's": in the first, that the Blessed Sacrament be given all the adoration and service, and so forth, that the sacrament deserves by the entire world; the "all" of the second loaf is for the salvation of all people; and the third "all" is for the complete and total well-being of my soul. I have spent much time in prayer asking for these three "all's."[25] But let us leave now this way of words formed interiorly.

UNFORMED INTERIOR WORDS

76. Let us come to the third way, that of unformed words, which are more correctly called interior *razones* [reasons].[26] They come to the soul not through formed words heard interiorly or exteriorly but by an interior presence perceived by the soul. These interior *razones* are given with such light that from them the soul is able to form other concepts,

seeking words by which to express them to herself. In this way, I have had many conversations not only with our Lord and our Lady but also with Mother Teresa of Jesus. There is a lot to tell that would be of much benefit and counsel for many souls.[27]

77. **Cyril:** *Don't fail to give me an example of this mode of proceeding in the spiritual life.*

78. **Anastasius:** Once when I was saying Mass, it seemed to me that Christ, our Lady, and Mother Teresa were present in my soul. They gave me to understand, by this third way of [unformed] words, the following messages: first, that I should be sure to have the greatest attention possible at Mass; second, that in all I do, I should seek the greater honor and glory of God; third, that for the rest of my life, I should always have the greatest care concerning the affairs and interests of the order; and fourth, that the extraordinary experiences of the soul, such as exterior visions, raptures, etc., are neither all from God nor all from the devil even though the one who receives them might be either a saint or a sinner and that to make a general rule about such things is the cause of much harm.

79. Another time, while I was holding a chapter with some nuns, it seemed that I had Mother Teresa at my side with the kind of presence of which I am speaking, although without any visible exterior or interior figure; the truth is, one of the sisters said she saw her with her bodily eyes. When a sister accused herself of a fault that seemed small to me, I understood this *razón* from Mother Teresa: "How small some imperfections and faults seem in this life, and how great they will be seen in the next, especially if they hinder the increase of charity; and how severely we will be judged for having made little account of them!" Another sister accused herself of doing things carelessly and that she did not suffer patiently the importunities of the sick. It seemed that Mother Teresa said to me that I should insist that things be done carefully; that the sick should not be judged (when they complain and importune) as imperfect, for they are not able to do more; and that in religious life, it is very

important to be patient with the sick and to care for them with much love.

80. I do not want to say anything else to you about this mode of intellectual visions and interior words because I might publish a book entitled "Saetas agudas y brasas encendidas" [Sharp arrows and burning embers] in which I say more about these teachings in a style that can be easily read and which will benefit all, without saying where the teaching comes from.[28]

DREAMS

81. I could tell you about many other *razónes*, concepts, and teachings that I have received in this third manner of interior words, which have been a regular part of my spiritual life, but let us discuss the dreams that come when a person is sleeping.

82. They come in three ways. Some are produced naturally by the vapors that rise from the stomach to the brain and awaken or stir up phantoms or interior images of the fantasy and place them in the imagination. Since these images are joined randomly, without order or agreement, it is a sin to believe in such dreams. There are other dreams that are produced by the good angel who joins these same interior figures with order and agreement and presents them to the imagination. Usually they are of hidden or prophetic things, as when the angel spoke in dreams to Joseph, the husband of Mary. The dreams of Joseph the patriarch, son of Jacob, and those of Pharaoh, Nebuchadnezzar, and so forth, were of this kind. Others are evil dreams from the devil. They very often represent twisted things, and some stir up the humors of the body so that sensual movements occur. The church sings against them: *Procul recedant somnia / et noctium phantasmata, / hostemque nostrum comprime, / ne polluantur corpora* ["Far off let dreams and phantoms of the night depart; restrain Thou our adversary, lest our bodies become defiled"].[29]

83. Usually, I do not care to ascertain how dreams come to me, whether they are from a good angel or the devil or are natural. If a dream is good, I profit from it when I wake up; if it is bad, I put it out of my mind, following the rule of St. Paul: "Test everything. Retain what is good. Avoid any semblance of evil" [1 Thess 5:21–22, NAB].

84. Many times I dreamed that I was debating in the lecture hall. Waking up, I would remember that the argument was very good and that I argued right to the conclusions. I have also dreamed that I sinned, and that I went to confession, examining my conscience about some sins that were hidden and intricate. Remembering that dream, I was able to write a good paper on cases of conscience based on it. Other times, I dreamed that I sinned, that I was awake, and that it was not a dream, which would at first cause me great pain; later, thinking over the dream and the nonsense mixed in, I would realize that I had been dreaming and my distress would go away. I once dreamed I was dying and was going to hell for my sins; when I awoke, the dream motivated me to do penance and make a general confession. Not long ago, I dreamed that I saw myself in the death agony and was forcing myself to make more heroic interior acts and the loftiest and firmest intentions of which I was capable. Remembering that dream, I continued exercising those same acts and intentions for a greater part of the night. It was a very beneficial prayer. Following the rule of St. Paul that I mentioned earlier, I don't concern myself with my dreams or the dreams that others tell me they have had. When I was among the Turks, some of the renegades often came to me to tell me their dreams—those of the sect of Muhammad pay great heed to dreams and they look for learned men to interpret them—and, although a dream might be crazy, I would interpret it to mean that it would be good [for them] to return to the Christian faith and flee those lands and go to Catholic lands in order to save themselves.[30] With such interpretations of their dreams, I was able to persuade some of them to do it and leave for Catholic lands, for it was my aim to save those souls.

STILLNESS OF SPIRIT

85. There is a way of stillness of spirit or interior attention in which the senses are not absorbed, lost, or enraptured, but their operation is forced to cease because of a certain interior presence of the living God. It seems like a rapture, but it really isn't because there is no alienation of the senses, nor is any great effort necessary to awaken the soul. When she wants to, the soul returns to herself and leaves the prayer easily enough by thinking about something other than what she was thinking. In this way of stillness of spirit, I have received great graces and mercies from the hand of God.

86. **Cyril:** *I would really like you to explain more about this way of proceeding in prayer since you said many times that you have experienced it.*

87. **Anastasius:** Remember the words the Bridegroom spoke to the bride: "She remained asleep." She says that the left hand of her Bridegroom was under her head, and with his right hand he embraced her [see Song 2:6]. When in another place, she says, "I sleep and my heart keeps vigil" [Song 5:2], the Spouse, holding her in his arms, says, "I adjure you, daughters of Jerusalem, do not awaken or make my bride keep vigil until she desires it" [Song 2:7]. By these words, the Holy Spirit is speaking about this way of sleep, for I am free to awaken when I want. In natural sleep or in rapture, we are not so free to awaken ourselves.

88. This divine sleep and interior attention is born of the presence of the living God, and of the Spouse—whom the bride calls her heart—watching His bride attentively and speaking with her. This presence is as different from the presence of exterior images, or from the imaginative or intellectual presence we ordinarily have, as the living thing is different from the painted thing. Suppose you were looking at a painting of a lion and it rouses your memory to recall the strength of a real lion and that it is good to be afraid of it. But if you see a real lion enter through the door of your room, it instantly causes in you such an effect of fear that it makes you scream and run. In the same way, you might be

meditating on Christ crucified, placing the figure within your imagination, and there you think of how good it is to serve and fear Him. But it is something altogether different when He is present within your heart, truly living, and you feel that He is speaking and looking at you, for this then causes such great emotion that the soul forgets all created things. This is what it means to put the left hand under the head, because the left hand signifies temporal things. Forgetful of them, the soul is raised to eternal things—signified by the right hand—with such strength that the soul no longer thinks of anything but God. With an interior impetus caused by this divine sleep, she is absorbed by and attentive to only the things pertaining to His service. Since the soul is distracted when she is called or spoken to, the Spouse abjures the daughters of Jerusalem, which are creatures, not to wake her. If she wants to discontinue that act and reflection, it is within her power to do so. It should be noted that the impetus does not last long, because sometimes it slows the breathing; if it did last long, the health might be harmed. But when it is the presence of the living God—the soul reflecting on diverse concepts, making acts of love, or speaking loving words to Christ—it is not unusual for the soul to continue in prayer for as much as three or four hours, which seem like only a moment. From time to time, the impetus comes during this sleep and gives even more fervor. It seems to me that my soul has experienced the greatest benefit from this way of prayer. But I know very well that I have not described what it is really like, because the divine interior impressions are so delicate that words cannot explain it. And so, leaving this, let us say something about ecstasies and raptures.

ECSTASIES AND RAPTURES

89. **Cyril:** *I have a great desire to know if you have had raptures and ecstasies often, since you write about them in many places in your books.*

90. **Anastasius:** Glory be to God, I have never seen myself with raptures or ecstasies, nor do I know from my own experience what they are. And I say glory be to God because—as I said at the beginning—I have

always abhorred exterior visions and revelations, miracles, ecstasies and raptures, and similar gifts and graces for myself. God gives these to humble souls and not to souls that are proud like mine. If I know something about these things, it is from what I read in Sacred Scripture and the doctors about the ecstasies of St. Peter, the raptures of St. Paul, and the dream of St. John the Evangelist on the breast of Christ. Having looked through many books by persons who have had great raptures, such as St. Hildegard and St. Angela di Foligno, and having examined and spoken with many persons who have experienced them—such as Mother Teresa of Jesus; Sister Ursula of Naples, who for twenty-five years was enraptured twelve hours every day; a *beata* of Burgos who passed sixteen hours in a rapture; Fray Melchor Cano, a Dominican who was sometimes twenty-four hours in a rapture; Fray Dominic Ruzola, a Carmelite;[31] and many others whose raptures I have known about in such detail—I was able to write about them in the books you mention.

91. But this is enough now about these twelve ways of the spirit and prayer in explanation of the twelve stars.

Sixteenth Dialogue: Revelations

This dialogue concerns some of the interior lights that devout persons—mainly the nuns of the Order of the Discalced of Our Lady of Carmel—have had about the things that happened to Gracián, particularly the principal revelations that Teresa of Jesus and some of her daughters have left in writing, represented by the emblem of the name of Mary in the shield.

1. **Cyril:** *I would very much like for you to tell me some of the revelations that other persons, servants of God, have had about you and your affairs.*

2. **Anastasius:** There cannot be any revelation truer or more certain than the one I had about myself one day when I was given to understand who I was in twelve D's:[1]

1. Disbelieving and lacking in faith, because just as a living faith is the origin of all good, so the lack of a living faith is the beginning of great abominations;
2. Distrusting, lacking in confidence, and being full of doubts, thus not putting my hand to doing great things for God; looking at my own weakness instead of God's strength and what I could do if I put myself in His strong arms, truly confiding in Him;
3. Disaffected and without the love of God; full of self-love, dryness, lukewarmness, and coldness of spirit;

4. Disobedient to divine inspirations and commands of superiors; full of rebellion and hardness of heart;
5. Disregardful of the innumerable favors and mercies I have received from God; and how my ingratitude has closed the door to grace, leaving me full of sins and misfortune;
6. Discomposed exteriorly and interiorly, giving bad example to all by my scandalous life;
7. Disagreeable and full of disgust and gloominess of heart, without that sweetness of spirit that enriches the soul with good things;
8. Disordered in all ways of living; loving creatures more than the Creator and not keeping the divine order that God asks of His servants;
9. Discloser of interior secrets of my heart, broadcasting them to the detriment of my humility;
10. Disrespectful and giving little reverence and adoration to God, His saints, and His images;
11. Distracted, forgetful, negligent, and lazy in the things that should be important to me for the sake of God's honor, the good of my soul, and the souls of my brothers and sisters;
12. Disdainful and full of murmurs, prejudice, and coldness toward others, which has caused me great harm with regard to attaining true union with Christ.

3. These are the virtues of my soul, the goods of my conscience, and what can be revealed to the world. If I were to recount at length the great evils, abominations, sins, and faults that follow from these twelve D's, it would be necessary to write a big book. No matter which one of these twelve fountains of all evil is found in the soul, innumerable misfortunes follow. Therefore, don't expect any revelation of good things in me but rather disbelief, distrust, disaffection, disobedience, disregard, discomposure, disagreeableness, disorder, disclosure, disrespect, distraction, and disdain.[2]

4. **Cyril:** *I already know there can't be any revelation more profitable than what God gives to the soul in order for her to know herself. When the water is*

clear, the stones and the tiniest pebbles over which it runs are visible, which is not so when it is cloudy. But I have read, and have in my possession, writings from the hand of Mother Teresa of Jesus and other great servants of God that speak about your person and many things that have befallen you, long before they actually happened. No one can explain them to me except you who have gone through them, since you know the inner workings of your heart and the events in which you were involved. Be patient so that I can read them, and please answer the questions I ask about them.

5. **Anastasius:** I will do so provided that if there is anything good said about me, you either take these revelations to be illusions or understand that God usually reveals good things about a person to other souls so they can be moved to imitate the example of that good thing, or so that the very person about whom the revelation is made will be confounded, seeing how differently he lives from what other people judge about him, or to encourage him to live up to the revelations about him. With this condition you can read what you wish, and I will listen and respond.

6. **Cyril:** *A document has come into my possession from Mother Teresa of Jesus, of which there are two copies. Mother said to take care that it be given to you after her death because the time would come when you would need it. This paper says, beginning with the superscription, "These are things of my soul and conscience. No one is to read it until after I am dead, and it is to be given to Father Fray Jerónimo Gracián."*[3]

> 7. In the year 1575 in the month of April, I was at the foundation of Beas when Master Fray Jerome Gracián of the Mother of God happened to come there. I confessed to him a few times, although I did not hold him in the place of my regular confessors such that I would be directed by him in everything. One day while I was eating, without any interior recollection, my soul began to be suspended and so recollected that I thought a rapture was coming on. A vision was represented to me with the usual swiftness, like that of a flash of lightning: I seemed to see at my side our Lord Jesus Christ in the form in which His Majesty usually appears to me, and on His right was

Master Gracián. The Lord took his right hand and mine and joined them, and He told me that He wanted me to take him in His place for the rest of my life and that there should be conformity between us in everything because this was fitting.

8. I felt very secure that it was God's doing. I thought about two of my long-time confessors to whom I owed much (the thought of one especially, for whom I have great affection, caused me terrible resistance); nevertheless, I was not able to persuade myself that the vision was a deception. This was due to the great power and strength produced in me along with my being told on two other occasions, in different words, that I should not be afraid and that our Lord desired this. In the end, I was determined to do it—understanding it to be God's will—and to follow [Gracián's] judgment as long as I lived. It is something I have never done with anyone, even though I have dealt with other persons of learning and holiness who looked after my soul with great care; but neither have I been given to understand that I should not change even though some of my confessors were beneficial for me, and I for them. Having made this decision, I remained with a peace and comfort so great that I was amazed and certain that it was our Lord's will. Such peace and consolation are so great that it does not seem that the devil can give them. Thus, when I think of it, I praise the Lord, remembering the verse, "He has placed peace on your borders" [Ps 147:14], and I wish I could wear myself out in the praises of God.

9. It must have been about a month after I made this decision when, on the second day of Pentecost, on our way to Seville to make the foundation, we heard Mass in a hermitage of Ecija and remained there for siesta.[4] While my companions were in the hermitage and I was alone in the sacristy there, I began to think about a great favor the Holy Spirit had once granted me on the eve of this feast, and a great desire came to me to render Him a most signal service.[5] I couldn't think of anything I had not yet done, or at least resolved upon for

to say all was done is surely incorrect; and I realized that although I had made a vow of obedience, it could still be made with greater perfection. The idea came to me that it would be pleasing to Him if I promised what I had already intended to do, namely, to obey Father Master Fray Jerome. On the one hand, it didn't seem that I was really offering anything because I had already resolved to do this. On the other hand, it seemed difficult, considering that our interior state is not revealed to the superiors who receive our vows, that superiors change (if things are not going well with one, another comes in his place), and that I would be without any liberty interiorly or exteriorly the rest of my life. This pressured me greatly not to do it.

10. The resistance of my will displeased me, for it seemed that now that I had something I could do for God, I was not doing it, which was hard to bear because of the determination I had to serve Him. The fact is, the difficulty pressured me so much that I do not think I ever did anything in my life, not even my profession, that was so hard, except leaving my father's house to become a nun. This is why I put out of my mind how much I loved him [Gracián] and how well suited he was for my plans. Rather, at the time, I considered him as a stranger—which surprised me—feeling nothing except a great fear as to whether it was in the service of God. And nature, which is a friend of liberty, must have been doing its duty. Although for years I had not enjoyed [liberty], it seemed to be something else altogether to give up one's liberty by a vow, which in truth it is.

11. The more I thought about it, the better it seemed, and after a long struggle, the Lord gave me great confidence. Since I was making that promise for the Holy Spirit, He was obliged to give Master Gracián light to guide me. I also remembered that the Lord had given him to me. With this—in order to render this service to the Holy Spirit—I went down on my knees and promised to do everything he [Gracián] told me the rest of my life, provided it was not contrary to God's will or that of my superiors, whom I was more bound to obey. I made note that the obligation did not extend to my amenities or to things

of little importance, such as if I importune him for something, he tells me to forget it, I don't heed him, and I ask again. Finally, it does not apply to little nothings that are done without a thought. Also, I was not to knowingly conceal from him any of my faults or sins or my interior state, which is more than we do with our superiors. In the end, I promised to hold him in the place of God, in exterior and interior matters.

12. I do not know if it is so, but it seems I have done a great thing for the Holy Spirit, at least, all that I knew how to do, which was very little compared to what I owe Him. I praise God who created a person fitted for this, and thus I remain confident that His Majesty will bestow upon him new favors. I am so happy and content that I seem to be free of myself in every way, and though I thought my obedience would be oppressive, I have found much greater freedom. May our Lord be praised by all.

13. *This is what is contained in the paper. Tell me, why did Mother Teresa say that after her death it was to be given to you, that you would need it?*

14. **Anastasius:** What I understand by this is that a time was to come when I would see myself so affronted, dishonored, and beaten that there would be no one to take my side, and some would examine this paper so that, with the good name of Mother Teresa, I would not completely lose my reputation, which also is sometimes necessary in order to serve God. However, the truth is, some of my rivals denied that it was written by Mother Teresa.[6] Others interpreted the words about Christ joining our hands in a way that was quite offensive. It seems to me, the joining of the hands was a prophecy of Mother Teresa of what happened afterward: that from the time I met her in Beas, where she had the revelation, until she died, in whatever business she or I had to undertake, whether of the order or other particular things, we were always in agreement. This is because I told her, as her superior, to study very carefully whatever business she was engaged in, commend it to God, and let me know if she had an opinion contrary to mine, explaining and defending

her reasons for it. I held her in such esteem, knowing her great prudence and holiness, that sometimes I yielded to her opinion; at other times, she understood my reasons and yielded to me. Thus, although we argued back and forth in order to figure out what was best, we always came to conformity of judgment, she keeping to the obedience that it says there she promised me.[7] I once showed this paper to the patriarch of Valencia, who was taking my testimony for the canonization process of the saintly Father Ignatius of Loyola, founder of the Company of Jesus, because the witness is asked if he has ever been sentenced. He recognized the handwriting of Mother Teresa and accepted me as a witness. Thus I saw fulfilled what she had said, that there would come a time when this document would be necessary.[8]

15. **Cyril:** *In a notebook of her writing, she says: "Being in sorrow on account of the illness our Father [Gracián] was enduring, I could not rest. Since our Lord had given him to me, I could not see myself without him. He told me, 'Have no fear.'" In the same notebook she adds:*

> 16. One night I was full of grief because it had been a long time that I had no news of my father, and he was not well the last time he wrote to me. It was not like the former grief I had about his illness—which I haven't had since then—because I was confident, but the worry hindered my prayer. Suddenly, it seemed (and it was such that it could not have been my imagination) that a light was presented in my interior, and I saw him coming down a path. He was joyful and his face shone white, although from the light I saw, his face could only have been white, as it seems to me are all those in heaven, and I have wondered if they are white from the splendor and light that comes from our Lord. I understood these words: "Tell him to begin now without fear, that his is the victory."

17. **Anastasius:** This occurred when I was given the brief from the nuncio Ormaneto along with letters from the king to make the visitation of the Calced in Andalusia, and I was going to Seville to present it.[9] I had been ill but not seriously ill.

18. **Cyril:** *It certainly seems that it was at that time, since she also writes these words, in her own hand:*

> 19. The day after he came, while I was praising our Lord at night for the many favors He had done for me, our Lord said, "What have you asked for that I have not done for you, my daughter?"
>
> 20. The day the brief was presented, I was filled with anxiety and so disturbed that I could not even pray because they came and told me that our Father was in great straits. They would not let him leave and there was much shouting and noise. I understood these words: "Oh, woman of little faith! Calm yourself, for everything is going well." It was the day of the Presentation of Our Lady in the year 1575. I promised myself that if the Virgin attained from her Son that we see our Father and ourselves free of those friars, I would ask permission for this feast to be celebrated with solemnity in every single one of our monasteries of Discalced nuns.

21. **Anastasius:** When I presented the brief of the visitation to the Calced friars of Seville—which was on the day of the Presentation—they did not want to accept it. I excommunicated them, and the chapter friars rose up in a great tumult and clamor and closed the doors of the monastery. I thought they were going to physically harm me. But I had forewarned the archbishop of Seville that there might be trouble, and when those who remained outside the monastery saw the doors close and heard the disturbance, they went to him for help. The archbishop immediately sent orders to the monastery to open the doors, and I was freed.

22. **Cyril:** *In a letter written in her hand, she says:*

> 23. The letters from Alcalá have frightened me and have made me very angry, especially the one [from Sega] written to Your Paternity [Gracián]. My God, how we do not know ourselves! Well, I am telling Your Paternity, as I have written you before, that now with what has been done, I have so much fear that I do not want to see you there

[with the Discalced], and this I believe will have to come about. Please God, you return to the Cats! The threat is for real.[10]

24. *I would like to know what Mother Teresa means by the words in this letter: whether it is a prophecy that you were to come and live with the Calced friars.*

25. **Anastasius:** When Mother Teresa and I wrote to each other, we changed the names according to a certain code. "*Gatos*" [cats] is what we sometimes called the Calced. What is going on in this case is that when I was arrested by the nuncio Sega on account of the visitation, he sent me to a monastery of the Calced in Madrid. They treated me well, with great courtesy and love, the whole time I was with them.[11] Afterward, when the nuncio sentenced me, he deprived me of voice and rank and sent me to the college of the Discalced Carmelites in Alcalá where I thought I was going to rest from my troubles. As it happened, Fray Elías de San Martín, who was the rector and was suffering from the quartan fever, sent me a few times to speak to the friars in chapter. Three of them wrote to the nuncio Sega that, in defiance of his orders, I had returned to governing the Discalced.[12] This made him very angry, and he wrote me a letter severely reprimanding me. So, what Mother said was like a prophecy because, having returned to the Calced, I have had greater peace. They have treated me with greater love, honor, and charity than I would have received from the Discalced had I stayed with them, as can be seen. Even my Discalced friends have been persecuted and marginalized by the same Discalced.

26. **Cyril:** *In another letter Mother writes, "I wrote last week by means of the mail service here, responding to Paul about those wagging tongues. Discussing the matter with Joseph, he told me to advise him to watch himself, that he had many enemies, visible and invisible. For this reason, and Your Reverence [Gracián] may tell him, I would not want him to trust too much those of Egypt or the night birds."*

27. **Anastasius:** Using the same code, Mother Teresa used to call me "Paul" and our Lord Jesus Christ "Joseph" when He said something to

her by way of revelation. She called the Calced [of Andalusia] "those of Egypt," and the "night birds" were the Calced nuns. This letter refers to my visitation of the Calced nuns of Paterna. I discovered that a friar had spread a shameful false accusation about three of them. To free them from the bad reputation they had throughout Seville, I castigated with a torrent of choice words the friar who caused it, as the constitutions require. Afterward, those three nuns whom I freed from this infamy, along with some Calced friars with whom I had formed a great friendship and in whom I had much trust, raised terrible, false accusations against me and sent their charges to the nuncio Sega.[13] From this, a great deal of trouble followed.

28. **Cyril:** *For heaven's sake, no wonder Mother Teresa says not to trust those of Egypt or the night birds!*

29. *But tell me why Mother says in another letter I have, written in her own hand, "I was wondering which of the two loves Your Paternity more: Doña Juana who I see has a husband and her other children to love, or poor Lorenza who has no one else in the world but this Father. May it please God to preserve him to her, amen, for I need this consolation. They tell me that Joseph has once again reassured her, and with this her life goes on, although with troubles without relief."*[14]

30. **Anastasius:** Here Mother Teresa calls herself "Lorenza." In order for you to understand this properly, you need to know that she loved me most tenderly and I loved her more than any other creature on earth, and after her, my mother Doña Juana Dantisco, who also loved me with a special love different from what she had for any of her other children. But this great love that Mother Teresa and I had for one another is a very different kind than the love that is usually in the world. Worldly love is dangerous and disconcerting and causes thoughts and temptations that are not good because they make a person unhappy and tepid and give rise to sensuality. But this love that Mother Teresa and I had for one another caused purity, fervor, and the love of God in me; in her, it gave consolation and comfort in her labors, as she told me many times. Thus,

she did not want even my mother to love me more than her. Blessed be God who gave me such a good friend! And as she is now in heaven, this love will not grow cool; I have confidence that it will greatly benefit me. But see how wicked the tongue is! [see Jas 3:6]. On account of the great communication and familiarity the two of us had, some malicious people judged that ours was an unholy love. Even if she were not the saint she was and if I were the most evil person in the world, there was no reason to suspect anything bad about a woman sixty years old who was quite enclosed and very modest. But, because of such gossip, we hid our intimate friendship so that it would not be taken the wrong way.

31. **Cyril:** *Blessed be God that such a holy person loved you so much and that God assured her in prayer that this consolation would not be taken from her! But what do these words mean, which I have read in another letter written by her?*

> 32. I consider it a great favor of God that, in the midst of all the storms, Paul should have the strength to make such great resolutions that even an hour a month is enough, there being so many occasions to lose his peace. Glory be to the One who gives this peace to him. If he completes his contract, there is nothing more to desire for my consolation, because all other trials will at last come to an end. Even if it were not so, it wouldn't matter. Your Paternity must advise him that I will keep that writing in order to question him if he fails. It comes in handy to quell the fears I have, since my only concern is that Paul do nothing against the will of God. Of this, Joseph has given Angela much assurance that he is doing well and is meriting more and more.

33. **Anastasius:** Here Mother Teresa of Jesus calls herself "Angela," Christ she calls "Joseph," and me she calls "Paul." You need to know that when the two of us were away from each other, I would give her an account of all that was going on in my soul, and many times she would send me what she had written in some notebooks that she kept. Once, when I saw myself full of contradictions and obstacles, the Lord gave me a great desire to make the same vow that Mother Teresa of Jesus had

made: to do in everything what was most pleasing to God; and I would give her my word that I would keep it. When I went about inquiring whether it would be good to make this vow, I was advised not to make it but to make a firm resolution instead, in order to avoid scruples.[15] So I wrote my resolution to Mother in the form of a contract. This desire to do what is most pleasing to God, even if I were to lose a thousand lives on account of it, increases more and more in me. This is how I understand what Mother Teresa writes in the letter.

34. **Cyril:** *I have seen many other letters in the handwriting of Mother Teresa that are bound in a book four fingers high. Though they give me many things about which to ask questions, I don't want to deal with them anymore so that you can tell me about another paper I have in my possession. In the handwriting of the same Holy Mother, it says:*

> 35. Once, in deep recollection, I was commending Eliseo [Gracián] to God and I heard this: "He is my true son. I will not fail to help him," or words to that effect, which I don't remember exactly.
>
> 36. On the eve of St. Lawrence, having just received Holy Communion, my mind was so distracted and inattentive that I had no power over it. I began to envy those who dwell in desert places, thinking that since they hear and see nothing, they are exempt from distractions, and I was given to understand: "You are greatly deceived, my daughter. On the contrary, in the desert the temptations of the devil are much greater. Have patience; while life lasts this cannot be helped." While thinking this over, I suddenly became recollected and saw a great light within me. It seemed that I was in another world. Interiorly, I found my spirit in a forest and a garden of delights, which made me remember the words of the canticle: "Let my beloved come into his garden" [Song 4:16]. I saw my Eliseo there, not at all black but rather with a strange beauty.[16] Around his head was a garland of precious stones. Many maidens went before him with palms in their hands singing hymns of praise to God. I did nothing except open my eyes to see if this would distract me, but it was not enough to divert

my attention. Rather, it seemed that there was music of little birds and angels. Although I did not hear it with my bodily ears, my soul delighted in it. I observed that no other man was there. It was said to me, "He has merited being among you, and all the rejoicing that you behold will take place on the day he establishes the feast in honor of my mother. Hurry if you want to reach the place where he is." This vision lasted more than an hour and a half, for I could not divert my attention from it. It gave me great delight and was different from other visions. The effect of the vision was a greater love for Eliseo and to hold him as more present in that beauty. I have feared whether it was a temptation, for it was certainly not my imagination.

37. **Anastasius:** I also fear that it could have been an illusion of the devil because I know very well what a difference there is between my soul and spirit and that of Holy Mother Teresa and how bad I am. What I can say in this case with certainty is that no one has desired the well-being and benefit of the Discalced Carmelite nuns as I have, nor suffered what I have suffered from persevering in maintaining the Rule and constitutions with which Holy Mother founded the nuns so that they would not be changed by superiors who governed the nuns after me. As for what is said about the feast of the Virgin Mary, I think it's because I ordained that the feast of the Presentation of Our Lady be instituted in all the monasteries in memory of the favor the Lord did for me the day I presented the brief to the Calced friars in Seville when, as I said before, I found myself in the greatest danger I have ever been in.

VISIONS OF OTHER HOLY NUNS

38. **Cyril:** *Other servants of God of great spirituality have written things in their own hand, which I would also like to ask about. Let the first be Mother María de San José [Salazar], prioress of Lisbon, who in a little notebook writes these words:*

39. At the time they imprisoned our Father [Gracián] in Madrid,[17] I was at prayer and saw a great serpent with seven heads. Father, with his hands folded and his face looking heavenward, was raised up so high that all those heads, which were going after him with their mouths open, could not reach him. It seemed to me that he was taken into a very resplendent city and the serpent was losing its heads one by one until only its body remained, which is what we now see fulfilled. When I saw Father taken into that city, I was sad because I thought it meant that he would die before he got out of prison and that the city was heaven.

40. *And she adds, "Being very afflicted one day because of the terrible sentence they gave that innocent and holy Father, the Lord gave me to understand that by means of the habit of the Calced fathers, the Lord would restore his honor and raise him up to what we never imagined. In this way, all my pain was taken away and I never again could feel any pain on account of his affairs. Such effects remained in my soul that I have no doubt about it."*

41. **Anastasius:** The serpent with seven heads probably signifies the *consulta* with its seven definitors. It is an amazing and fearful thing that while I suffered and was imprisoned in the land of the Turks—before I joined the Calced—most of the fathers who sentenced me died.[18] Although afterward the government of the *consulta* continued, it was not as it was before.[19] And I have experienced that in the habit of the Calced, the Lord has kept me occupied with very important things in His service.

42. **Cyril:** *Similar to these words are those written by Mother Ana de San Bartolomé, the companion of Mother Teresa: "While he was in prison, after the time he was provincial, I saw a lamb that had been ousted from the flock by many wolves and had fallen into the hands of other enemies. Our Lord snatched him from there and returned him to the order, and he was over them all."*

43. *Another nun had many indications of your rescue and return to the order. And to still another, our Lord said many words to the effect that He would restore you, His servant, before your death when the time was right.*

44. *In a notebook in the handwriting of Mother María de San José,*[20] *prioress of Consuegra, are these words: "In those days, upon entering a cave we had in Madrid, Mother Ana de San Bartolomé saw a multitude of demons that were making a great clamor with papers."*

45. **Anastasius:** They have told me many things that this Ana de San Bartolomé has experienced regarding what has happened to me. But these papers in the cave probably signify the multitude of charges they wrote against me that, as I learned afterward, Father Fray Elías de San Martín burned when he was general of the order so that all those calumnies would be forgotten.[21]

46. **Cyril:** *The same María de San José writes in her own hand the following:*

> 47. A very trustworthy nun, who is now deceased [María del Nacimiento, d. 1597], told me that a certain spiritual person with many spiritual experiences in prayer [Ana de Jesús], while commending him [Gracián] to God a few years before the troubles came to pass in Madrid, saw him in the form of a very bright star moving from one place to another, and she heard, "This one gives as much light here as over there." And this person said to the nun, "Make note and remember this for the future, because I don't know what will become of this father."

48. **Anastasius:** God can easily arrange that a person does as much good in one order as in another, as I have seen from experience.

49. **Cyril:** *The same María de San José adds in the same notebook:*

> 50. Also, I was told by Dr. Bernabé del Mármol that when he was passing through Alba at the time the turmoil began in Madrid, a nun who was a great servant of God in our Discalced monastery insisted on speaking with him. When she got the opportunity, she told him

to warn Anastasius [Gracián] to prepare himself to suffer three great trials that would soon come to him and that although he desired to suffer much, he could never have anticipated these. And so it was, for he was stripped of the habit, had troubles with the pope in Rome, and was a captive. Dr. Mármol would later understand that it was these three things to which the nun was referring.

51. I also learned from Father Juan Díaz, a disciple of Master Ávila,[22] that around this time he was saying Mass one day and commending him [Gracián] to God with sorrow at seeing him with such troubles. Our Lord said these words to him: "Leave him be with all his troubles, for this is what he desires, and he is content with this."

52. **Anastasius:** This Father Juan Díaz was a great servant of God and a man of prayer. He was a nephew of Father Master Ávila who left all his papers to him, and he published *Audi filia* and other books.[23] What he says, "Leave him be with all his troubles," is true; for when I had the most troubles, the words said by Jeremiah regarding Christ would come to mind: "Let him be filled with disgrace" [Lam 3:30, NAB], and with these words I was greatly consoled.

53. **Cyril:** *In the same notebook Mother [María de San José] adds these words:*

54. One of our Discalced fathers told me that in the time of persecution by the Calced, while accompanying our Reverend Father [Gracián] as his companion and sorrowful to see him so persecuted, our Reverend Father said to him, "Brother, are you afflicted by this? This is nothing. I will have to suffer greater tribulations from our Discalced in due time." In reply he said, "How can it be, Father, that your own sons will give you tribulations?" Our Reverend Father answered that our Holy Mother had told him so, and thus he held it for certain.

55. *She adds on the same page:*

56. Being with much sorrow because of Father's troubles, a nun complained to the Lord of how He could permit the order to lose such a

father. His Majesty gave her to understand that all would come out well and that he would reap great benefits from those infamies and his valor would be better known by all. Afterward, when news of his captivity arrived in Madrid and this nun was commending him to God with great weariness on the day of the martyr St. Catherine, she seemed to see our Lady. At her feet was this Father, whom she was protecting, and she said, "You will see him in the order soon." She remained so consoled and certain of this that, however difficult they said his rescue would be, she never stopped hoping to see him free and with the habit of Our Lady of Carmel, as she did see him.[24]

57. **Anastasius:** Great are the blessings and favors I have received at the feet of our Lady. Placing my mouth and my heart there, I reflected that the big toe signifies and reminds me of the Virgin's great power, which is greater than that of any creature. The second toe signifies her wisdom; the middle toe, her goodness and fairness; the fourth toe, her mercy; and the little toe, her humility. Since this way of prayer has greatly benefited me for many years, I am pleased to hear this account of that servant of God.

58. **Cyril:** *I have many other things in my possession written by the holiest nuns of the order, but I do not want to tell you of them because most do not speak of things that happened to you. Rather, they are words of warning that Mother Teresa of Jesus said to them in prayer and that were to be told to you for the good of the order or the benefit of souls.*

59. **Anastasius:** It is not right for you to keep them from me, for I would much rather hear them than those other words. Words that speak well of me, I take to be deceptive, according to the words of the Holy Spirit, which is true and certain revelation: "O my people, those who call you good are misleading you" [Isa 3:12]. The admonitions of Mother Teresa, when she teaches, are of greater benefit.

60. **Cyril:** *Well then, listen to what I have in my possession written by the hand of Catalina de Jesús [Sandoval y Godínez],[25] foundress of the*

monastery of Beas and one of the holiest nuns in the order, who has had many supernatural experiences. In one of her papers she says, speaking of what she has experienced:

> 61. While hearing Mass, I was commending our Reverend Father [Gracián] and the foundations to God. It seemed that Holy Mother said to tell him not to part with the relic of her finger nor to give it to anyone else while he lived, because it would help him in the foundations and in particular things concerning our Reverend Father, and also keep him safe and be of help to him in virtue. This was communicated with so much clarity that it made me long to also possess a relic of the body of our Holy Mother.[26]

62. **Anastasius:** It would be necessary for me to write on many reams of paper in order to relate what has happened to me with this finger, which I cut off more than twenty-six years ago and carry with me, so let us move on to something else.

63. **Cyril:** *In the same notebook she says:*

> 64. For [the benefit of] His Reverence, she [St. Teresa] told me what usually worries him regarding his obligations: that he is failing in his office because he is remiss in punishing and that he is too gentle and lacks verve to be a provincial. I was to tell him not to be distressed about it, regardless of what others say, nor is he to make any effort to change his natural disposition or the way he does things, because instead of setting things right, he would do harm. He is to always keep that customary fear of God before him and aim at advancing the greater honor and glory of God. In this way, he will render great service to our Lord and will be successful in all his undertakings. Let others think what they wish. As regards punishments, lean toward charity and forgiveness—as God Himself does—and let there be less publicity and more secrecy about the affairs of our neighbors.

ADDITIONAL COUNSELS FROM MOTHER TERESA

65. In sermons, let there be great insistence upon confessions being well made, which is very important, for the devil is always trying to mix poison with our medicine.[27]

66. It is very wrong for confessors to relate anything that passes in the confessional, for nothing connected with it—either good or bad—should be discussed.

67. Let the bad custom of speaking ill of *beatas* be stopped, for many of them are very pleasing to God.

68. Let no one criticize the spiritual way of others because everyone can ascertain their own way; much harm is done by criticizing one another.

69. Let no provincial believe too readily all that is said or written to him about the faults of his subjects, but let him withhold his judgment until he is well informed about the matter.

70. Make sure to instill in all the monasteries that an increase of temporal goods is not to be sought after by the same means used by people in the world but that the religious trust in God and live in recollection. Many times, under the pretext of maintaining the monastery or benefiting souls, too much communication with people in the world is introduced, which does great harm to the spiritual life.

71. The provincial should be sure to pray before making important decisions and teach his subjects to do the same because in this way good results usually follow.

72. As far as possible, the provincial should involve himself in new foundations. This is important for many reasons, one of which is to prevent his subjects from claiming a right over foundations made by themselves, which would lead to disputes and divisions and cause much time to be lost, there being too many in charge.

73. In a newly founded monastery of nuns, the prioress should be someone experienced in government even if she has to be taken from another house; an inexperienced prioress would do less harm in a monastery that has already been founded than in a new one.

74. Let the prioress who is put in charge of a monastery be notably obedient to the provincial; thus will the community grow in obedience.

75. Let the prioresses be taught to form their subjects in such a way that they become detached from all things, exterior and interior, as she herself should be, since they are all brides of so great a king as Christ.

76. The provincial is not to let foundations be made without some means of support, for the nuns cannot begin by requiring help from laypeople without causing a loss of esteem for religious life.

77. Let the provincial visit the monasteries personally. If, however, he has to send a delegate, let it be someone who is humble, experienced, and spiritual and has great respect for him. Otherwise, the delegate will want to introduce new modes of government that cause great harm to religious life.

78. Let the provincial, wherever he finds himself, praise penance and reprimand excesses in meals, for—as long as health is not injured—penance, austerity, and self-contempt greatly help the spiritual life.

79. It is not wise to reelect priors in the monasteries of the friars because, although sometimes it is necessary to reelect those who have experience, normally it is better that those who have been superiors become subjects so that they too will know how to be humble and obey. They will thus do much good for the brethren by their example of these two virtues and be greatly able to assist new priors with good advice. When they are perhaps reelected, they will fulfill their office all the better.

80. Let the custom be kept of having days of spiritual exercises and recollection for spiritual growth.

81. Provincials will be called to render an account on the Day of Judgment, and many will have a long time in purgatory—and some even hell—on account of others' sins that they did not condemn.

82. Do not make much account of visions and revelations, for although some are true, many are false and deceptive, and it is very difficult and risky to separate uncertain truths from falsehoods. Besides, souls who follow private revelations are liable to deviate from faith, which is the sure and certain virtue. There are many persons who like to be sanctified by revelations while at the same time denying the means God has established for the sanctification of the soul, namely, the practice of virtue and obedience to the laws and commandments of God. Since women are credulous, they are easily deceived. When they speak with confessors who have little learning or the discretion to put things in proper perspective, great harm can follow. Also, Mother Teresa said that the reward she has in heaven was given to her not for her revelations but for her virtues.

83. Catalina de Cristo, prioress of Pamplona, had this revelation: It is very important in monasteries of nuns that there be great transparency with the confessors, because sometimes too much familiarity between the prioress and the confessor can be harmful to the community. Let whoever governs make sure there is much purity in the order of the Discalced Carmelites, for God wants to do many good works with it, and God does His works with pure souls.

84. While a prioress [María de San Angelo, at Beas] was commending the provincial to God and fearing whether the order would lose the spirit it had, Mother Teresa appeared to her and told her not to be afraid because God would watch over it since it was founded in His blood and it pleased Him; rather, she should tell the provincial to place great emphasis on the observance of the Rule and constitutions and enforce them as much as possible.

85. On another occasion, while a nun [Catalina de Jesús] was asking our Lord to give her the virtues of Holy Mother Teresa, this very Mother appeared to her, saying that God would give them to whomever disposed herself for them and that she was to tell the provincial to assign particular virtues to various sisters so that all might exercise one or another.

86. There is a nun whom Mother Teresa was particularly fond of when she was alive because, besides being saintly since her childhood and advanced in heroic virtue, she asked our Lord for a share in His passion. He appeared to her and placed a crown of thorns on her head, which caused an extraordinary pain that never left her. It is a mystery how she was able to fulfill her duties unfailingly in spite of that pain. After the death of Holy Mother Teresa, still desiring to suffer for Christ in remembrance of His passion, she was given such great pains in her hands, feet, and side that it is amazing. Many things have happened to this servant of God that are worthy of consideration.

87. **Anastasius:** I know this nun very well. She is a native of Molina and her name is María de Jesús [Rivas],[28] and she has been the prioress of Toledo. I could tell you so many things about her that you would be amazed. But tell me what counsels you have found recorded by her that might be from Holy Mother Teresa after her death.

88. **Cyril:** *Once she appeared to her [María de Jesús] in an interior vision and told her that it was important to persevere in the poverty in which the Discalced nuns began because God would bestow a double spirit upon the houses that were poor. As long as they trusted in Christ the Bridegroom, they would never come to want.*

> 89. Tell the provincial that he should try to found as many monasteries of the Discalced nuns as possible, for they are pleasing to God, and let him try to be involved in these foundations himself.
>
> 90. Do not let professed nuns be taken from other houses for houses that lack nuns. Rather, let those houses receive new candidates. Or let those who are given the habit in a monastery where many candidates

are received be sent to other houses where not so many come, or send them when they are still in their secular dress. To send those who are discontented in one place to another place, or to take them on a new foundation because they are unhappy where they are, would open the door to restlessness and want of religious spirit.

91. Let the provincial make sure that there are pleasant vistas in all the monasteries of the nuns, and let no austerities be introduced beyond what is prescribed in the Rule and constitutions. For if the nuns do not have the possibility of recreation inside the monastery, they will seek it outside; and although they might not be doing this at the present time, those who come later could very well become lax in this regard.

92. *On another occasion, this servant of God [María de Jesús] saw our Lord and Holy Mother next to Him in great splendor and beauty. She was given to understand that the time would come when the sanctity of that soul [Mother Teresa] would become known and that she was to tell the provincial he would be repaid for having reburied her body more decently than it was found;*[29] *Holy Mother told her the same thing. And they gave her to understand that there were to be martyrs in the order.*

93. *Another great servant of God [Ana de San Bartolomé] was lamenting that Mother Teresa was absent, having gone to heaven, when Mother appeared to her and said she would help the order more now that she was in heaven than she had done on earth. She was to tell the provincial that he was to watch most carefully over the order and that he was to always keep at his side in spirit the glorious Virgin Mary and the glorious St. Joseph, for they would give him light.*

94. *Another time when the same nun was grieving at having no one to whom she could open her soul as she had done with Holy Mother Teresa, she appeared to her and told her to communicate with the provincial and have the same openness and confidence with him as if she were alive, and that he should see to it that the nuns preserve great concord, union, and joy, and always give an account of their spirit to the prioress.*

95. *She also saw, with her bodily eyes, Holy Mother going about in the garden planning hermitages. Holy Mother instructed her to tell the provincial to make the vow of greater perfection he wanted to make and that he strive to have great conformity with the spirit of Mother Teresa.*[30]

96. *I have read many other things written by different Discalced nuns and other spiritual persons. Tell me how you feel about all of this.*

97. **Anastasius:** There is so much to say about what has happened in which the warnings of Mother Teresa have been fulfilled that a big book could be written. For now, it is enough to say that after she died, she has taken great care to give warnings in revelations regarding many little things that might not seem very important. A prioress even told me that Holy Mother told her to warn me that when going along a bad road, not to be lazy about dismounting so that nothing unfortunate would happen to me. Not long after, coming from Galicia on a horse, when crossing a little wooden bridge not far from El Escorial, I dismounted, remembering the warning of Mother Teresa that I was lazy when it came to dismounting. In the middle of the bridge, the nag put its foot in a hole, stumbled, and broke its leg. I would have been broken to pieces had I been on it because the bridge was high above some huge rocks. My companion, Fray Domingo, blamed the devil who—he said—in the form of an altar boy, threw him down some stairs the night before. Then we saw some fishermen who suddenly disappeared, and he judged them also to be devils. But I reprimanded him for this nonsense and encouraged him to carry the saddle and the saddlebags on his back. I carried the rest of the gear with much difficulty because we went on foot with these things for more than three leagues in the rain.[31]

98. So that you can fully understand these warnings about which you have been reading, you should know that they all occurred while I was provincial; therefore, they are speaking about me when Mother Teresa tells the nuns to warn the provincial.[32]

Appendixes

Appendix I

Letter to a Friend

BRUSSELS, MID-1612

[*Taken from a manuscript, folios 176–86, from the Royal Carmel of the Discalced Carmelite nuns, Brussels.*]

A COPY OF A LETTER THAT FATHER JEROME GRACIÁN DE LA MADRE DE DIOS WROTE TO ONE OF HIS FRIENDS, IN WHICH HE GIVES AN ACCOUNT OF THE ORIGIN AND GROWTH OF THE ORDER OF THE DISCALCED OF OUR LADY OF CARMEL AND OF THE FIRST FOUNDATIONS OF MONASTERIES OF THIS ORDER IN SOME KINGDOMS. IT ALSO TELLS HOW THE PROVINCE WAS FOUNDED AND SEPARATED FROM THE CALCED AND RELATES SOME OF THE TRIALS AND PERSECUTIONS THAT GAVE SOLIDITY AND INCREASE TO THIS ORDER.

Your honor writes me that I should tell you about the beginning and rise of this order of the Discalced Carmelites, the growth and increase it has had, its expansion in diverse kingdoms, the first monasteries established in each kingdom, and the trials, persecutions, and important events that I experienced, since you believe no one else is more qualified to write about these things or has more experience of them.

2. Read the book of the *Life* of the blessed Mother Teresa and *The Book of Her Foundations*, both of which she wrote, and the books that Father Ribera of the Company of Jesus, the bishop of Tarazona [Diego de Yepes], and others have written. There you will find what you desire to know discussed at length. I wrote a large book about the foundations of the monasteries of the friars, with many events and details worth knowing. But

when I was freed from the power of the Turks, who had held me captive, I did not find it among my papers. If it ever appears, you can read in it the things you ask me about. Or if someone took and reworked its material like old metal in order to write his own history, you will also see it there; I hope to God that the work that cost me so much to write was not for nothing. But in order not to entirely fail to reply to what you are asking me, I will write a few words about what I know regarding the beginning and growth of this order, especially what I have experienced.

3. Blessed Mother Teresa of Jesus founded a monastery of Discalced Carmelite nuns in the city of Ávila with all the fervor, poverty, contradictions, and zeal that she recounts. And seeing that the rigor and obedience she desired could not be preserved if the nuns were not governed and administered by Discalced friars of the same order, she persuaded Fathers Fray Antonio de Jesús, known as de Heredia, and Fray John of the Cross, Calced Carmelites, to become Discalced. For this purpose she secured from the general, Fray Juan Bautista Rubeo de Ravena, permission to found two monasteries of Discalced friars. She already had permission to found as many monasteries of nuns as she had hairs on her head. I have the original patents in my possession. The two fathers founded a monastery in a village called Duruelo, near Salamanca, in a very poor house; to be more precise, it was a hay barn of a farmer. This was a blessing because just as Jesus Christ was born in a manger and St. Francis in a stable, so this order was born in a hay barn.

4. The prince of Éboli, Ruy Gómez de Silva, sent for blessed Mother Teresa to make a foundation of nuns in his town of Pastrana. She came to Madrid and stayed at the Monastery of the Angels, which at the time was a foundation of Franciscan nuns made by Doña Leonor Mascareñas, who used to be the governess of King Philip II. It so happened that Father Fray Ambrosio Mariano de San Benito, accompanied by Fray Juan de la Miseria, came to Madrid. Although he was a learned doctor of the law, in order to better serve the Lord he left the world and became a hermit with others who were in the mountains of Tardón, near Córdoba, whose leader was Father Matheus. He was going to Rome to procure

the pope's approval of their eremitical life and that he give them a rule. He happened to speak with Mother Teresa, who said these words to him: "If Your Reverence is going to Rome looking for a rule by which to serve God, living an eremitical way of life and professing austerity, spirit, prayer, and manual labor, I will show you one given and confirmed by many popes." And she gave him the Primitive Rule of Carmel to read, since it used to be printed in the old breviaries we had, and she shared with him her intentions and plans to make foundations of Discalced Carmelite friars. Father Mariano was convinced, believing that he had found what he desired. From Madrid they went to Pastrana and, with the help of Prince Ruy Gómez, founded a monastery of nuns (which later was moved to Segovia) and the monastery of friars at San Pedro of Pastrana, which has been the principal nursery of the whole order. From there the house of studies, the College of St. Cyril of Alcalá, was founded. As the first of the desert houses, a monastery was founded near Almonacil de Zurita, called Nuestra Señora de Altomira, benefiting in the beginning from some Calced friars who became Discalced, such as Fray Baltasar Nieto and Fray Francisco de Jesús [Gómez]; others entered as novices.

5. A lady named Doña Catalina de Cardona came from Naples with the duchess of Calabria. She stayed in Spain at the house of Prince Ruy Gómez de Silva. With the consent of a priest named Father Piña, who was a hermit of Vera Cruz of Alcalá de Henares,[1] she left the world and became a hermit in the wilderness of La Mancha, a place near La Roda abounding in rosemary shrubs.[2] She led a life of extraordinary penance. One day while praying, she asked the Lord to give her light as to what habit [i.e., religious order] He wanted her to serve Him in. Jesus Christ Himself appeared to her in the Discalced Carmelite habit. She did not know what order it was, nor were the Trinitarian friars in the monastery of Fuensanta—two leagues away from her cave where she went to confession and received Holy Communion—able to tell her which order it was. One day, after this revelation, Father Mariano happened to pass through that region. Since she recognized the habit he was wearing, she got information from him about the foundations and the beginning

of the order. She then went from her desert retreat to court where she collected money, vestments, and relics from prominent ladies there and used these items to found the monastery of Nuestra Señora del Socorro near La Roda, at the very place where her cave was located. She wore the habit and cowl of a lay brother and lived in a cell built for her near the monastery until she died, having lived a holy life that included the working of miracles.

6. Shortly after the foundations of Pastrana, Altomira, and Alcalá were made, I took the habit at San Pedro of Pastrana with an extraordinary and wondrous vocation, together with others who studied in Alcalá, where I finished my studies and the required acts to be a doctor of theology. The Virgin Mary did well to disillusion me during the novitiate year, since I entered to have many trials and affronts for love of her and her order. And after professing my vows, news came to Father Mariano and me that certain Calced fathers in Andalusia had founded a monastery of Discalced Carmelites. But that was due to the jealousy and dissension between them and their superior rather than a true spirit of observance. We went immediately to Andalusia. Upon arriving, Father Fray Francisco de Vargas, provincial of the Order of St. Dominic, gave me the original brief he had from Pope Pius V that empowered him to make visitations and reform the Calced Carmelite fathers of Andalusia, substituting me in his place with the commission to carry it out.

7. It was with this authority that I went to San Juan del Puerto where the new monastery of the Discalced was located. Ordering the founders to return to their first order, I arranged with the Calced, whose they were before, to give them all the rights and privileges that they formerly had. I took with me to Seville the seven or eight who were novices or recently professed, since they had never been Calced. With much poverty and many trials and contradictions from the Calced but being favored by the archbishop (Don Cristóbal de Rojas, who was the uncle of the duke of Lerma), I founded the monastery of Nuestra Señora de los Remedios of Seville. It became the seedbed of all the other monasteries in Andalusia.

8. A little while after this foundation was made, it so happened that Mother Teresa of Jesus came to found a monastery of nuns in Beas de

los Comendadores,[3] and I went to see her (for we didn't know each other except by letters). There we discussed at length the plans she and I had for guiding the Discalced Order forward. I gave her an account of all my thoughts, my life, and method of prayer. She shared with me her spirit and desires and everything she had done since she was born. During the time in which these conversations took place, one of my companions by chance said that when he was a secular, he had come from Seville with the [Franciscan] provincial of Andalusia to visit a convent of the Order of St. Francis located in that village [Beas]. I asked him if the town was in the jurisdiction of Castile or Andalusia. Inquiring from authorities greater than him, I discovered that in business pertaining to courts and civil matters it belonged to Castile, and in ecclesiastical business it belonged to Andalusia. I thus ascertained that the new monastery that blessed Mother Teresa had founded was under my jurisdiction. So I showed her the brief I had for visitator of Andalusia, which meant that she was subject to my authority. She did not know what to think or do because the commission she had to make foundations did not extend beyond Castile, nor did mine extend beyond Andalusia. But God allowed this mistake for the great good that I will relate. Not only did she then obey me as visitator of Andalusia, but she even made a vow to obey me the rest of her life and never to conceal things of her interior or the exterior works she might do, provided that what I commanded was not against God or her superiors. I have this vow written and signed by her.

9. Thus, having her as my subject, I commanded her to ask the Lord in prayer for light in order to know where we should go from there to make a foundation, that is, whether we should go to Madrid or Seville. She replied that what was revealed to her was Madrid. In spite of this, I commanded her to found in Seville; thus the first monastery of [Discalced] nuns was founded in Andalusia; from it many others have multiplied in that province.

10. And because at this time Pope Pius V had died, making my commission doubtful and uncertain and leaving the Discalced friars without the support and favor they had received from the Dominican visitators so that they were to return to the authority of the Calced, I went to Madrid

to inform the king what was happening. By his order, the papal nuncio Ormaneto, who had authority from Pope Gregory XIII to reform the religious orders of Spain, gave me a new commission as apostolic visitator and reformer of all the Discalced friars and nuns of Andalusia and Castile, as well as of the Calced of Andalusia. I accepted, knowing the troubles and dangers in which I was being placed, because it seemed to me that in order for the Discalced to go forward, it was better to have the Calced for subjects and let them fight to defend themselves from me rather than the other way around because they would surely disband the Discalced.

11. With this commission in hand I returned to Andalusia. Amid life-threatening dangers—what with strong condemnations, calumnies, false testimonies, hardships, and fatigues, I can't tell you how much I suffered, glory to God—I began to carry out the brief. One day I came so close to losing my life that Mother Teresa of Jesus promised that the feast of the Presentation of Our Lady [November 21] would be celebrated throughout the order so that I might escape victoriously with my life, because I was in the greatest danger that day when I presented the brief of visitation to the Calced of the monastery of Seville.[4] I saw that the best way to reform the Calced was to multiply the Discalced and found new seedbeds of the order; although I worked to put some things of the Calced in order—studies, principally, which later bore fruit—my principal care was to govern the Discalced and multiply their monasteries so that if my commission ended, the Calced who wanted to disband them could better be resisted since the Discalced would then be more numerous. Thus I founded a number of monasteries in Andalusia and Castile.

12. At this time God called the nuncio Ormaneto to Himself. The nuncio [Sega] that succeeded him sent for me and ordered me to proceed with the visitations with his new commission. But the king, Don Philip, ordered that the commission be suspended until he wrote the pope and found out what authority the new nuncio had from the pope and the purpose of his coming. The decision came from the pope that the nuncio was not to concern himself with the friars and nuns of Spain. He was very offended by this and blamed me, saying that I had caused this faculty

to be taken away from him. He carried on a judicial process against my person as a judge, hearing the complaints and accusations the Calced friars and nuns of Andalusia were making against me. They presented many lawsuits containing calumnies of such insolence and excesses imputed to me that even if the judge were well disposed, he couldn't help but be indignant. It came to light what the devil and the Calced were trying to do, namely, restore the jurisdiction of the Calced over the Discalced in order to do away with this new way of life that the Discalced were following, saying it was a novelty and hypocrisy not known in the Order of Carmel, and in this way disband them. The king, Don Philip, wanted the order of the Discalced to be conserved and thus managed to get the nuncio to inform the pope how good their way of life was.[5] The business came to such an end that all the indignation settled upon me because the nuncio decided that before writing to the pope about conserving the Discalced, he must sentence and punish me. Thus, catching me in the web of the judicial process, he ordered that a new inquiry was to be made about my life and conduct and new judges appointed to address and examine my rebuttals, unless I wanted to be amenable and admit what was said in the charges the Calced had made against me on their own authority.

13. Here I found myself in the greatest conflict I had ever been in. If I wanted to expedite the business by letting them sentence me so they would petition Rome to restore the Discalced and remove them from obedience to the Calced, I would remain dishonored and ruined for the rest of my life and my labors and studies would come to nothing. And this was no small thing, trading my honor and life to achieve such a great good as that of securing the order and the Discalced way of life. But my conscience troubled me greatly, knowing it is a mortal sin for a public man to allow his honor to be lost, especially since with its loss, the honor of other holy persons such as the Discalced nuns is also lost since they were falsely accused as accomplices in my sins. I was forcefully struck by the verse of David: "Unless thy law had been my meditation, I had then perished in my abjection" [Ps 119(118):92]. On the other hand, I wrestled in my heart, seeing clearly that establishing the province of the Discalced would be

delayed on account of a new inquiry into my innocence. It might never be done because the nuncio was determined to write to Rome in their [i.e., the Calced] favor, and the king and his almoner,[6] Don Luis Manrique, and the rest wanted to send for the patents immediately. If too much time were taken to check my information and make charges and acquittals, the opportunity to establish the province would be lost, thus destroying the new manner of life followed by the Discalced and compelling them to follow a mediocre religious life, a manifest beginning of relaxation.

14. I tell Your Honor that I found myself in a great conflict. But the Lord delivered me from it because, leaving aside my own opinion and desire and placing my case in the hands of learned, devout, and spiritual persons who understood it well, I held myself to what they thought best. They judged that, without my giving offense to God, I could—trusting in God and throwing myself in His arms—let the judges do what they wanted without waiting for the results of another investigation based on my appeal. I was sentenced to be deprived of voice and place of all dignity and office, and confined to a monastery with some particular penances of fasts, disciplines, and prayers. And when I accepted the sentence, they wrote to Rome asking that the patents be sent for the erection of the province. It was of no little advantage, perhaps the greatest, that Fray Juan de Jesús and Fray Diego de la Trinidad went to Rome, disguised in secular clothes, under the pretext that they were going there to obtain certain dispensations. They thoroughly informed the cardinals of the Congregation of Religious and other ministers of Rome who were handling the matter, giving them points on how to respond to the opponents, and there were plenty of both points and opponents.

15. At the time of my greatest persecution, when I was in hiding before they sentenced me,[7] and afterward, when I was imprisoned in the Carmen of the Calced [in Madrid],[8] I had three consolations. One was a saint of our order—whom I hold as such anyway—named Fray Benito de Jesús y la Virgen, who had attained such simplicity by means of his abundant prayer that he even forgot the name of tangible things and in a roundabout way would ask for water by calling it "*la blanca*" ["the white"]. Trusting in

his great sanctity—as if he were the wisest and most discreet man in the world—I placed before him the state of our affairs and all our doubts, especially whether we should obey the Calced who came with the brief of the nuncio saying that we were to render them obedience, or take it away from them by means of the provision from the royal council that the king had given us not to obey them. He answered me in these grave words: "Look, pretty boy, if you now displease the little treasurer, the big treasurer will be displeased and then the little black one, neither thing nor thing. And if you do not displease him, a little effort and another little effort, a little step and another little step, you will see thing and thing." I understood very well these words, and I received them as from an angel from heaven. What he wished to say is that if I displeased the nuncio, whom he called the little treasurer, by taking away his patent with the provision of the royal council and not obeying the Calced, the pope, whom he called the big treasurer, would be displeased and the king, whom he always called the little black one, would do nothing in our defense—nor could he defend us—and all would be lost. But if we now obeyed the nuncio and the Calced, although it would cost us some trouble, negotiating step-by-step, the province would be created, as did happen. Thus I made the determination that we would obey them, and all the chief Discalced who were with me in the Pastrana monastery followed me. Everything turned out well, albeit with trials, because the whole point was that the nuncio, pacified by this obedience, would write to the pope in our favor.

16. Mother Teresa also consoled me with her letters, which I received frequently, assuring me of success.

17. I was no less encouraged by my mother, Doña Juana Dantisco. Certain important persons went to her saying I wanted to change orders, leaving that of the Discalced Carmelites, and that this would be a good means of escaping the insults and disturbances that enveloped me, adding that it was not suitable for a person of my caliber to be treated in that manner. My mother replied to them in her usual sweet words, but to me she said, "They tell me that you want to take off the habit of the Virgin Mary [i.e., leave the order] because you fear persecutions and insults. If such a thing

has entered your mind, I will not look at you again, nor may you ever see or write to me, nor do I hold you as my son because I don't want a son who would not give his life, his honor, and a thousand lives if he had them for the Virgin Mary and suffer whatever trials for her order." I assured her that what they told her about me was not true. I understood that it was a scheme of my rivals who wanted me thrown out of the order because they judged that I resisted them more than anyone else and fought them so forcefully that they could not disband the Discalced, whereas if I were out of the order, they could easily disperse the rest.

18. These and many other things occurred in the persecution against me before I was sentenced. Then they sentenced me. I found myself out of favor, humiliated, insulted, and confined in the College of Alcalá. Although the flesh felt this very much—it couldn't be otherwise—I confess that I then received from our Lord delights and interior consolations so lofty that I am not even able to speak of them. A soul who suffers a great affront for God and rejection by the whole world yet seeks consolation with the afflicted and crucified Christ is not able to explain the interior consolations that result. I am referring to a book I wrote on the Apocalypse that describes the consolations and desolations of afflicted souls. If it is ever printed you will see it discussed there.[9]

19. This trial—or I should say comfort, consolation, quiet, and rest—lasted a short time, because the sentence was revoked soon afterward and I was reinstated to my previous state and reputation. The provincial of the Calced, Master Fray Angel Salazar, a prudent man with good intentions, governed and visited the Discalced at that time. Knowing that the king, in agreement with the nuncio, had sent to Rome for patents in order to establish the province of the Discalced and seeing that his authority might not last long and that it would not be in the service of God if the Discalced were disbanded, he called for me to be his companion and transmitted to me the authority to govern and order all the business of the Discalced. He even gave me news of the Calced and named me prior of the Discalced of Seville.

20. The brief of Gregory XIII for the establishment of the province of the Discalced separate from the Calced arrived, accompanied by another brief for Father Fray Pedro Fernández, provincial of the Dominicans of Castile, to execute it. The king commanded me to bring these briefs with his own letters to the same Fray Pedro Fernández so that he could carry it out. I carried these messages to Salamanca, and I found the father dying. The Lord took him a few days after I arrived. It seemed as though all that had been done in Rome would be fruitless. I traveled from Salamanca to Portugal where the king was, to notify him of the death of Fray Pedro Fernández. When I arrived at Elvas, the queen, Doña Ana, had just died. The same day that the queen died, I saw the king, and His Majesty again sent dispatches to Rome asking for a new commission. I went to my monastery in Seville.

21. His Holiness returned the same dispatches, commissioning Fray Juan de las Cuevas [to execute the brief]. He was the prior of the Dominican friars of San Ginés de Talavera at the time and later became Cardinal Archduke Albert's confessor and bishop of Ávila. They ordered me to carry the messages from Seville to Talavera. I suffered, glory to God, great discomforts and troubles from the weather, rains, and bad roads, together with Fray Bartolomé de Jesús. He helped me write all the announcements and letters for the convening of the chapter, which was held in Alcalá de Henares.[10] There the Discalced province was founded separate from the Calced, and I was elected its first provincial.

22. Seeing myself with the ordinary authority of a provincial with faculties to found monasteries without opposition and free of the responsibility of visiting the Calced, I founded many monasteries of friars and nuns in Castile and Andalusia. I accompanied Mother Teresa of Jesus on some foundations. I sent Father Fray Ambrosio Mariano to Portugal where the first monastery of friars, San Felipe of Lisbon, was founded in that kingdom. I brought Mother María de San José, who had been prioress of the nuns in Seville, to the same city with four other nuns,

and they founded the first monastery of nuns called San Alberto. While waiting for it to be made ready, they stayed for some days in the convent of the Dominican nuns, where the prioress was said to have the wounds of Christ. It was no small thing for this servant of God, María de San José, to be there during those days since afterward she disclosed some things by which it was realized that those wounds were false; thus the deception was discovered. Also, I sent Father Fray Nicolás Doria de Jesús María to Genoa, where he founded the first monastery in Italy. A monastery of nuns was afterward founded in the same city.

23. Shortly after the death of Mother Teresa of Jesus, I was given the opportunity to visit the nuns of Soria in my capacity as provincial. Martín Cruzat, a hermit and great servant of God who had been one of the important magistrates of the city of Pamplona, came to see me to ask for a foundation of nuns in his city. I brought from Soria for foundress Mother Catalina de Cristo, a great saint who in life and death has worked miracles, and, with her, Mother Leonor de la Misericordia. They founded a monastery in Pamplona with the help of Don Francés de Ayanz, brother of Mother Leanor, and his wife Doña Catalina Xavier, niece of Father Francisco Xavier of the Company [of Jesus, i.e., the Jesuits]. Because of the communication I had with this servant of God, Martín Cruzat, he took the habit of the Discalced friar and later founded the monastery of Discalced friars of Pamplona, the first in the kingdom of Navarre, just as Catalina de Cristo was beginning the foundations of nuns in Barcelona; thus the order expanded into the kingdoms of Catalonia and Aragon.

24. Seeing that there was hardly a kingdom in Spain where there was not a monastery, and they were already present in Italy, I was moved by zeal to extend the order to still further regions. Thus, in a chapter held in Lisbon where Father Fray Nicolás Doria was elected provincial (my term as provincial had come to an end, but because he was away in Italy, I continued governing the province as first definitor), I sent twelve Discalced friars from there to Mexico, where they founded a monastery. It was the origin of all the monasteries of the order that are in the West Indies.

25. I had sent friars for the conversion of the gentiles in the Congo of Ethiopia, where they began to win many souls for God. If the superiors who succeeded me had not recalled them, I believe there would have been much good done in the kingdoms of the African peoples. The order of the Company of Jesus, as we can see, has expanded to many kingdoms of the world with the good they have done and are doing. Likewise, according to my communications with Mother Teresa, the Virgin Mary His Mother was desirous that her order expand. I have always had and always will have this zeal, spirit, and desire.

26. Having finished my term as provincial, they elected me vicar provincial of Portugal. While exercising this office, the uprising of Drake, Don Antonio, and the English came upon that kingdom, and in order that the Calced Carmelite friars not become disquieted, Cardinal Archduke Albert named me apostolic visitator and reformer of the Calced Carmelites of that kingdom with the authority that the cardinal had from His Holiness.

27. While exercising this office, the superiors of the Discalced who succeeded me invented a new mode of government, which they were calling the *consulta*, and they began to change the laws that Holy Mother Teresa of Jesus had left her nuns. It seemed to me that if that mode of governing were not stopped, the sincerity, simplicity, and genuine spirit that up till then had been followed would be lost. I wrote some arguments against the *consulta* in order to give light to the religious about the harm that would follow. I sent Fray Pedro de la Purificación to Rome to inform the protector of the order and the pope of this so that the government of the *consulta* would not advance. Also, some of the Discalced prioresses authorized Dr. Bernabé del Mármol to negotiate for a brief from Pope Sixtus V that confirmed their customs and constitutions and ordered that they not be changed. I was able to do this very easily because, besides the obligation I had to my order that I had governed up till then, with the new commission of apostolic visitator and reformer I then had, I was not obligated to follow the opinions of the ordinary [Discalced] superiors, especially in

a matter so grave, and was able to have recourse to the pope and the protector of the order to whom we are all subject.

28. For this reason, and for reasons known to the Lord, when my visitations were finished, I found myself a prisoner, sentenced and condemned by them [the superiors] with the greatest public reproach and effrontery that can befall a religious. Seeking a remedy, I went to Rome in the habit of a hermit, so foreign from the one of my profession that I was a stranger to my brothers and a castoff from my mother order. I arrived, having suffered great trials by sea and by land. (I saw myself in evident danger of drowning five times.) But the greatest persecution of the brothers was in Rome, where with many letters of recommendation, they were so diligent and solicitous in bringing judicial processes and sentences against me that I had no defense other than innocence, silence, and hope. Father José de Acosta of the Company of Jesus counseled me to leave the affair in the hands of God and His Holiness and let my rivals do as they wished with me. I went in the same clothes of a hermit to preach in the kingdom of Sicily and spent seven months residing at the Hospital of St. James for the Spanish in Palermo, favored and supported in some fashion by the countess of Olivares, wife of the viceroy of Sicily. I also occupied myself with writing some books.

29. At the end of this time, they sent me a brief from His Holiness that I was to take the habit of the Discalced Augustinians in order to found, with a companion and patent sent to me from the Augustinian procurator general, the monastery of Saints Peter and Marcellinus in Rome and another Discalced Augustinian monastery in Naples. Here was presented to me the greatest spiritual trial of interior darkness and battle of conflicting reasons that I had ever faced. I was unable to decide what I should do to please God and our Lady and do their will. On the one hand, I saw that the pope, Vicar of Christ, was commanding it of me;[11] my adversaries had sought it with the intention of expelling me totally from the Carmelite Order without any hope of my return; my relatives and friends implored it of me, already seeing me with its honor and

peace; I myself was tired of going around for so long in peregrinations and exile; and I was slightly tempted by the honor of being the first founder of a newly reformed order and one so holy as that of St. Augustine. On the other hand, I couldn't get out of my sight the Virgin Mary whom I held as always present, as if I saw her admonishing me with her eyes not to set her habit aside and threatening me if I did, reminding me of the reasons I had for taking it in the first place and entering her order. This battle was of such strength and efficacy that I would not know how to describe it. In the end however, the contrary side in my heart won and I determined to take the habit of St. Augustine, yet with such great contradiction, fear, and shame on account of the Virgin Mary that death seemed more desirable than returning to Rome to clothe myself with the black habit of an Augustinian friar and make the foundations that I was charged to make.

30. My determination did not last more than four hours when, leaving from Gaeta in a frigate headed for Rome, we encountered a *galeota* of Turks who captured us. They stripped me of all my clothes, manacled my hands with irons, lifted me out of the frigate, and put me in the hold of the *galeota*. I confess to Your Honor that this event, which is normally the most disastrous that can happen in this world, was then for me a great relief, contentment, and joy. My heart expanded, seeing it clearly to be the will of God that I be dressed in the habit in which I was born and die rowing a Turkish oar.

31. They brought me to Tunis. For almost two years I was with four twenty-five pound irons at my feet in a dark and stinky *baño,* or underground prison. But after a few days, the feet became accustomed to the irons, the nose to the stench, the eyes to the darkness, and the body to being stretched upon a poor, miserable bed. I could not rise from it except to say Mass, which I said each day with much difficulty, tying the weight of the irons to my neck with a rope. Our Lord consoled me with the great good I was able to do in confessing and preaching each day to the six hundred Christian captives inside the dungeon and to others

who came in from outside. And with the ruminations I made with my mind and spirit, having all day and night for this without anything else to occupy me, many books could be filled up with diverse concepts if I were to write about the things I thought about.

32. Our Lord rescued me by a miracle or a mystery, for I never thought I would leave that *baño*. That was because they initially asked for thirty thousand *escudos* for my release, believing they were holding a great archbishop going to Rome to be a cardinal. This false testimony about me was started by the Turks, but it was beneficial to me in that the *janissaries*, who accused me of being an inquisitor in the land of the Christians, didn't burn me at the stake. I returned to Rome in the clothes of a poor priest slave, covered with a dyed *barragán* made into a cape. The same day I arrived, Father Francisco de Soto, cantor of His Holiness, had settled on a house, which he purchased to convert into a monastery of Discalced Carmelite nuns. And as they had known nothing about the order, nor was there in Rome at that time a single Discalced friar or nun or anyone else who knew about it, I helped him refurbish the house in the mode of a monastery and taught the young ladies, servants of God, whom he had gathered together, explaining the Rule to them and showing them the ceremonies and customs. With the help of the marquise of Rangona and the duchess of Aquasparta, and Pope Clement VIII also helping with money, the monastery of the Discalced Carmelite nuns of Rome was founded, subject immediately to the pope.

33. It was at this time that I asked His Holiness, with a veritable determination to submit to whatever the Vicar of Christ should command of me, to give me an order in which to live and to put me in the habit that he pleased. The cardinals of the Congregation for Religious determined that I should return to the Discalced Carmelites, and by their decree a brief was drawn up, of which I have an official translation in my possession to this day. His Holiness revoked the previous sentence that had laid down that I could not return to the Calced or the Discalced Orders. An official copy was sent to Spain. The Discalced challenged the brief, stirring

up dissension and persecutions against me with the result that the pope commanded, as the final solution, that I take the habit of the Calced. His secretary, [Msgr. Barbiano] Vestrio, advised me that it was not in my best interest to return to the Discalced, even if they begged me to return.

34. I was graciously and lovingly received by the Calced even though I had no other brief to be received by them except that of the *vivae vocis oraculo* ["by the oracle of a live voice"], which the pope said to the protector Pinelli. I was given a place to stay in the apartments of the general in the monastery of San Martín in Montibus, where I was but a short time because Cardinal Deza, protector of Spain and one of the oldest members of the Inquisition,[12] brought me to his house by order of His Holiness for the office of theologian. For five years, I was thus engaged in serious matters not only of the Inquisition but also of religious orders and cases involving Spanish friars who were brought back from apostasy, working with my general and the protector to settle various concerns of the order. During this time, glory to God, I helped with the foundation of the orders of the Discalced Augustinians and the Discalced Trinitarians of Spain, assisting Fathers Fray Miguel, Discalced Augustinian, and Fray Juan Bautista, Discalced Trinitarian, and helping them to put their constitutions in conformity with those of the Discalced Carmelites and the Council of Trent. I also helped to procure the well-being of Christians who were held captive in the land of the Moors, and I wrote some books that I then had printed in Rome.

35. Being thus occupied, it so happened that two Discalced friars, superiors from the monastery in Genoa, came to Rome. I told them to found a monastery in Rome since it is the head of the church and that if they didn't, I would do it and no honor would come to them; without a doubt I would have founded it. They must have feared this because by then I was much accredited and favored in Rome by many lords and cardinals, as well as by the ambassador and courtiers of Spain. So they came and founded the monastery of Nuestra Señora de la Scala of the Discalced Carmelites of Rome. This monastery was the beginning of

the congregation of the Discalced Carmelites of Italy, distinct from the Discalced Carmelites of Spain. From the religious of this monastery, other monasteries of friars and nuns have multiplied in Italy. And since they profess zeal for souls, they have gone to Persia by order of Pope Paul V and have founded a monastery in the principal city of that kingdom, which is called Isfahan. Although the king [Shah Abbas I] is a Muslim [*de la ley de Mahoma*], he shows them much favor and they are doing much good. For the conversion of Persia and other kingdoms of those regions, Pope Paul V named me bishop of the Armenians without my knowing it since I was in Flanders at the time; however, the mission he wanted to make for these conversions was terminated. From this monastery in Persia, Discalced friars have gone to the celebrated kingdom of Mogor,[13] where they have established a hospice. Though a monastery was not founded, one could be—if it pleases God—and in this way the order will spread throughout the East Indies. Would that I had space to send Your Honor copies of the letters from the king of Persia and the fathers of the Company of Jesus who are in Mogor, Java,[14] and other parts of the East Indies, where they write of the good that ours are doing in Persia and what they can do in that new world.

36. From this same monastery in Persia, in the year in which I now write, 1612, friars have also gone to the grand dominion of Moscow, which is inhabited by Greek schismatics, and I hope in God that, with the help of the Discalced friars who are in the kingdom of Poland, they will do good. It is now seven years since Fray Matías de San Francisco, a Spaniard,[15] went from the monastery of the Scala of Rome to the city of Kraków, Poland, to found a very good monastery. It is located on a most pleasant site, spacious, with many trees, and fountains and ponds with a great abundance of fish, more than enough for their monastery and many more. And in these ponds they made islands on which they have built hermitages, for greater prayer and devotion. This monastery is called the Concepción de Nuestra Señora; it is the novitiate, with a good number of Polish novices. From there they founded another monastery in the town of Ziblia, four days' journey

from Moscow, which they call San José. There they study arts and theology and have more than twenty student religious. Within the city of Kraków itself, in one of the best locations, a nobleman of that kingdom is now constructing a great monastery called San Miguel Arcángel, which will serve as a house for the professed. Young men from the noblest families of that kingdom, such as the nephew of the grand chancellor, and others who are already preaching in the Polish language, have entered these monasteries as religious. Many regions of Poland are asking for foundations of monasteries of friars. The reason I said that the monastery in Moscow could be helped from Poland is that the king of Poland, who is a great Catholic and loves our friars very much, has conquered a great part of the dominion of Moscow and is trying to make a foundation there. And although there are many heretics in the kingdom of Poland, in the main, especially in the Poland they call Minor, the people are very devout Catholics, generous with alms, and friends of reformed orders.

37. I want to return to what I was talking about when I was working in Rome in the house of Cardinal Deza. At that time, a friend of mine wrote to me from the town of Rouen, France. His name is Don Juan Quintanadueñas Brétigny, and we were great friends in Seville. He wrote that in his town of Rouen they wanted a monastery of Discalced Carmelite nuns; that the sisters of Cardinal Joyosa and the cardinal himself would construct it; and that some ladies, relatives of Brétigny and Monsignor de Quesada, having been informed of the order, desired to become religious. For a long time I conferred with him through letters as to how we might manage to bring nuns to Rouen. Since he was not able to reach any agreement with the Discalced friars of Spain to give nuns, I wrote that there was no other remedy but to get a brief from His Holiness and a letter from the king and queen of France addressed to the king and queen of Spain asking for nuns for this foundation and for others in their dominions. Through these letters, it was agreed that Mothers Ana de Jesús, Ana de San Bartolomé, Isabel de Los Ángeles, Beatriz de la Concepción, Isabel de San Pablo, and Leonor de San Bernardo would go to France. They

founded the first monastery in Paris, a renowned monastery called Nuestra Señora del Campo, the construction of which was helped by the duchess of Longueville.[16] From this monastery, which was made in 1604, a monastery was founded in Poitiers in 1605; another in the town of Dijon that same year; another in Amiens in 1606; and in 1608, another in Tours. And they are multiplying in other parts of France.

38. Seeing the great good that this same order could do in Flanders, the most serene archduke and archduchess of Austria, Albert and Isabel, brought Mother Ana de Jesús and others of her companions from France and founded the celebrated monastery of Santa Ana y San José of Brussels, endowing it very well and enriching it with splendid sacred vestments. They say that the construction will cost them more than 150,000 *escudos*. From this monastery, Mother Ana de Jesús founded another monastery in the town of Louvain; Lady Constancia Helman helped fund its construction. Another monastery was founded in the town of Mons de Henao where the example of their religious life has borne much fruit, especially in a celebrated cathedral church of canonesses in that town.

39. These nuns were, as the ones in France are now, subject to the visitation and government of the secular clergy—servants of God—by the bull of Pope Clement VIII. The nuns in Flanders, desiring to be subject to the government of the Discalced friars of their order, have never been able to succeed—although they have made great efforts at various times—in getting the Discalced friars of Spain to come to these parts.

40. Our Lord ordained that in the year 1600, which was the year of the Great Jubilee, Pope Clement VIII would send me—by order of the cardinals of the Congregation of the Propagation of the Faith, to whom I had given many memorials regarding the redemption of Christian souls captive in Africa—to all the regions of Barbary and other regions subject to the Grand Turk with the faculty to announce the jubilee of the holy year, in order to put up altars and churches and appoint confessors. With this commission, which is one of great honor as can be seen in the brief that was given to me, I went about Africa with letters from

King Philip III of Spain and did what I could. When I was in Tétouan, the alcalde talked with me about getting involved in the peace initiative of the great sharif, king of Morocco, with the king of Spain; the sharif desired to give the king the Al-Arache River.[17] I left Africa to attend to this important negotiation. Intending to go inform the pope about the status of things in Africa, I was just about to embark from Alicante when His Holiness went to heaven. I remained preaching in the kingdom of Valencia, where my general ordered me to print my books.

41. It came about that the marquis of Guadaleste, whom I knew, told me he was going as ambassador to Flanders. He wanted me to go with him. Thinking I would have better resources there for my printing, as I indeed have had, I came to Brussels. I began to preach and deal with the Discalced fathers as I was accustomed to do. And seeing that the Discalced friars of Spain did not want to come to these countries, I wrote at various times to the Italian congregation in Rome, primarily to Father Tomás de Jesús [Sánchez Dávila]. He left Rome with some companions and founded their monastery in Brussels at the best site they could find. Prominent gentlemen helped with donations for its construction, while Madame de Lachau and Countess Jodamia helped with that of two good hermitages. From here the College of Louvain was founded, a seminary connected to the renowned university of the States of Flanders.[18] Our Lord furnished them with a very good house built on a very good site, and Father Fray Nicolás de la Concepción came from Rome to be prior and rector of that college.

42. When Father Fray Tomás passed through Paris, he left the beginnings of a monastery of Discalced friars in that city. Its foundation was preceded by no little contradiction from parliament and many other public and secret adversaries, since they feared that the obedience of the nuns in France would be taken from the secular clergy, where it is placed now, and given to the friars. This monastery of Paris will be the primary seminary of those kingdoms, although there was another one already in Bononia of France,[19] founded by friars from Italy.

43. The last monastery founded by the nuns of this order has been in Kraków, because a canon of that city who was living in Rome asked His Holiness for nuns. The fathers wrote Father Fray Tomás in Flanders that he should make the foundation. Thus, on April 27 of this year in which I write this letter, 1612, Father Tomás took Mother María de la Trinidad from the Brussels monastery for prioress, and Sisters Margarita de Jesús and Teresa of Jesus from the monastery of Mons de Henao and Sister Cristina de San José from the Louvain monastery. They are all very noble, servants of God, and among the first who have professed in these regions, and they know how to speak many languages. They were suitably accompanied by the superior of Brussels and a priest servant of God as well as a lay woman who became a nun there. They had letters from their highnesses for the princes of Alemania [Germany] where they would pass. Upon their arrival in Nuremberg, some gentlemen were waiting with two large coaches to accompany them to Kraków. They arrived the second of June. A Polish gentleman who came for them paid for the cost of the journey. They traveled with the same modesty with which Mother [St. Teresa of Jesus] used to make her foundations. Although they passed through many lands of heretics, the friars and nuns never had to remove their habits, nor were they mistreated by the heretics, but only received reproaches, affronts, and insults.

44. Our fathers of Kraków went out to meet them with many lords of the kingdom. Since the house for the foundation was not yet ready and the foundress was away at the time, the nuns stayed in the convent of Santa Clara, which had more than forty Franciscan nuns. Their example bore much fruit, such that the nuns there desired to reform their own order in those kingdoms and attempted to do so. After spending nineteen days in that convent, they moved into the house that the duchess of Arloslavia had given them. The dean of the main church celebrated Mass for them and reserved the Blessed Sacrament. In the name of the foundress, he assured in writing 450 ducats of rent. Many distinguished young ladies ask for the habit, and there is great devotion in other towns of Poland where monasteries of the order might be established. God

provided them with a young lady, the first of that kingdom, who knows Polish, French, and Italian, and serves as their translator. Blessed be our Lord, that from the east to the west and the south to the far north, where lies this kingdom of Poland, the order has expanded.

45. I hope in His Divine Majesty—and they are even planning now with letters and negotiations with the most serene electors of Cologne and Mainz, and the new emperor Mathias, that the order will soon be established in Alemania, Bohemia, and Hungary, where the heresy of Luther and his bad nun Doña Catalina Bora began, which has caused so much damage. In this way, may the good nun, Mother Teresa, be a part of the upholding of the faith and the increase of religious life by means of her friars and nuns, in company with holy Ignatius of Loyola who, by means of the fathers of his Company, is doing incredible good in all of Christianity in those kingdoms. Why, this holy Ignatius converted in the same year that Luther began to preach [his heresy], and Holy Mother became a nun in the same year that Luther married the abbess Doña Catalina Bora. By means of these two columns of the church, Ignatius and Teresa of Jesus, and the Virgin Mary their mother, the fruit that is desired and prayed for will certainly be produced.

46. There are many things I could tell Your Honor in this letter that I have written in a book entitled *Peregrinación de Anastasio,* in which I write at greater length about my affronts and trials. And do not be taken aback that I want to manifest them to all the world because "we glory in our tribulations" [Rom 5:3], knowing that the road of the cross is the most direct for attaining blessedness. May our Lord grant you such blessedness, after many years of a healthy, spirit-filled life.

Appendix II

Letter 185 to Francisca de Las Llagas and María de San José[1]

ANTWERP
MARCH 14, 1610

[Gracián] preaches during Lent at the Antwerp Castle. He prints the *Life* of Mother Teresa in Latin because of a certain persecution against her by the Discalced of Spain. The finger of the saint will be for the monastery of Seville; he tells of something that happened with it. The Pilgrimage of Anastasius is nearly finished. The statement of the canonization of Mother Teresa is now prepared, but he is awaiting the arrival of Father Tomás to declare it. The disillusions of Mother Ana de Jesús. His own plans to return to Spain.

+
Jesus Mary

I went to preach this morning, the Sunday of the "mute little demon,"[2] at the Castle of Antwerp (where I am preaching to many people this Lent with good results), and I was given an envelope with a letter from Doña Luisa Faxardo and two from Your Reverences.[3] Without a doubt, I believe a mute little devil has been meddling because from the time I sent you my captivity portrait until now I have not received a letter from you, nor, I believe from what you say in yours, have you received mine.[4] So it will be helpful to state generally what I wrote, namely, that I am doing well, my health is good, and I am occupied with good works.

2. They write me from Rome that our Discalced in Spain do not want to call Mother Teresa foundress of the friars, but rather John of the Cross. They also want to remove from the *rótulo* what it says about her zeal for souls.[5] And they are trying to have other things removed, as you will see from the letter of Father Tomás. In order to counter this persecution, I have printed a book in Latin of the life of Mother Teresa taken from the *rótulo* for her canonization; if we need it for the authentic *rótulo,* it can be used with just a few words added. The nuncio [Cardinal Guido Bentivoglio] here has received a commission to gather information. He has the authority to delegate whomever he wants in any part of the world (as the nuncio in Toledo delegated that canon to take testimonies), authorizing him to carry out the commission as the nuncio's representative, sending him to all parts of Spain, to prelates, dignitaries, and friends, so they can give their testimonies. The Discalced Carmelites in Spain are not happy about this. When these testimonies have been gathered, they will serve as a book with a prologue by me, and we will send it to England, France, Germany, and Poland so that Catholics and heretics alike will profit and have information about Mother Teresa. We have already begun to send the *Life* in Latin. Although it cost me fifty ducats to print, it is money well spent.

3. With regard to the finger,[6] many days ago I promised it to Mother Juliana for the monastery of Seville. Although she pressured me to send it right away, since they have made a reliquary of silver for it, I replied to her with Mother Teresa's revelation that I should not part with it until I die. The things that have happened with it and that are still happening every day are certainly amazing. A married man once asked me to give it to him so he could bring it to his wife who was giving birth. Not entrusting it to him, I said I would go with him and read the gospel. I brought it to her and asked her if she had made her confession. She said she had but that once she had failed to confess something out of shame. She said that fourteen years ago she committed a grave sin that

she never confessed because of her shame. I heard her general confession there where she was giving birth. As soon as I absolved her, she died. So it is enough that my daughters in Consuegra get my body and papers.[7] Leave the finger for the nuns of Seville.

4. Regarding the request of Your Reverences about how to understand Mother Teresa when she writes to me of Alcalá and the Cats,[8] I would like you to read the "Pilgrimage of Anastasius," which is almost finished and will be around eighty sheets of paper. In it I tell about all the tribulations I have had during my life, the spirit by which God has led me, the offices I have had, and the revelations there have been about me and what has come of them. I will try to send it as soon as possible so that it can be put with my other papers.

5. It has been many days since I wrote my testimony for the canonization process of Mother Teresa. It is some twelve sheets of paper. Although I have taken great pains that testimonies be gathered in these countries—the testimonies of Mother Ana de Jesús, Mother Ana de San Bartolomé, and of persons who have had miracles granted in France, Mons de Henao, Cambray, and other places—I am waiting for the arrival of Father Tomás who asked me to wait for him so that he can make a declaration. From his letter you will see the purpose of his coming here.

6. I have come to Antwerp to deal with the foundation of his college in this city, which is the important thing. As for one in Brussels, Mother Ana has promised much. She is disillusioned by how they have duped her and how little it has profited her in this business of the order to distance herself from me.[9] I have much to say about this, but it is not for a letter. See how I am fasting from the things of over there except for the letter Secretary Pero Rodríguez wrote informing me that Doña Teresa was married and Your Reverences didn't even know about it.[10] I greatly suspect that they have much affection for each other. Now that the Marquise of Guadaleste is there,[11] I will write by way of Doña Luisa, by whom this goes.

7. If the ambassador does not return, I plan to go by sea with good weather. Once I arrive there, my first visit will be to my monastery of Consuegra, and there I will decide where I should go to die. But first the Discalced fathers must arrive from Rome and we will see what God wants to do with us. May God guide things well. To all the sisters, whom I don't want to name in particular because I love them all so much, Your Reverences give my greetings and divide the holy cards for their breviaries. May our Lord give you the grace and spirit I desire for you. From Antwerp, Third Sunday of Lent, 1610.

Appendix III

Letter 222 to Alfonso de Narvaez, Captain of the Artillery of Pamplona

BRUSSELS, DECEMBER 28, 1612

[*From the National Library of Madrid*]

[Gracián] tells him his present situation in the habit of a Calced Carmelite and the reason the efforts of Father Tomás de Jesús inviting him to return to the Discalced have not so far been successful. In the meantime, he helps the order with its activity. He tells how he goes about reforming the friars and nuns of the Calced according to the norms of the Council of Trent. He tells of the manner and mode of life of the Flemish beguines and the danger they run of falling into the new heresy of the "perfectionists." Instructions for receiving his books.

+

Jesus Mary

I received much pleasure from Your Honor's letter of November 23. May the Lord reward you for remembering me, for the favors you have done for me, and for the desire for my well-being that you have shown to me. As for this business regarding my religious order, it is my practice never to speak of it (as with all other things that have happened) because it has been twenty years now since it happened and I have turned it all over to the Lord.[1] Nevertheless, I want to give you a brief account about what is going on with me so that you can give a report to Father Prior of the Discalced there and to the Discalced nuns.[2]

2. When Father Tomás de Jesús arrived here to found the Discalced Carmelite friars, he told me personally to give him in writing what my will was regarding my return to the Discalced. I consulted the Lord about this and also other persons of the Discalced Order. I replied in writing that in something that touched me so personally, I did not have nor did I want to have my own will or preference but only God's will. I was in this habit of the Calced by the command of obedience that Pope Clement VIII gave me, and with the same apostolic obedience I would be happy to change it, assured that this would be the will of God. I wrote this to the communities in Spain and to many persons who loved me dearly and knew about my affairs. It seemed like a good idea to all of them. They were sure that if the Discalced fathers wanted me (though not even my will or theirs would be enough without the pope's), they would draw up the necessary documents or give instructions as to how they were to be drawn up, so that I could return to them. Thus the matter stood. I understood very well what was at the root of this business.[3] Namely, there were two generals of the Discalced, one for the friars of Italy and the other for the friars of Spain, and if I were to return to those of Italy, it would entail renouncing, maybe by a vow, ever to return or place eyes on the Discalced of Spain, forever saying goodbye to Spain, and never again visiting the monasteries there. Since I professed as a Discalced of Spain with the customs and rules that we follow, it would be hard for me to follow others that are new such as those they follow in Italy, separating myself from my dear Spanish Discalced and my country and native place,[4] and finishing my life among Italians whom I do not know. I know well that there are some (perhaps many) in Spain who love me very much, but to this day no one has written to me on behalf of the general or communicated with me in any way, asking that I do what Father Tomás asked me on behalf of those of Italy.[5]

3. I am on the watch to help in all that I can with writings and books for the whole order, the Calced and the two branches of the Discalced,

fighting against heretics and supporting the foundations of the Discalced here and in Germany, which I hope in God will be made soon for the increase of the faith. I am more useful to them in this habit [of the Calced] for their temporal (and even spiritual) good than I would be if I were among them. My life is eremitical inasmuch as I live in a cell in the garden of the monastery of the Calced in Brussels. Since they are Flemish, it is as if they were painted on a tapestry. They have reformed their manner of life considerably since I came, and they follow the Council of Trent. Formerly, women ate in the refectory with the friars. In the same way, in a monastery of fifty very holy Calced Carmelite nuns two leagues from here,[6] men and women enter the cloister as if it were a house for seculars. They care for thirty girls who come and go, and the friars who confess them live inside the cloister with them. When there is a feast day, friars from outside go there to sing with the nuns in the choir. Through the goodness of God, never has the slightest weakness of the world been heard of or seen (which is a thing of admiration).[7] Our Lord was served when they, merely by hearing the provincial read to them the decrees of the Council of Trent, immediately installed the turns,[8] grilles, and doors as if they were Discalced (the provincial had brought me along as a companion of the visitation). Please God there could be some Discalced nuns here to show them how to pray, because without a doubt ours would help them much. What gives the fathers of the Company of Jesus and me, who deal with some of them, the most difficulty is their excess in mental prayer and indiscreet penances.

4. It is mainly in this way that much service is rendered to our Lord in these lands. The books that have been translated from Spanish to Flemish and are circulating among the beguines and monasteries of nuns and friars of all orders are bearing much fruit. Two books of Mother Teresa are already distributed in Flemish and French and are bearing much fruit. To whomever has not seen the beguinages of these countries,[9] it might seem hard to believe—given the lack of cloister, as I said, in this monastery of the Carmelite nuns of Vilvoorde (as in other orders)—that purity and chastity is guarded. There are congregations

of women, most of them young and beautiful, numbering five hundred and even a thousand in some places, each with their own little house and the main gate closed only at night. Whosoever wants, friars and laity, may enter the house of whatever beguine. They go out for all their own business and for festivals. In spite of the number of beguines and so many occasions,[10] there are no disasters to chastity. Even the laity is eager about prayer and perfection. Since there is no one to teach them, a new heresy of those called "perfectionists" has made inroads under the pretext of seeking greater union with God. Against these we are busily occupied. I had one of their heresiarchs, who goes about in these parts teaching spirituality, imprisoned.[11] I would very much like to send to Your Honor the books I have already printed against them two years ago and many others. They cannot be sent by regular mail. Please write your brother Ensign Narvaez, who is in Dunkirk, to send them, as I will send them to him and give notice to those of the Inquisition to let them enter. Our brothers can use them. Please give my greetings to them and also to the Discalced nuns and the ladies, principally to Doña Marta and her companions. May our Lord grant Your Honor, Doña Marta, and all our friends there the grace, life, health, and spirit that I desire and pray for them.

From Brussels, December 28, 1612
Father Jerome Gracián of the Mother of God

Appendix IV

Illness and Happy Death of Jerome Gracián

Written by a person who was present for most of what is related here, and the rest was told to him either by the deceased or his companion.[1]

Having gone out in a carriage at three o'clock in the afternoon on September 20 with a lay brother of his order named Aloste to a village five leagues from Brussels, where he was doing works of charity for the common good (holy works that he spent most of his life doing), Father Master Jerome Gracián arrived very late at the gates of Brussels and found them closed, as was customary at nightfall in all the villages of Flanders. For that reason, it was necessary to lodge that night in a house on the outskirts of the parish of St. John.

2. This same night, Father Master became very ill with a sickness that began to attack him around two o'clock. From then on, he was not able to rest, so he called his companion. He got up to see if he could get some relief by vomiting. Although he vomited some phlegm, he was seized with such physical distress from the effort of getting up that it was not possible to get back in bed again even with the help of five other persons. It was necessary to leave him in another bed on the floor to see if he would get better. The rest of the night was spent like this. At daybreak, Father Master sent the owner of the carriage to his monastery to advise them of his illness. This man met a Dominican friar in the streets of Brussels. Since it was Sunday and the feast of St. Matthew, this very devout and good religious was on his way to preach in one of the neighborhoods as this was what the friars of the Order of Preachers did. Since the owner of the carriage did not know

much about the difference between the two religious habits, he told the Dominican friar to go quickly to the house, where he would find a friar of his order very ill and that he would continue on to the monastery to inform them of the situation.

3. When this religious arrived at the house, Father Gracián was greatly relieved. Although he did not know the Dominican friar, except by the laws of charity, he seemed to him to be an angel from heaven who came to visit him on that occasion. With this happiness, he made his confession in Latin. This being accomplished, the religious left to do his preaching. Meanwhile, the coachman arrived at the monastery of St. Dominic with the news. A certain religious who knew and dealt with Father Gracián for years grabbed his mantle. Passing by the house of the Spanish ambassador, who lived near the monastery and had confessed to Father Gracián for many years,[2] he asked for a small carriage that was set aside for the use of Father Gracián. It was seven o'clock in the morning. This religious got into the carriage and headed out to get Gracián and bring him back to the monastery. Father Gracián rejoiced at seeing this religious and the concern he showed. He thought they could return to the monastery at a slow pace. But it was not possible. As much as he tried to get up from the bed, he could not do it, even with five men who helped his desire more than his strength, which was completely gone. After all this effort, he could no longer move without fainting and falling as if they had cut off his legs. His color was changed, and he showed other signs of death in his eyes and mouth. Having tried this twice on account of his pleading, and seeing that he got worse with these movements, they fixed him a comfortable bed so he would not be on the ground. After making the bed, they tried to put him in it. The same thing happened as before, and it even seemed that the signs of death were increasing. So it was necessary to leave him there in that position and not move him again since moving him appeared to be hastening death.

4. The Dominican religious then persuaded Father Master to recognize that he was in a very bad way; that there were signs of death; and

that if he fell again, he could die before he knew it. So it would be very wise to put himself right with God and to look at himself to see if he had some scruple or remorse with which he could help him. Father Gracián responded that he had confessed that morning, and he found nothing in his conscience that troubled him. The Dominican friar said since this was so, it was fitting to receive the Blessed Sacrament and prepare for what might come to pass. This counsel seemed very good, and so they brought him the Blessed Sacrament from the parish church of St. John outside the walls of Brussels; he received it with notable tenderness and devotion. Before receiving, he professed the Catholic faith, pardoned all, and asked pardon for himself. Assisted by the already-mentioned religious, he called to mind blessed Mother Teresa of Jesus whom he knew and dealt with very particularly and then he continued his other prayers. As an act of thanksgiving to God who really and truly had come to visit Gracián in the sacrament and for whom the hour had arrived to enjoy Him forever, the two of them said the Te Deum. After having received Communion and requesting the holy anointing, which was given very soon after, and having given thanks, he never tired of repeating many times, "Glory to the Father, and to the Son, and to the Holy Spirit." He also repeated a saying of a holy bishop who, at the hour of his death, responded to his good friend St. Augustine who had asked him to ask God to let him live longer for the good of the church: "*Si numquam, bene; si aliquando, quare non modo*" ["If I am never to die, well and good; but if I am to die, why not now"]. Father Gracián repeated this several times, wherein he showed his great desire to enjoy God and the assurance he had of this.

5. All this took place at nine o'clock in the morning. Then the ambassador of Spain arrived from Brussels to visit Gracián. Father Provincial of the [Calced] order had come with a doctor and a pharmacist shortly before. Although they gave him certain remedies, they were of little use. At midmorning, many of the important and principal persons of the court and others devoted to him came to visit, as well as the prior of the Carmel of the Discalced. They were sorry to see him on the ground. The aged holy man replied that the bed of Christ on the cross was much

harder. He rejoiced with everyone and spoke with much happiness to all as one on the eve of his wedding with Christ, his Spouse. Being so happy with all present, he recited some devout couplets composed by Mother Teresa of Jesus. Then he asked that his *"Metresas"* be taken from his breast so he could see them.[3] These were two very beautiful images engraved on little copper plates, one of our Lady and the other of Mother Teresa of Jesus. He wore these images for many years along with a relic of Holy Mother Teresa, a finger from her hand. The chief doctor of His Excellency visited him a second time at three o'clock in the afternoon. It seemed to the doctor that he would surely die in a few more hours. It was decided that they would take him to the monastery because, whether he lived or died, it was much better to be inside rather than outside it.

6. Father Gracián was much relieved with this decision. So, having readied a bed inside the carriage, he was placed in it by six people carrying him by the bedsheets on which he was lying. All the doors of the coach were wide open. Two religious of his order accompanied him, and the other important persons of the court followed in their coaches. In this way, he entered his cell at the monastery. He arrived very changed, almost unconscious, or so it seemed because he did not speak. At six o'clock in the afternoon, he expired very gently without much pain or suffering because God, who had given him so much suffering in life, wanted to grant him a peaceful death and bring him to Himself in an extraordinary way without grave sickness or suffering except that which served to let him know he was being called home.

7. The following day, after the feast of St. Matthew, the court honored him with a solemn burial. Father Provincial of the Carmelites said the Mass, and a Dominican of the royal court preached in Spanish. They buried him in his habit in a tomb before the altar of the chapter room of the monastery. There were many people present. All showed honor and esteem as so much was owed to Gracián in life and death for his rare virtues. This was clear from the testimony of a great authority, Mother Teresa of Jesus, who says many good things about Gracián in chapter

23 of the book she called *Foundations*. And there were other writings that were found on the deceased written in the hand of Mother Teresa wherein was related a revelation in which Christ, Our Lord, told her to take in His place in all things Father Master Gracián, who lives and reigns in blessedness. Amen.[4]

Appendix V

Official Declaration of the Rehabilitation of Father Jerome Gracián of the Mother of God, O.C.D.

ROME, CHRISTMAS 1999

Protocol number 289/99 DF[1]

At our 1991 general chapter, in the atmosphere of the fourth centenary of our holy father St. John of the Cross, a proposal was presented by the provincial chapter and the association of our nuns in Andalusia, which in the *Actas* (p. 209 of the printed text) bears the title *De causis beatificationis et canonizationis Servorum Dei Annae a Iesu (Lobera), Mariae a Sancto Joseph (Salazar) necnon P. Hieronymi Gracián a Matre Dei introducendis* (To Introduce the Cause for the Beatification and Canonization of the Servants of God: Ana de Jesús (Lobera), María de San José (Salazar), and Father Jerome Gracián of the Mother of God).[2]

2. Concerning Father Gracián, it was also proposed that the chapter revoke the sentence expelling him from the order as an official gesture of rehabilitation and reparation for the injustice of which he was the victim. The chapter thought it appropriate to delegate to the definitory and to the postulation the topic of the causes for beatification and canonization, while requesting that the rehabilitation of Father Gracián be examined further from the historical point of view.

3. In its forty-seventh session on December 15, 1999, the general definitory, following the example of the Holy Father in this jubilee

year, judged it appropriate to make an official declaration *revoking the sentence of expulsion from the order issued against Father Jerome Gracián,* the spiritual son and beloved disciple of our mother St. Teresa of Jesus, as an official gesture of rehabilitation and reparation for the injustice he suffered.

4. In examining studies made before and after the 1991 general chapter, the historical facts causing particular grief are the expulsion from the order of Father Jerome Gracián and his secretary, Father Bartolomé de Jesús, as well as the grave punishments imposed on Mothers Ana de Jesús and María de San José, all people trusted implicitly by our Holy Mother and examples of the highest order in the founding group.

5. Also to be lamented, in addition to the injustices they suffered during life, is the unjust treatment they received throughout much of our history, canceling the important place they ought to have or attributing to them defects that in reality they did not have.

6. Shortly after being liberated from captivity in April 1595, Father Gracián petitioned the general to be readmitted to the order.[3] The then general, Father Elías de San Martín, replied,

> As Your Reverence also knows, as one who has governed, the superior must place the good of the community before all other things, even if this means his own life and the counsel of his friends. That is why I have delayed answering: to seek advice and see if what Your Reverence asks would lead to peace among the religious. And I found great evidence that doing so would cause great discord and division, which I, as head, though unworthy, am obliged to avoid as far as possible. And because of this, I ask Your Reverence that, since you considered and still consider yourself a true son of the order and have such love for it, in exchange for its good you would accept staying separated. I well believe that on occasion you will have prayed to the Lord as St. Paul did: "That I might be accursed and cut off from Christ if this could benefit my brothers" [Rom 9:3]. And, since His Majesty has fulfilled this in you, there is no need to be distressed,

> since your crown is not lost but rather, I believe, doubled . . . and I am confident that when His Divine Majesty would have seen what was suitable for the greater good of Your Reverence's soul, being cut off from us, He ordained this as He is accustomed to ordain other things, except that people such as I provide the means.[4]

7. At the same time, Father Gracián obtained from Pope Clement VIII a brief entitled *Apostolicae Sedis benignitas* in which it was ordained that he be readmitted, something that was never realized. In the brief, it was stated,

> We grant and give permission that you be able to return to the said order of Discalced Carmelite friars and once more be received into it, and that you be able to use and enjoy all the graces, privileges, indults, favors, as well as active and passive voice, as though you had never been cut off and deprived of them. I order this of the said vicar and definitors and other superiors and friars of the said order, that they receive and treat you kindly and permit you to use and enjoy peacefully the said privileges, graces, and other things. Notwithstanding the abovementioned letters of ours or any other constitutions or apostolic ordinances whatsoever, etc.

8. Though late and not wishing to raise new polemics, the present definitory thought the moment had arrived to make a declaration that does justice to a religious so important to the Teresian refoundation plan.

9. Paraphrasing the words pronounced by Pope John Paul II on December 17, 1999, in his discourse to those taking part at the International Congress on Jan Hus celebrated in Rome, the definitory also wishes to say: Today, on the eve of the great jubilee, we feel the duty to express profound regret for the expulsion from the order inflicted on Father Jerome Gracián of the Mother of God, and for the resulting wound that has been a source of conflict and division in the minds and hearts of the sons and daughters of St. Teresa of Jesus.

10. As successors of Elías de San Martín and his definitory who denied Father Gracián readmission to the order, taking into account all that we owe to Father Gracián, faithful and indefatigable collaborator of our Holy Mother Teresa, and desiring to follow the example of John Paul II and the universal church, we want, as the Teresian Carmel, to enter the third millennium with a memory reconciled with our past and a renewed enthusiasm in looking to the future.

11. Referring back to the pope's discourse previously mentioned, we make his words our own:

> Of capital importance, from this viewpoint, is the effort that scholars can spend to reach a deeper and more complete understanding of historical truth. Faith has nothing to fear from commitment to historical research, since research is, in the final analysis, directed toward the truth that has its source in God. . . . Truth can be uncomfortable when it asks us to abandon our prejudices and deeply rooted stereotypes. This goes for churches, ecclesial communities, and religious orders as much as for nations and individuals. Yet, the truth that sets us free from error is also *the truth setting us free to love.*[5]

In the name of the General Definitory:

Father Camilo Maccise, O.C.D.
superior general

Father Silvano Vescovi, O.C.D.
secretary general

Notes

Preface

1. "Unshod" translates *descalzo*. Reformed orders take the name "Discalced" to indicate their renewed austerity or poverty, signified by bare or shoeless feet.
2. Since the descriptions of the dialogues in Gracián's table of contents duplicate the descriptions at the beginning of each dialogue, I have replaced them with a single word description. The shield elements and their corresponding dialogues are listed at the end of my Introduction (pp. xxxiii–xxxiv).

Prologue

1. The shield above is composed of elements taken from two different versions of Gracian's shield, one from Astigarraga's edition of *Peregrinación de Anastasio* (p. 3) and the other from Morales' edition of *The Burning Lamp*.
2. Bernard of Clairvaux, "On the Song of Songs II," sermon 23, 9, in *The Works of Bernard of Clairvaux*, trans. Kilian Walsh, vol. 3, 33–34 (Kalamazoo, Mich.: Cistercian Publications, 1976), 34 (although the translation there is "My secret to myself"). The phrase originated in the Latin Vulgate translation of Isaiah 24:16. St. John of the Cross also makes use of it in maxim 74 or *Sayings of Light and Love* 153, in *The Collected Works of St. John of the Cross*, trans. Kieran Kavanaugh and Otilio Rodriguez, 83–97 (Washington, D.C.: ICS Publications, 1991), 96: "Be silent concerning what God may have given you and recall that saying of the bride: 'My secret for myself.'"

First Dialogue: Vocation

1. Gracián received the habit at the monastery of San Pedro on April 25, 1572. He notified his mother that same day that he had entered the Carmelite Order.
2. Diego Gracián de Alderete and Juana Dantisco. A renowned humanist, Diego Gracián had been secretary to King Charles I (known also as Holy Roman Emperor Charles V) and King Philip II.
3. Antonio Gracián was secretary for Philip for five or six years.
4. The first foundation of the Discalced Carmelite friars was made at Duruelo on November 28, 1568. Gracián knew the history of the Carmelite Order very well. Although he speaks here of the reformation of the order, he is aware of the special role that St. Teresa of Jesus has as foundress (see PA 13).

5. Miguel Cervantes (1544–1616), a contemporary of Gracián, parodies this kind of chivalric love in *Don Quixote*.
6. The monastery of Pastrana (Guadalajara) was founded July 9, 1569.
7. San Bábilas is named for St. Babylas of Antioch (d. 253).
8. Gracián was ordained to the priesthood on March 25, 1570, at the age of twenty-four, before he entered the order.
9. Baltasar de Jesús (Nieto) received the habit of the reform at Pastrana with Ambrosio Mariano and Juan de la Miseria and was prior from July 1570 to November 1573. In 1577, he joined Miguel de la Columna in a campaign of calumny against Gracián. For more biographical details about him and other friars and nuns who are mentioned in *Pilgrimage of Anastasius*, see the invaluable work of Peers, *Handbook to the Life*.
10. St. Teresa did not meet Gracián in person until he visited her at her monastery in Beas de Segura in April 1575.
11. The theme of "holy liberty" is important in recent studies of the Teresian charism.
12. St. John of the Cross was sent to Pastrana to rectify the deplorable situation of the poor formation being given in this novitiate, which was destined to become the cradle of the Discalced Carmelites (F 23.9–10).
13. His mother did not die at this time. She died October 6, 1601, with her son Jerome at her bedside.
14. Ana de Mendoza. After the death of her husband, Mendoza joined the Discalced at the Pastrana monastery of which she was patroness. She caused so much commotion and consternation that the nuns left stealthily at night, leaving the princess behind with her servants. See F 17.16–17.
15. A monastery that already belonged to the Carmelite Order. See Peers's *Handbook to the Life*, 23.
16. *El Carmen* invariably means a church or monastery that is dedicated to Our Lady of Mount Carmel.
17. The founding of the Discalced in Andalusia is discussed in more detail in PA 13.32–38.
18. One doubloon, which was a denomination of the *escudo* worth 2 *escudos*, equaled thirty-two *reales*.
19. Pius V died May 1, 1572.
20. Nicolò Ormaneto, born in Verona in 1515, had worked with St. Charles Borromeo in executing the Tridentine decrees. He was named bishop of Padua in 1570 and the nuncio in Spain two years later.
21. The brief of Ormaneto naming Gracián as commissary and reformer of the Order of Carmel in the province of Andalusia and of the Discalced of Castile is dated August 3, 1575 (see MHCT 1, doc. 84).

22. Gracián discusses these twenty foundations of the friars in dialogue 13.
23. See St. Teresa's *Spiritual Testimonies* 55, 417. St. Teresa says she made a promise to the Virgin that if Father Gracián were liberated from the Calced monastery in Seville, she would order that the feast of the Presentation of Our Lady (November 21) be celebrated with solemnity in all the Discalced monasteries. (See also PA 16.20–21, 37).
24. Gracián as visitator is implementing the decrees of the Council of Trent.
25. A bezoar is a hard, indigestible mass found in the intestines of certain ruminant animals and once considered an antidote to poison.
26. This concerns the monastery of the Carmelite nuns of Paterna. A lay brother named Fray Juan falsely reported throughout the province that four of those nuns were pregnant. Among the accusations presented by the nuncio Filippo Sega, Gracián had to defend himself regarding this one. There is much about this in Teresa's letters. Gracián mentions this incident again in PA 16.27.

Second Dialogue: Discalced

1. Suetonius reports this in *Julius Caesar*. Shakespeare made this famous in the English-speaking world in his play by the same name (act 3, scene 1). He even uses the Latin: "*Et tu, Brute?*"
2. In the margin of the Madrid manuscript, it continues, "But you that are a friend of mine . . ." which completes Gracián's point.
3. This story appears in Eusebius's *History of the Church*, trans. G. A. Williamson (Baltimore: Penguin, 1965), chap. 3, no. 29. He quotes it from Clement of Alexandria's Book III of *Miscellanies*. I have translated *por sensualidad* as "on account of jealous love."
4. Cardinal Archduke Albert of Austria made Gracián apostolic visitator of the Carmelites of the Ancient Observance in the kingdom of Portugal in November 1588. See PA 3.34.
5. Father Pedro de la Purificación, prior of Genoa, went to Rome in the summer of 1590.
6. Gracián was elected the first provincial of the order and governed from March 1581 to May 1585.
7. See MHCT 4 wherein most of the documents of the years 1590–1591 deal with this question. The papal brief *Salvatoris* was dated June 5, 1590. Knowledge of the circumstances of this brief and the reaction of Nicolás Doria is crucial to understanding the subsequent history of the Discalced Carmelites. Ana de Jesús (Lobera) and María de San José (Salazar) were actually imprisoned in their own monasteries for their part in seeking this papal brief.
8. The sentence of expulsion of Gracián from the order, February 17, 1592.
9. Doria helped the king solve his financial problems. See PA 13.35.

10. Gracián founded the Discalced priory of Los Remedios on January 6, 1574. See PA 1.23.
11. See PA 10.38–41 and PA 16.25–27.
12. In dialogue 3. Gracián writes again of this Mondéjar event in PA 15.65.
13. María de San José (Salazar, 1548–1603). More of her revelations are recorded in PA 16.38–40.
14. Juan Velázquez de las Cuevas, a Dominican, who executed the Brief of Separation in 1580 and presided at the first Discalced chapter in 1581.
15. A Carmelite, Father Gregorio received the habit from Gracián in Beas and made his profession in Gracián's hands in Seville.
16. Ormaneto died June 16, 1577.
17. Sega arrived in Madrid on August 29, 1577.
18. Sega presented fifteen charges to Gracián on December 1, 1578 (see docs. 157 and 158 of MHCT 2). Doc. 175 (MHCT 2) is Gracián's reply to those charges. The nature of these charges and Gracián's response to them are in PA 4.19–29.
19. All three were initially confined at the Madrid Carmen. See doc. 423 (pp. 609–11) of MHCT 3.
20. The decree of the nuncio Sega dated October 16, 1578, subjected all the Discalced to the government of the Calced provincials.
21. King Philip II appointed a commission of five theologians to study the matter, and they recommended that a separate province be made for the Discalced. Sega agreed. Otilio Rodriguez, *A History of the Teresian Carmel: An Abridgement of Its Origins and Development 1562–1979* (Darlington, UK: Darlington Carmel, n.d.), 63.
22. The sentence of Sega against Gracián was given on December 20, 1578. Gracián was deposed of the office of visitator and confined to the monastery in Alcalá de Henares where he was to do penance. Blessed Ana de San Bartolomé said that his tender devotion to those who persecuted him was supernatural and that he prayed for his persecutors day and night. See Ana de San Bartolomé, *Noticias sobre los comienzos del Carmelo Teresiano,* n. 28, in *Obras completas de Ana de San Bartolomé,* ed. Julián Urkiza (Burgos, Spain: Editorial Monte Carmelo, 1998).
23. Gracián discusses this incident again in PA 16.25.
24. The Brief of Separation was issued on June 22, 1580, and reached Spain in August.
25. See PA 3.11–15.

Third Dialogue: Visitator

1. A patent of Angel de Salazar dated April 10, 1580, designated Gracián as commissary and visitator of the monasteries of the Discalced friars and nuns of Andalusia since he was not able to make visitations due to his illness and other duties.
2. The king received the Brief of Separation on August 15, 1580.

3. The brief *Nuper iustis* dated August 30, 1580, named Fernández to carry out the erection of the Discalced province and the election of its first provincial.
4. Gracián had left before Fernández died on November 22, 1580. On October 25, 1580, St. Teresa had written to María de San José: "See that all the nuns commend Padre Fray Pedro Fernández who is at the point of dying; look how much we owe him and what a loss to us his death would be." (See letter 357 in *The Collected Letters of St. Teresa of Avila*, trans. Kieran Kavanaugh, vol. 2 [Washington, D.C.: ICS Publications, 2007]).
5. Queen Anna of Austria died on October 26, a victim of an epidemic. She was King Philip's niece and his fourth wife. He married her in 1570 and she bore him five children, only one of whom survived beyond the age of eight, a feeble son who would become the next king.
6. Gracián was elected unanimously (ten votes) by the community of Los Remedios on February 19, 1580; Angel de Salazar confirmed his election on March 10.
7. The brief was dated November 20, 1580.
8. Gabriel de la Asumptión got one vote; Nicolás Doria one vote; Antonio de Jesús seven votes; and Jerome Gracián eleven votes.
9. King Philip II of Spain sent the duke to secure the Portuguese Crown, which he claimed was rightfully his due to his mother's Portuguese royal lineage (Isabella was the daughter of King Manuel I).
10. Although Sega issued a brief that subjected the Discalced to the authority of the Calced, dated October 16, 1578 (see PA 2.27), the brief that Gracián mentions here was issued some months earlier (July 23, 1578) by which Sega annulled all patents and faculties given to Gracián by his predecessor, Ormaneto. He also forbade the Discalced from obeying Gracián and took upon himself their governance, which of course he was expected to place into the hands of the Calced. See Peers, *Handbook to the Life*, 51–55.
11. Gracián tells us a little more about this holy friar in PA 13.41–42 in his discussion of the foundation of Almódovar del Campo.
12. The word translated as "pretty boy" is *boniquito*. It is a diminutive typical of the Catalan dialect of Fray Benito. It might also be rendered "pretty child" or maybe even "dear little one." One can see that Fray Benito has a peculiar way of speaking.
13. The provisor of the abbot is like the vicar or second in charge.
14. The Calced were already there and felt encroached upon by the Discalced. This event actually occurred a year before Gracián was provincial. The foundation was successfully made in May 1581. See PA 13.64 for more details.
15. The princess of Éboli (Ana de Mendoza) was implicated in the 1578 assassination of Juan Escobedo by her involvement with Antonio Pérez, secretary of King Philip II (see note 46 below). Santorcaz is near Pastrana.
16. Founded by the Discalced Carmelite friars in November 1570.

17. Gracián's use of the term "Congo" refers to all of sub-Saharan West Africa, while "Ethiopia" seems to include the same area but also regions on the east side of Africa. In other words, the names do not correspond to present-day geographical nomenclature. Gracián's figure of one hundred thousand baptisms is exaggerated. Three reports were sent from the Congo about this missionary expedition, and they speak of thousands of baptisms. Because of Doria's lack of support, the missionaries returned to Spain within five years. The Carmelites did not return to sub-Saharan Africa until the middle of the twentieth century. See Florencio del Niño Jesus, *La Orden de Sta. Teresa, la fundación de Propaganda Fide y las misiones carmelitanas* (Madrid: Nieto, 1923).
18. The Lisbon chapter was continued in Pastrana in October 1585. Gracián was elected definitor, vicar provincial of Portugal, and prior of the monastery in Lisbon.
19. Gracián was a firm believer in missionary activity for the Discalced Carmelites and says this was St. Teresa's spirit. The friars' present-day constitutions bear this out: "Our Holy Mother St. Teresa passed on to the order the ardent missionary zeal that burned within her heart, and it was her wish that her friars should also undertake missionary activity" (*Discalced Carmelites: Constitutions and Norms* [Dublin: Conference of English-speaking Provincials, 1988], 94).
20. This curious reference is perhaps an allusion to the widow in 1 Kings 17:7–24 and the Shulammite of Song 7:1.
21. Gracián seems to have enjoyed an extraordinary friendship with this holy bishop. They often conversed for two hours after lunch and again after supper.
22. Lorenzo Gracián made a note in the margin: "Gaspar Lucas, heretical cleric of the alumbrados, chastised by the Inquisition." See PA 14.36.
23. See Alison Weber, "Demonizing Ecstasy: Alonso de la Fuente and the Alumbrados of Extremadura," in *The Mystical Gesture: Essays on Medieval and Early Modern Spiritual Culture in Honor of Mary E. Giles,* ed. Robert Boenig (Aldershot, UK: Ashgate, 2000), 147–65.
24. Teutonio Braganza was a great admirer of St. Teresa. *The Way of Perfection* was first published at his expense in 1583. He had once been a Jesuit. St. Ignatius wrote him a letter expressing his disappointment with his decision to leave the Society of Jesus.
25. Son of Prince Don Juan of Portugal and Doña Juana of Austria, sister of Philip II. At age twenty-four, King Don Sebastián invaded Morocco and was last seen charging into enemy lines in the Battle of Alcazarquivir on August 4, 1578. Many believed he would return to Portugal to reclaim his throne. He never did, nor did he leave an heir. See PA 14.35 for details about Gracián's work in Evora.
26. Indeed, it is too long to recount the story of Sister María de la Visitación, who was a Dominican nun. When the Carmelite nuns first came to Lisbon at Christmas in 1584, they stayed at the Dominican convent of the Annunciation where Sister María was prioress. Mother María de San José (Salazar) was suspicious of this stigmatic from the beginning.

27. Cardinal Archduke Albert of Austria, governor of Portugal at this time, was the son of Emperor Maximilian II and María of Austria, the sister of Philip II. He received a dispensation in order to marry his cousin, Philip's daughter Isabel Clara Eugenia, with whom he was coregent of the Lowlands. They attended Gracián's funeral.
28. The false wounds were clearly a ruse to get sympathy for the Antonistas whom the English had agreed to help. By "Lutherans," Gracián means Protestants but most particularly here the English.
29. Don Antonio, prior of Crato, was a Portuguese prince contending against Philip II for the Portuguese Crown.
30. Cristóbal de Moura was a Portuguese member of the Spanish court.
31. There was quite an uproar in October 1588, when news spread that the falsehood of the stigmata was discovered.
32. Gracián quotes in Portuguese.
33. Sir Francis Drake, the famous English corsair and admiral of the English Armada sent by Queen Elizabeth I in April 1589, was assisting Don Antonio to seize the Crown of Portugal.
34. Conflict between Gracián and Doria over Doria's highly centralized government of the Discalced escalated to the point that on June 17, 1588, Gracián was ordered to go to Mexico as a simple friar, but prelates in Portugal, including Cardinal Albert, interceded to keep him from leaving.
35. Luis de Granada died in Lisbon on December 31, 1588.
36. See MHCT 3, doc. 381 (pp. 383–85) and PA 14.29.
37. The monastery of San Felipe was founded on November 14, 1581, and the monastery of San Alberto was founded on January 19, 1585.
38. The news of the English Armada's approach came to the city in the middle of May 1589.
39. St. Nuño Alvarez Pereira (1360–1431) was a national hero of the Portuguese who became a Carmelite in 1423. He was canonized on April 26, 2009.
40. The harquebus was a matchlock gun invented in the fifteenth century that was portable but heavy and usually fired from a tripod or forked rest.
41. The English Armada left Plymouth on April 13, 1589, and arrived at Peniche a month and a half later and at Torres Vedras on May 29. When it received notice to head for Alvalade, it formed a camp at Alcántara—on the coast just south of Lisbon—where it was until the first of June. Today Alvalade and Alcántara are part of the city of Lisbon.
42. *Donados* were laymen who worked for a religious order as volunteers. It was often a lifelong commitment.
43. Stubborn or obstinate people.

44. Needless to say, a passage like this is quite disturbing to our sensibilities today.
45. In view of the previous note it is somewhat reassuring that Gracián does not allow revenge and indiscriminate killing.
46. Antonio Pérez, secretary to King Philip II, plotted against Don Juan of Austria to the point of having Don Juan's secretary killed. In April 1590, he escaped from prison in Madrid and fled to Aragon. When the king's troops invaded Aragon twenty months later, Pérez fled to France where he remained until his death in 1611.

Fourth Dialogue: Expulsion

1. Pedro de la Purificación was Gracián's secretary. He was well known to both St. John of the Cross and St. Teresa. See Peers, *Handbook to the Life*, 212–13.
2. He means he had the authority to act in virtue of the office he held (apostolic visitator of the Calced in Portugal).
3. With a patent dated June 3, 1591. Gracián arrived in Madrid on June 28.
4. This offer to Gracián was similar to a patent (for vicar provincial of Mexico) that he was given four years earlier for much the same reason, that is, to put an end to his interference with the *consulta* (See Rohrbach, *Journey to Carith*, p. 213). St. John of the Cross, after defending Gracián and the nuns at the June 1591 general chapter, was also ordered to Mexico (June 25) but died six months later in Úbeda (see Peers, *Handbook to the Life*, pp. 92–95).
5. See the mandate of the nuncio Cesare Speziano that kept Gracián from going to Mexico (MHCT 4, doc. 338).
6. The Spanish word is *preñadas*, which means pregnant, that is, insinuating.
7. This is taken from the Gospel of John: "A time will come when anyone who puts you to death will claim to be serving God" (16:2, NAB). Gracián is very skillful in quoting the Bible.
8. Gracián was confined for over six months in the prison of the monastery of San Hermenegildo in Madrid, just prior to his expulsion in February of 1592.
9. Fathers Bartolomé Muñoz (prior of the monastery of Santo Tomás) and Francisco de Segovia (prior of the monastery of San Jerónimo).
10. Nicolás Doria (Nicolao de Oria) had been a Genoese merchant and was something of a financial genius.
11. Doria wrote a letter to the king to this effect in early 1589, three years before Gracián was expelled from the order.
12. Her husband and two of her sons had been secretaries to the king, and she herself was the daughter of the Polish ambassador to Spain.
13. The papal nuncio for Spain at that time was Pietro Millino. He absolved Gracián of the censures contained in the sentence for six months, during which time he was

to go and see the pope. See Jerome Gracián, *Cartas,* ed. Juan Luis Astigarraga, MHCT 9, MHG 1 (Rome: Institutum Historicum Teresianum, 1989), no. 36.

14. In other words, just as a sick sheep must be taken away from the flock, so must a rebellious religious be expelled from his congregation.
15. Don Iñigo López de Mendoza, fifth duke of Infantado, who accompanied King Philip II when he went to England to marry Mary Tudor in 1556.
16. He must be referring to the Father Tomás de Aquino mentioned in the superscription, who was indeed one of the judges that expelled Gracián from the order. Father Tomás made his profession as a Discalced Carmelite in Seville in 1580 and died in Madrid while serving as definitor.
17. Doria is also reported to have been remorseful on his deathbed of his treatment of Gracián. See Peter-Thomas Rohrbach, *Journey to Carith: The Story of the Carmelite Order* (Washington, D.C.: ICS Publications, 2001), 226.
18. Faults and punishments were enumerated in the constitutions of the religious orders. Even today they are given in the Discalced Carmelite constitutions but in a way that is in keeping with modern sensibilities regarding punishment.
19. See PA 3.34.

Fifth Dialogue: Appeal

1. One of these laymen was Juan de Palacios. Gracián left Madrid on February 27, 1592, ten days after the sentence, and arrived at Alicante March 5 and Rome at the beginning of June. In a long letter to his sister Adriana (a Discalced Carmelite nun) dated October 1592, he narrates his adventure over land and sea from Madrid to Rome touching on much that follows here. See *Cartas,* no. 46.
2. He was close to turning forty-seven.
3. Pedro Luis Garcerán de Borja was the last master to govern the military order of Montesa; he governed from 1545 to March 20, 1592.
4. See *Cartas,* no. 46, p. 156.
5. One of these friars was Diego Evangelista who, as a member of the *consulta,* had investigated Gracián's conduct and used the opportunity of visiting numerous monasteries to gather incriminating testimony about St. John of the Cross. The other was Luis de San Jerónimo, provincial of Lower Andalusia.
6. Gracián alludes to the same event in *Dialogues of Eliseo* (*1592–1595*) [MHCT 19 (Rome: Institutum Historicum Teresianum, 2001), 340] but writes in the margin that it wasn't true.
7. See the petition that Gracián made to Pope Clement VIII on August 16, 1592: Juan Luis Astigarraga, ed., *Expulsión del P. Gracián, Documentos de un Proceso* (*1587–1601*), MHCT 21, MHG 3 (Rome: Institutum Historicum Teresianum, 2004). See also *Cartas,* no. 38.

8. Francisco de Toledo was a Jesuit and the pope's preacher. Father Francisco Alexandre, a Dominican, was the pope's confessor.
9. This Italo-Spanish Dominican House of Studies was founded at the monastery of the Santa Maria Sopra Minerva, the church dedicated to the Blessed Virgin Mary, built over the temple of Minerva in Rome; St. Catherine of Siena and Fra Angelico are buried there. See Gracián's letter to Francisco Alexandre, September 1592 (*Cartas*, no. 42).
10. This Jesuit, José de Acosta (1540–1600), was a celebrated missionary, geographer, ethnologist, and historian.
11. This important person was the viceroy of Naples. Naples was a vice regency of the Spanish Crown.
12. This brings to mind the autobiographical narrative of St. Ignatius of Loyola who, like Gracián, called himself "the Pilgrim" and let go of the reins of the mule he was riding in order to determine, like the wandering knight errant, in which direction he should go.
13. These women would have been accompanying the captain and the soldiers.
14. Gracián was in Naples five years later for the first ten months of 1598. During that time he was instrumental in founding such a convent.
15. It was actually barely six months that Gracián was in Palermo, from February to mid-August 1593. See PA 10.59–61 for more about his stay there. The autograph of "Flores Carmeli" is in the Discalced Carmelite General Archives in Rome, sec. 304, c.
16. The brief *Uberes fructus* was issued in Rome on January 27, 1593, and confirmed the sentence of Gracián's expulsion from the order. He was prohibited from being received in any monastery of the order and could not present himself in Rome unless he first joined the Discalced Augustinians.
17. Gracián's choice of words is touching. *Partirse*, for "departed," also means to be torn apart, suggesting how he felt interiorly.
18. The superiors of the Discalced Augustinians were waiting for him to come to Rome to begin a new foundation at the church of Saints Peter and Marcellinus. See PA 8.36.
19. At a later date, January 14, 1598, he writes to his mother about these relatives (see *Cartas*, no. 72).
20. Gracian introduces the elements of his shield in the PA Pref.5.

Sixth Dialogue: Captive

1. Only in the margins of the manuscript is the name of this "visionary" revealed. Recommended to St. Teresa by St. Peter of Alcántara, Antonia del Espíritu Santo (Henao) was one of the first four nuns to be clothed in the habit of the reform at St.

Joseph's, Ávila. She accompanied St. Teresa on some of her foundations, going to Granada in 1581 and Málaga in 1585.

2. The humorous name of a person who makes solemn pronouncements about obvious things is *Perogrullo*. The origin of this expression is difficult to determine, but Miguel de Cervantes used it in *Don Quixote* (vol. 2, chapter LXII, trans. John Ormsby, p. 434): "Good, by God!" said Sancho Panza; "I could have told myself that; the prophet Perogrullo could have said no more."
3. These healers were supposed to cure or guard against sicknesses, especially rabies, using certain prayers and rituals.
4. The viceroy of India and a great friend of Gracián's (see PA 4.5).
5. The Madrid autograph says five times.
6. Gracián goes on to mention not five but eight times he was in danger at sea.
7. Apparently, this is not true, as noted earlier (PA 5, note 6).
8. Captain Moraterráez of Algiers was one of the many pirates of the Barbary Coast and evidently well known.
9. These friends were in fact the Lomellinis, a Genoese firm doing business in Tabarka.
10. *Papaz* is what the Turks called Gracián.
11. He is referring to the feast day of the Assumption of Our Lady, August 15.
12. Corsica and Sardinia.
13. The feast day of the Presentation of Our Lord, February 2.
14. A *galeota* is like a galley (a long, low ship using oars), only smaller in some respects in order to be faster and more agile at sea.
15. An *escopeta* is a small single- or double-barreled gun like a shotgun, smaller than the harquebus.
16. The Spanish is *y un criado que iba conmigo soldado*. This interesting detail shows that Gracián didn't travel alone.
17. Gracián is making a play on words here. *Áspero* is a Turkish coin, that is, money, whereas in Spanish *áspero* means rough, unpleasant, or bitter.
18. *Mezzanìa* (Italian), or the hold, indicates the central section of the ship.
19. *Bizcocho* is a biscuit or kind of sponge cake, but in this context, probably sea biscuits or hardtack.
20. Bizerte is on the northern coast of Tunisia.
21. The two copper engravings were returned to their legitimate owner, Gracián, on March 20, 1596, in Rome.
22. Gracián makes a play on the word *cazar*, which means both to hunt and to chase.
23. The *baños* were prisons. As Carlos Ros explains, "The name comes from Constantinople, where the Christian prisoners were piled in the ancient [Roman] baths of large patios and high walls" (*El hombre de Teresa de Jesús*, 436).

24. Gracián uses the title Grand Turk for the sultan, the emperor of the Turks residing in Constantinople.
25. "Swimming the horse" means making a horse swim when the water is too deep to wade through.
26. The redemption or ransom of captives is a corporal work of mercy.
27. Gracián mentions this Lutheran, Master Guillermo, again in PA 10.72.
28. *Barberos,* from which the English word "barbers" derives, were practical surgeons who did a variety of "operations" that included removing molars and healing burns and wounds.
29. *Oráculo,* or oracle, figuratively means a person everyone listens to with respect and veneration for his wisdom and learning (Real Academia Española, *Diccionario de lengua española* [Madrid: Editorial Espasa-Calpe, 1947]). Gracián is saying in all seriousness that these Turks respected him for his judgment, fairness, wisdom, and so forth.
30. *Nóminas,* which were among the earliest books to be printed, consisted of Scripture passages, prayers, or simply the names of saints. They were used by Muslims and Christians alike and were often carried on one's person (Owen Davies, *Grimoires: A History of Magic Books* [Oxford: Oxford University Press, 2009], 45).
31. *De vehementi* must be a technical term used in the courts meaning that the abjuration, that is, the renunciation of the Muslim creed by the Christian renegade, must be strong, even vehement we could say.
32. The names and circumstances of twelve Christian captives who had been ransomed by Gracián are listed in the appendix (number 9) of Gracián, *Peregrinación de Anastasio*.
33. A *janissary* is a soldier in the army of the Grand Turk, that is, the sultan.
34. The *cerraje* was the place where the women were kept in the palace, that is, the *seraglio* or harem.
35. It is still the tradition of the Latin church for priests to say three Masses on Christmas.
36. This expression *en seco* refers to an act made without the actual circumstances or necessary means for its accomplishment.
37. *Bey* is a Turkish title for the governor of a city, district, or region.

Seventh Dialogue: Freedom

1. This Mami is not to be confused with Mami (Mohamet), the pasha of Tunis.
2. Gracián picks up where he left off at the end of dialogue 6: he remains in the *baño,* alive, after his escape from being burned on Christmas Day.
3. The dominant ethnic group of Hungary.

4. *Valiente* means brave or valiant.
5. Gracián has a play on words here: they are *renegando*, that is, reneging or reproaching, because he converts a renegade.
6. Leg armor, known as greaves, to protect the shins.
7. The pad or *rodete* might have been the kind that was used for carrying things on one's head. The irons consisted of four twenty-five pound weights (see p. 333).
8. The other captain is Captain Asán, as mentioned in PA 6.53.
9. A marabout is a Muslim holy man, often a hermit, similar to Christian anchorites in their mode of religious life.
10. An alcaide is the commander of a castle or fortress.
11. King Sebastián of Portugal was defeated in a terrible battle (see PA 3, note 25). The two men mentioned here must have fled to Lisbon for siding with King Sebastián.
12. Gracián is alluding to Jesus of Nazareth.
13. The last name Escanasi probably means he was an Ashkenazi Jew, descended from Jews of the diaspora living in the region around the Middle East, rather than a Sephardic Jew from Spain or Portugal.
14. The Lomellinis were a Genoese family known throughout Europe for their banking, merchandising, and coral fishing grounds.
15. Gracián frequently refers to Simón Escanasi as "the Jew," but in many of these cases I use his name instead.
16. Gracián uses ducats and *escudos* interchangeably.
17. This letter of ransom is preserved in the National Historical Archives of Spain. It is dated April 11, 1595.
18. An *alcalde* is a chief magistrate or mayor, though the Brussels manuscript uses *alcaide*, meaning commander.
19. The brief was the bull *Ex omnibus*, dated January 9, 1596. Earlier, on October 25, 1595, Gracián had written to Father Elías de San Martín asking to be readmitted to the Discalced (see *Cartas*, no. 56). Father Elías responded the following spring (March 21, 1596) with a polite refusal. Father Elías commiserated with Gracián's desire but did not want to provoke the friars.
20. San Martín in Montibus was and still is the general house of the Calced in Rome. Gracián was given a patent by the vicar general of the Calced dated April 6, 1596, exactly one month after the papal brief readmitting him to the Discalced Carmelite Order (March 6, 1596). This patent states that Gracián presented the papal brief to the vicar general as well as a letter from Cardinal Caesar Baronius stating that the pope permits Gracián to be charitably received by the Calced and to live with them since his own order will not take him back. The patent also states that he can wear the habit of the Discalced and follow their observances. See Astigarraga, *Expulsión del P. Gracián.*

21. This congregation was evolving and wasn't wholly established until 1622. See Tarsicio del Ssmo. Sacramento, "Los carmelitas descalzos y la Sagrada Congregación de Propaganda Fide," *Monte Carmelo*, vol. 60 (1952): 37–68.
22. The commission was given June 10, 1600, by Clement VIII, for Gracián to preach the holy year and to arrange the rescue of Christian captives, in company with two Capuchin fathers (see PA 14, note 26).
23. The king was King Philip III of Spain. Gracián had been gone from Spain for eight years.
24. Gracián's mother, Doña Juana Dantisco, died October 6, 1601, in Madrid. See the precious letter of Gracián where he narrates the last days and death of his mother (*Cartas*, no. 116).
25. Ceuta, located at the northeast tip of Morocco 24 miles north of Tétouan, belonged to Portugal and is today an autonomous city of Spain.
26. A sharif is a descendant of Muhammad through his daughter Fatima and a title of honor among the Moors. The sharif at this time was Ahmad al-Mansur (1578–1610), the sultan of Morocco. Gracián discusses this event in detail in PA 14.25. See also *Cartas*, nos. 118–24.
27. The Carmen of the Calced Carmelites. Gracián went there on May 15, 1602 (see *Cartas*, no. 122).
28. After two and a half years in Madrid, he arrived in Valencia on November 19, 1604 (*Cartas*, no. 132). Clement VIII died on March 3, 1605.
29. Father Juan de Heredia, O.Carm., was the provincial of Aragon under whose jurisdiction Gracián was at that time. See *Cartas*, no. 147.
30. He arrived in the Spanish Netherlands in the summer of 1607 and lived there until his death in 1614. In the last five paragraphs to end this dialogue, Gracián has compressed a dozen years.

Eighth Dialogue: Afflictions

1. Father Astigarraga's Spanish edition of *Pilgrimage of Anastasius* used the Brussels manuscript for the basic text from this point on, except for the titles and various notes that are taken from the Toledo manuscript.
2. The Spanish is *niebla interior*. *Niebla* literally means fog or mist; figuratively, it means confusion or obscurity. Gracián explains his use of the term in PA 8.25.
3. Recall that Gracián is framing the whole of this work according to the various parts of his shield.
4. The Company of Jesus, that is, the Jesuits.
5. He quotes Habakkuk in Spanish: *Entre, Señor, podre en mís huesos para que yo suba ceñido a nuestro pueblo*. The Toledo manuscript provides the Latin: *Ingrediatur putredo in ossibus meis et subter me scateat, ut ascendam ad populum accinctum nostrum* (Hab 3:16); this citation of the old Latin Vulgate does not correspond to a modern translation.

6. His older brother was Antonio Gracián, who died on April 6, 1576, at the age of thirty-four or thirty-five. See the precious description he wrote of Gracián in MCHT 3 (pp. 587–88).
7. Gracian framed his shield with this passage, as a motto. See page 3 of Astigarraga's edition of *Peregrinación de Anastasio.*
8. Alfonso de Deza, who was also Gracián's master of scholastic theology.
9. He means permanent teaching positions, which are called *cátedras* (i.e., chairs), such as the chair of dogmatic theology.
10. Gracián says more about his studies in PA 12.4. See also MHCT 3 (pp. 537–38).
11. Agustín de Cazalla was the preacher of Emperor Charles V. He became involved in Lutheranism and was burned at the stake during the infamous auto-de-fé in Valladolid. The young Gracián, at fourteen years, witnessed these events (PA 13.43). St. Francis Borgia also witnessed these events in Valladolid (see Margaret Yeo, *St. Francis Borgia: The Greatest of the Borgias* [Milwaukee: Bruce, 1936], 209).
12. Gracián mentions this book in several places, but it seems that it was never printed.
13. This is not the scrupulosity that afflicts the beginner, but a serious matter for the advanced soul. See St. Ignatius's rules regarding scruples (*Spiritual Exercises*, #346–347).
14. Gracián is surprised to find his brethren treating him so poorly, as though he is a really bad person, when he had been a father to them.
15. I take him to be speaking figuratively about his reputation as an expelled religious, that is, a bad friar.
16. Gracián writes of this earlier (PA 5.20).
17. Gracián writes of his capture by the Turks in greater detail in PA 6.8.
18. See PA 10.66–67.
19. See PA 2.11.
20. This is really saying a lot. St. Teresa had much to say about melancholy, but Gracián no doubt must have been an expert in this matter.

Ninth Dialogue: Calced

1. At the base of the heart in Gracián's shield.
2. The "Latins" were crusaders and pilgrims from Europe who lived as hermits on Mount Carmel in the Holy Land. They banded together and obtained a rule from Saint Albert, patriarch of Jerusalem, in the early 13th century.
3. Gracián gives additional meaning to the twelve stars in dialogue 12 where he discusses his studies and writings.
4. It is interesting to compare this list to St. John of the Cross's *Sayings of Light and Love* 154: "Twelve stars to arrive at perfection: Love of God, love of neighbor, obedience, chastity, poverty, choir, penance, humility, mortification, prayer, silence, peace."

5. See PA 5, note 15, regarding "Flores Carmeli." *Disciplina regular*, a commentary on the Rule of St. Albert, was written at the request of the prior general of the Carmelites, Enrico Silvio, and printed in Venice in 1600.
6. Printed in Madrid (1604).
7. This apocryphal story is very charming. Agabus's disappointment is masterfully depicted by Raphael in *The Marriage of the Virgin* (1504). The great Carmelite humanist Blessed Baptist Spagnoli of Mantua (1447–1516) writes of Agabus in his poem "Partenicae marianae." See Teófanes Egido Lopez, "La devoción a san José," *Estudios Josefinos* 61, n. 121: (2007), 83–104. Agabus is mentioned in the Acts of the Apostles 11:28 and 21:10–14.
8. See Louis Saggi, ed., *Saints of Carmel*, trans. Gabriel Pausback (Aylesford, Ill.: Carmelite Fathers, 1975).
9. Gil González Dávila (1532–1596). Gracián was sixteen years old when he made this agreement with the Jesuits.
10. Gracián was greatly influenced by his Jesuit confessors. See Enrique Llamas Martínez, "Jerónimo Gracián Dantisco (de la Madre de Dios) en la Universidad de Alcalá (1560–1572)," *EphCarm* 26, no. 1 (1975): 176–212.
11. See PA 1.1.
12. April 25, 1573, in Pastrana (MHCT 1, doc. 49).
13. See PA 1.14–35.
14. Gracián is referring to the persecutions by the Calced that were especially severe in the last months of 1578 when the nuncio Sega arrived, in their effort to destroy the Discalced movement (see PA 2.24–34). The division that eventually came about was the formation of a separate province—and later congregation and order—of the Discalced from the Calced.
15. See PA 4.6, 30. A lapse of nearly fourteen years separates what follows from what has preceded. Here Gracián is referring to the sentence of expulsion from the Discalced Carmelite Congregation pronounced by the Discalced on February 17, 1592.
16. See PA 5.14–21.
17. See PA 16, note 18.
18. See PA 7.33. The general refused to accept Gracián on account of his debt from his ransom.
19. Gracián is referring to the white mantle worn by the Carmelites.
20. The Apostolic Camera served as an ecclesiastical court of appeals. Today its main purpose is to manage the Vatican when the pope dies.
21. The papal brief, *Apostolicae Sedis benignitas*, revoking the sentence against Gracián, was given by Pope Clement VIII on March 6, 1596. An incredible opposition was raised against him by the Discalced in Spain in complete disregard of the papal

Brief of Rehabilitation. For more on this, see Moriones, *Papal Rehabilitation.* See also *Cartas,* nos. 111–12.

22. The superior general of the Order of Carmel even today lives at San Martín in Montibus.
23. See PA 7.35.
24. A separate order of the Discalced was established on December 20, 1593, by a bull of Clement VIII.
25. *Barragan* was a Spanish term for various types of cloth, derived from the Arabic *barrakan,* a heavy cotton or woolen cloth or long mantle (Maureen Mazzaoui, *The Italian Cotton Industry In the Later Middle Ages, 1100–1600* [Cambridge: Cambridge University Press, 1981], 199.
26. For Gracián's description of *gamberes,* see PA 7.7.
27. An *almaizar* is a head covering made of gauze or chiffon used by Muslims.
28. *Vivae vocis oraculo* literally means "by the oracle of a live voice." Here it means that the pope gave an oral, not written, pronouncement or directive. See Moriones, *Papal Rehabilitation,* 34–35.

Tenth Dialogue: Consolations

1. Aristeas was a Jewish scholar of the second century. It is interesting to note that Pope Benedict XVI mentions the *Letter of Aristeas to Philocrates* in his book *Jesus of Nazareth: From the Baptism in the Jordan to the Transfiguration,* trans. Adrian J. Walker (New York: Doubleday, 2007), 179.
2. St. Teresa is said to have repeated this verse when she was dying.
3. See dialogues 15 and 16, respectively.
4. Although there was an extraordinary general chapter in 1590, it was at a chapter held two years earlier that Doria was elected vicar general (a six-year term) and the *consulta* was put into effect (see MHCT 3, doc. 343; and Rohrbach, *Journey to Carith,* 214). Gracián was working in Evora the latter half of 1588.
5. These two events were related in PA 8.10–18.
6. See PA 8.12–13.
7. Orlando is the knight-hero in *Orlando Furioso,* which is considered one of the most influential works in the whole of European literature. It is a romance of chivalry. St. Teresa says her mother was attached to this popular literature. Cervantes effectively puts an end to this sort of literature with his *Don Quixote,* a spoof of books on chivalry.
8. See PA 1.4.
9. *Zupia* means the dregs of the wine, having an awful color and taste.
10. This is the same Benito written about in PA 3.13–14. See the biographical note about this brother who was renowned in the novitiate of Pastrana for his simplicity (MHCT 3, doc. 423, p. 604).

11. See PA 1.7–13.
12. Among the collected letters of St. Teresa, the letters to Jerome Gracián are by far the most numerous.
13. Francisco de Ribera was a scholarly Jesuit whose life of St. Teresa was published in 1590. The second author mentioned is Diego de Yepes, bishop of Tarazona. However, it is believed that Tomás de Jesús is the principal author. Gracián is evidently aware that the bishop is not the actual author.
14. May 23, 1575, less than a month after her first meeting with Father Gracián in Beas.
15. The resolution that St. Teresa writes of is the substance of her *Spiritual Testimonies* 36.5–8, in *The Collected Works of St. Teresa of Avila,* trans. Kieran Kavanaugh and Otilio Rodriguez, 1:369–438 (Washington, D.C.: ICS Publications, 1976).
16. St. Teresa is referring to a vision she had, which Gracián relates in PA 16.6–12. See St. Teresa of Avila, *Spiritual Testimonies* 36.1–4.
17. St. Teresa of Avila, *Spiritual Testimonies* 36.1–4.
18. The document is still conserved there.
19. The holy Juan de Ribera, who has been canonized, was the patriarch of Valencia.
20. Gracián's testimony was given in Valencia on November 8, 1606, and he is listed as witness four in volume 6 of the canonization proceedings of St. Ignatius. He writes about this to his sister María de San José on November 24, 1606 (see *Cartas,* no. 146, MHCT 9).
21. Gracián thinks it is better to stay away from Madrid because of its power and influence, being the capital city (see MHCT 3, doc. 423, p. 574).
22. See PA 2.32.
23. In 1580, King Philip II sent the duke to lead the invasion of Portugal when Philip was claiming the Portuguese Crown. The duke invited Gracián to go with him. See PA 3.10.
24. St. Ignatius also addressed persons he met in the direct form of "you" (*vos*), as he says in his autobiography, "piously holding that Christ and the Apostles had spoken in this way" (Ignatius of Loyola, *Autobiography,* trans. Parmananda Divarkar, in *Spiritual Exercises and Selected Works,* Classics of Western Spirituality, ed. George Ganss [Mahwah, NJ: Paulist Press, 1991], 90.). *Señoría* means "lordship," or rather, "Your Lordship."
25. The Dutch didn't think much of the duke either after his six years of ruthless rule in the Netherlands. He died two months after St. Teresa and was attended by Luis de Granada in his last hours.
26. This absurd calumny was a source of humor when recounted many years later. Juliana was the youngest of Gracián's sisters, almost twenty years his junior, and she went to live at the Seville monastery when she was only seven. The prioress in question is María de San José. For more on María de San José's petition, see PA 2, note 7.

27. See PA 2.10 and PA 4.11.
28. Gracián wrote a monograph in 1586 entitled "An Argument for Charity: Against Some Who, under the Pretext of Observance of Rules, Weaken and Disturb It in Religious Orders" (see Rohrbach, *Journey to Carith,* 212; and Smet, *Mirror of Carmel,* 115).
29. See PA 5.6–9.
30. Grace and Justice was a tribunal of the church at that time. Sotomayor was probably a canon lawyer for the Discalced.
31. See the letter Gracián wrote in September 1592 (*Cartas,* no. 44).
32. In his letters, Gracián writes of the unconditional support he received in Rome from this Capuchin, Father Pedro Trigoso (1533–1593), who was the first systematizer of the theology of St. Bonaventure.
33. The ambassador of King Philip II in Rome at that time was Don Antonio Fernández de Córdoba. His wife was Doña Juana, and she had a sister who was a Discalced Carmelite nun in Barcelona.
34. In a letter of the king to the ambassador, dated November 9, 1592, the king instructed his ambassador not to help Gracián in his appeal to the pope (MCHT 4, doc. 569).
35. This Italian expression could be rendered "Oh, that's friars' stuff," but it was no laughing matter for Giordano Bruno, a Dominican friar, who was burned at the stake in a central Roman market square on February 17, 1600. It happened only a few months before Gracián left Rome for good.
36. See PA 5.14–16.
37. The countess had tried to obtain Gracián's release when he was being held by the Turks (PA 7.18).
38. Gracián is wryly alluding to his being named—though never consecrated—a bishop for the Armenian Christians in Persia. See PA 14.26.
39. See PA 5, note 15.
40. See PA 6.9 and PA 8.36–37.
41. Gracián discusses his prayer and spirituality in dialogue 15.
42. See also PA 6.40.
43. Gracián stated earlier that there were six hundred Christians in the *baño* and 1,600 slaves in Tunis (PA 6.44).
44. A term moralists use for taking something ("stealing") from one who rightfully owes it to the one who takes it.
45. *Aguardiente* (literally "firewater") is "raw brandy" and was probably distilled from grapes or sugar cane.
46. See PA 6.35–37, for details about the other priest and this church.
47. Gracián names two priests who were burned alive in Algiers (PA 6.43, 48); apparently they were not part of this group.

48. Gracián mentions earlier having nearly drowned eight times (see PA 6.4–7).
49. See dialogues 11 (the six letters), 15 (the name of Jesus), and 16 (the name of Mary).

Eleventh Dialogue: Succor

1. A stands for *amor* (love), F for *fe* (faith), and I for *juicio* (judgment) and *justicia* (justice).
2. This is surely St. Anthony of the Desert, who often skirmished with the devil in his temptations. The temptations of Anthony in the desert were a favorite subject in Christian art.
3. *Amate* is the imperative of *amare,* a love that is passionate and sensual, but it could also simply mean to like someone or something. The Lord is not saying we have to like our enemies.
4. *Diligere* means a love by choice and has the connotation of esteem. *Diligere* and *amare* are commonly rendered as love in English.
5. Zeuxis and Apeles were painters of ancient Greece.
6. A monastic practice involving self-flagellation.
7. "Martinico" could be a little statue of a saint.
8. See PA 4.11–17, for Gracián's previous discussion on the will and the understanding.
9. Gracián dedicates dialogue 13 to his "good deeds" in making foundations for the Discalced Carmelites. The examples that come at this point in the text are from the Toledo manuscript.
10. See PA 13.102–104 for more details. See also *Cartas,* no. 62.
11. The countess of Castellar was Doña Beatriz Ramírez de Mendoza. See PA 13.110 and *Cartas,* no. 127, about this foundation.
12. The monastery of Santa Maria della Scala (see *Cartas,* no. 66).
13. Gracian is making a reference here to Phil 1:18: "But what then? So that by all means, whether by occasion or by truth, Christ be preached: in this also I rejoice, yea, and will rejoice" (Douay-Rheims).
14. *Aborrecimiento y abatimiento propio* is the Spanish.
15. See PA 8, note 7.
16. *A rio vuelto pesca buenos peces* ("Good fish are caught in a churning river") is a popular expression.
17. St. Ignatius of Loyola says similarly: "Interior penance consists in grieving for one's sins" (*Spiritual Exercises,* #82).
18. That is, Psalm 51(50): "Have mercy on me, God, in Your kindness. . . ."
19. Gracián's father was Diego Gracián de Alderete (d. 1584), a noted humanist who studied under Vives at Louvain and became secretary to Charles V and, afterwards, to Philip II.

20. This passage calls to mind Gracián's prayer at age 20, that God lead him by the sure road of the cross. See PA 8.2.
21. See PA 4.29; 5.10; and 13.100.
22. Gracián is likely referring to the difficulty he had with Father Doria and the *consulta* that resulted in his expulsion from the order.
23. See the letter, dated July 6, 1591, from St. John of the Cross to Maria de la Encarnación, prioress of the Discalced Carmelites of Segovia (Letter 26, *Collected Works of St. John of the Cross*, 760).
24. Compare what Gracián says here with St. John of the Cross's *Spiritual Canticle* 29. 2–3.
25. Gracián gives us her name, María de Jesús (Rivas), a Blessed, in PA 16.86–87.
26. What follows is actually a consideration of the "Four Last Things."
27. See PA 6.8–9.
28. This is an allusion to a popular saying: "There is no better surgeon than one who has himself been under the knife" (see PA 8.20).
29. The letters correspond to the first letters of the first words of these verses in Latin.

Twelfth Dialogue: Writings

1. Gracián mentions other meanings of the twelve stars in PA 9.4–5.
2. See PA 8.4 for Gracián's earlier discussion of his education. See also Llamas Martínez, "Jerónimo Gracián Dantisco."
3. Francisco de Jesús (Hernández, (1529–1601), a disciple of St. John of Ávila, professed in Seville in 1583. Gracián sent him to the Congo (see PA 3.19).
4. See PA 13.70 and 14.20.
5. Father Astigarraga lists these works alphabetically, along with a complete record of each book or writing, in *Cartas* (MHCT 9), at the end of the bibliography (pp. xxii–xxiv). See also Antonio Fortes Rodríguez, "Bibliografia del P. Jerónimo Gracián de la Madre de Dios" in *Archivum Bibliographicum Carmelitanum* 15 (Rome: Teresianum, 1973), 175–203.
6. See Morales, *Burning Lamp.*
7. The full title of this work is *Josefina: Summario de las excelencias del glorioso san José, esposo de virgen Maria* [Joseph: Summary of the Excellences of the Glorious St. Joseph, Husband of the Virgin Mary]. An English translation of a portion of this work appears in Gracián, *Just Man.*
8. Gracián fails to mention here that this book was printed in Lisbon in 1586 and was the beginning of his problems with Nicolás Doria, who objected to its publication. As regards the congregation that is mentioned, see PA 13.106 and 14.19, 23, 26.
9. See Enrique García Hernán, "El soldado católico de Jerónimo Gracián de la Madre de Dios," Rome: Teresianism, no. 1 (2011): 181–93.

10. "El Cerro" is an imaginary monastery. See the fine translation of this humorous short work: Jerome Gracián, *Jerome Gracian: Treatise on Melancholy,* trans. Michael Dodd (Wisconsin Dells, Wisc.: Pileated Press, 2009). It reminds one of the *Screwtape Letters* of C. S. Lewis.
11. This remarkable work gives great insights into the relationship Gracián had with St. Teresa.

Thirteenth Dialogue: Foundations

1. "The favors of the Lord I will sing forever" (Ps 89[88]:2). St. Teresa liked to repeat this verse.
2. This is an important writing of Gracián that has been published in MHCT 3, doc. 423 (pp. 533–694). It was meant to be a companion to St. Teresa's *Book of Foundations.* In fact, when Gracián asked Teresa to finish her *Foundations,* she said she would if he would write a similar account of the friars.
3. See Peers, *Handbook to the Life,* for dates of the foundations of the Discalced Carmelites, nuns and friars.
4. That St. Teresa is rightly called "foundress" of the friars is a key assertion of Gracián's that was not held by those who eventually had him expelled from the Discalced.
5. See MHCT 1, doc. 21.
6. It was Ana de Peñalosa who got the papal brief. It is thought by some that this transfer of the body of St. John of the Cross was the inspiration for one of the stories recounted by Cervantes in *Don Quixote* (vol. I, chapter XIX).
7. This was a common belief about the birth of Saint Francis.
8. Ruy Gómez de Silva was the husband of the princess of Éboli. He was one of the richest men in Spain and one of the most powerful in the Spanish court, and much favored by King Philip II. He was a good friend of the Teresian Carmelites.
9. St. Ignatius knew Doña Leonor and even wrote to her in a letter, "You are engraved on my heart."
10. Although I have translated *seminario* as seminary, Gracián means the novitiate. The Pastrana novitiate was really the seedbed, that is, seminario, of the Discalced Carmelite friars.
11. Elías de San Martín was the first elected general of the new Discalced Carmelite Order (1594–1600).
12. Pope Clement VIII made him visitator, and hence superior, of this new congregation that was begun with the reform initiated in Spain by St. Juan Bautista García, who was canonized in 1975. Gracián discusses Bautista's reform in PA 14.7.
13. Father Elías was professed with Father Gracián at Pastrana on April 25, 1573.
14. Fray Elías's brother was Fray Francisco de la Concepción; he professed at Pastrana on April 11, 1572.

15. St. Teresa's nickname for Fray Elías was "Clemente." See her letter to Gracián of October 23, 1576 (LE 1.136.8).
16. See PA 1.23.
17. Pius V was a Dominican pope (1566–1572) who implemented the decrees of the Council of Trent. He is a canonized saint.
18. Nuestra Señora de los Remedios was known as Los Remedios.
19. Doria entered Los Remedios on March 24, 1577.
20. See PA 4.35 for Gracián's earlier discussion of Doria's help to the king.
21. Gracián's praise of Doria's uprightness is all the more striking considering the injustice of his expulsion by Doria.
22. St. John of Ávila (1500–1569), known as the "Apostle of Andalusia," was born in Almodóvar del Campo. He was declared a Doctor of the Church in 2012.
23. See the letter of St. John of the Cross to the vicar general, Father Nicolás Doria, dated September 21, 1589 (Letter 18, *Collected Works of St. John of the Cross*, 753).
24. This would have been the auto-de-fé in Valladolid, May 24, 1559. See PA 8, note 11.
25. The silks were either vestments or material for making vestments. See "Letter to a Friend," p. 322.
26. See St. Teresa's interesting account of this in her *Book of Foundations* (F 28.20–36).
27. I.e., monasteries in remote places.
28. The Alhambra in Granada was the palace of the Moorish kings.
29. The count of Tendilla was Don Luis Hurtado de Mendoza, later the marquis of Mondéjar.
30. Gonzalo de Zúñiga, bishop of Jaén (1422–1456), is considered a martyr who died in a Moorish prison.
31. This is the same number of years that Gracián was provincial. Nothing else is known about this faithful servant and lay brother except the grateful remembrance of Gracián.
32. The *Miserere mei* is Psalm 51(50), which is one of the traditional penitential psalms and the one usually recited while taking the discipline.
33. Eliseo de los Mártires [1550–1620] came into frequent contact with St. John of the Cross. Later he became a leading figure of the Discalced Carmelites in Mexico where he was provincial for some time. It was he who sent the three Discalced Carmelites on the Vizcaíno expedition to California in 1602.
34. Catalina de Jesús (Sandoval y Godínez; 1540–1586) was a Discalced nun whom St. Teresa writes about in her *Book of Foundations* (F 22). St. John of the Cross was her spiritual director. See further mention of her in PA 16.60, 85.
35. The auto-de-fé was the ceremony accompanying the pronouncement of judgment by the Inquisition and followed by the execution of sentence by the secular authorities.

36. *Fuensanta* means "holy fountain."
37. *Percheles* refers to an apparatus on which to hang fishing nets, commonly seen around Málaga, or the place where the nets are hung.
38. *Jábega* is a dragnet or a sailing boat used for fishing.
39. Gracián makes a brief reference to this event in PA 3.16.
40. See PA 13.57.
41. The Magdalene was a religious and military order of Alcántara founded in 1154.
42. The location of this foundation in Salamanca was of concern to St. Teresa. She gives her opinion in letters to Gracián and Mariano (see LE 1.134–135).
43. See PA 14.10.
44. Erysipelas is a serious skin infection caused by bacteria.
45. Gracián tells of "el Indigno" also in PA 3.19 and 14.20.
46. Luis de Granada and Luis Muñoz, *Vida del Padre Maestro Juan de Ávila,* ed. Luis Sala Balust (Barcelona: Juan Flors, 1964).
47. Unfortunately, he never does tell us more about this but see note 45 above.
48. See PA 14.36; see also 3.26.
49. Gracián tells of the friars helping him hear the confessions of the soldiers (PA 3.39).
50. The difference between these two congregations is captured here in a few words and is a topic of great importance. Gracián was attracted to the Italian congregation's apostolate of the missions, but he declined to join them because he still hoped to reenter the Spanish congregation, and members of one were not allowed to transfer to the other, according to papal decree; besides, Gracián understood that St. Teresa did not want two orders of Discalced Carmelites.
51. Doria, the newly elected provincial, was opposed to the missions.
52. Published as *Historia de las fundaciones* [History of the foundations].
53. Father Francisco de Ribera, S.J., was the first biographer of St. Teresa (1590). He was a professor at the Jesuit college in Salamanca, hence the customary address of doctor. What we do now in giving precedence to clerical and religious titles over academic titles is different from what was the practice back then.
54. See PA 10, note 13.
55. See PA 16.7–12 and St. Teresa's *Spiritual Testimonies* 36, 405–408.
56. A speak room is a room where cloistered nuns meet their visitors, separated from them by a grille.
57. Julián de Ávila (1527–1605) served as chaplain for the monastery of San José for almost forty years. His sister was María de San José (Dávila).
58. This is no small praise to speak of María de San José (Salazar) in the same breath as St. Teresa. In one of her last letters (LE 1.435), St. Teresa speaks of her as a fit successor to herself. However, María de San José's close friendship with Gracián would

be used against her by Father Doria and his successors. This outstanding nun suffered tremendously.

59. Lorenzo de Cepeda (1519–1580) went to America in 1540. It was a moving reunion after thirty-five years to see his big sister Mother Teresa again. From then on, Teresita, his daughter, was brought up in the monastery in Seville until she later became a nun herself in Ávila. Lorenzo was a great consolation to his sister, and she helped him greatly to become a man of prayer. "Teresica" is an endearing diminutive of Teresa.
60. This "rule" was in the constitutions of 1581. The nuns were indeed supposed to give an account of their prayer to the prioress once a month.
61. The prior of the Carthusians was Fernando de Pantoja, prior of Las Cuevas, whom St. Teresa frequently mentions with words of thanks. Gracián draws an exquisite portrait of him in *Escolias*.
62. About this mortification, see *Escolias*, 398.
63. This is one of the most famous quips of St. Teresa. We can certainly be grateful that Fray Juan painted her portrait, because it is the only one we have of her that was actually made from a sitting. The portrait is kept by the nuns in Seville.
64. In Palencia, Suero de Vega was called "father of the poor."
65. St. John of the Cross went to Ávila to get St. Teresa to go to Granada for the foundation there but she went to Burgos instead. It was the last time the two saints saw each other. St. John of the Cross accompanied Mother Ana to Granada.
66. St. Teresa went to Soria six months before Mother Ana went to Granada.
67. They left Ávila on January 2, 1582.
68. Gracián gives us more information about this interesting proposal in *Escolias* (416), where he says that St. Teresa would have made this foundation if the abbot had not insisted that the nuns be under his jurisdiction. St. Teresa was serious about the good formation and education of girls.
69. There is certain pathos behind the phrase, "This was the last . . . returning from Burgos, the Lord took her." St. Teresa begged Gracián to accompany her as much as he possibly could. He couldn't have left at a worse time. He was in Beas when he got word of St. Teresa's death in Alba de Tormes. See *Escolias*, 423.
70. See PA 3, notes 27 and 37.
71. See PA 14.34; see also 3.28–32.
72. See PA 3.37.
73. The best biography of Catalina de Cristo was written by Leonor de la Misericordia. A critical edition of this work is *Relación de la vida de la venerable Catalina de Cristo*, ed. Pedro Rodríguez and Ildefonso Adeva, Biblioteca Mística Carmelitana 28 (Burgos, Spain: Editorial Monte Carmelo, 1995). Gracián writes admiringly of these two nuns in *Escolias*, 407–9.

74. Her husband was her first cousin. Apparently, a dispensation had not been given for this marriage. In any case, it was never consummated.
75. Martín de Cruzat was the lord of Oriz. He founded the monastery of the friars in Pamplona (see PA 13.74).
76. Francis Xavier was canonized with Teresa of Ávila, Ignatius of Loyola, and Philip Neri in 1622.
77. Francisco Soto, a Spanish priest, was an Oratorian. The founder of the Congregation of the Oratory, St. Philip Neri, very much supported the idea of a foundation of Discalced Carmelite nuns in Rome.
78. César Baronio was an Oratorian and protégé of St. Philip Neri.
79. This encounter with St. Philip Neri (1515–1595) must have occurred in the latter part of 1592, since the saint would have been dead when Gracián returned to Rome after his captivity.
80. Nuestra Señora de la Scala was the principal monastery of the Discalced Carmelites in Rome and the general house of the Italian congregation for nearly three centuries. Gracián also tells of this event in PA 11.22.
81. Pope Paul V issued a papal bull in 1608 that instituted a new missionary congregation of Discalced Carmelites—the Congregation of St. Paul—and put it under his immediate jurisdiction with Father Tomás de Jesús, O.C.D., as the commissary general. Any Discalced Carmelite of Spain or Italy was free to join it for the purpose of going to the missions. This third Discalced Carmelite congregation (there were already the Spanish and Italian congregations) was like a missionary society within the order. It caused so much inconvenience and disturbance that it was discontinued after six months, although the papal bull instituting it was not revoked until 1613.
82. Monsignor Juan Bautista Vives y Maria (1545–1632), a Spanish priest residing in Rome, founded the first pontifical College of Propaganda Fide, donating a small palace in Rome for its use. When Pope Gregory XV established the Sacred Congregation for the Propagation of the Faith in 1622, Vives was one of its first members. Umberto Benigni, "Propaganda, Sacred Congregation of," in *The Catholic Encyclopedia*, ed. Charles Herbermann, Edward Pace, Condé Pallen, Thomas Shahan, and John Wynne (New York: Encyclopedia Press, 1913), 456–61. See PA 12, note 8.
83. Juan de Brétigny (1556–1634) first met María de San José (Salazar) and the Discalced Carmelite nuns in Seville as early as 1583. Almost from that time he tried to get the nuns to make a foundation in France. See Julián Urkiza, *Comienzos del Carmelo Teresiano Francés* (Burgos, Spain: Editorial Monte Carmelo, 2004).
84. Pierre de Bérulle (1575–1629) later became a cardinal and one of the most important churchmen of his time in France.
85. Catherine d'Orleans-Longueville (1566–1638), whose letters to the king of Spain (Philip III), the superior general of the Discalced Carmelites, and the papal nuncio in Spain were a decisive influence in getting the Teresian Carmelite nuns to France.

The first foundation was made in Paris in 1604; Madame Barbara Acarie was much involved.

86. The Paris foundation was made on October 18, 1604; a foundation was never made in Rouan.
87. La Concepción monastery was founded in 1563. Gracián says more about it in *Escolias*, 368–69.
88. This is the same superior general who welcomed Gracián into the Order of the Calced in Rome in 1596.
89. This is a rather interesting comment regarding the original purpose of the Discalced. In fact, it is something that is still being discussed, namely, the purpose and charism of the Teresian Carmelites. Did St. Teresa think of herself as a reformer? Gracián's statement here needs to be put in context. He more than anyone understood that St. Teresa was the foundress of the Discalced Carmelite friars and nuns and that this was something new and original.

Fourteenth Dialogue: Fruits

1. The Second Vatican Council's Dogmatic Constitution on the Church *Lumen Gentium* teaches, "Those also can attain to salvation who through no fault of their own do not know the Gospel of Christ or His Church, yet sincerely seek God and moved by grace strive by their deeds to do His will as it is known to them through the dictates of conscience" (LG 16).
2. This was just four months after his profession. See PA 1.20.
3. This is a good example of how Gracián proceeded in the work of the reform of the monasteries of the Calced, applying the norms of the Council of Trent. His report of his visitation of the monastery of the Calced in Seville in 1576 (February 21–April 1) is preserved (see MHCT 1, doc. 107).
4. Gracián writes of this PA 3.34.
5. A master was one who had a permanent office of teacher or an academic chair in the university.
6. In fact, the Augustinians are still present in Nostra Señora del Popolo in Piazza del Popolo. There are two Caravaggio paintings that draw a continual stream of tourists to the church.
7. There is a reference to this appointment in PA 13.29.
8. The countess had also founded the monastery of the Discalced Carmelite nuns in Alcalá (PA 13.110), and a monastery for the Discalced Jeronimites (PA 14.11).
9. Cardinal Alejandrino was Michele Bonelli, a Dominican like his uncle, Pope Pius V.
10. Gracián alluded to the difficulties regarding this foundation in PA 13.67.
11. See *Cartas*, no. 127, about the foundation plans that Gracián made with the countess, Doña Beatriz Ramírez de Mendoza.

12. "Caballero de Gracia" was a famous Italian priest, Jacobo de Gratiis (1517–1619), who in Madrid was dubbed the "Knight of Grace." He founded an association to promote devotion to the Eucharist. See *Cartas*, no. 60, July 2, 1596, the only letter of Gracián's to him that has been conserved.
13. Colón had dealt with St. Teresa about her foundation in Salamanca.
14. See Tomás Alvarez, "Reviven las Constituciones de Santa Teresa entre Doria, San Juan de Ribera y Gracián," *Monte Carmelo* 88 (1980): 67–86. See also *Cartas*, no. 146 (pp. 384–85).
15. Gracián discusses these foundations in his letter dated November 24, 1606 (*Cartas*, no. 146).
16. The Brothers of Obregón were founded in 1567 by Bernardino de Obregón (1540–1599) of Madrid and staffed hospitals throughout Spain, Belgium, and the Indies, and in Lisbon. Gracián had also considered asking the Brothers of John of God in Granada to come.
17. Various letters of Gracián (1610–1611) attest to his accompaniment of the visitation of the Calced provincial, whose intention was to apply all the norms of the Council of Trent about enclosure, for both the nuns and the friars.
18. Licentiate Padilla, or Juan Cavallo de Padilla (b. 1520), a Castilian priest, was held in high regard by Philip II and the royal council, who often worked on behalf of the Discalced for St. Teresa and for Gracián. He was a graduate of the University of Barcelona, hence his title *el licenciado*, that is, licentiate. He spent some time in the West Indies and in Guinea. His zeal exceeded his discretion, and this was an "intolerable cross" for Gracián. See MHCT 3 (p. 580), and *Cartas*, no. 6.
19. The written document of this concord, *Vínculo de hermandad* [Bond of Brotherhood], was drawn up in Lisbon in April of 1585. This was one month before the end of Gracián's term as provincial. It was signed by himself and Martín Ignacio de Loyola, provincial of the Discalced Franciscans founded by St. Peter of Alcántara. Martín de Loyola was a nephew of St. Ignatius of Loyola. He went around the world three times and had been to the Philippines and China before signing this accord with Gracián.
20. It is interesting that Gracián knows about the martyrs of Nagasaki, who were martyred in 1597.
21. The book that Gracián wrote caused many problems with his successor, Father Doria, and was the beginning of his troubles (see MHCT 3, doc. 282; and *Cartas*, no. 15).
22. See chapter 17 of Gracián's *Historia de las fundaciones* (MCHT 3, doc. 423) where he recounts the missions he sent between 1582 and 1585. See also PA 3.19.
23. See MHCT 3, pp. 670–78.
24. Gracián is referring to a commission of three cardinals, headed by Giulio Antonio Santori (1532–1602), archbishop of Santa Severina, which was initially established

during the pontificate of Gregory XIII (1572–1585) and revitalized by Clement VIII (1592–1605), who retained Santori as its president. This commission was the principal forerunner of the Sacred Congregation for the Propagation of the Faith (known as the Congregation for the Evangelization of Peoples since 1982) that was instituted on June 22, 1622, by Pope Gregory XV. See also PA 13.106.

25. This was the Order of Friars Minor, Capuchins.
26. Clement VIII gave Gracián a brief authorizing him to go to Africa and to preach the jubilee year and work for the redemption of captives. Two Capuchins were to accompany him, but they did not recognize his commission and even tried to have it revoked. See *Cartas*, nos. 88, 97.
27. Ceuta, on the northeastern tip of Morocco, belonged to Portugal (1415–1668). When Philip II assumed the Portuguese throne in 1580, Spanish people began to populate that city.
28. Mumen ben Abdelquirin El Mesuar was the commander's name, according a letter of Gracián (*Cartas*, no. 121).
29. The sharif at that time was Ahmad al-Mansur (1578–1610), and the king of Spain was Philip III.
30. The duke of Medina Sidonia was Alonso Pérez de Guzman (1559–1615), commander of the Spanish Armada.
31. This duke, Francisco Gómez de Sandoval y Rojas (1553–1625), who was very close to the Carmelites, practically ruled Spain under Philip III, who was rather weak.
32. Toledo is just thirty miles southwest of Aranjuez, so he was indeed waiting. He writes about this proposed peace deal in *Cartas*, nos. 118–22.
33. On April 25, 1607, a Dutch fleet destroyed twenty-one Spanish ships anchored in the Bay of Gibraltar. Three years later, the Spanish captured the town and port of L'Arrache (Larache or El Araich today), located on the west coast of northern Morocco.
34. See PA 13.106 for Gracián's previous reference to this congregation and also his letter dated December 26, 1608 (*Cartas*, no. 164).
35. The martyr St. Anastasius (d. 628), whose name Gracián takes for himself in these dialogues, was a convert from Persia following his participation in the capture of the True Cross from Jerusalem.
36. Shah Abbas of the Safavi dynasty was the king of Persia. He built his royal capital in Isfahan and set aside an entire quarter for thousands of Christian Armenians brought in from northwest Persia. It was to these people that Pope Clement VIII sent Father Paolo Simone (Rivarola) and his companions. They left Rome in 1604 but did not arrive until 1607, having been imprisoned for a year in Moscow. The Armenians were asking for a bishop. Gracián was told that he had been nominated, but he never received official notification of it.

37. The Discalced Carmelites made a foundation in Kraków on December 7, 1605.
38. See *Cartas*, no. 148.
39. Here and four sentences later, Gracián uses the word *Negro*, which indicates a sub-Saharan man as opposed to a North African.
40. See *Cartas*, nos. 74, 75.
41. Establishing houses for women in these difficulties was one of Gracián's special works of mercy. He did this in Lisbon, Seville, and Naples. This reminds one of St. Ignatius's special care of converted prostitutes.
42. This Melchor Cano (1541–1607) is the nephew of the famous Dominican theologian of the same name. The nephew was a great friend of the Discalced Carmelite nuns in Consuegra where Gracián's sister María de San José was. St. Teresa praises this Dominican in a letter to Father Domingo Báñez, O.P., dated February 28, 1574: "Yesterday I was with a padre named Fray Melchor Cano, who is from your order. I tell you that if there were many spirits in your order like his, they could found some contemplative monasteries " (LE 1.61.8).
43. This most famous spiritual guide had believed María de la Visitación, whose story follows.
44. The kingdom of Portugal could have been lost to Spain due to the rebellion at hand and the help the English were giving it (see PA 3.28–32). Gracián was very concerned that there would be loss to the Catholic faith if the Protestant English succeeded in their invasion.
45. This was in June and again in August of 1588. The archbishop was very pleased with the results (see MCHT 3, doc. 419, p. 524).
46. King Henry III of France was assassinated in 1589.
47. He married four times; Mary Tudor was his second wife.
48. The woman was examined by doctors and theologians of the Inquisition for six months, but they found nothing wrong with her. See MHCT 3, doc. 423 (pp. 585–86) for a longer account of this strange episode in Seville.
49. This was mentioned in PA 3.26.
50. Regarding these two books, see *Cartas*, no. 158 (p. 412). *Vida del alma y verdadera imitación de Cristo* (Life of the soul and true imitation of Christ) was dedicated to the prior of the Carthusians in Brussels.
51. See *Cartas*, no. 189 (May 8, 1610). This priest, Carlos Fevre, said that fifty Discalced Carmelite nuns were pregnant by the Holy Spirit and their sons would be the principal preachers and captains to regain the Holy Land.
52. This sounds like the same case that Gracián discusses in greater detail in PA 3.18 except that his view of the outcome here is not as grim as it is there.
53. Alessandro de Medici (1535–1605) was Pope Leo XI. His pontificate began in 1605 and lasted only a few months.

54. Just after founding Los Remedios in Seville in 1574, the archbishop gave him this responsibility. See MHCT 3, doc. 423 (p. 567).

Fifteenth Dialogue: Prayer

1. See PA Pref.5 for Gracián's explanation of his shield.
2. This is an allusion to the parable of the talents (see Mt 25:14–30).
3. *Scivias* means "you know the ways." St. Hildegard of Bingen was declared a Doctor of the Church along with St. John of Ávila in October of 2012.
4. He mentions this in *Historia de las fundaciones*, MHCT 3, p. 536. Father Master Deza, S.J., was his professor (see PA 8.10).
5. The Pauline text is referring to speaking in tongues in assemblies of the faithful.
6. Gracián doesn't say what he prayed "nine" of, but it might have been the Glory Be.
7. Such meditations, ordered according to the days of the week, can be found in many manuals on prayer of the period.
8. This is the doctrine of St. Thomas Aquinas and the teaching of the church (see *Summa Theologiae* I-II, q. 112, a. 5). St. Teresa at times adverts to this truth. However, St. Thomas does say a person can have certain knowledge of grace by its effects.
9. Held in June 529, this council was directed against semi-pelagianism.
10. Ambergris is used in the making of perfume.
11. See PA 2.16.
12. It is sometimes said that Gracián was too fond of visions and revelations and such things. This is false as shown here. In fact, in many places in his writings he insists on these points, which are in agreement with St. John of the Cross.
13. There are numerous versions of this vision. Knowledge of it must have been widespread. It is even related by María de San José in "Instrucción de novicias." There is some discrepancy about when it actually happened (see MHCT 3, p. 646). It is interesting to compare the coupling of "purity and love" (*pureza y amor*) with this coupling in St. John of the Cross. For instance, he writes, "Consequently, we understand with greater clarity that the preparation for this union, as we said, is not an understanding by the soul, not the taste, feeling, or imagining of God or any other object, but purity and love, which is the stripping off and perfect renunciation of all these experiences for God alone" (A 2.5.8).
14. Gracián writes at length about these four desires impressed upon his heart in *Diálogos del tránsito de la M. Teresa de Jesús*, ed. Juan Luis Astigarraga, Otilio Rodriguez, and Eulogio Pacho (Rome: Institutum Historicum Teresianum, 1982) (dialogue 5 in MHCT 6, p. 96).
15. See PA 2.16.
16. What Gracián says here seems to contradict what he said previously about reprimanding those who said they saw souls in heaven or hell, but the difference is

that he doesn't "see" these saints to be in either place but rather he is "given to know" where they are, that is, through a concept accompanying the vision, thus qualifying it as "intellectual." As Gracián says later, intellectual visions, per se, are imageless.

17. This scenario is possible in a Spanish home that is built with an inner courtyard.
18. "I don't know what" (*Un no sé qué*) sounds like St. John of the Cross.
19. This is according to classical astronomy.
20. These bodies are visible to the naked eye, as is Uranus (if one knows exactly where to look), which wasn't discovered until 1781. Neptune was discovered via telescope in 1846.
21. Aristotle's idea of the encyclopedia was not a collection of books such as the French later developed; rather, it was a theory of the unity of all things knowable.
22. Gracián was famous throughout Spain for his preaching, but this frequent activity in the pulpit was something for which he was often criticized by Doria and others.
23. This occurred when Gracián and Father Mariano were in Mondéjar. See PA 2.17.
24. There were many such treatises written throughout Europe before the seventeenth century, including one by Erasmus.
25. As Gracián said earlier, *pan* is both the Greek word for "all" and the Spanish word for "bread" or "loaf." St. John of the Cross interprets the three loaves as the three theological virtues that are necessary for union with God (see A 2.6.5). Perhaps the two diverse interpretations are an illustration of the different spirits of these two sons of St. Teresa. Gracián is oriented to the service of Christ and the salvation of souls; John of the Cross is oriented to union with God.
26. It is difficult to translate *razones* in this context, but perhaps the words "notions," "impressions," and "apprehensions" come close to Gracián's meaning.
27. Gracián writes about this in *Diálogo de Angela y Eliseo*, ed. Juan Luis Astigarraga, Otilio Rodriguez, and Eulogio Pacho, MHCT 6 (Rome: Institutum Historicum Teresianum, 1982); and *Tránsito y ultima jornada de Teresa*, ed. Juan Luis Astigarraga, Otilio Rodriguez, and Eulogio Pacho, MHCT 6 (Rome: Institutum Historicum Teresianum, 1982). Both of these were written within a year of St. Teresa's death (see MHCT 6).
28. As far as we know, this work was never published.
29. This is a verse from a hymn that was sung at Compline (night prayer) before retiring to sleep. The translation is from Matthew Britt, *The Hymns of the Breviary and Missal* (New York: Benzinger Brothers, 1924), 39.
30. I don't think Gracián was deceitful in doing this, because guilt shows up in our dreams. No doubt there was legitimate matter in their dreams for him to work with.
31. Dominic Ruzola was one of the great Carmelite friars of the Italian congregation.

Sixteenth Dialogue: Revelations

1. In Spanish, these "twelve D's" are *descreído, desconfiado, desamorado, desobediente, desagradecido, descompuesto, desabrido, desordenado, descubridor, desacatado, descuidado, desdeñoso.*
2. This is a typical disclaimer before telling us about some pretty amazing revelations. Many of the texts cited by Gracián in this last dialogue are those he took from notebooks sent to him at his request by his sister, María de San José, O.C.D., from Consuegra (see *Cartas*, no. 172, May 4, 1609). These notebooks, sown together in one volume, are presently in the monastery archives of Consuegra (Toledo).
3. There is an autograph of this text in the archives of the monastery of Consuegra. St. Teresa has written at the top, "This is a thing concerning my soul and conscience. No one is to read it even when I die, but instead, it is to be given to P. Gracián / Teresa of Jesus." Gracián seems to have had his own copy that he always kept with him. His copy is now—after the closure of the monastery of Chichester—in the archives of the monastery of Notting Hill in England.
4. See St. Teresa's *Spiritual Testimonies* 36.
5. The expression in Spanish is *señalado servicio*, which sounds a lot like the *señalar en todo servicio* [to singularize yourself in all service] found in the *Spiritual Exercises* of St. Ignatius, in the meditation of the Call of Christ the King at the beginning of the second week. I cannot help detecting here, in the way St. Teresa relates her decision to make the vow to Gracián, a certain influence of the Ignatian spirit of *agere contra* [to work against] and the Ignatian notion of obedience of mind and will. See St. Ignatius's Letter #3304, dated March 26, 1553.
6. Gracián says otherwise in PA 10.30.
7. This passage is the most cogent reason why Jerome Gracián should be given his just due in the history of the Teresian Carmelites. It is also interesting to note that thanks to Jean de Brétigny's translation of the writings of St. Teresa into French as early as 1602, St. Francis de Sales knew of and discussed St. Teresa's vow to Gracián with St. Jane Frances de Chantal. St. Jane made a vow of obedience to St. Francis de Sales in 1604. See note 17 of the Introduction (p. xviii).
8. Gracián writes of this in more detail in PA 10.31.
9. Gracián mentions the visitation briefly in PA 1.32.
10. The background here, as Gracián will explain, is that St. Teresa was so upset by how his own brethren were treating him at Alcalá that she wished he was back with the Calced, who had treated him so well just a short time before while he was with them in Madrid waiting to be sentenced by Sega. Of course, Gracián, as he is remembering these things while writing his autobiography, interprets Teresa's words as foretelling his present circumstances.
11. Gracián writes differently of his experience with the Calced in PA 2.26.
12. Gracián writes briefly of this incident in PA 2.33.

13. This incident is mentioned in PA 1.35, and many of the charges brought against Gracián are listed in PA 4.19–28. See also MHCT 3, doc. 423 (pp. 586–87); and MHCT 2, doc. 175 (pp. 66–67).
14. Gracián lovingly saved all of Teresa's letters. The letter cited here is dated September 20, 1576.
15. See PA 16.95 where St. Teresa appears to Ana de San Bartolomé and instructs her to tell Gracián to make the vow he intended.
16. St. Teresa is thinking of the Bride in Song of Songs who describes herself as black (i.e., sunburned) but lovely (1:5–6).
17. This would have been when he was arrested by the Discalced and imprisoned at the Madrid priory from the end of June 1591 to February 17, 1592, the day he was expelled from the order.
18. Gracián was a captive of the Turks from October 11, 1593, to April 11, 1595. In that time, among those who died were Nicolás Doria (May 1594), vicar general; Ambrosio Mariano (1594), a witness at Gracián's trial; and Diego Evangelista (June 1594), a definitor who, although he wasn't present at Gracián's trial (Juan Baptista, the prior at Madrid, took his place) was directly instrumental in gathering charges against him. Luis de San Jeronimo, who had gone to Rome with Diego Evangelista to obstruct Gracián's appeal, died unexpectedly in 1593.
19. Elías de San Martín, general of the new order from 1594 to 1600, "dismantled the machinery of the Consulta" (Rohrbach, *Journey to Carith*, 227).
20. This is Gracián's blood sister.
21. This same general also burned the calumnies written up by Fray Diego Evangelista against St. John of the Cross.
22. St. John of Ávila (see PA 13.70).
23. *Audi filia* [Listen, O daughter] is a major work of this new Doctor of the Church.
24. Gracián was readmitted to the Discalced Order by a papal brief dated March 6, 1596, but the Discalced declined to receive him. A month later, again by papal order, he was admitted to the Calced Order of Carmel and allowed to live as a Discalced.
25. See PA 13, note 34.
26. References to the little finger of the right hand of St. Teresa are numerous in the letters of Gracián. He acquired her finger when he exhumed her body in 1583. He carried it with him for the rest of his life, even in captivity. It is now kept by the Carmel of the Discalced Carmelite nuns of Brussels. See MHCT 9, *Cartas* (under the index of names, see Teresa de Jesús, *Reliquias: dedo*).
27. This and the following counsels of St. Teresa were not part of Catalina's notebook but were taken from the notebook that Gracián asked his sister to send from

Consuegra. See note 2 above. However, he copies them rather freely. He was aware of these counsels since the early 1580s when he wrote *Diálogos del tránsito de la M. Teresa de Jesús*. See MHCT 6, pp. 137–42.

28. Here Gracián names the nun he mentioned in PA 11.44 in connection with the same marvelous grace of receiving the mystical crown of thorns. María de Jesús took the habit at Toledo in 1577. St. Teresa, who thought highly of her, declared that she wanted her "even if she had to stay in bed all her life long." She is now a Blessed, and her memorial is September 12.
29. Mother Teresa's body was exhumed in 1584 for examination and reburied afterwards. Her casket was found to have caved in and filled with a mix of lime and wet soil, the body intact and supple but blackened by the lime and exuding a strong sweetly-fragrant odor (MHCT, vol 6 [Rome: Teresianum, 1982], 73–74).
30. Before receiving St. Teresa's posthumous instruction, Gracián had settled upon making a resolution instead of a vow (PA 16.33).
31. How quixotic of Gracián, an old nag stumbling, leaving him to carry his stuff with his Sancho-like companion-friar.
32. Although this seems to be a rather inglorious and abrupt ending to his autobiography, it might help to keep in mind that Gracián arranged all this material—written over a ten-year period—as it related to various aspects of his shield, the last of which is the emblem of Mary, perhaps the most upbeat or uplifting dialogue, since it encourages hope of Gracián's eventual return to the Carmelite Order, whether Calced, as was indeed the case four years after his expulsion, or the Discalced, as has actually happened in our day with the generalate's "Official Declaration of the Rehabilitation of Father Jerome Gracián of the Mother of God, O.C.D." in 1999 (see this document in Appendix V).

Appendix I: Letter to a Friend

1. Vera Cruz is a hill east of Alcalá de Henares.
2. La Mancha is a plateau region in central Spain.
3. This is Beas de Segura. Some towns were given special privileges because of their participation in the Crusades. *De los comendadores* means "of the commanders," i.e., knights.
4. Gracian writes of this episode in PA 16.20–21, 37.
5. The Discalced Carmelites were not yet a formed religious order at this point.
6. The almoner has the duty of distributing alms on behalf of the king.
7. He spent a year "lying low" in Pastrana.
8. See Peers, *Handbook to the Life,* 54.
9. It seems it was never printed.
10. The Chapter of Alcalá was held in March of 1581.

11. The pope was commanding Gracián to join the Discalced Augustinians.
12. This was presumably the Roman Inquisition.
13. The Mughal Empire, to which Mogor refers, was the dominant power on the Indian subcontinent between the mid-sixteenth century and the early eighteenth century.
14. Java was often associated with India at that time.
15. Fray Matías was elected general of the Italian congregation in 1620.
16. The duchess of Longueville was Catherine d'Orleans-Longueville (1566–1638). See PA 13, note 85.
17. Spain contested and fought for territory in North Africa over many years. See *Cartas,* no. 121, MHCT 9 (1989). See also PA 14.25.
18. The University of Louvain was founded in 1425.
19. Bononia is the old Roman designation for Bologna, and there were several places bearing the name.

Appendix II: Letter 185 to Francisca de Las Llagas and María de San José

1. Gracian is writing to Francisca de Las Llagas (1560–1612) and María de San José (his sister) at the monastery in Consuegra, which they founded in May 1597. Each had held the office of prioress over the years; Francisca was prioress at this time.
2. The "mute little demon" (*diablillo mudo* in Spanish) is a reference to Lk 11:14–28 ("He was driving out a demon that was mute"), which was the Gospel reading for the Third Sunday of Lent.
3. Doña Luisa Faxardo is the daughter of the Marquise de Almazán and a sister of Francisca de Las Llagas, to whom Gracián is writing. The sisters were cousins to Luisa de Carvajal, who came to live with them in Pamplona when she was ten years old.
4. This is a portrait of Gracián that was done while he was a captive in Tunis. The original is still preserved in the monastery of Consuegra, and an identical copy is in the monastery of Seville. It is printed on the cover of this book.
5. A *rótulo* is a circular letter regarding the life and virtues of a person sent by the Congregation for the Causes of the Saints in the name of the pope before the person is beatified. This reference to Mother Teresa's zeal for souls disturbed the Spanish Discalced because it was understood to mean her zeal for the missions, a zeal which that was not much in evidence in the Spanish Discalced at the time.
6. This was the little finger of St. Teresa's right hand that Gracián took when her body was exhumed the first time in 1583. He carried it with him, even in his captivity, until the end of his life.
7. Gracián's body was buried at the Brussels monastery, which was destroyed in the Napoleonic Wars. See the account of Gracián's death in Appendix IV: "Illness and Happy Death of Jerome Gracián."

8. See PA 16.25, where he explains what happened in Alcalá and how he and Teresa used code names. "Cats" was the name they used for the Calced Carmelite friars.
9. Ana de Jesús was practically obstinate in her insistence that she only wanted the friars to come from the Spanish congregation and not from the Italian congregation as Gracián tried to advise her. The Discalced Carmelites were divided into two congregations in 1600.
10. Most likely this Teresa is the daughter of Tomás Gracián who remarried after the death of his first wife.
11. This was Don Felipe Folch de Cardona y Borja, the ambassador of King Philip III to Flanders, whom Gracián accompanied from Spain to Flanders in late May of 1607.

Appendix III: Letter 222 to Alfonso de Narvaez, Captain of the Artillery of Pamplona

1. On February 17, 1592, Father Jerome Gracián was sentenced and expelled from the Order of the Discalced Carmelites. When he refers to "this business regarding my habit," he means the business of what order he belongs to.
2. The prior of the monastery in Pamplona was Father Alonso de San Bautista.
3. In other letters he says that the friars in Spain are stalling, basically giving him the runaround.
4. Gracian's "*Emanciparme de mis queridos*" (that is, to be liberated from those he loves) is, I suppose, melancholic humor.
5. Namely, Father Tomás asked Gracián to manifest in writing his desire to return to the Discalced Order—in this case, the order in Spain. The Discalced Carmelites in Italy, on the other hand, were willing, even anxious, to receive Gracián into their congregation.
6. As he will say further on in the letter, he is talking about the monastery in Vilvoorde. Established in 1468 by the superior general John Soreth, this was the first community of Carmelite nuns. In 1966, the community transferred to the Discalced Carmelite Order.
7. "Weakness of the world" seems to be a euphemism for weakness of the flesh.
8. A turn is like a turnstile for goods to be passed in and out of the monastery. It helps the nuns avoid unnecessary contact with the public and maintain their recollection.
9. The beguines were women who dedicated their lives to God without retiring from the world. In the thirteenth century, they founded the beguinages, enclosed communities designed to meet their spiritual and material needs. The Flemish beguinages are architectural ensembles composed of houses, churches, ancillary buildings, and green spaces, with a layout of either urban or rural origin and built-in styles specific to the Flemish cultural region.

10. That is, Gracián seems to think that the lifestyle of the beguines is fraught with occasions of sin. His observation about this situation reflects his Spanish mentality regarding the relations of the sexes, that is, the need for strict segregation and cloister.
11. Gracián would have had some canonical authority to do this. The "spirituality" he speaks of was a form of perfectionism.

Appendix IV: Illness and Happy Death of Jerome Gracián

1. This appendix is taken from "An Account of the Brief Illness and Happy Death of Jerome Gracián," trans. Stephen Watson, *Carmelite Digest* 24, no. 3 (fall 2009), 43–48, and reprinted with permission. It was originally published as "Relación de la Breve Enfermedad y Dichosa Muerte de Jerónimo Gracián," in MHCT, appendix 29, *Cartas*. This account is found at the end of a résumé of the life of Father Jerome Gracián written by his younger brother, Father Lorenzo de la Madre de Dios, who was also a Discalced Carmelite. A copy is found in the archives of the Discalced Carmelite friars in Ávila. Who actually wrote the account is not known. It might have been written by Father Tomás de Jesús, O.C.D., who was the superior of the Discalced Carmelites in Brussels at that time.
2. The Spanish ambassador was Don Felipe Folch de Cardona y Borja, the fourth marquis of Guadaleste. He had obtained a patent from the Spanish nuncio for Gracián to accompany him to Brussels (capital city of the Spanish Netherlands) when he was appointed ambassador there. Father Gracián was his confessor. See PA 14.27; and a "Circular Letter to His Friends," May 1607, in *Cartas*, no. 148.
3. *Metresas*, or mistresses in English, is a term derived from the French that in Spanish means ladies whom the gallants serve.
4. In a letter that Blessed Ana de San Bartolomé wrote to Mother Leonor de la Misericordia in April of 1615, she says, "I believe I already wrote to Your Reverence regarding the death of Father Gracián. He died eight days before the feast of the beatification of our Holy Mother. [Note: This was the liturgical and popular celebration in Antwerp that Blessed Ana had prepared for her beloved Mother Teresa who had been beatified on April 24, 1614.] He was coming in late from a village outside Brussels. The gates of the city were locked, and there was a terrible chill. He had to stay in a poor hospice, and he got a bad stomachache. He could see that he was going to die. He made his confession. The confessor said he would not die, but Gracián said he would because "*La Santa*" [The Saint] had appeared to him. Mother Teresa told him that God wanted him to celebrate her feast in heaven. And so, this same day, he died at three o'clock in the afternoon. He made a general confession to Father Tomás de Jesús who gave him all the sacraments. He is the prior of the fathers of Brussels, and all of us nuns are under his jurisdiction, subjects of the province of Italy since those of ours in Spain have not wanted to take this province." Blessed Ana de San Bartolomé was very devoted to Father Gracián and often said that he was in heaven. In a letter written to

Juliana de la Madre de Dios, who was Father Gracián's sister and a Discalced Carmelite, Blessed Ana ends by saying, "We of this community commend ourselves to you, and we consider ourselves daughters of our Father Gracián who is in glory" (Letter 176 dated August 2, 1616, from Ana de San Bartolomé, *Cartas,* in *Ana de San Bartolomé obras completas,* ed. Julián Urkiza [Burgos, Spain: Editorial Monte Carmelo, 1999], 1078). To the prioress of Pamplona she writes, "I believe Your Reverence will take pleasure in the printed images of Father Jerónimo Gracián de la Madre de Dios, and since he is a saint you can with good reason esteem them" (Letter 171 dated January 15, 1616, from Ana de San Bartolomé, *Cartas,* 1068).

Appendix V: Declaration of the Rehabilitation

1. Taken from Camilo Maccise and Silvano Vescovi, "Official Declaration of the Rehabilitation of Father Jerome Gracián of the Mother of God, O.C.D.," *Carmelite Digest* 15, no. 3 (summer 2000), 73–76, and reprinted with permission. Originally published in Rome: Acta Ordinis Carmelitarum Discalceatorum (Anno 44), 1999, 46–49.
2. *Actas* refers to the acts of the general chapter.
3. See MHCT 9, pp. 184–85.
4. MHCT 9, pp. 599–600.
5. *L'Osservatore Romano,* December 18, 1999, p. 5.

Bibliography

Alvarez, Tomás. "Reviven las Constituciones de Santa Teresa entre Doria, San Juan de Ribera y Gracián." *Monte Carmelo* 88 (1980): 67–86.

Astigarraga, J. L., E. Pacho, and O. Rodriguez, eds. *Fuentes históricas sobre la muerte y el cuerpo de Santa Teresa de Jesús (1582–1596)*. Monumenta Historica Carmeli Teresiani (MHCT) 6. Rome: Institutum Historicum Teresianum, 1982.

Astigarraga, Juan Luis, ed. *Expulsión del P. Gracián: Documentos de un Proceso (1587–1601)*. MHCT 21; Monumenta Hieronymi Gracián (MHG) 3. Rome: Institutum Historicum Teresianum, 2004.

———. *Páginas de María de San José (Salazar)*. Contains the original of her "Instrucción de novicias." *Ephemerides Carmeliticae* (*EphCarm*) 29 (1978): 469–506.

Benedict XVI. *Jesus of Nazareth: From the Baptism in the Jordan to the Transfiguration.* New York: Doubleday, 2007.

Benigni, Umberto. "Propaganda, Sacred Congregation of." In *The Catholic Encyclopedia,* edited by Charles Herbermann, Edward Pace, Condé Pallen, Thomas Shahan, and John Wynne, 456–61. New York: Encyclopedia Press, 1913.

Bernard of Clairvaux. "On the Song of Songs II." Sermon 23, 9. In *The Works of Bernard of Clairvaux,* translated by Kilian Walsh, vol. 3, 33–34. Kalamazoo, Mich.: Cistercian Publications, 1976.

Britt, Matthew. *The Hymns of the Breviary and Missal.* New York: Benzinger Brothers, 1924.

Cervantes Saavedra, Miguel De. *Don Quixote of La Mancha.* Translated by John Ormsby. New York: Thomas Y. Crowell Co, 1920.

Florencio del Niño Jesús. *La Orden de Sta. Teresa, la fundación de Propaganda Fide y las misiones carmelitanas.* Madrid: Nieto, 1923.

García Hernán, Enrique. "El soldado católico de Jerónimo Gracián de la Madre de Dios." *Teresianism,* no. 1 (2011): 181–93.

Gracián, Jerome of the Mother of God. *Apología y avisos acerca del gobierno.* Rome: Institutum Historicum Teresianum, 1977.

———.*The Burning Lamp, or A Short Summary of Christian Perfection.* Edited by José L. Morales. Translated by Mary Regina Larkin. New York: Brooklyn Carmel, 1971.

———. *Cartas.* Edited by Juan Luis Astigarraga. MHCT 9; MHG 1. Rome: Institutum Historicum Teresianum, 1989.

———. *Diálogo de Angela y Eliseo*. Edited by Juan Luis Astigarraga, Otilio Rodriguez, and Eulogio Pacho. MHCT 6. Rome: Institutum Historicum Teresianum, 1982.

———. *Diálogos del tránsito de la M. Teresa de Jesús*. Edited by Juan Luis Astigarraga, Otilio Rodriguez, and Eulogio Pacho. MHCT 6. Rome: Institutum Historicum Teresianum, 1982.

———. *Escolias: A la vida de Santa Teresa compuesta por el P. Ribera*. Edited by Juan Luis Astigarraga. MHCT, Fontes selecti 3. *EphCarm* 32 (1981): 343–430.

———. *Historia de las fundaciones*. MHCT, Fontes selecti 1; MHCT 3, doc. 423, pp. 533–694. Rome: Institutum Historicum Teresianum, 1977.

———. *Just Man, Husband of Mary, Guardian of Christ: An Anthology of Readings from Jerónimo Gracián's Summary of the Excellencies of St. Joseph (1597)*. Edited and translated by Joseph Chorpenning. 2nd ed. Philadelphia: St. Joseph's University Press, 1993.

———. *Peregrinación de Anastasio*. Edited by Juan Luis Astigarraga. MHCT 19; MHG 2. Rome: Institutum Historicum Teresianum, 2001.

———. *Tránsito y ultima jornada de Teresa*. Edited by Juan Luis Astigarraga, Otilio Rodriguez, and Eulogio Pacho. MHCT 6. Rome: Institutum Historicum Teresianum, 1982.

———. *Jerome Gracian: Treatise on Melancholy*. Translated by Michael Dodd. Wisconsin Dells, Wisc.: Pileated Press, 2009.

Granada, Luis de, and Luis Muñoz. *Vida del Padre Maestro Juan de Ávila*. Edited by Luis Sala Balust. Barcelona: Juan Flors, 1964.

Gregory of St. Joseph. *Father Jerome Gratian O.C.D. and Those Who Judged Him*. Translated by John McGowan. Oxford, UK: Joshua Horgan Print and Design, 2014.

Henry-Coüannier, Maurice. *St. Francis de Sales and His Friends*. Translated by Veronica Morrow. New York: St. Paul Publications, 1964.

Ignatius of Loyola. *Spiritual Exercises*. Translated by George Ganss. In *Ignatius of Loyola: Spiritual Exercises and Selected Works*, The Classics of Western Spirituality, 113–214. Mahwah, NJ: Paulist Press, 1991.

———. *Autobiography*. Translated by Parmananda Divarkar. In *Ignatius of Loyola: Spiritual Exercises and Selected Works*, The Classics of Western Spirituality, 65–111. Edited by George Ganss. Mahwah, NJ: Paulist Press, 1991.

———. *St. Ignatius' Own Story as Told by Luis Gonzalez de Camara*. Translated by William J. Young. Chicago: Loyola Press, 1982.

Institutum Historicum Teresianum. *Documenta primigenia*. MHCT 1–4. Rome: 1973–1985.

John of the Cross. *The Ascent of Mount Carmel*. In *The Collected Works of St. John of the Cross*, translated by Kieran Kavanaugh and Otilio Rodriguez, 101–349. Washington, D.C.: ICS Publications, 1991.

———. *Sayings of Light and Love*. In *The Collected Works of St. John of the Cross*, translated by Kieran Kavanaugh and Otilio Rodriguez, 83–97. Washington, D.C.: ICS Publications, 1991.

———. *The Spiritual Canticle*. In *The Collected Works of St. John of the Cross*, translated by Kieran Kavanaugh and Otilio Rodriguez, 461–630. Washington, D.C.: ICS Publications, 1991.

———. *The Letters*. In *The Collected Works of St. John of the Cross*, translated by Kieran Kavanaugh and Otilio Rodriguez, 735–764. Washington, D.C.: ICS Publications, 1991.

Leonor de la Misericordia. *Relación de la vida de la venerable Catalina de Cristo*. Edited by Pedro Rodríguez and Ildefonso Adeva. Biblioteca Mística Carmelitana 28. Burgos, Spain: Editorial Monte Carmelo, 1995.

Llamas Martínez, Enrique. "Jerónimo Gracián Dantisco (de la Madre de Dios) en la Universidad de Alcalá (1560–1572)." *EphCarm* 26 (1975): 176–212.

———. "La 'Peregrinación de Anastasio' del Padre Jerónimo Gracián de la Madre de Dios: Nuevo manuscrito." *EphCarm* 28, no. 2 (1977): 278–310.

Maccise, Camilo, and Silvano Vescovi. "Official Declaration of the Rehabilitation of Father Jerome Gracián of the Mother of God, O.C.D." *Carmelite Digest* 15, no. 3 (summer 2000): 73–76.

Márquez, Cristóbal. *Excellencias, vida y trabajos del padre fray Gerónimo Gracián de la Madre de Dios, carmelita*. Valladolid, Spain: Francisco Fernández de Córdoba, 1619.

Mazzaoui, Maureen. *The Italian Cotton Industry In the Later Middle Ages, 1100–1600*. Cambridge: Cambridge University Press, 1981.

Moriones, Ildefonso. *The Papal Rehabilitation of Father Jerome Gracián in 1595*. Translated by John McGowan. Rome: Postulazione Generale O.C.D., 2006.

Pacho, Eulogio. *El Padre Gracián: Discípulo, amigo, provincial de Santa Teresa*. Burgos, Spain: Editorial Monte Carmelo, 1984.

Peers, E. Allison. *Handbook to the Life and Times of St. Teresa and St. John of the Cross*. London: Burns Oates, 1954.

Real Academia Española. *Diccionario de lengua española*. Madrid: Editorial Espasa-Calpe, 1947.

Rodriguez, Otilio. *A History of the Teresian Carmel: An Abridgement of Its Origins and Development, 1562–1979*. Darlington, UK: Darlington Carmel, n.d.

Rohrbach, Peter-Thomas. *Journey to Carith: The Story of the Carmelite Order*. Washington, D.C.: ICS Publications, 2001.

Ros, Carlos. *El hombre de Teresa de Jesús: Jerónimo Gracián*. Seville, Spain: Rosalibros, 2006.

Saggi, Louis. *Saints of Carmel*. Translated by Gabriel Pausback. Aylesford, Ill.: Carmelite Fathers, 1975.

San Bartolomé, Ana de. *Ana de San Bartolomé obras completas.* Edited by Julián Urkiza. Burgos, Spain: Editorial Monte Carmelo, 1998.

Shakespeare, William. *Julius Caesar.* In *Complete Works of William Shakespeare.* Garden City, N.Y.: Doubleday, 1936.

Smet, Joachim. *The Mirror of Carmel: A Brief History of the Carmelite Order.* Darien, Ill.: Carmelite Media, 2011.

Teresa of Jesus. *The Book of Her Foundations.* In *The Collected Works of St. Teresa of Avila,* translated by Kieran Kavanaugh and Otilio Rodriguez, 3:3–309. Washington, D.C.: ICS Publications, 1985.

———. *The Collected Letters of St. Teresa of Avila.* Translated by Kieran Kavanaugh. 2 vols. Washington, D.C.: ICS Publications, 2001–2007.

———. *Spiritual Testimonies.* In *The Collected Works of St. Teresa of Avila,* translated by Kieran Kavanaugh and Otilio Rodriguez, 1:369–438. Washington, D.C.: ICS Publications, 1976.

Urkiza, Julián. *Comienzos del Carmelo Teresiano Francés.* Burgos, Spain: Editorial Monte Carmelo, 2004.

———. *Noticias sobre los comienzos del Carmelo Teresiano. Obras completas.* Burgos, Spain: Editorial Monte Carmelo, 1998.

Watson, Stephen, trans. "An Account of the Brief Illness and Happy Death of Jerome Gracián." *Carmelite Digest* 24, no. 3 (fall 2009).

Weber, Alison. "Demonizing Ecstasy: Alonso de la Fuente and the Alumbrados of Extremadura." In *The Mystical Gesture: Essays on Medieval and Early Modern Spiritual Culture in Honor of Mary E. Giles,* edited by Robert Boenig, 147–65. Aldershot, UK: Ashgate, 2000.

Yeo, Margaret. *The Greatest of the Borgias.* Milwaukee: Bruce, 1936.

Biblical Index

Entries listed in bold refer to page numbers, all other entries list the dialogue (or appendix) followed by the paragraph. For example: **387n36** refers to note 36 on p. 387; **ixn2** refers to note 2 on p. ix; 15.5 refers to the Fifteenth Dialogue, paragraph 5; I.35 refers to Appendix I, paragraph 35.

Genesis
18:1–2 15.34
32:25–31 15.19

Exodus
3:2 15.34
28:29 15.5

Numbers
21:6–9 11.49

Joshua
1:8 15.16

1 Kings
10:1–13 10.2
17:7–24 **364n20**
18:30–38 1.9

Job
1:1–42:17 4.10, 4.14, 11.34
1:6–12 11.41

Psalms
4 11.62
7 11.62
9 11.62
19(18):4(5) 3.23
31(30):2 11.32
37:24 10.9
39(38):3 11.35
39(38):4 15.17
51(50) 11.30, **378n18**, **381n32**
51(50):6 11.34
55:13 2.1
71(70):1 11.32
87(86) 11.62
89(88):2 10.8
91(90):11–12 10.9
94(93):20 10.84
106(105) 11.62
119(118):17 11.62
119(118):67 11.29
119(118):71 8.9, 11.27
119(118):92 11.36, I.13
119(118):121 11.46
120(119) 11.62
120(119):2 11.62
120(119):4 11.62
122(121):3 15.73
146(145):3 11.32
147(146):10 13.4
147:14 16.8

Proverbs
24:16 2.4, 4.39, 10.47

Song of Songs
1:1–8:14 15.60
1:5–6 **392n16**
2:5 11.50
2:6 15.87
2:7 15.87
4:4 11.1
4:16 16.36
5:2 15.87
7:1 **364n20**
7:2 2.12

Wisdom
5:1 5.5, 11.42
7:11 15.21

Sirach
41:12 2.3

Isaiah
3:12 16.59
5:2, 4 13.2
24:16 **359n2**
30:15 11.35
55:4 11.1

Jeremiah
17:5 11.32

Lamentations
3:30 16.52

Micah
6:8 11.47

Habakkuk
2:4 15.33
3:16 8.7, **372n5**

Matthew
3:9 15.24
5:13 13.2
5:15 9.26
5:15–16 15.3
5:44 11.9, 11.17, 11.24
5:45 11.18
6:9 15.74
7:2 11.24
7:3–5 4.15
7:14 11.33
7:18 13.2
14:1–12 2.12
15:1–20 4.15
20:22 8.7
23:37 10.82
26:39 8.5, 11.39
26:42 11.39

Mark
10:38 8.7

Luke
2:41–47 11.2
6:27 11.9, 11.19
6:35 11.9
6:41–42 4.15
7:36–50 4.15
7:37–38 2.12
11:2 15.74
11:5 15.75
14:26 11.26
19:1–10 2.12

John
3:8 15.18
3:14 11.49
6:13 15.72
8:49 2.3
9 4.15
9:2 4.37
9:3 4.38, 4.44
11:50 2.10
12:24 13.1
16:2 **366n7**

Acts of the Apostles
11:28 **374n7**
21:10–14 **374n7**

Romans
1:16 11.6
5:3 Pref 1, I.46
5:3–5 8.8
8:18 11.55
9:3 **xxiii**, 2.26, V.6
10:18 3.23
11:36 15.72

1 Corinthians
2:11 15.3
4:2 15.3
13:3 9.22

13:4 9.22, 11.43
14:19 15.10

2 Corinthians
1:3–6 Prol 3
1:4 11.3, 15.3
1:6 8.20
5:7 15.33
11:14 11.5
12:1–2 15.34
12:2 15.24
12:6 Prol 3

Ephesians
6:12 11.1

Philippians
1:18 **378n13**
2:8–9 11.26
3:8 11.45

1 Thessalonians
5:21–22 15.83

2 Timothy
2:5 11.55
3:12 3.16

Hebrews
4:15 8.40, 11.49
11:1 15.33
12:4 11.52

James
1:17 15.3
3:6 16.30

Revelation
3:19 11.17
12:1 9.4, 12.2
21:10–13 15.5
21:27 11.55

Index

Entries listed in bold refer to page numbers, all other entries list the dialogue (or appendix) followed by the paragraph. For example: **387n36** refers to note 36 on p. 387; **ixn2** refers to note 2 on p. ix; 15.5 refers to the Fifteenth Dialogue, paragraph 5; I.35 refers to Appendix I, paragraph 35.

A

Aaron, 15.5
abandonment, interior and exterior, 8.34–8.36
Abbas I, I.35, **387n36**
Abbey of Saints Vincent and Anastasius, **ixn2**
abbot provisor (Valladolid), 3.16, 13.64, **363n13**
Abdelquirin El Mesuar, Mumen ben, 14.25, **387n28**
Acarie, Barbara, **385n85**
accusations. *See also* persecution
  about relationship with a repentant woman, 8.15–8.16
  about relationship with María de San José, 10.46, **376n26**, **383n58**
  by the Calced friars of Andalusia, 1.14–1.15, 1.29–1.31, 2.10, 2.25, 2.29–2.30, 2.32, 4.19–4.28, 10.39, I.12–I.14, **362n18**
  by the Discalced, 2.33, 4.6–4.8, 10.45, 16.45, **392n18**
  false testimonies, 7.15–7.21
  leading to expulsion, 4.19–4.28
  by Miguel de la Columna, 2.22
  by nuns, 1.35, 2.3–2.4, 16.27, **361n26**
  by Pedro de San Angel, 2.23
ACFRIC hieroglyph, 10.2–10.7, 11.2, 11.60–11.62, **378n1**, **379n29**
  A: love of enemies and contempt of self, 11.9–11.27
  C: contrition and confidence, 11.28–11.32
  F: living faith and fortitude, 11.33–11.37
  R: resignation and renunciation, 11.38–11.45
  I: justice and judgment, and imitation of Christ, 11.46–11.50
  C: consideration and counsel, 11.51–11.59
Acosta, José de, SJ, 5.16, I.28, **368n10**
afflictions. *See* trials and tribulations
Aga, Abrahim (*casaca* of the Pasha), 6.31–6.32
Agabus, 9.5, **374n7**
Aguilera, Catalina de, 13.66
Alonso de la Cruz, 7.4, 7.6, 7.8–7.9. *See also* Mami
Alarcón, Juan de, 14.10
Albert, St. (patriarch of Jerusalem), 9.5, 12.9, **373n2**, **374n5**
Albert VII of Austria (cardinal archduke), **xv**, 2.9, 3.31–3.32, 3.34, 3.44, 4.1, 13.94, 13.107, 14.5, 14.16, 14.29, 14.39, I.21, I.26, I.38, **361n4**, **365n27**, **365n34**
Alberto, Brother, 2.18–2.19
Albucarín, Cid (alcaide), 7.24, 11.18

Albuquerque, Matías de (viceroy of India), 4.5, 6.3, **369n4**

Alcalá de Henares (Madrid), *chapter* 2.9, 3.8, I.21, **394n10**; *university* **xi**, **xvin14**, 1.4, 5.16, 8.10, 8.14, 8.16, 10.13, 12.4, 13.25, I.6; *College of St. Cyril* 2.32, 3.18, 13.11, 13.25, 13.51, 16.25, I.4, I.18, **363n16**; *hermitage of Vera Cruz* 13.44, I.5, **393n1**; *OCD nuns La Concepción monastery* 11.21, 13.41, 13.110, **385n87**, **386n8**; *OCD friars monastery* 2.32–2.33, 13.63, 14.40, 16.25, I.6, I.21, II.4, **362n22**, **392n10**, **395n8**

Alejandrino,(Alessandrino), Cardinal (Michele Bonelli, OP), 14.9, **386n9**

Alexandre, Francisco, OP, 5.14, **368n8**

Alexis, St., 13.64

Alhambra, 13.49, **381n28**

Aljubarrota, battle of, 3.34

Almodóvar del Campo (Ciudad Real), *OCD friars monastery* 13.39–13.40, **363n11**

Altomira (Albacete), *OCD friars monastery* 13.11, 13.27–13.29, I.4

Alvarez de Toledo, Fernando (duke of Alba), 3.10, 10.42, **376n23**, **376n25**

Alvaro (king of the Congo), 3.19

Amatarráez, Bey, 6.53, 7.11

Ambrosio Mariano de San Benito (Azaro), 1.9, 1.19, 2.17, 2.23, 2.26, 3.12, 6.2, 13.18–13.19, 13.23–13.24, 13.32–13.37, 13.46, 13.72, 13.94, 15.65, I.4–I.6, I.22, **360n9**, **392n18**

Ambrosio de San Pedro, 13.26

Amiens (France), *OCD nuns monastery*, 13.109, I.37

Ana de Jesús (Lobera), **xxiv**, 13.55, 13.83, 13.90, 13.107–13.108, 13.109, 16.47, I.37–I.38, II.5–6, V.1, V.4, **361n7**, **383nn64–67**, **395n9**

Ana de San Bartolomé, Blessed, **xix**, **xxiv**, 16.42, 16.44–16.45, 16.93–16.95, I.37, II.5, **362n22**, **392n15**, **396n4**

Anastasius of Persia, St., **ix**, **387n35**

Andalusia, *Calced friars* 2.26–2.34, 16.22–16.25; *O.Carm. Visitation* **xiii**, 1.20, 1.24–1.27, 1.29–1.35, 3.35, 14.4, 16.21, 16.37, I.10–I.12, **385n5**

Angela di Foligno, St., 15.3, 15.90

Angelus of Jerusalem, St., 9.5, 12.12

Anna of Austria (queen), 3.6, **363n5**

Anthony of the Desert, St., 11.5, **378n2**

Antonia del Espíritu Santo (Henao), 6.1, **368n1**

Antonio, Fray (Portuguese friar), 13.39

Antonio, prior of Crato, 3.31, 3.33–3.34, 13.72, 13.94, 14.5, 14.39, I.26, **365n29**, **365n33**

Antonio de Jesús (Heredia), **xiii**, 2.18, 2.26, 13.14, 13.17, 13.94, I.3, **363n8**

Antonistas, 3.31–3.32, 3.46, **365n28**

Apeles, 11.12, **378n5**

Apología (Gracián), 14.37

Apología y avisos acerca del gobierno (Gracián), **xx**, **xxii**

Apostolic Camera, 9.11, **374n20**

Apostolicae Sedis benignitas (papal brief), V.7, **375n21**

Aquasparta, duchess of, 13.102, I.32

Aquino, Tomás de, 4.42, **367n16**

al-Arache (river), 14.25, I.40

Arbol prodigioso (Gracián), 12.10, 12.12

"An Argument for Charity" (Gracián), **377n28**

Aristeas, 10.2, **375n1**

Aristotle, 15.59, **390n21**

Armenian Christians, **xxv**, I.35, **377n38**, **388n36**

Armonía mística (Gracián), 5.19, 6.10

Arras, *O.Carm. friars* 13.112, 14.16

Asán, Captain, 6.53, 7.11, **371n8**

Assumption, Feast of the, 6.7, **369n11**

Astigarraga, Juan Luis, **vii**, **xxxv–xxxviii**, **359n1**, **372n1**, **373n7**, **379n5**
Astorga vision, 2.16, 15.32, 15.43
Audi filia (John of Ávila), 16.52, **392n23**
Augustine, St., Pref 2, 4.12, 8.7, 11.26, 14.8, 15.3, I.29, V.4
Augustinians, 14.6, **385n6**; *Augustinian canonesses* 14.13–14.14. *See also* Discalced Augustinians
Auñón, marquis of, 14.12
Ávila, *OCD nuns monastery* 13.81, 13.90, I.3, **383n59**; *OCD friars* **396n1**
Ávila, Julián de, 13.81–13.82, **383n57**
Ayala, Inés de, 14.29
Ayala, Juan de, 14.29
Ayanz, Francés de, 13.96–13.97, I.23
Ayanz, Jerónimo de, 13.96
Azevedo, Pedro Enríquiz de, 3.33

B

Babylas of Antioch, St., **360n7**
Baeza (Jaén), *OCD college* 13.52, 13.63; *Disc. Fran. nuns monastery* 13.53
Balboa, Pedro de San Angel de, 2.23
Ballibrera, Captain, 14.13
Baltasar de Jesús (Nieto), 1.7, 1.13, I.4, **360n9**
Baltasara (Franciscan or Poor Clare nun), 14.12
Báñez, Domingo, OP, **388n42**
baños. *See* Turkish capture and imprisonment
barberos, 6.41, **370n28**
Barcelona, *OCD nuns monastery*, I.23, **377n33**; *university*, **386n18**
Barnabas, St., 4.12–4.13, 4.37
Baronio, César (cardinal), 13.102, 13.104, **371n20**, **384n78**
Barreto, Francisco, 14.29
Bartolomé de Jesús, 13.49, I.21, V.4
Basil, St., 9.5
Basilio, Fray, 13.39, 13.48
Bautista de la Trinidad, 3.35
Bazán, Alvaro de (marquis of Santa Cruz), 3.33
Beamonte, Beatriz de, 13.96
Beas de Segura (Jaén), *OCD nuns monastery* **xiii**, 10.33, 13.55, 13.78, 13.80, 16.7, 16.14, 16.60, 16.84, I.8, **360n10**, **362n15**, **376n14**, **393n3**
Beatriz de la Concepción, I.37
beguines and beguinages, III.4, **396nn9–10**
Bellarmine, Robert, St. (cardinal), 13.73
Benedict XVI, **375n1**
Benito de Jesús y la Virgen, 3.13–3.14, 10.21, 13.41–13.42, I.15, **363n12**, **375n10**
Bentivoglio, Guido (nuncio in Flanders), 13.112, II.2
bezoars, 1.34, **361n25**
Bernard, St., Prol 2, 10.18
Bernardine nuns (of Odivelas and Toledo), 3.46, 13.67, 14.10
Berthold, 9.3
Bérulle, Pierre de, 13.109, **385n84**
bizcocho, 6.11, 6.15, **369n19**
Blas de San Alberto, 13.51
Bobadilla, Andrés de, 1.4, 10.18
Bonaventure, St., 10.55, 12.10, **377n32**
Bond of Brotherhood. *See* Vinculo de hermandad
Bonelli, Michele. *See* Alejandrino, cardinal
Book of Her Foundations (Teresa of Ávila), **x**, **xxi**, I.2, V.7, **380n2**, **381n26**, **381n34**
Bora, Catalina (wife of Martin Luther), I.45
Borja, Pedro Luis Garcerán de (master of Montesa), 5.7, **367n3**
Borromeo, Federico (cardinal), **xxviii**
Bouyer, Louis, **xxxi–xxxii**

Braganza, Teutonio de (archbishop of Evora), 3.27, 14.35, **364n24**
Brétigny, Juan de Quintanadueñas, 13.109, I.37, **384n83**, **391n7**
breviary, loss of, 6.26–6.28
Bridget, St., Prol 3, 15.3
Bridgetine nuns (Tournai, Flanders), 14.38
Brief of Separation (*Pia consideratione*), 2.34, 3.2, 3.5–3.7, **362n2**, **362n14**, **362n24**
Brothers of John of God, **386n16**
Brothers of Obregón, 14.15, **386n16**
Bruno, Giordano, **377n35**
Brussels, *OCD friars monastery* I.41, II.6, **396n1**, **397n4**; *OCD nuns monastery* **xxxvi**, 13.108, **319**, I.38, I.43, **393n26**; *O.Carm. friars monastery* **xxv**, III.3, **395n7**; *Carthusians* **388n50**
Brutus, 2.1
Bujalance (Córdoba), *OCD friars monastery* 13.57
Burgos, *OCD nuns monastery* **xix**, 13.78, 13.90, 13.92–13.93, **383n65**

C

cabezones, 3.41, **365n43**
Caballero de Gracia. *See* Gratiis, Jacobo de
Cabria, Fernando de, 13.64
Caffardo, Giovanni Battista (O.Carm. general), 3.47
Calancha, Juana, 13.55
Calced Carmelites, *passim*
  of Andalusia, 1.20, 3.35, I.10
  of Portugal, 3.34–3.35
  reform of, 14.4–14.6, **385n3**
  of San Martín in Montibus (Rome), 7.34, 9.18, I.34, **371n20**, **375n22**
Calderón, Father (O.Carm.), 3.34
Cano, Melchor, OP, 14.33, 15.90, **388n42**
captivity. *See* Turkish capture and imprisonment
Capuchins, 5.14, 10.49–10.50, 10.55, 13.73, 13.107, 14.24, 14.37–14.38, **372n22**, **377n32**, **387nn25–26**
Caravaca (Murcia), *OCD nuns monastery* 13.78, 13.83
Caravaggio, **385n6**
Cardona, Catalina de, 13.43–13.47, I.5
Cardona y Borja, Felipe Folch de (marquis of Guadaleste, ambassador to Flanders), II.6, **395n11**, **396n2**
Carmelite Order, **xx**, **xiin8**. *See also* Calced Carmelites; Discalced Carmelites
  Rule of, xxxii, 9.4, 9.19, 13.19, 13.69, 13.102, 13.106, 15.16, 16.37, 16.84, 16.91, I.4, I.32, **373n2**, **374n5**, **383n60**
  writings about, 12.12
Carranza, Miguel de, O.Carm., 3.47
"Cartas a príncipes y señores" (Gracián), 12.11
Carthusians, 3.24, 5.14, 10.49–10.50, 13.86, 14.37–14.38, **383n61**
Carvajal, Jerónimo de, 13.65
Carvajal, Luisa, **xxix**, **394n3**
Casaz, Juan, 6.31
Castellar, countess of. *See* Ramírez de Mendoza, Beatriz
Castelo Branco, Duarte de, count of Sabugal (Meirinho-mor), 14.29
Castilla, Juana de, 14.9
Castro del Río (Córdoba), *O.Carm. friars monastery* 14.4
Catalina de Cristo (Balmaseda), 13.95, 16.83, I.23, **384n73**
Catalina de Jesús (Sandoval y Godínez), 13.55, 16.60–16.64, 16.85, **381n34**
Catherine (duchess of Longueville), 13.109, I.37, **385n85**, **394n16**

Catherine of Alexandria, St. (martyr), 16.56
Catherine of Genoa, St., 15.3
Catherine of Siena, St., **xvii**, 15.3, **368n9**
Cazalla, Agustín de, 8.15, 13.43, **373n11**
Cepeda, Lorenzo de, 13.84, **383n59**
Cepeda, Teresita de, 13.84, **383n59**
cerraje, 6.44, **370n34**
Cervantes, Miguel, **360n5**, **369n2**, **375n7**, **380n6**
Céspedes, Alonso de, Captain, 14.29
charity, **xxii**, **xxxii**, 9.22, 10.48, 11.43, 14.2, 15.21–15.30, 15.36, 15.79, **377n28**, **389n8**
Charles Borromeo, St., **xxviii**, **360n20**
Charles I, **xin6**, **359n2**
Charles V, **373n11**, **378n19**
Chinchón, count and countess of, 1.4
Chorpenning, Joseph, **xxvi**
Clement VIII, **xxiii**, 7.37, 8.33, 9.30, 10.31, 12.10, 13.14, 13.73, 13.102, 14.6, 14.9, 14.13, 14.23, I.32, I.39–I.40, III.2, V.7, **367n7**, **372n22**, **372n28**, **375n21**, **375n24**, **380n12**, **387n24**, **387n26**, **388n36**
clothing, types of, 9.22–9.25, 10.75, **375nn25–27**
College of Alcalá. *See* Alcalá de Henares/College of St. Cyril
College of Baeza. *See* Baeza/college
College of Cuenca. *See* Salamanca/College of Cuenca
College of Louvain, I.41
Colón, Cristóbal, 14.13, **386n13**
commissions
  by Cardinal Albert, to Portugal, 2.9, 3.34, 4.1, 4.43, 14.5, I.26, **361n4**
  by Clement VIII, to Africa, **xxiv**, 3.39, 7.36–7.37, 14.13, **372n22**, **387n26**
  by Francisco de Vargas (from Pius V), to Andalusia, 1.20, 13.80, I.6; *cessation of* 1.25, I.10
  for Fray Juan de las Cuevas, 3.6–3.7, I.21
  for Fray Pedro Fernández, 3.5–3.6, I.20, **363n4**
  by Ormaneto (from Gregory XIII), to Andalusia and Castile, 1.26–1.27, 2.24, I.10, I.12, **360n21**
  for Teresa of Jesus, to found Discalced friars, I.9
Company of Jesus. *see* Jesuits
confidence in God, 6.30, 13.34, 13.36, 11.31–11.32
Congregation for Religious, 9.11, 14.9, I.33
Congregation for the Causes of the Saints, **394n5**
Congregation for the Propagation of the Faith, **xxvii**, 7.36, 12.10, 13.106, 14.19, 14.23, 14.26, I.40, **372n21**, **384n82**, **387n24**, **387n34**
Congregation of St. Paul, OCD, 13.106, **384n81**
Congregation of the Oratory of Our Lady of Vallicella, 13.103
conscience
  perplexity of, as a cross, 2.29–2.31
  security of, 15.28
consolations, **xvii**, **xxviii**, 2.11, 8.21, I.15; *interior* 11.1–11.62, I.18; *exterior* 10.1–10.85
Consuegra (Toledo), *OCD nuns monastery* 10.30, II.3, II.7, **388n42**, **391n2**, **391n3**, **393n97**, **394n1**, **393n4**
"Consuelos y desconsuelos interiores de las almas atribuladas" (Gracián), 12.11
consulta, 2.9–2.10, 4.1–4.5, 4.13, 4.28, 4.32, 4.35, 4.41, 4.43–4.44, 7.34, 8.31, 9.19–9.21,10.11, 10.47, 11.14, 11.18, 16.41, I.27, **366n4**, **367n5**, **375n4**
contemplation, 10.6, 11.43, 15.6, 15.19–15.30, 15.50–15.51

Contemptus mundi, 15.66, **390n24**
Contreras, 14.29
contrition for past sins, 6.50, 11.2, 11.28–11.30
conversions, **xx**, 3.19–3.22, 7.1–7.9, 10.72, 13.59, 13.73, 13.94, 13.106, 14.17–14.32, I.25, I.35
Copernicus, Nicolaus, **xi**
Córdoba, Andrés de (auditor of the Rota), 13.57, 13.66
Córdoba, Antonio Fernández de, 10.56, **377nn33–34**
Córdoba, Juana de, 10.56, **377n33**
Córdoba, *OCD friars monastery* 13.56–13.57
Coria, Diego de, 3.12
"Corona de doce estrellas" (Gracián), 15.27, 12.12
Council of Orange, 15.24, **389n9**
Council of Trent, **xxix**, 1.8, I.34, III.3, **361n24**, **381n17**, **385n3**, **386n17**
counsel, 5.16, 8.32, 10.36, 10.51, 11.2–11.3, 11.58–11.59,14.15–14.16, 16.65–16.85, 16.87–16.91, 16.93–16.95, I.28, **393n27**
Count of Fuentes. *See* Azevedo, Pedro Enríquiz de
Count of Osorno, 13.89
Count of Tendilla. *See* Mendoza, Luis Hurtado de
Cristina de San José, I.43
Cristóbal de Moura, 3.31, **365n30**
Cristóbal de San Alberto, 13.68
Cruzat, Margarita de, 13.74
Cruzat, Martín de Jesús María, 13.74, 13.97, I.23, **384n75**
Cuevas, Juan de las, OP, 2.9, 2.23, 3.6–3.7, I.21, **362n14**
Cyprian, St., 11.63
Cyril of Constantinople, St., **ix**

D

Damiel (Ciudad Real), *OCD friars monastery* 13.50
Dantisco, Juana (mother of J. Gracián), **x–xi**, **xvii**, **xxiv**, 1.13, 2.27, 4.35, 7.36, 9.8, 10.35, 10.37, 16.29–16.30, I.17, **359n2**, **360n13**, **366n12**, **368n19**, **372n24**
Dantyszek, Jan (Juan Dantisco, Gracián's grandfather), **x–xi**
David (king), 2.1, 10.9, 11.46, 11.61–11.63, 13.5, 13.70, 15.29, I.13, **361n2**, **380n1**
Dávila, Gil González, SJ, 9.6, **374n9**
"De la ceguedad de Babilonia" (Gracián), 12.11
De la disciplina regular (Gracián), 9.4, 12.11, **374n5**
"De potestate Papae" (Gracián), 12.11
De redención de cautivos (Gracián), 12.10, 14.23
death, remembrance of, 1.26–1.27, 3.36, 3.41, 6.9, 6.49–6.50, 7.6, 11.53, 15.12, 15.15, 15.84
Denia (Alicante), *Discalced Augustinian nuns Monastery* 14.14
Denis the Carthusian, 11.56
devil
  and Catalina de Cardona, 13.46
  deceptions of, 1.6, 8.30, 11.5, 13.55, 14.33, 14.36, 15.23, 15.33, 15.43, 15.78, 16.65
  dreams from, 15.82–15.83, **391n29**
  fighting, with God's defenses, 10.82, 11.1
  Lucifer's threats, 2.11
  temptations of, 8.38, 16.36, **378n2**
  visions of, 2.14–2.21
  works of, 2.7–2.10, 2.13, 2.23, 3.26, 4.10, 9.1, 10.23, 11.42, 11.46, 13.24, 14.2, 14.20, 16.97, I.12

Deza, Alfonso de, SJ, 8.10, **373n8**
Deza, Pedro (cardinal, protector of Spain), **xxiv**, 7.35, 9.18, 10.53, 11.22, 13.105, 14.6, 14.32, 14.41, I.34, I.37
Dialogues of Eliseo (Gracián), **xxxviii**, **367n6**
Díaz, Juan, 16.51–16.52
Diego (silversmith), 10.80
Diego de la Trinidad, 3.3, 13.41, I.14
Diego del Sacramento, 3.19
Diego Evangelista, 13.39, **367n5**, **392n18**, **392n21**
Dilucidario del verdadero espíritu (Gracián), **xxvii**, 9.4, 12.9, 15.27, 15.64
Dionysius the Areopagite, St., 6.8
Discalced Augustinians, **xxiii**, 5.20–5.21, 7.33, 8.36, 9.9, 9.11, 9.24, 10.66, 14.6–14.8, 14.13–14.14, I.29, I.34, **368n16**, **368n18**, **394n11**
Discalced Carmelites, **ix**, **x**, **xi**, **xiv–xv**, **xx–xxi**, **xxiii–xxv**
  Brief of Separation, 2.34, 3.2, 3.5–3.7, **362n2**, **362n14**, **362n24**
  expulsion from. *See* expulsion
  faults and punishments in constitution of, **367n18**
  fears of dissolution of, 2.27–2.31, 3.11, **362nn20–21**
  foundations made while prelate, 13.32–13.76
  foundations of, *nuns* 13.77–13.112; *friars, before made prelate* 13.10–13.31
  good deeds done for, 11.19–11.23, **378n9**
  growth of, 10.36
  habits worn, 9.22–9.24
  letter to a friend giving an account of, I
  obedience to the Calced, 3.14–3.15
  order established by Clement VIII, **375n24**
  persecution of by the Calced, 9.8, **374n14**
  profession to, 9.7, 13.29, **380n13**
  purpose of, 13.112, **385n89**
  readmittance to, 9.11, 9.28–9.30, **371n20**, **375n21**, **392n24**
  vocation of, 10.50
Discalced Dominicans, 14.9
Discalced Franciscans, 13.24, 13.53, 14.19, **386n19**
Discalced Jeronimites, 14.11, **386n8**
Discalced Mercerdarians, **xxix**, 14.8
Discalced Trinitarians, **xxix**, 13.29, 14.7, 14.8, I.34, **380n12**
"Disciplina regular" (Gracián), 12.11, **374n5**
Domingo, Fray, 16.97
Dominicans, 5.15, 13.62, 13.94, 14.9. *See also* Discalced Dominicans
Don Quixote (Cervantes), **xxx**, **360n5**, **369n2**, **375n7**, **380n6**
donados, 3.36, **365n42**
Doria, Nicolás de Jesús María, **xv**, **xix**, **xx**, 2.23, 3.19, 4.35, 10.11, 13.35, 13.73, 13.75, 14.21, I.22, I.24, **361n7**, **361n9**, **363n8**, **364n17**, **365n34**, **366n10–11**, **367n17**, **375n4**, **379n8**, **379n22**, **381nn19–21**, **381n23**, **382n51**, **383n58**, **387n21**, **390n22**, **392n18**
doubloons, value of, 1.23, 3.43, 5.7, 10.80, **360n18**
Drake, Francis, **xv**, 3.33, 3.43, 13.72, 13.94, 14.5, I.26, **365n33**
dreams, 15.6, 15.81–15.84, 15.90, **391n30**
drowning at sea, multiple dangers of, 6.4–6.7, 10.51, 10.82, I.28, **369nn5–6**, **378n48**

Duralí, Captain, 6.21, 6.26
Duruelo (Ávila), *OCD friars monastery* 13.15–17, I.3, **359n4**

E

ecstasies, 15.6, 15.32, 15.89–15.90
El Calvario, *OCD friars monastery* 13.61
El devoto peregrino (Gracián), 12.10
"El soldado católico" (Gracián), 12.11
Elías de San Martín (Hériz), xxiii, 2.33, 13.29–13.30, 14.7, 16.25, 16.45, V.6, V.10, **371n19**, **380n11–15**, **392n19**
Elijah (prophet), 1.9, 3.25, 9.3, 9.5, 13.35
Elisbey, Captain, 6.21–6.22, 6.25–6.26
Elisha (prophet), 3.25, 9.5
Eliseo de los Mártires, 13.54, **381n33**
enemies, love of, 11.2, 11.9–11.24, **378n3**
English Armada, **xv**, 3.33–3.34, 3.36, 3.43, **365n33**, **365n38**, **365n41**
Enríquez, Enrico Silvio (O.Carm. general), 13.112, **385n88**
Erasmus, **390n24**
Escanasi, Simón, 7.25–7.32, 10.83, **371n13**, **371n15**
Escobedo, Juan, **363n15**
escopetas, 6.8, 6.10–6.11, **369n15**
Estímulo de la propagación de la fe (Gracián), **xxvii**, 12.10, 14.19, **387n21**
Eugene IV, 9.22
Euphrasia, St., 9.5
Ex omnibus, **371n19**
"Excelencia y valor de nuestra santa fe católica" (Gracián), 12.11
excommunication, 2.26, 3.16, 4.36, 5.4, 9.9, 13.64, 16.21
expulsion, **xv**, **xxi**, **xxiii**, **xxviii**, **xxxvi**, 2.3, **361n8**, **368n16**, **379n22**, **381n21**, **393n32**, **395n1**
  affronts suffered in Naples, 5.17
  affronts suffered in Rome, 5.10–5.16
  charges leading to, 4.18–4.28, 4.39, 4.43
  departure from Rome, 5.17–5.20
  fruits of, 13.99–13.112
  habit taken away, 4.30, 13.100
  innocence, proof of, 4.41–4.42
  patent to be vicar general of the Indies, 4.4–4.5
  rejection by other orders, 5.14–5.16
    as a result of the *consulta*, 4.1–4.6, 9.9, **374n15**
  revoking of, 9.11–9.16, V.3
  rumors following from, 4.31–4.32
  sentence of, 4.6, **366n6**
  travel from Madrid to Rome following, 4.36, 5.2, 5.6–5.10, **367n1**

F

Fadrique, Don, 10.42, 14.9
faith, living, 11.2, 11.33–11.34, 15.70, 16.1
Faxardo, Luisa, II.1, **394n3**
fear, as a cross, 8.26
Febronia, St., 9.5
Fernández, Pedro, 3.5–3.6, I.20, **363nn3–4**
Ferrer, Jerónimo, 14.4
Fevre, Carlos, 14.38, **389n51**
Flores, María, 13.53
"Flores Carmeli" (Gracián), 5.19, 9.4, 10.61, 12.11, **368n15**
food, 1.4, 1.11, 1.34, 3.39, 6.16, 6.21, 6.38, 9.22, 10.16–10.21, 10.69, 10.75, 10.80
fortitude, 11.35–11.37
The Foundations of the Discalced (Gracián). *See Fundaciones de los Carmelitas Descalzos*
Francis, St., **xvii**, 13.16, I.3, **380n7**
Francis Borgia, St., **373n11**
Francis de Sales, St., **xvii–xviii**, **391n7**
Francis Xavier, St., 13.97, I.23, **384n76**
Francisco, Fray, 13.68, 13.112

Francisco de Jesús el Indigno (Hernández), 3.19, 12.5–12.6, 13.70, 14.20, **379n3**
Francisco de la Concepción, **381n14**
Frígola, Dean, 14.15
Fuensanta monastery, 13.58–13.61
Fundaciones de los Carmelitas Descalzos (Gracián), **xxi**, 13.8, **380n2**, **382n52**, **387n22**, **389n4**

G

Gabriel de la Asumptión, **363n8**
Gabriel de la Asunción, 13.26
Gaitán, Antonio, 13.83
galeotas, 6.8, 6.15–6.19, 6.21, 10.74, 11.56, I.30, **369n14**
gamberes, 7.7, 9.24, **371n6**, **375n26**
García, Fray, 13.48
García, Pedro, 9.6
Garro, Miguel, 14.6
Gebre, Abraham, 7.24
Genoa, *OCD friars monastery* xv, 13.73, 13.75, 13.105, I.22, I.35, **361n5**; *OCD nuns monastery* 13.102; *O.Carm. friars monastery* 5.8
Gesualdo, Cardinal, 14.30
glory, consideration of, 11.55
Godoy, Juan Pérez de, 13.71
Gómez, Francisco de Jesús, 13.28–13.30, I.4
Gómez de Silva, Ruy (prince), 1.13, 1.16–1.18, 13.18, 13.20, 13.44, I.4–I.5, **380n8**
Grace and Justice tribunal, 10.54, 13.106, **377n30**
Gracián, Adriana del Espíritu Santo, **367n1**
Gracián, Antonio, 8.9, 10.34, **359n3**, **373n6**
Gracián de Alderete, Diego (J. Gracián's father), **x**, 10.60–11.32, **359n2**, **378n19**
Gracián, Jerome
acquaintances, **xxviii–xxix**
apostolic visitations. *See* commissions
attempts to make him bishop, 4.33–4.35
burial, V.7, **395n7**
capture and imprisonment, **xxiii**. *See also* Turkish capture and imprisonment
as a Carmelite, **xi–xv**
charges against Gracián, 4.18–4.28, 4.39, 4.43
chronology, **xli–lviii**
clothing of, 4.30, 5.2, 6.16, 9.22–9.25, 10.75, I.28–I.30, I.33, **375nn25–27**
death, **xxv**, V.6, **372n30**, **396n4**
desires impressed upon by God, 14.2–14.3
as a Discalced Carmelite, **ix**, **xiv–xv**
early years, **x–xi**, 8.4
education, 8.4, 8.10–8.14, 10.13, 12.3–12.4, 15.9, **373nn9–10**
expulsion, **xv–xvi**, **xxi**, **xxii**, **xxx**, **361n8**. *See also* expulsion
faults, 16.2–16.3
good works, **xxix**, **xxxii**, 13.1–13.10, 15.47, 16.83, II.1
and his brothers, **xix–xxi**
illness, V.2–V.5
imprisonment before expulsion, **xv**, 4.30, **366n8**
joining of the Calced Carmelites, 9.17–9.19, 9.22–9.23, 9.28–9.30, I.34, III.2–III.3
ordination, **xi**, 8.15, **360n8**
pilgrimage, **xxii–xxv**, 10.64
rehabilitation, **xxx–xxxii**, V.1–V.11, **375n21**, **393n32**
restoration to Discalced Carmelites, **xxiii–xxv**, 9.11–9.18, 9.24, 9.28–9.30, **371n20**, **375n28**

sentenced and imprisoned by Sega, **xv**, 2.26, I.15, **392n17**
and Teresa of Ávila, **xii**, **xiii–xiv**, **xvi–xix**, **xxiv**, **xxv**, **xxx**, 3.8, 8.39, 13.80, **360n10**
and Teresian charism, **xx–xxii**
writings, **xxv–xxvii**, 12.1–12.12. *See also* specific titles
Gracián, Jerome–correspondence
to Alfonso de Narvaez, III
to Francisca de Las Llagas and María de San José, II
to a friend, I
with Teresa of Ávila, **xvii**, 10.26, 10.37, 16.4–16.37, II.4, **376n12**, **376nn14–18**, **381n15**, **395n8**
Gracián, Lorenzo, **xxxvii**, **364n22**, **396n1**
Gracián, Luis, 13.68
Gracián, Teresa, II.10, **395n10**
Gracián, Tomás, **xxx**, **395n10**
Granada, Luis de, 3.33, 10.42, 13.70, 14.34, 15.13, **365n35**, **376n25**, **388n43**
Granada, *OCD nuns monastery* 13.90, **383n65**
Gratiis, Jacobo de, 14.12, **386n12**
Gregory of Nyssa, St., Pref 3
Gregory XIII, 1.26, 2.9, 2.34, 10.38, I.10, I.20, **387n24**
Gregory XV, **384n82**, **387n24**
Guadalcázar, *OCD friars monastery* 13.57, 13.66
Guerrero, Pedro, 13.49
Guzman, Alonso Pérez de (duke of Medina Sidonia), 14.25, **387n30**
Guzmán, Sancha de, 13.56–13.57

H

Habakkuk, 8.7, **372n5**
harquebuses, 3.34–3.35, 3.40, 6.11, 14.5, **365n40**
healers, 3.33, 6.2, 13.94, **369n3**
heaven, consideration of, 11.55
hell
consideration of, 11.56
foretaste of, 8.39
Helman, Constancia, I.38
Henry III, 14.35, **388n46**
Heredia, Diego, 3.47
Heredia, Juan de, O. Carm, **372n29**
heresies, 14.27
Hériz, Elías de San Martín. *See* Elías de San Martín (Heriz)
Hermas, 15.3
Hernández, Francisco. *See* Francisco de Jesus (Hernandez)
Higuera loca (Gracián), 14.36
Hildegard of Bingen, St., 15.3, 15.44, 15.53, 15.90, **389n3**
Historia de las fundaciones (Gracián). *See Fundaciones de los Carmelitas Descalzos*
Holdax, Ramadán, 7.20
holy liberty, 1.8, 2.9, **360n11**
honor
defense of, 2.3–2.5
false testimony of by Turkish captors. *See Papazquivir*
loss of, in exchange for Discalced province, 2.31
Hospital of St. James (Palermo), 10.59–10.60, I.28
Hospital of St. Lucy (Valencia), 5.6
Hospital of the Misericordia (Valencia), 14.15

I

I Promessi Sposi (Manzoni), **xxviii**
Ibros, Teresa de, 13.53
Ignatius of Antioch, St., 2.7
Ignatius of Loyola, St., 10.31, 16.14, I.45, **364n24**, **368n12**, **373n13**, **376n20**, **376n24**, **378n17**, **380n9**, **384n76**, **386n19**, **388n41**, **391n5**

"Illness and Happy Death of Jerome Gracián," V
imitation of Christ, 11.26, 11.49–11.50, 11.56
imprisonment, **xv**, 2.26, 4.30, I.15, **366n8**, **392n17**. *See also* Turkish capture and imprisonment
indecisiveness, as a cross, 8.30–8.31
"Instrucción de novicias" (María de San José Salazar), **389n13**
The Interior Castle (Teresa of Ávila), **xviii**
interior fog, 8.23–8.26, **372n2**
Isabel Clara Eugenia, **365n27**
Isabel de Los Ángeles, I.37
Isabel de San Francisco, 13.94
Isabel de San Jerónimo, 13.86
Isabel de San Pablo, I.37
Isabel de Santo Domingo, **xvi**, 1.10, 10.22
Isaiah, 11.1, 13.2, **359n2**

J

Jaén, *OCD friars monastery* 3.26, 13.71
James, St., 8.7
Jane Frances de Chantal, St., **xvii–xviii**, **391n7**
janissaries, 6.44, 6.47–6.48, 6.51–6.54, 7.11, 7.27–7.29, 7.31, 10.75, I.32, **370n33**
Jerome, St., Prol 3, 1.9, 4.12, 9.5, 15.3
Jeronimites, 14.11
Jerónimo de San José Ezquerra (OCD historian), **xxxvii**
Jesuits, **xi–xii**, **xxix**, 1.25, 3.38, 8.4, 9.6, 10.31, 10.49–10.50, 13.63, 13.107, 16.14, I.25, I.35, III.3, **372n4**, **374nn9–10**
Jiménez de Pedro Corona, Juan, 13.21
Job, 4.10, 4.14, 11.34, 11.41
Jodamia, Countess, I.41
John, St., 8.7, 8.21, 9.4, 12.2, 12.11, 15.44, 15.72, 15.90
John Chrysostom, St., Pref 1, 8.5
John of Ávila, St., 13.40, 13.52, 13.57, 13.70, 16.51–16.52, **379n3**, **381n22**, **389n3**, **392nn22–23**
John of the Cross, St., **xviin16**, **xx–xxi**, **xxxiv**, 13.14, I.3, V.1, **359n2**, **360n12**, **366n1**, **366n4**, **367n5**, **374n4**, **379nn23–24**, **380n6**, **381n23**, **381nn33–34**, **383n65**, **389n12**, **389n13**, **390n18**, **390n25**, **392n21**
John Paul II, St., **xxxi**, V.9–V.11
John the Baptist, St., 2.12, 9.3, 9.5
Josefina (Gracián), **xxvii**, 12.9, **379n7**
Joseph, St., **xvii**, **xxvii**, 2.6, 4.37, 12.9, 16.93
Joyeuse, François de, 13.109
Joyosa, Cardinal, I.37
Fray Juan de la Miseria (painter), 13.24, 13.88
Fray Juan (Augustinian), 14.6
Fray Juan (OCD lay brother), 13.94
Fray Juan (Mercedarian sacristan), 14.8
Fray Juan (Cistercian), 14.10
Juan Bautista de la Concepción García López-Rico, St. (Discalced Trinitarian), 14.7, I.34, **380n12**
Juan de Jesús (Roca), 3.3, 13.41, I.14
Juan de Ribera, St., **xxiv**
Juan del Espíritu Santo, 13.69
Juanillo, 14.28
"Jubileo del Año Santo" (Gracián), 12.11
judgment, 11.2, 11.46–11.47, 11.54, **378n1**
Juliana de la Madre de Dios (Gracián), Mother, 10.46, II.3, **376n26**, **397n4**
Julius Caesar, 2.1, **361n1**
justice, 11.2, 11.46–11.48, **378n1**

K

Kraków (Poland), *OCD friars monastery* 14.26, I.36, **388n37**; *OCD nuns monastery* I.43–I.44

L

La Concepción monastery. *See* Alcalá de Henares
La Laura monastery, 14.9
La Mancheula monastery, 13.51
La Peñuela monastery, 13.47–13.48
La Roda monastery, 13.47, 321–322
Lachau, Madame de, I.41
Lámpara encendida (Gracián), **xxvii**, 12.9, 15.15, 15.27
Las Huelgas monastery (Burgos), *Discalced Bernardine nuns*, 14.10
Las Llagas, Francisca de, II, **394n1**, **394n3**
Las Recogidas del Nombre de Jesús monastery, 14.28
Latins, 9.3, **373n2**
Le Mire, Jean, 13.107
Leiva, Antonio de, 6.8, 6.22, 6.52
Leiva, Pedro de, 10.62
Leo XI, 14.41, **389n53**
Leonor de la Misericordia (Ayanz), 13.96, I.23, **384nn73–74**, **396n4**
Leonor de San Bernardo, I.37
Lisbon, Siege of, 3.38–3.43, 13.94, 14.5, 14.34, **388n44**
Lisbon, *Chapter* 3.19; *OCD friars monastery* 2.23, 3.33, 3.37–3.38, 13.72, I.24, **364n18**; *OCD nuns monastery* 3.37–3.38, 4.22, 13.83, 13.94, 13.109, 14.29, 14.34, I.22, **364n26**; *O.Carm. friars monastery* 3.34–3.35, 3.37, 3.39–3.41, 14.5; *OP nuns Annunciation convent* 3.28, 13.94, 14.34, **364n26**
Lomellinis, 7.26, 7.32, **369n9**, **371n14**
Los Mártires monastery, 13.49–13.50
Louvain, *OCD nuns monastery* I.38, I.43; *college* I.41; *university* **x**, **378n19**, **394n18**
love
  amare, 11.11, **378n3**
  consolation in the exercise of, 11.43
  diligere, 11.11, **378n4**
  effects of, 15.22–15.30
  of enemies, 11.9–11.24
Loyola, Martin Ignacio de, **386n19**
Lucas, Gaspar, 3.26, 14.36, **364n22**
Lucifer. *See* devil
Luis, Father (priest, canon of Lipari), 6.35, 6.44, 6.50, 10.80
Luis de San Jerónimo, **367n5**, **392n18**
Lumen Gentium, **385n1**
Luther, Martin, I.45
Lutherans (Protestants), 3.19, 3.31, 3.44–3.46, 8.15, 10.72, 12.11, 14.27, 14.37, **365n28**, **373n11**

M

Macarius, St., Pref 1, 8.7
Machuca, Gonzalo, 6.32
Maccise, Camilo, V
Madrid, *O.Carm. friars monastery* 7.37, I.15, **362n19**, **372n27**; *Franciscan nuns monastery* 14.12
Magdalena de la Cruz, 13.56–13.57
Magdalene order, 13.66, **382n41**
Magyars, 7.7, **370n3**
Málaga monastery, 13.61–13.62, 369n1
Mami (Alonso de la Cruz), 7.1–7.9, **370n1**
Mami (Mahamet), Pasha of Tunis, 6.5, 6.15, 6.24, 6.26, 6.29, 6.31–6.37, 6.40, 6.47–6.48, 6.53, 7.2, 7.8–7.11, 7.14, 7.20, 7.27–7.31, 10.72, 10.75, **370n1**
Manrique, Jerónimo, 13.66
Manrique, Luis, 10.40, I.13
al-Mansur, Ahmad (sharif), 14.25, **372n26**, **387n29**
Manzoni, Alessandro, **xxviii**
Manzur, 7.13
marabouts, 7.14, **371n9**
Margarita de Jesús, I.43

María Bautista (Cepeda y Ocampo), 13.65
María de Jesús, 13.110, **379n25**
María de Jesús (Rivas), 11.44, 16.86–16.92, **379n25**, **393n28**
María de la Trinidad, I.43
María de la Visitación, 14.34, **364n26**, **388n43**
María de San Angelo, 16.84
María de San José (Dávila), **383n57**
María de San José (Gracián), 16.44–16.56, II, **376n20**, **388n42**, **391n2**, **392n20**, **394n1**
María de San José (Salazar), 2.20, 10.46, 13.83, 13.94, 13.109, 14.34, 16.38–16.41, I.22, V.1, V.4, **361n7**, **362n13**, **363n4**, **364n26**, **376n26**, **383n58**, **384n83**, **389n13**, **392n17**,
María of Austria, **365n27**
Mark, St., 4.12
Mark the Hermit, St., 8.39
Mármol, Andrés de, **xxxviii**
Mármol, Bernabé del, 16.50, I.27
Márquez, Cristóbal, **xxxviin6**
Martínez, Ana, 10.11
Martínez, Gregorio Nacianceno, 2.23, 13.81, **362n15**
martyrdom, impending, 6.50, 7.1–7.9, 13.68, 15.21
martyrs of Nagasaki, **xxix**, **386n20**
Mary Magdalene, St., 4.15, 9.5, 10.48
Mascareñas, Leonor, 13.18, I.4, **380n9**
Masses, said in captivity, 6.35–6.37, 6.40, 6.44, 6.50, 7.6–7.7, 10.77–10.79, 10.81, I.31, **370n35**
Matheus, Father, 13.23, I.4
Mathias, I.45
Matías de San Francisco, Fray, I.36, **394n15**
Maximillian II, **365n27**
Medici, Alessandro de, **389n53**
Medina, María de, 8.15–8.18, 10.13
meditation, 11.2, 11.51, 13.51, 15.6, 15.13–15.18, **389n7**
Mendoza, Alonso de, 8.14
Mendoza, Alvaro de, 13.64, 14.30
Mendoza, Ana de (princess of Éboli), 1.19, 3.17, 13.32, 13.43, **360n14**, **363n15**, **380n8**
Mendoza, Beatriz Ramírez de (countess of Castellar), 11.21, 13.110, 14.8, 14.11, **378n11**, **386n8**, **386n11**
Mendoza, Elvira de, 13.89
Mendoza, Francisco Sarmiento de (bishop of Jaén), 3.26, 14.36, 13.71, **364n21**
Mendoza, Iñigo López de, 14.30, **367n15**
Mendoza, Luis Hurtado de, 13.49, **381n29**
Mendoza, María de, 13.64
Mercedarians, **xxix**, 1.25, 13.44, 14.8
mercies of God, Pref 3, Prol 3–4, 10.8–10.10, 10.28, 15.2–15.3, 15.34, 15.49, 15.85, 16.5
Micah, 11.47
Mieres, Antonio, 10.58
Miguel, Fray (OCD lay brother), 13.50, **381n31**
Miguel, Fray (Discalced Augustinian), I.34
Miguel de la Columna, 2.22, **360n9**
Miguel de la Virgen, 10.20
Millino, Pietro, **366n13**
miraculous images, 6.18, **369n12**
Miserere Mei psalm, 11.30, 13.51, **378n18**, **381n32**
Miseria, Juan de la, 13.18, 13.24, 13.88, I.4, **360n9**, **383n63**
missionary activity, **xv**, **xix–xx**, **xxiv**, **xxix**
  in Africa, 3.19–21, 7.36, 13.70, 14.18–14.20, I.25, I.40, **364n17**, **372n22**, **379n3**, **387n22**, **387n26**
  in Mexico, 13.75, 14.21, I.24, **382n51**
  in Persia, 14.26, I.35, **388n36**

Teresa of Ávila's zeal for, **xix**, **xxvii**, 3.22, **364n19**

mistakes, made without fault, 2.6–2.8

Mística teología (Gracián), 12.10

Molina, Dr., 14.42

Molina, Juan Vázquez de (secretary), 13.70

Mondéjar voices, 2.17, 15.65, **362n12**

Mons de Henao, *OCD nuns monastery* I.39, I.43

Montesa, Master. *See* Borja, Pedro Luis Garcerán de

Moraterráez, Captain, 6.5–6.7, **369n8**

mortification, 8.7, 9.22–9.24, 10.24, 10.41, 13.39, 13.52, 13.87, 15.70, **374n4**, **383n62**

Mother Teresa. *See* Teresa of Ávila, St.

Muñoz, Bartolomé, OP, **366n9**

N

Nacianceno, Gregorio. *See* Martínez, Gregorio Nacianceno

Nacimiento, María del, 16.47

Narvaez, Alfonso de, III

Nicholas of Antioch, St., 2.7

Nicolás de Jesús María. *See* Doria, Nicolás de Jesús María

Nicolás de la Concepción, I.41

Nieto, Baltasar de Jesús, 1.7, 1.13, I.4, **360n9**

Niño, Gabriel, 14.15

nóminas, 6.43, 14.22, 15.66, **370n30**

Nostra Señora del Populo, Church of (Augustinians), 14.6, **385n6**

novitiate duties, **xii**, 1.7–1.8, 1.11, 9.7

Nuestra Señora de Altomira monastery (Altomira, OCD friars), 13.11, 13.27–29, I.4

Nuestra Señora de Gloria monastery (Lisbon, for repentant women), 14.29

Nuestra Señora de la Cabeza monastery (near Andújar, OCD friars), 13.71

Nuestra Señora de la Scala monastery (Rome, OCD friars), 11.22, 13.105, I.35, **378n12**

Nuestra Señora de los Remedios monastery (Seville, OCD friars), **xiii**, 1.23–1.24, 2.13, 3.6, 13.32–13.38, 14.18, I.7, **362n10**, **363n6**, **381nn18–19**, **389n54**

Nuestra Señora del Campo monastery (Paris, OCD nuns), I.37

Nuestra Señora del Socorro monastery (La Roda, OCD friars), I.5

Nuño Alvarez Pereira, St., 3.34, **365n39**

nuns

- accusations by, 1.35, 2.3–2.4, **361n26**
- Bernardine, of Odivelas, 3.46
- Bernardine, of Toledo, 13.67, 14.10
- charges of improper dealings with, 4.20–4.27, 4.39, 4.41
- foundations of monasteries of Discalced Carmelite, 13.77–13.112
- founding of convent for repentant women in Naples, 5.18, **368n14**
- government of Discalced Carmelites of Pastrana, 1.8
- mortification of nun who concealed her thoughts, 10.24
- procession to castle in Lisbon, 3.37
- stigmatic, 3.28–3.32, 14.34, **364n26**, **365n31**
- unusual spiritual experiences of, 14.33
- visions of, 16.38–16.64

Nuper iustis (brief), **363n3**

O

Obregón, Bernardino de, **386n16**

occupations, good works as, 13.7. *See also* good works

Odivelas (Portugal), *Bernardine nuns* 3.46

"Official Declaration of the Rehabilitation of Father Jerome Gracián of the Mother of God, O.C.D.," V

Olea, Father, 1.25
Olivares, Countess of, 5.19, 7.18, 10.59, I.28, **377n37**
"Opúsculos" (Gracián), 12.11
oracles, 6.42, **370n29**
Order of Carmel of the Ancient Observance, **xxxi**, **xiiin9**
Orlando, 10.14, **375n7**
Ormaneto, Nicolò (nuncio), **xiv**, 1.26, 2.24, 14.18, 16.17, I.10, I.12, **360nn20–21**, **362n16**, **363n10**
Ortiz, Dr., 8.14
Osorio, Father (Discalced Franciscan), 14.19
Our Lady of Altomira hermitage, 13.27
Our Lady of Atocha monastery (Madrid), 2.26
Our Lady of August. *See* Virgin Mary, Feast of the Assumption

P

Pablo Simón de Jesús María (Paolo Simone Rivarola), 14.26, **388n36**
Pacheco, Juan, 13.62
Padilla, Juan Calvo de, Licentiate, 14.18, **386n18**
Palacios, Juan de, **367n1**
Palavesino, Damián, 7.26
Palencia monastery (OCD nuns), 13.78, 13.89
Pamplona monastery, *OCD friars* 13.74, 330, **384n75**, **395n2**; *OCD nuns* 13.74, 13.78, 13.95–13.97, **330**
Pantoja, Fernando de (Carthusian), **383n61**
Papareta, 6.45–6.47
Papazquivir ("*Papaz*"), as Turkish title for Gracián, 6.5, 6.23, 6.26, 6.29–6.30, 6.32, 6.37, 6.42, 6.45, 6.53, 7.2, 7.4–7.5, 7.13, 7.20, 7.29, **369n10**
Pardo, Pedro Cerezo, 10.52, 13.38, 13.94
Paris monastery, *OCD friars* I.42; *OCD nuns* 13.108–13.109, I.37, **385nn85–86**
Pastrana monastery, *OCD friars* **ix**, **xii**, 1.1, 1.5, 1.7–1.8, 3.12, 13.11, 13.19–13.21, 13.25, 13.27, 13.29–13.30, 13.40–13.41, 13.50, 13.69, 14.4, I.4, I.6, I.15, **360n6**, **360n9**, **360n12**, **364n18**, **374n12**, **375n10**, **380n10**, **380n13**, **381n14**, **394n7**; *OCD nuns* 1.8, 1.10, 1.19, 10.22, 13.18, I.4, I.6, **360n14**
Paul, St., **xxiii**, Prol 3, 2.26, 4.12–4.13, 4.37, 8.8, 8.40, 9.22, 15.3, 15.10, 15.33, 15.34, 15.72, 15.83–15.84, 15.90, V.6
Paul V, 13.106, 14.26, I.35, **384n81**
peace negotiations, 14.25, **387n32**
Pedro de la Madre de Dios, 11.22, 13.73, 13.105
Pedro de la Purificación, 4.1, 4.43, I.27, **361n5**, **366n1**
Pedro de San Angel (de Balboa), 2.23
Pena, Felipe, 7.32
Peñalosa, Ana de, **380n6**
"Pentecosmia" (Gracián), 15.59
Peñuela, Gabriel de la, 13.62
Peregrinación de Anastasio. *See Pilgrimage of Anastasius* (Gracián)
Pérez, Antonio, 3.47, **363n15**, **366n46**
perfection, 10.48, III.4, **396n11**
Perogrullo, 6.1, **369n2**
persecution. *See also* accusations; trials and tribulations
  of the Discalced Carmelites, 2.9–2.10, 9.8, **374n14**
  from a false report, 2.22
  of friars, 10.57, **377n35**
  by God, 4.10–4.11, 4.14
  just, of the innocent, 4.11–4.14
  by one's brothers, 2.1–2.2

permitted by God, 2.12
by Sega, 2.17, 2.24–2.28, 2.32–2.34, 3.11, **361n26**, **362nn17–18**, **362nn20–22**, **363n10**, **374n14**
strength in silence and hope during times of, 11.35–11.37
Peter, St., 2.7, 15.90
Peter of Alcántara, St., **xxix**, **368n1**, **386n19**
Pharisees, 4.15–4.17
Philip II, **x**, **xi**, 1.25, 3.17, 3.31, 10.38–10.41, 10.56, 13.18, 13.35, 14.18, 14.20, 14.35, I.4, I.12, **359n2**, **362n21**, **363n5**, **363n9**, **363n15**, **364n25**, **365n27**, **365n29**, **366n46**, **367n15**, **376n23**, **377nn33–34**, **378n19**, **380n8**, **386n18**, **387n27**
Philip III, **xxiv**, 14.25, I.40, **372n23**, **385n84**, **387n29**, **387n31**, **395n11**
Philip Neri, St., **xxviii**, 13.103, **384nn76–79**
Pilgrimage of Anastasius (Gracián), **ix–x**, **xvi**, **xxi**, **xxviii**, **xxxii–xxxiv**, I.46, II.4, **372n1**
Piña, Father, 13.44, I.5
Pinelli, Domenico, 4.1, 7.35, 8.31, 9.30, II.34
Pirula, 13.96
Pius V, 1.20, 1.24–1.25, 13.33, 14.9, 14.18, I.6, I.10, **360n19**, **381n17**, **386n9**
poisoning
dangers of, 1.34
of Ruy Gómez, 1.16–1.18
Portugal, *O.Carm. visitation* 3.34–3.35, 3.37, 3.39, 3.47,14.5
Potel, Francisco, 13.112, 14.16
prayer and praying
captivity as a time of, 10.82
contemplation, 15.19–15.30
for enemies and adversaries, 11.24
Gracián's, at age 20, 8.2, **379n20**
as interior words from God, 15.66–15.75
meditation, 15.13–15.18, **389n7**
purpose of, 11.38
stillness of spirit, 15.85–15.88
Teresa of Ávila's for Gracián's vocation, 1.2
for trials and tribulations, 8.5–8.7
vocal, 15.8–15.12
Presentation of Our Lady, Feast of the, 1.32, 16.20–16.21, 16.37, I.11, **361n23**
Ptolemy Philadelphus, 10.2
pusillanimity, as a cross, 8.26

Q

Quesada, Dr., 13.109, I.37
Quintanadueñas Brétigny, Juan de. *See* Brétigny, Juan de Quintanadueñas
Quiroga, Gaspar de, 1.27

R

Rangona, marquise of, 13.102–13.103, I.32
ransom/redemption of captives, 6.33, 6.44, 7.15, 7.32, 10.80, 10.83, I.31, **370n26**, **370n32**, **387n26**
ransom/redemption of Gracián, **xxiii–xxiv**, 6.21, 6.33, 6.53, 7.11, 7.29–7.31, 7.33–7.34, 9.24, I.32, **371n17**, **374n18**
raptures, 15.89–15.90
Ravena, Juan Bautista Rubeo de. *See* Rubeo de Ravena, Juan Bautista
Redención de cautivos (Gracián), 12.10, 14.23
rehabilitation, **xxx–xxxii**, V, **375n21**, **393n32**
Reloj de Acab (Gracián), 12.10
renunciation of worldly goods, 11.2, 11.45
resignation to the will of God, 11.38–11.44

restoration to Discalced Carmelites, xxiii–xxv, 9.11–9.18, 9.24, 9.28–9.30, **371n21, 375n28**
revelations. *See also* visions; words
exterior visions and, 15.31–15.43
of Teresa of Ávila, 16.4–16.37, 16.97–16.68, **391n3–392n16**
twelve D's, 16.2–16.3, **391n1**
types of, 11.5–11.6
Ribera, Francisco de, 10.26, 13.78, I.2, **376n13, 382n53**
Ribera, Juan de, St., **xxiv**, 14.14, **376.19**
Rivarola, Paolo Simone. *See* Pablo Simón de Jesús María
Roca, Juan de Jesús. *See* Juan de Jesús (Roca)
Rodríguez, Ana, 6.3, 14.34
Rodríguez, Pero, II.6
Rojas y Sandoval, Cristóbal de (archbishop of Seville), 1.23, 13.34, 14.18, I.7
Roman Inquisition, I.34, III.4, **394n12**
Rome, *O.Carm. friars monastery of San Martin in Montibus* 7.34, 9.18, I.34, **371n21, 375n22**;
Ros, Carlos, **369n23**
Rossi, Giovanni Battista. *See* Rubeo de Ravena, Juan Bautista
rótulo, I.2, **394n5**
Rubeo de Ravena, Juan Bautista (O.Carm. general), **xivn12**, 9.19, 13.13, I.3
Ruiz, Alonso, 6.2
Ruiz, Juan, O.Carm., 6.48
Rule of St. Albert (Carmelite Rule). *See* Carmelite Order, Rule of
Ruzola, Dominic, 15.90, **391n31**

S

"Saetas agudas y brasas encendidas" (Gracián), 15.80, **390n28**
Saints Peter and Marcellinus monastery (Rome, Discalced Augustinians) 8.36, I.29, **368n18**
Salamanca, *OCD friars monastery* 13.65–13.66, **382n42**; *OCD nuns monastery* 13.65; *College of Cuenca* 8.13, 10.13
Salazar, Angel de, O.Carm., 2.34, 3.4–3.6, I.19, **362n1, 363n6**
Salinier, Stéfano, 7.32
Salvador de la Cruz, 6.43
salvation, distrust of, 8.29
Salvatoris (Sixtus V), **361n7**
San Alberto monastery (Lisbon, OCD nuns), 3.33, 3.37–3.38, 13.94, I.22, **365n37**
San Bautista, Alonso de, **395n2**
San Felipe monastery (Lisbon, OCD friars), 3.33, 3.37–3.38, 13.72, I.22, **365n37, 382n49**
San Hermenegildo monastery (Madrid, OCD friars), **xv, 366n8**
San Jerónimo, Lussía Dermana de, 14.36
San José monastery, *Alcalá (OCD nuns)* 11.21, **383.57**; *Avila (OCD nuns)* 13.81; *Brussels (OCD nuns)* I.38; *Ziblia (Poland, OCD friars)* I.36
San Juan del Puerto monastery (Seville, OCD/O.Carm. friars), 1.19, 1.21, 13.32–13.34, I.7, **360n15**
San Lázaro church and monastery (Salamanca, OCD friars), 13.66
San Martín, Elías de. *See* Elías de San Martín (Heriz)
San Martín in Montibus monastery (Rome, O.Carm.), 7.34, 9.18, I.34, **371n20, 375n22**
San Miguel Arcángel monastery (Kraków, Poland, OCD friars) I.36
San Pedro monastery (Pastrana), *OCD friars* **ix, xii**, 1.1, 1.5, 1.7–1.8, 3.12, 13.11, 13.19–13.21, 13.25, 13.27, 13.29–13.30, 13.40–13.41, 13.50,

13.69, 14.4, I.4, I.6, I.15, **360n6**, **360n9**, **360n12**, **364n18**, **374n12**, **375n10**, **380n10**, **380n13**, **381n14**, **394n7**; *OCD nuns* 1.8, 1.10, 1.19, 10.22, 13.18, I.4, **360n14**
San Vitores, Hernando de, 14.16
Sandoval y Rojas, Francisco Gómez de (duke of Lerma), 14.25, **387n31**
Sanlúcar de Alpechín monastery (OCD nuns), 13.94
Santa Ana y San José monastery (Brussels, OCD nuns), I.38
Santa Clara monastery (Franciscan nuns), 14.12
Santa Maria della Scala monastery. *See* Nuestra Señora de la Scala monastery
Santa Maria Sopra Minerva monastery (Rome, Dominican friars), 5.15, **368n9**
Santa Ursula monastery (Valencia, Discalced Augustinian canonesses) 14.14
Santori, Giulio Antonio (Cardinal Santa Severina), 14.23, **387n24**
Sarmiento, Francisco. *See* Mendoza, Francisco Sarmiento de
Satan. *See* devil
Sayings of Light and Love (John of the Cross), **359n2**, **374n4**
Scivias (Hildegard of Bingen), 15.3, 15.44, **389n3**
scrupulosity, 8.27–8.28, **373n13**
Sebastián of Portugal, 3.27, 7.24, **364n25**, **371n11**
Sega, Filippo (nuncio), 2.17, 2.24–2.28, 2.32–2.34, 3.2, 3.11, 4.28, 10.37–10.41, 15.65, 16.23, 16.25, 16.27, I.12, **361n26**, **362nn17–18**, **362nn20–22**, **363n10**, **374n14**, **392n10**
Segovia, Francisco de (Jeronimite), **366n9**
Segura, Pedro de, 13.70
self-loathing and abasement, 11.25–11.27
sermons, 3.8, 6.45, 12.7, 13.37, 13.41, 13.43, 14.22, 14.27, 15.40, 15.56, 15.61,16.65
Severina, Santa (cardinal). *See* Santori, Guilio Antonio
Seville, *OCD friars Los Remedios monastery* **xiii**, 1.23–1.24, 3.6, 12.5, 13.11, 13.32–13.39, 13.60, 13.63, 14.18–14.19, I.7, I.19–I.20, **362n15**, **367n16**, **379n3**, **389n54**; *OCD nuns monastery* **xxx**, 4.26, 10.28, 10.33, 10.46, 13.78, 13.83–13.84, 13.94, 16.9, I.9, I.22, II.3, **376n26**, **383n59**, **383n63**, **384n83**, **394n4**; *O.Carm. monastery* 1.21, 1.31, 2.13, 14.4, **361n23**; *O.Carm. visitation* 16.17, 16.21, 16.37, I.11, **385n3**; *house for wayward girls* 14.28, 14.31, **388n41**
Shakespeare, William, **361n1**
Sheba, Queen of, 10.2, 10.6
shield, elements of
    about, **xxxiii–xxxiv**, Pref 5, Prol 1–4, **359nProl1**, **372n3**
    ACFRIC, 11.1–11.62. *See also* ACFRIC hieroglyph
    chains, 6.1–6.54, 7.1–7.37
    cross in heart, 8.1–8.40
    jewels in crown, 13.1–13.112, 14.1–14.42
    name of Jesus, 15.1–15.91
    name of Mary, 16.1–16.97
    shield and three stars, 9.1–9.30, **373n1**
    thorns and jewels, 10.1–10.85
    twelve stars, 9.4–9.5, 12.1–12.12
    unshod feet, 1.1–1.35, 2.1–2.34, 3.1–3.47, 4.1–4.46, 5.1–5.22
Shulammite of Zaraphath, 3.25, **364n20**
Sigismund I, **xn5**
Silverio de Santa Teresa (Gómez), **xxvi**, **xxviii**, **xxxvi**
Simón (hospital attendant), 10.60

Simón Stock, Fray, 13.60
Simon Stock, St., 9.5
sins, contrition for past, 11.28–11.30
Sixtus V, 2.9, 10.46, 10.57, 14.33, I.27
Soledad convent (Naples, for poor girls), 14.30
Solomon, 10.2–10.6
Soncino, Ambrosio de (Capuchin), 14.24
Soto, Francisco de (Oratorian), 11.20, 13.102, I.32, **384n77**
Sotomayor, Antonio de, 10.54–10.55, 10.58, **377n30**
Spanish Inquisition, 2.23, 2.27, 3.26, 3.31–3.33, 5.21, 6.43, 6.50–6.52, 9.18, 10.71, 13.55, 13.84–13.86, 14.22, 14.34, **364n22**, **382n35**, **388n48**
Speravi, sive de falsa et vera spe (Diego Gracián de Alderete), 11.32
Speziano, Cesare (nuncio), 4.5, **366n5**
spirit
- harmony from centering of, 10.18–10.19
- as a mercy of God, 15.1–15.7
- stillness of, 15.85–15.88

spiritual experiences, examination of unusual, 14.33–14.38
spiritual reading, 15.9
Spiritual Testimonies (Teresa of Ávila), **361n23**, **376n15–376n17**, **382n55**, **391n4**
stabbing incident, 1.22–1.23
strength in silence and hope, 11.35–11.37
Suetonius, **361n1**
suffering. *See also* trials and tribulations
- in the *baños*, 6.21, 6.33–6.35, 6.38–6.41, 7.5, 7.7, 7.13, 10.80–10.81, I.31
- caused by expulsion, 5.5
- caused by friends and family, 1.12
- caused by shackles, 7.5, 7.7
- desire for, 8.1, 8.5–8.7, 11.44
- old lady of San Bábilas on, 1.6
- physical, 1.11, 1.28, 10.14
- of the saints, 11.52

"Sufragio de las ánimas de purgatorio" (Gracián), 12.11
Suma de los siete ángeles príncipes (Gracián), 12.10

T

temptations of the flesh, 8.38
Teresa of Ávila, St., **xiin7**, **xv**, **xx**, **xxxiv**, Prol 3, 4.41, **375n7**
- and Antonia del Espíritu Santo, **368n1**
- beatification, **xxiv–xxv**
- *Book of Her Foundations*, **x**, **xxi**, I.2, V.7, **380n2**, **381n26**, **381n34**
- on Cano, **388n42**
- canonization, II.2, II.5, **384n76**, **394n5**
- charism of, **xxi–xxii**, **360n11**
- and Colón, 14.13, **386n13**
- correspondence with Gracián, 10.26–10.27, 10.37, II.4, **376n12**, **381n15**, **395n8**
- counsels from, 16.65–16.97
- death, 13.93, **383n69**
- exhumation and reburial, 16.92, **393n29**
- and foundations of monasteries of Discalced Carmelite nuns, 13.77–13.112, I.3–I.4, I.8
- as foundress of the Carmelite Order, 2.9, 13.13–13.19, **359n4**, **380n4**
- on Fray Fernández, **363n4**
- and Gracián, **x**, **xii–xxii**, **xxx**, 3.8, 8.39, 13.80, **360n10**
- Gracián's visions of, 15.32, 15.39–15.41, 15.79, **376n16**, **389n13**, **396n4**
- *The Interior Castle*, **xviii**
- on Miseria's portrait of her, 13.88, **383n63**

missionary spirit, **xix**, **xxvii**, 3.22, **364n19**
prayer for Gracián's vocation, 1.2
prayer to Catalina de Cardona, 13.47
relics of, 13.104, 16.61–16.62, II.3, V.5, **393n26**, **395n6**
revelations, 16.4–16.37, 16.97–16.98, **391n3–392n16**
Spiritual Testimonies, **361n23**, **376n15–376n17**, **382n55**, **391n4**
The Way of Perfection, **364n24**
vow of obedience to Gracián, **xvi**, **xviii**, **xix**, 10.28–10.33, **376nn14–18**, **391n7**
Tertullian, 2.7
Thérèse of Lisieux, St., **xxxiv**
Thomas Aquinas, St., 15.9, **389n8**
Toledo, Fadrique de, 10.42, 14.9
Toledo, Father, SJ, 5.10, 13.73
Toledo, Fernando Alvarez de (duke of Alba), 3.10, 10.42, **376n23**, **376n25**
Toledo, Francisco de, 5.10, **368n8**
Toledo, Luis de, 13.17
Toledo, María de, 14.9
Toledo monastery (OCD friars), 13.67–13.70, **393n28**
Toledo visions, 2.18–2.19
Tomás de Jesús (Sánchez Dávila), 13.106–13.107, 14.26, I.41–I.43, II.2, II.5, III.2, **376n13**, **384n81**, **395n5**, **396n1**, **396–397n4**
Tomás de la Ascensión, 13.65
"Tratado de la melancolía" (Gracián), 12.12, **380n10**
Tratado del Jubileo del Año Santo (Gracián), 12.9
trials and tribulations. *See also* persecution; suffering
abandonment, interior and exterior, 8.34–8.36
afflictions asked for, 8.2, 8.5–8.10
benefits received from, 8.8
compelling zeal, 8.32–8.33
distrust of salvation, 8.29
dryness of spirit, 8.39
fear and pusillanimity, 8.26
indecisiveness and indetermination, 8.30–8.31
interior, 8.19–8.24, 8.40
interior fog, 8.23–8.26, **372n2**
permitted by God, Pref 1–3
psalms of David for times of, 11.61–11.63
recounting of, Pref 1–3, Prol 3–4
rest from during captivity, 10.67–10.71
scruples, 8.27–8.28, **373n13**
spiritual defenses to avoid faltering in, 11.1–11.8. *See also* ACFRIC hieroglyph
temptations of the flesh, 8.38
whether one should pray for, 8.5, 8.9
Trigoso, Pedro (Capuchin), 10.55, **377n32**
Trinidad, Diego de la, 3.3, 13.41, I.14
Turkish capture and imprisonment
in the *baños*, 6.21, 6.33–6.35, 6.41, 10.74, 10.77, I.31–I.32, **369n23**, **377n43**
in Bizerte, 6.20–6.30, **369n20**
clothing worn, 9.24, 10.75, **375nn25–26**
confessions and conversions of other captives, 10.71–10.74
escape rumors, 7.12–7.13
false testimonies by others, 7.15–7.21
fruits from, 14.22–14.23
in Gaeta, 6.8–6.12, 6.16–6.17
gifts received, 10.75–10.76
at Island of San Pietro, 6.18–6.19
Masses said during, 6.35–6.37, 6.40, 6.44, 6.50, 7.6–7.7, 10.78–10.79, 10.81, I.31, **370n35**

in Naples, 6.17
passing of time during, 10.81
portrait made during, II.1, **394n4**
prisoner exchange offers, 7.11
ransom and freedom, 7.22–7.33, **371n17**
rest from interior trials during, 10.67–10.71
spared from burning at the stake, 6.46–6.54, 7.6–7.9
as a time of prayer and reflection, 10.82–10.84
in Tunis, 6.31–6.54, 7.1–7.32, I.31
at Ventotene, 6.13–6.15, 10.69

U

Úbeda monastery (OCD friars), 13.70
Uberes fructus (brief), **368n16**
Ursina, Olimpia (duchess of Aquasparta), 13.102, I.32
Ursula, Sister, 14.33, 15.90
Utiel, Master, 7.32
University of Alcalá de Henares, **xi**, **xvin14**, 1.4, 5.16, 8.10, 8.14, 8.16, 10.13, 12.4, 13.25, I.6
University of Louvain, **x**, **378n19**, **394n18**
University of Salamanca, 8.13, 13.66. *See also College of Cuenca*

V

Valiente, Juan, 7.7, **371n4**
Valladolid monastery (OCD friars), 3.16, 13.50, 13.63–13.64, **363n14**
Vanegas, Juan, O. Carm, 6.48
Vargas, Francisco de, OP, **xii–xiii**, 1.20, 13.33, 13.80, I.6
Vega, Juan de, 13.89
Vega, Suero de, 13.89, **383n64**
Vela, Cristóbal, 13.90
Vescovi, Silvano, V
Vestrio, Barbiano, 9.11, 9.16–9.17, 9.28, I.33
Vicente, Juan, 5.15
Victoria de la fe (Gracián), 10.77
Vida del alma y verdadera imitación de Cristo (Gracián), 14.37, 15.64, **388n50**
Vida en Cristo (Gracián), 12.10
[*Vida*] *de san Andrés* (Gracián), 12.12
Vida y doctrina de Nuestra Señora (Gracián), 12.12
Villavicencio, Lorenzo de (Augustinian), 10.40
Vilvoorde monastery (Flanders, OCD nuns), III.4, **395n6**
Vinculo de hermandad (Bond of Brotherhood), **xxix**, **386n19**
Virgin Mary
consolation of, 10.19
and conversion of king of Iznatorafe, 13.59
faultless in loss of Child Jesus, 2.6, 4.37
Feast of the Assumption ("Our Lady of August"), 6.7, **369n11**
Feast of the Presentation, 1.32, 16.20–16.21, 16.37, I.11, **361n23**
Our Lady of the Purification, 6.7, **369n13**
vocational calling by, 1.1, 1.5, 8.37
as the woman clothed with the sun, 9.4
virtues exercised, 15.15
visions
of Ana de Jesús (Lobera), 16.47
of Ana de San Bartolomé, 16.42, 16.44–16.45
of Ana Martínez, 10.11
of Antonia del Espíritu Santo, 6.1

in Astorga, 2.16, 15.32, 15.43
of Brother Alberto, 2.19
of Catalina de Cardona, 13.43, 13.46–13.47, I.5
of Catalina de Jesús (Sandoval y Godínez), 16.60–16.64, 16.85, **393nn26–27**
dreams, 15.81–15.84
ecstasies and raptures, 15.89–15.90
exterior, 15.31–15.43
of Gracián of Teresa of Ávila, 15.32, 15.39–15.41, 15.79, **376n16**, **389n13**, **396n4**
of holy nuns, 16.43, 16.50, 16.56
imaginative, 15.44–15.48
intellectual, 15.49–15.64, **390n16**
interior, 15.44–15.48, **390n16**
interior *razones*, 15.76–15.80, **390n26**
of Juan Jiménez, 13.21
of Juana Calancha, 13.55
of María de Jesús (Rivas), 16.86–16.92, **393n28**
of María de San José (Salazar), 2.20, 16.38–16.41
of the queen of Iznatorafe, 13.59
of Sancha de Guzmán, 13.56–13.57
of St. Anthony, 11.5, **378n2**
of St. Hildegard, 15.3, 15.44, 15.53, 15.90
in Toledo, 2.18–2.19
types of, 11.5–11.6
Vives, Juan Bautista (Monsignor), 12.10, 13.106, 14.19, 14.26, **384n82**
Vives, Juan Luis, **x**, 12.10
vocation
following one's, 10.50
struggles with, 1.1–1.6, 1.12–1.13
Teresa of Ávila's prayer for, 1.2
Virgin Mary's calling to, 1.1, 1.5, 8.36–8.37

W

The Way of Perfection (Teresa of Ávila), **364n24**
ways of the spirit, 15.1–15.91
will
resignation to God's, 11.38–11.44
understanding and, 4.11–4.17, 11.18
words, 15.6
formed interior, 15.66–15.75
heard exteriorly, 15.65
unformed interior (*razones*), 15.76–15.80, **390n26**
works of humans, ways of viewing, 4.15–4.29

X

Xavier, Catalina, 13.97, I.23
Xuárez, Hernando, 3.12

Y

Yanguas, Diego de, 14.9
Yepes, Diego de, I.2, **376n13**

Z

Zafonte, Joaquín, 10.51
Zalimamet, 7.2
Zambalí, 6.24, 6.26, 6.30
Zaragoza, Dean, 14.13
Zayas, Gabriel de, 2.23
zeal, and persecution of the innocent, 4.11–4.29, 4.32, 4.44, 10.47, **366n7**
zealousness, as a cross, 8.32–8.33
Zeuxis, 11.12, **378n5**
Zúñiga, Gonzalo de, 13.49, **381n30**
zupia, 10.20, **375n9**

About Us

ICS Publications, based in Washington, D.C., is the publishing house of the Institute of Carmelite Studies (ICS) and a ministry of the Discalced Carmelite Friars of the Washington Province (U.S.A.). The Institute of Carmelite Studies promotes research and publication in the field of Carmelite spirituality, especially about Carmelite saints and related topics. Its members are friars of the Washington Province.

The Discalced Carmelites are a worldwide Roman Catholic religious order comprised of friars, nuns, and laity—men and women who are heirs to the teaching and way of life of Teresa of Avila and John of the Cross, dedicated to contemplation and to ministry in the church and the world.

Information about their way of life is available through local diocesan vocation offices, or from the Discalced Carmelite Friars vocation directors at the following addresses:

Washington Province:
1525 Carmel Road, Hubertus, WI 53033

California-Arizona Province:
P.O. Box 3420, San Jose, CA 95156

Oklahoma Province:
5151 Marylake Drive, Little Rock, AR 72206

Visit our websites at:

www.icspublications.org and *http://ocdfriarsvocation.org*